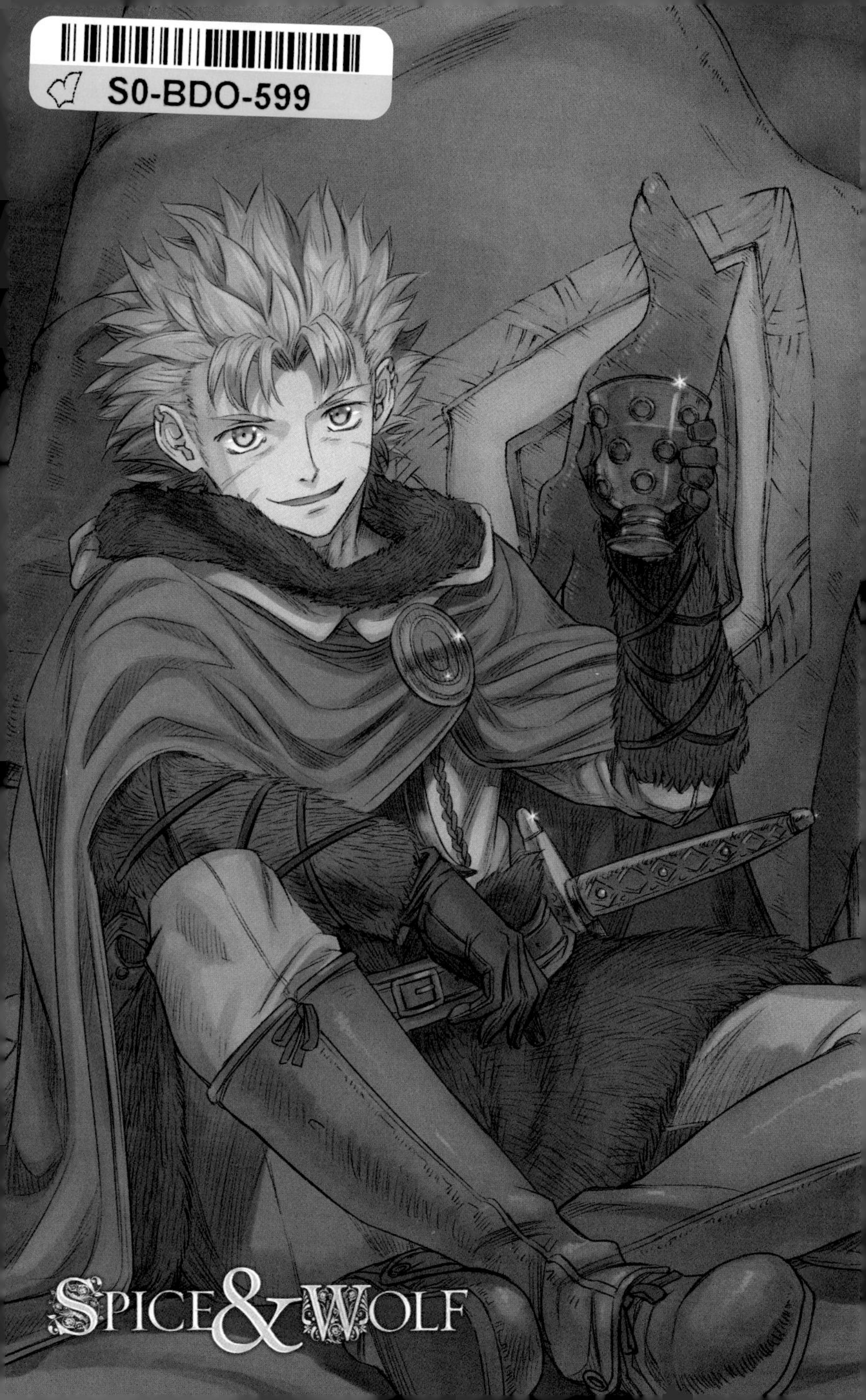
SPICE & WOLF

SPICE & WOLF
CONTENTS

Chapter 87 ·································· *3*

Chapter 88 ·································· *27*

Chapter 89 ·································· *57*

Chapter 90 ·································· *79*

Chapter 91 ·································· *105*

Chapter 92 ·································· *131*

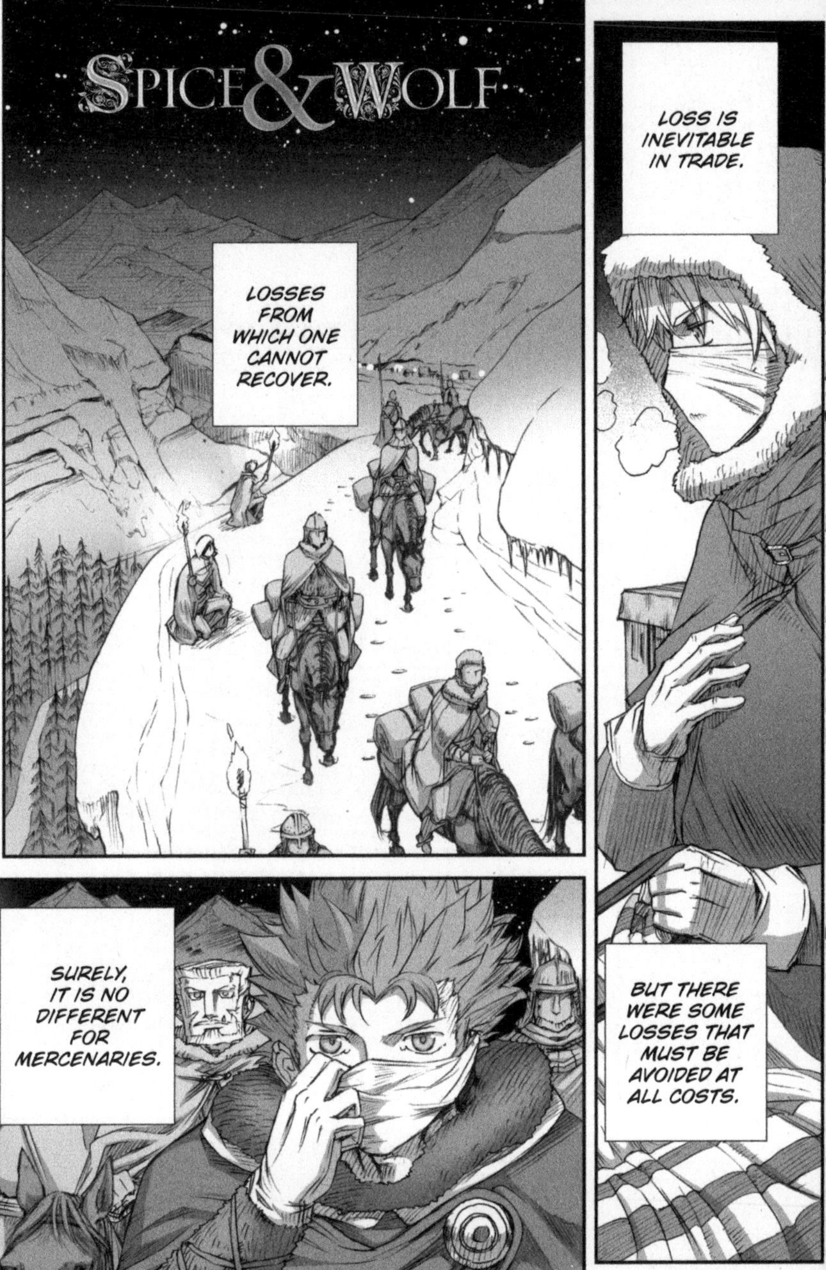
LOSS IS INEVITABLE IN TRADE.
BUT THERE WERE SOME LOSSES THAT MUST BE AVOIDED AT ALL COSTS.
SPICE & WOLF
LOSSES FROM WHICH ONE CANNOT RECOVER.
SURELY, IT IS NO DIFFERENT FOR MERCENARIES.

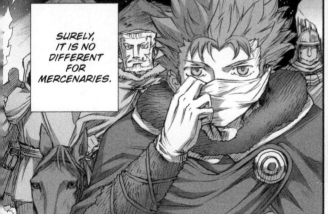

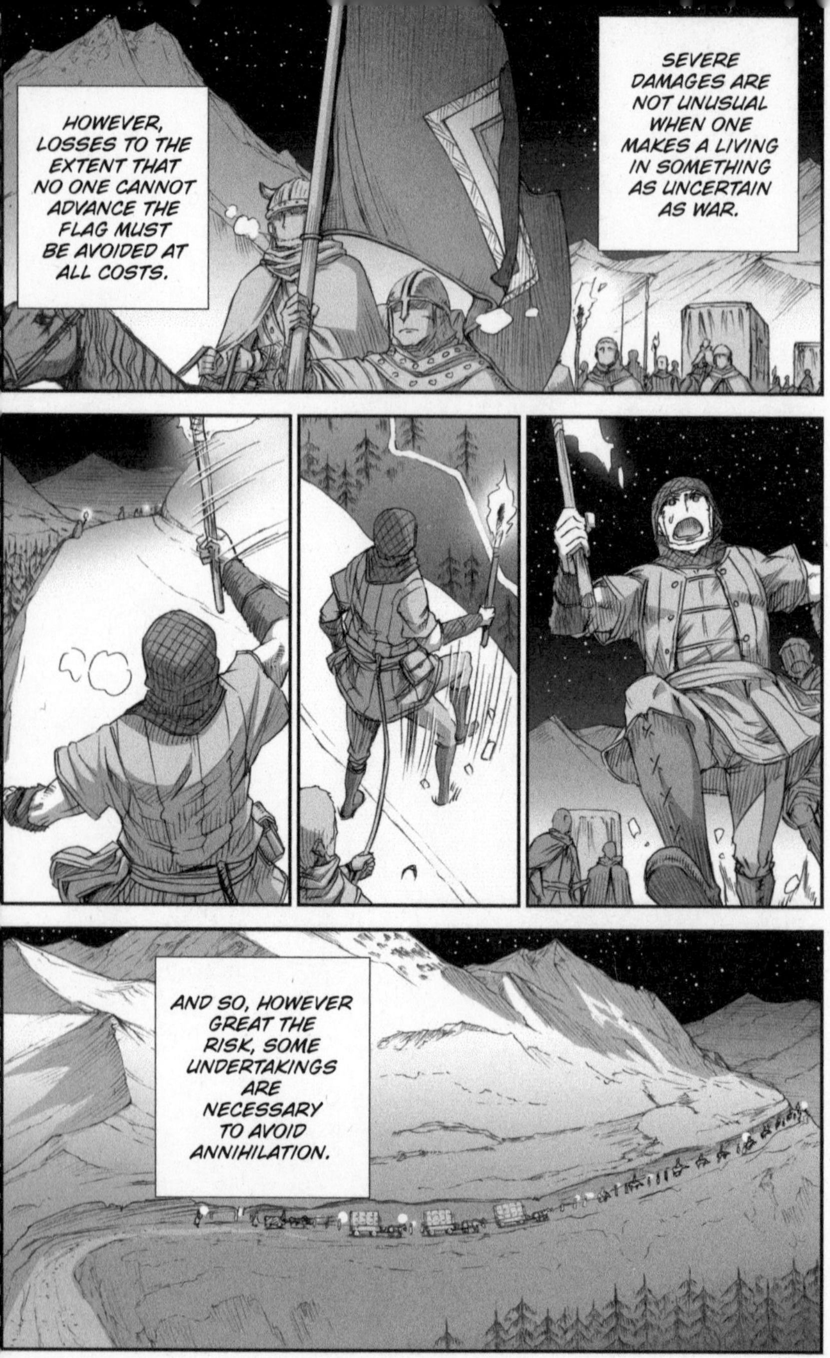
SEVERE DAMAGES ARE NOT UNUSUAL WHEN ONE MAKES A LIVING IN SOMETHING AS UNCERTAIN AS WAR.
HOWEVER, LOSSES TO THE EXTENT THAT NO ONE CANNOT ADVANCE THE FLAG MUST BE AVOIDED AT ALL COSTS.
AND SO, HOWEVER GREAT THE RISK, SOME UNDERTAKINGS ARE NECESSARY TO AVOID ANNIHILATION.

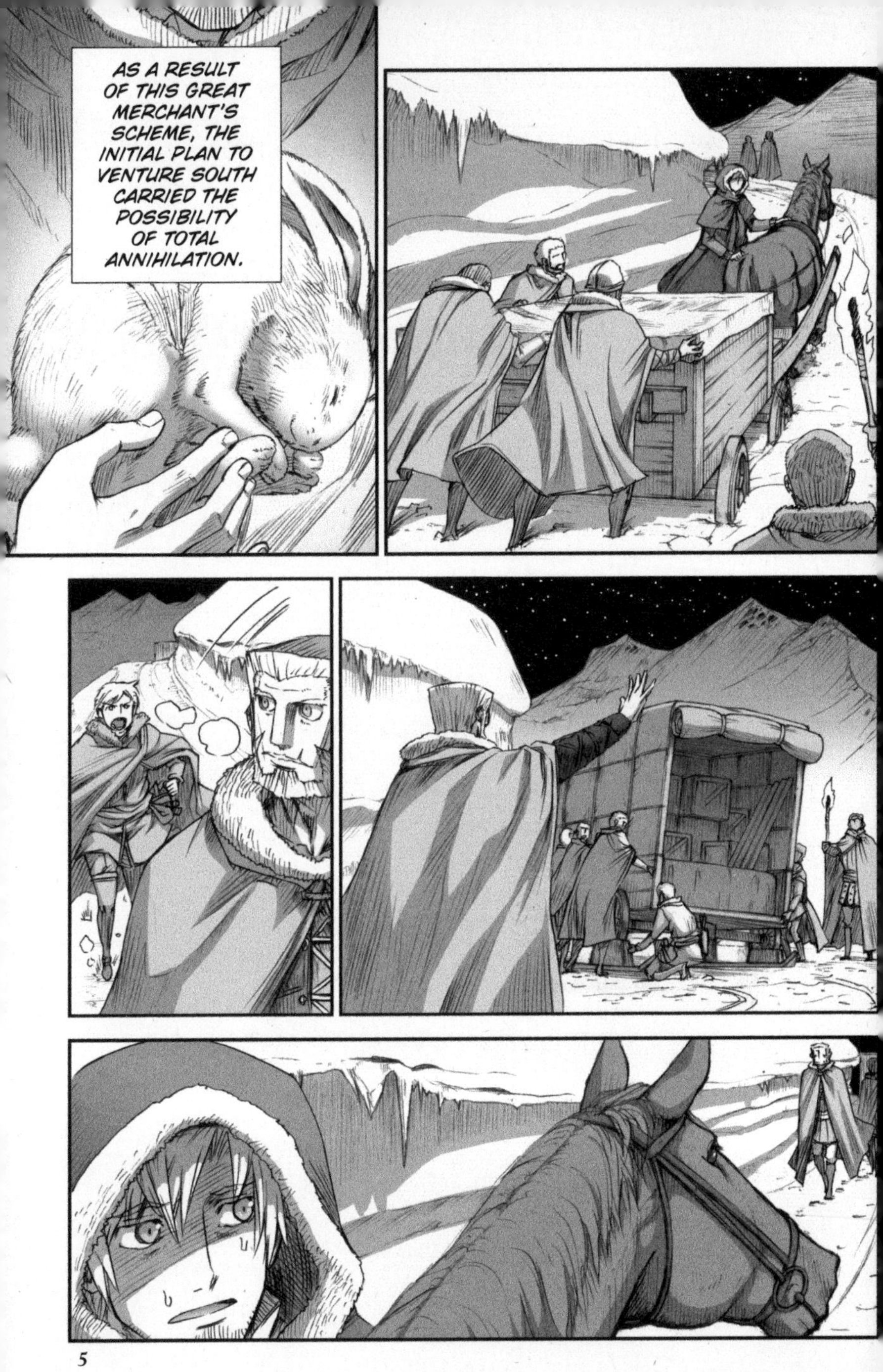
AS A RESULT OF THIS GREAT MERCHANT'S SCHEME, THE INITIAL PLAN TO VENTURE SOUTH CARRIED THE POSSIBILITY OF TOTAL ANNIHILATION.

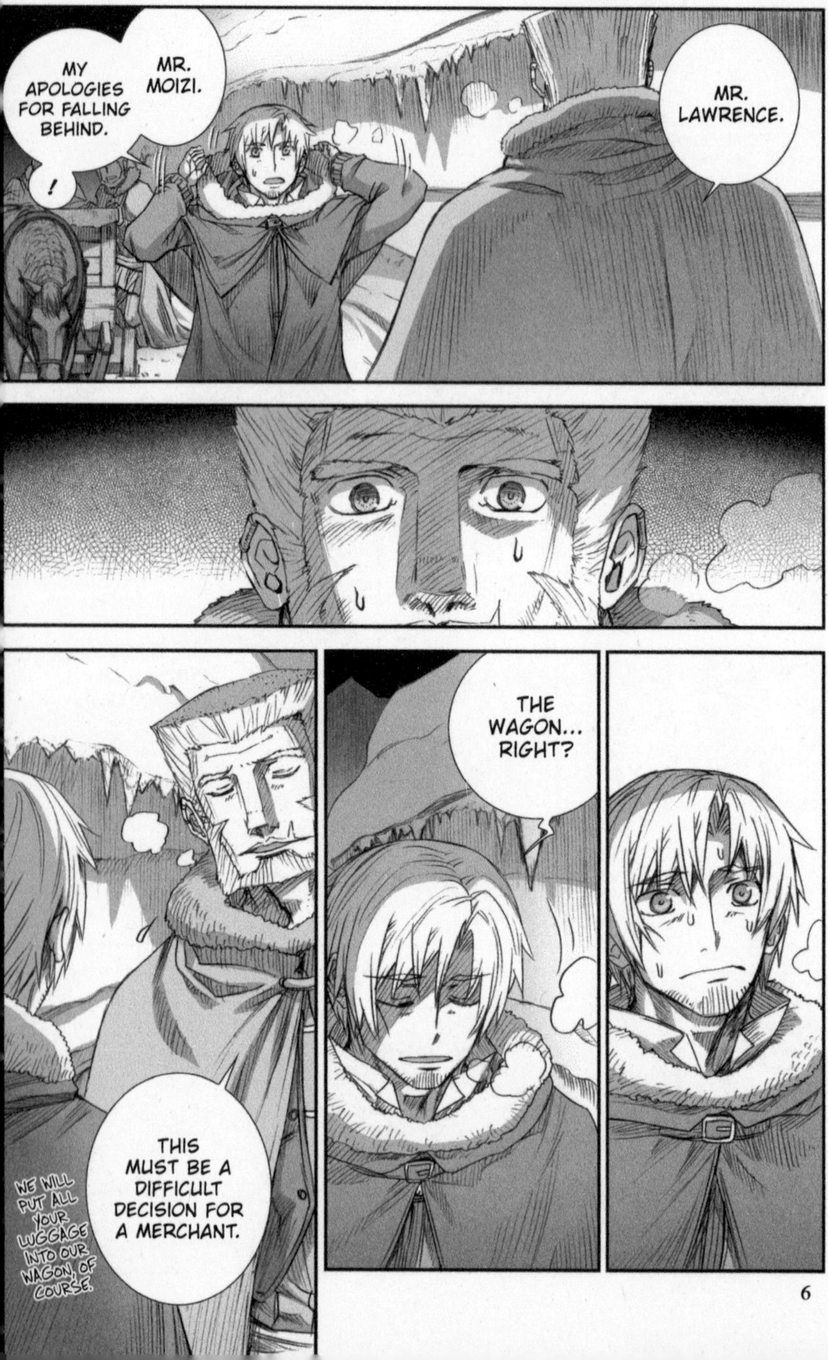
MR. LAWRENCE.
MR. MOIZI.
MY APOLOGIES FOR FALLING BEHIND.
!
THE WAGON... RIGHT?
THIS MUST BE A DIFFICULT DECISION FOR A MERCHANT.
WE WILL PUT ALL YOUR LUGGAGE INTO OUR WAGON, OF COURSE.

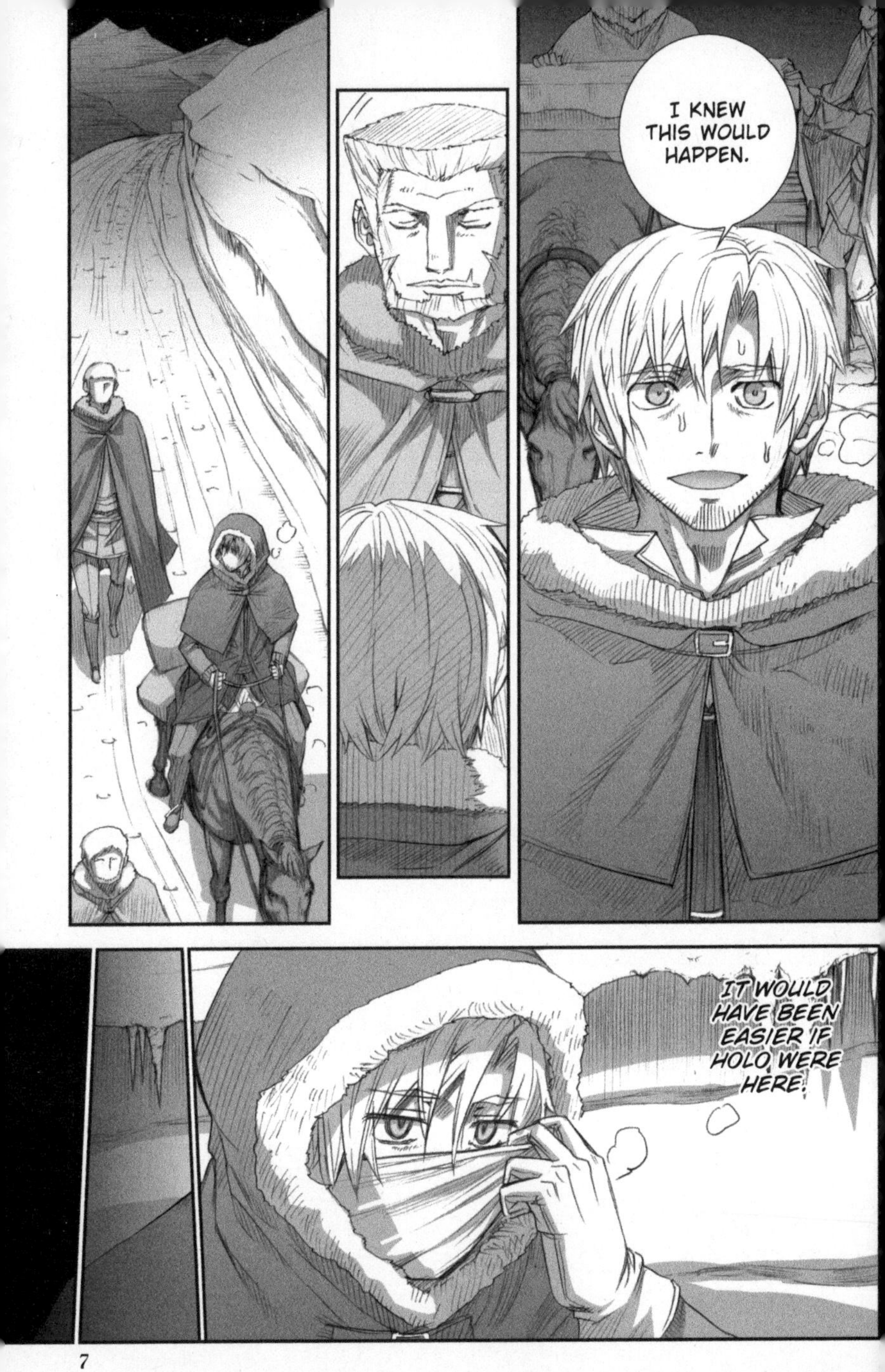
I KNEW THIS WOULD HAPPEN.
IT WOULD HAVE BEEN EASIER IF HOLO WERE HERE.

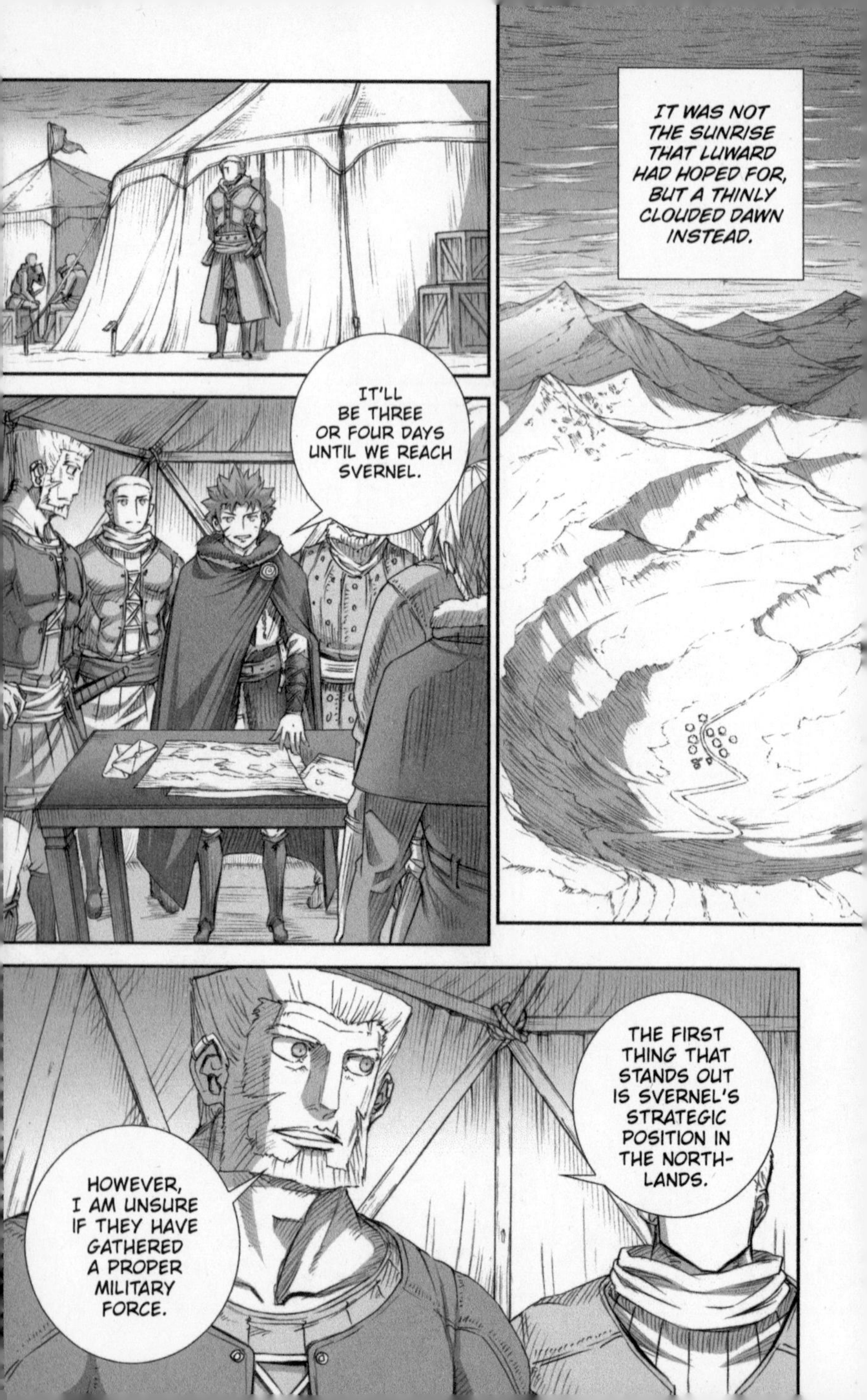
IT WAS NOT THE SUNRISE THAT LUWARD HAD HOPED FOR, BUT A THINLY CLOUDED DAWN INSTEAD.
IT'LL BE THREE OR FOUR DAYS UNTIL WE REACH SVERNEL.
THE FIRST THING THAT STANDS OUT IS SVERNEL'S STRATEGIC POSITION IN THE NORTH-LANDS.
HOWEVER, I AM UNSURE IF THEY HAVE GATHERED A PROPER MILITARY FORCE.

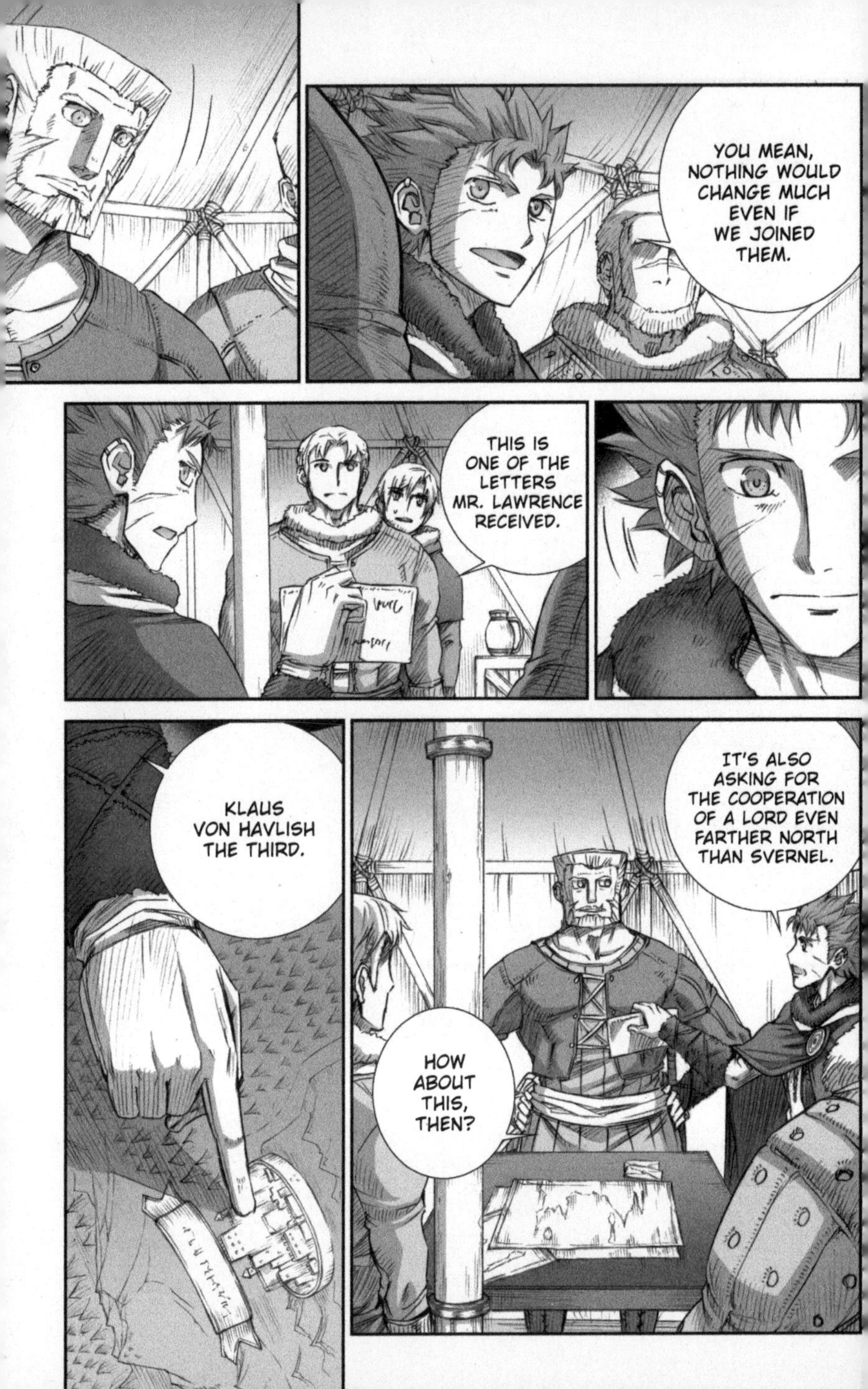
YOU MEAN, NOTHING WOULD CHANGE MUCH EVEN IF WE JOINED THEM.
THIS IS ONE OF THE LETTERS MR. LAWRENCE RECEIVED.
IT'S ALSO ASKING FOR THE COOPERATION OF A LORD EVEN FARTHER NORTH THAN SVERNEL.
HOW ABOUT THIS, THEN?
KLAUS VON HAVLISH THE THIRD.

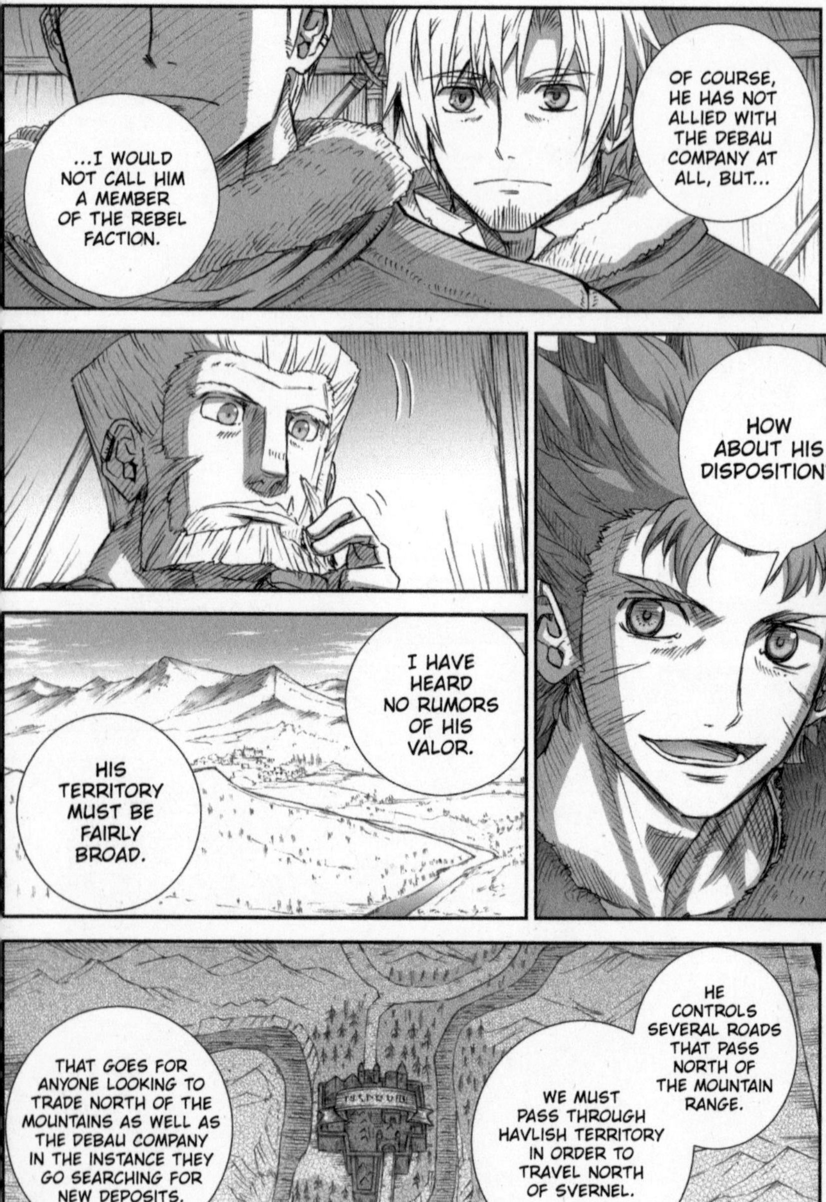
OF COURSE, HE HAS NOT ALLIED WITH THE DEBAU COMPANY AT ALL, BUT...
...I WOULD NOT CALL HIM A MEMBER OF THE REBEL FACTION.
HOW ABOUT HIS DISPOSITION?
I HAVE HEARD NO RUMORS OF HIS VALOR.
HIS TERRITORY MUST BE FAIRLY BROAD.
HE CONTROLS SEVERAL ROADS THAT PASS NORTH OF THE MOUNTAIN RANGE.
WE MUST PASS THROUGH HAVLISH TERRITORY IN ORDER TO TRAVEL NORTH OF SVERNEL.
THAT GOES FOR ANYONE LOOKING TO TRADE NORTH OF THE MOUNTAINS AS WELL AS THE DEBAU COMPANY IN THE INSTANCE THEY GO SEARCHING FOR NEW DEPOSITS.

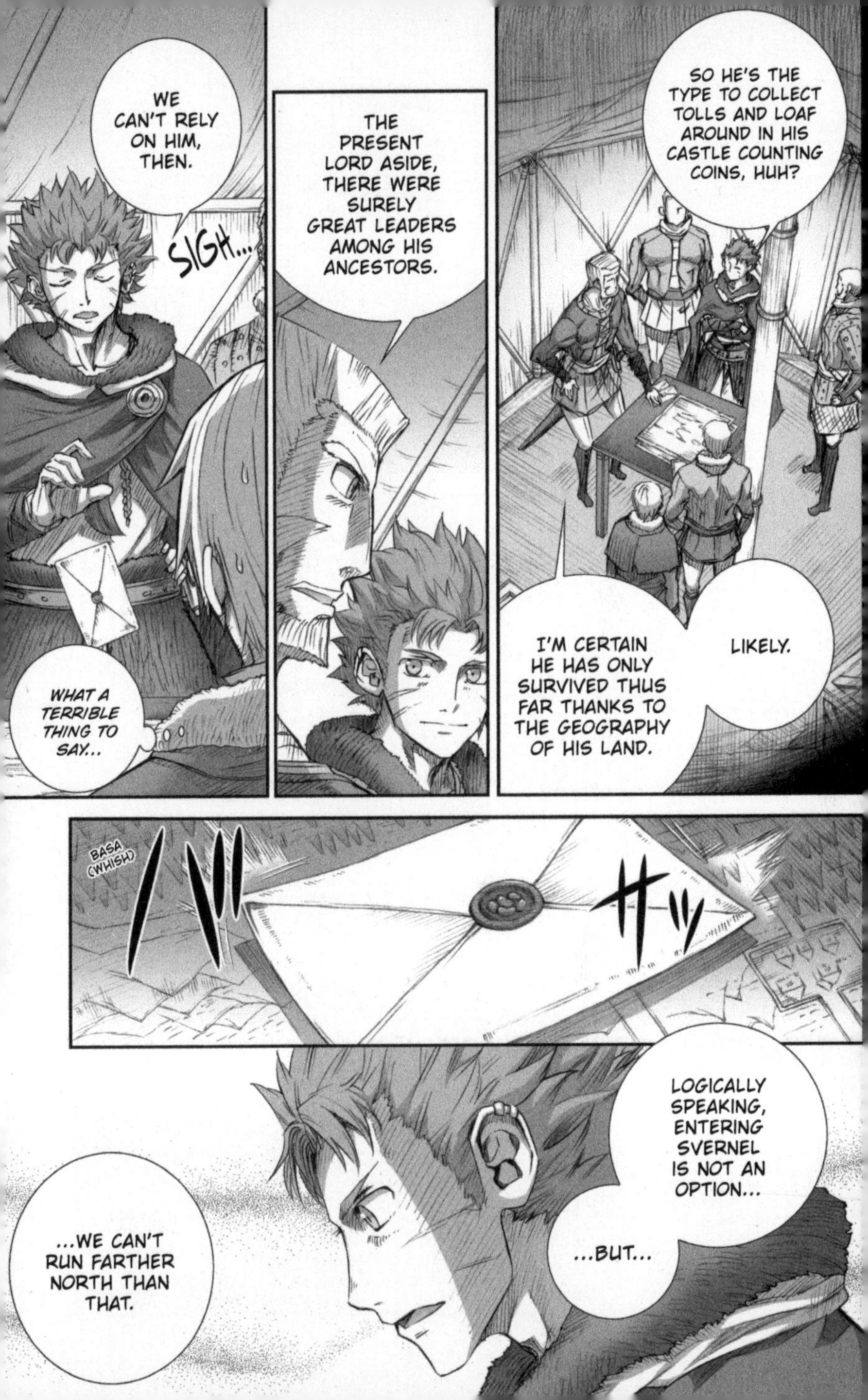
SO HE'S THE TYPE TO COLLECT TOLLS AND LOAF AROUND IN HIS CASTLE COUNTING COINS, HUH?
LIKELY.
I'M CERTAIN HE HAS ONLY SURVIVED THUS FAR THANKS TO THE GEOGRAPHY OF HIS LAND.
THE PRESENT LORD ASIDE, THERE WERE SURELY GREAT LEADERS AMONG HIS ANCESTORS.
WE CAN'T RELY ON HIM, THEN.
SIGH...
WHAT A TERRIBLE THING TO SAY...
BASA (WHISH)
LOGICALLY SPEAKING, ENTERING SVERNEL IS NOT AN OPTION...
...BUT...
...WE CAN'T RUN FARTHER NORTH THAN THAT.

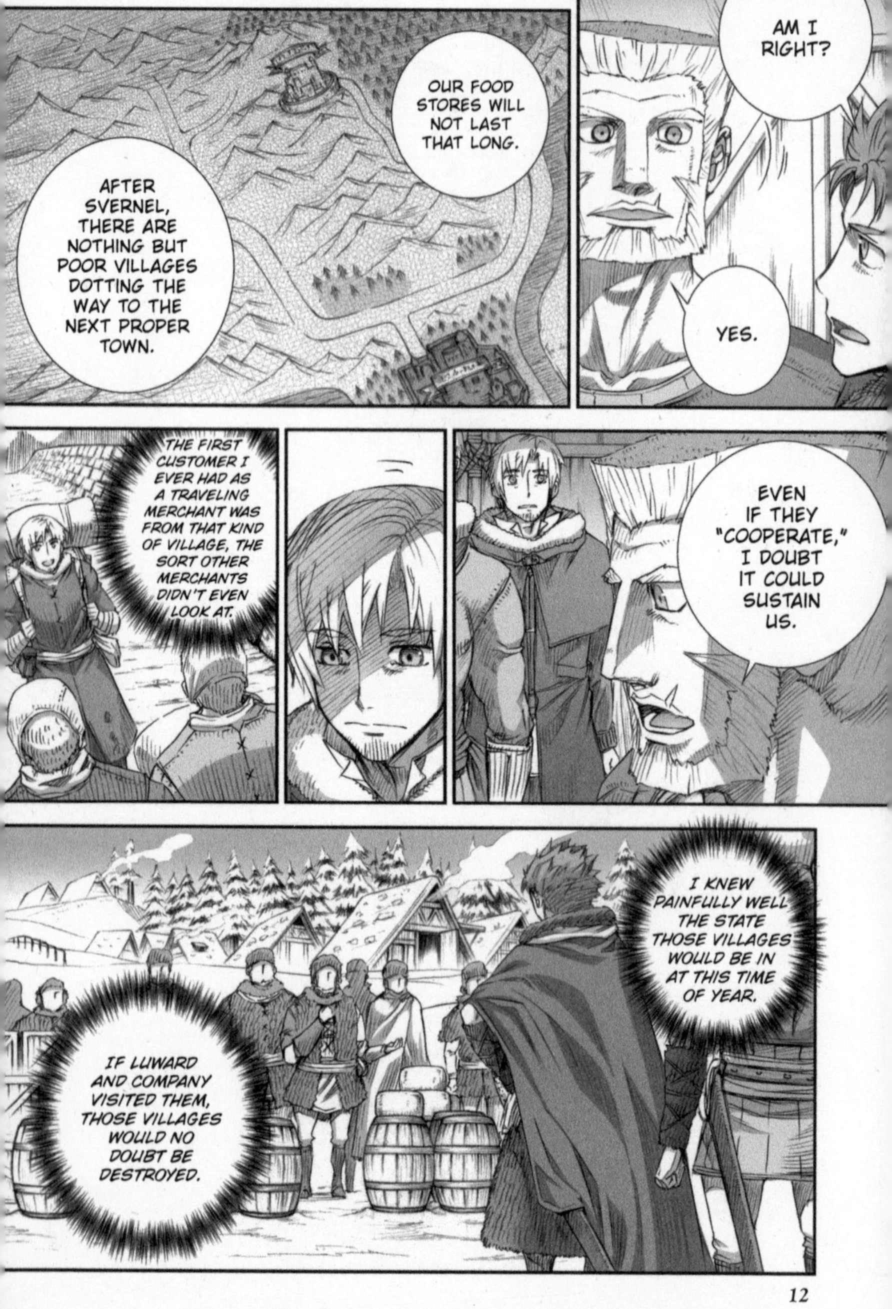
AM I RIGHT?
YES.
OUR FOOD STORES WILL NOT LAST THAT LONG.
AFTER SVERNEL, THERE ARE NOTHING BUT POOR VILLAGES DOTTING THE WAY TO THE NEXT PROPER TOWN.
EVEN IF THEY "COOPERATE," I DOUBT IT COULD SUSTAIN US.
THE FIRST CUSTOMER I EVER HAD AS A TRAVELING MERCHANT WAS FROM THAT KIND OF VILLAGE, THE SORT OTHER MERCHANTS DIDN'T EVEN LOOK AT.
I KNEW PAINFULLY WELL THE STATE THOSE VILLAGES WOULD BE IN AT THIS TIME OF YEAR.
IF LUWARD AND COMPANY VISITED THEM, THOSE VILLAGES WOULD NO DOUBT BE DESTROYED.

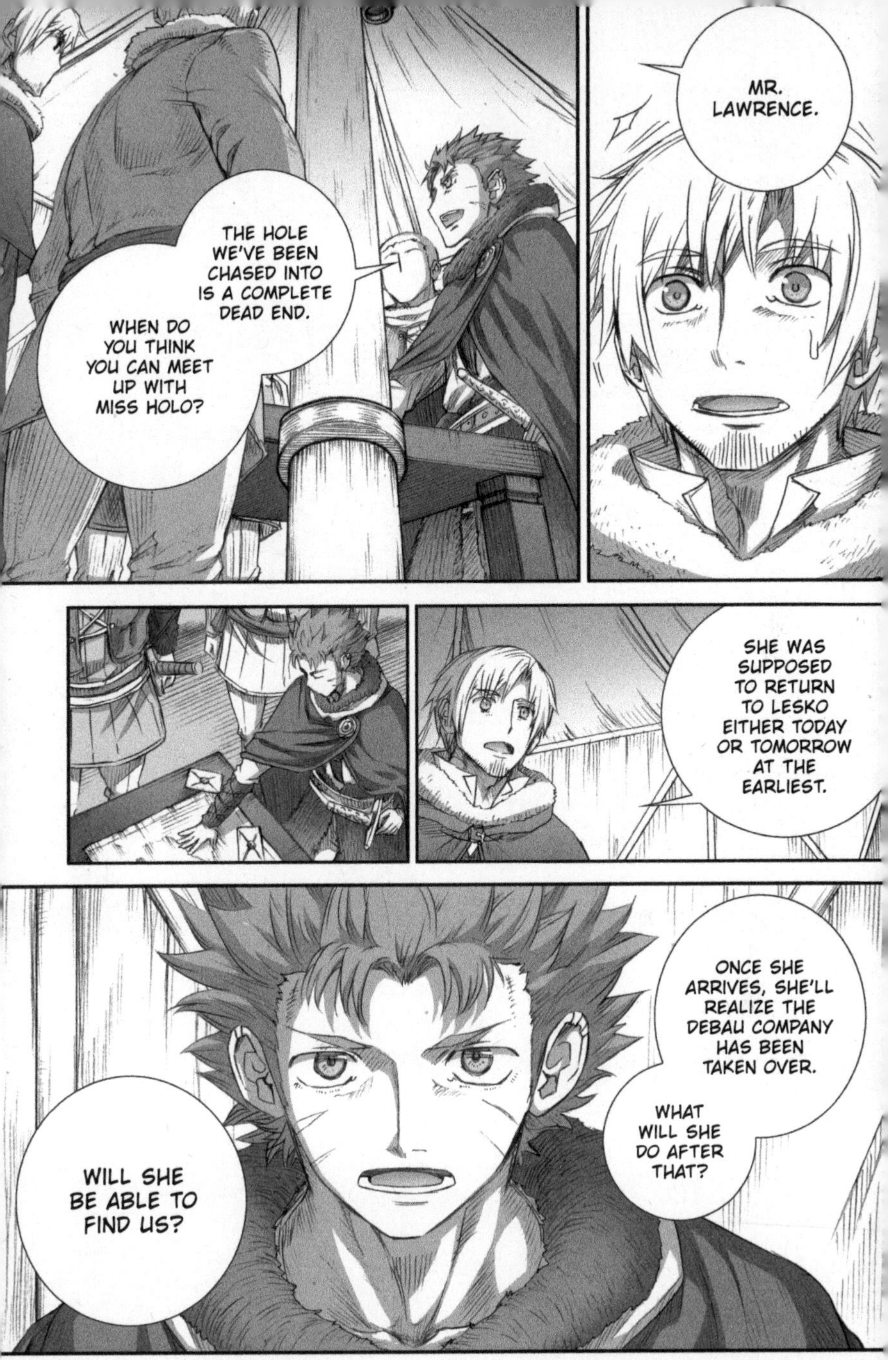
MR. LAWRENCE.
THE HOLE WE'VE BEEN CHASED INTO IS A COMPLETE DEAD END.
WHEN DO YOU THINK YOU CAN MEET UP WITH MISS HOLO?
SHE WAS SUPPOSED TO RETURN TO LESKO EITHER TODAY OR TOMORROW AT THE EARLIEST.
ONCE SHE ARRIVES, SHE'LL REALIZE THE DEBAU COMPANY HAS BEEN TAKEN OVER.
WHAT WILL SHE DO AFTER THAT?
WILL SHE BE ABLE TO FIND US?

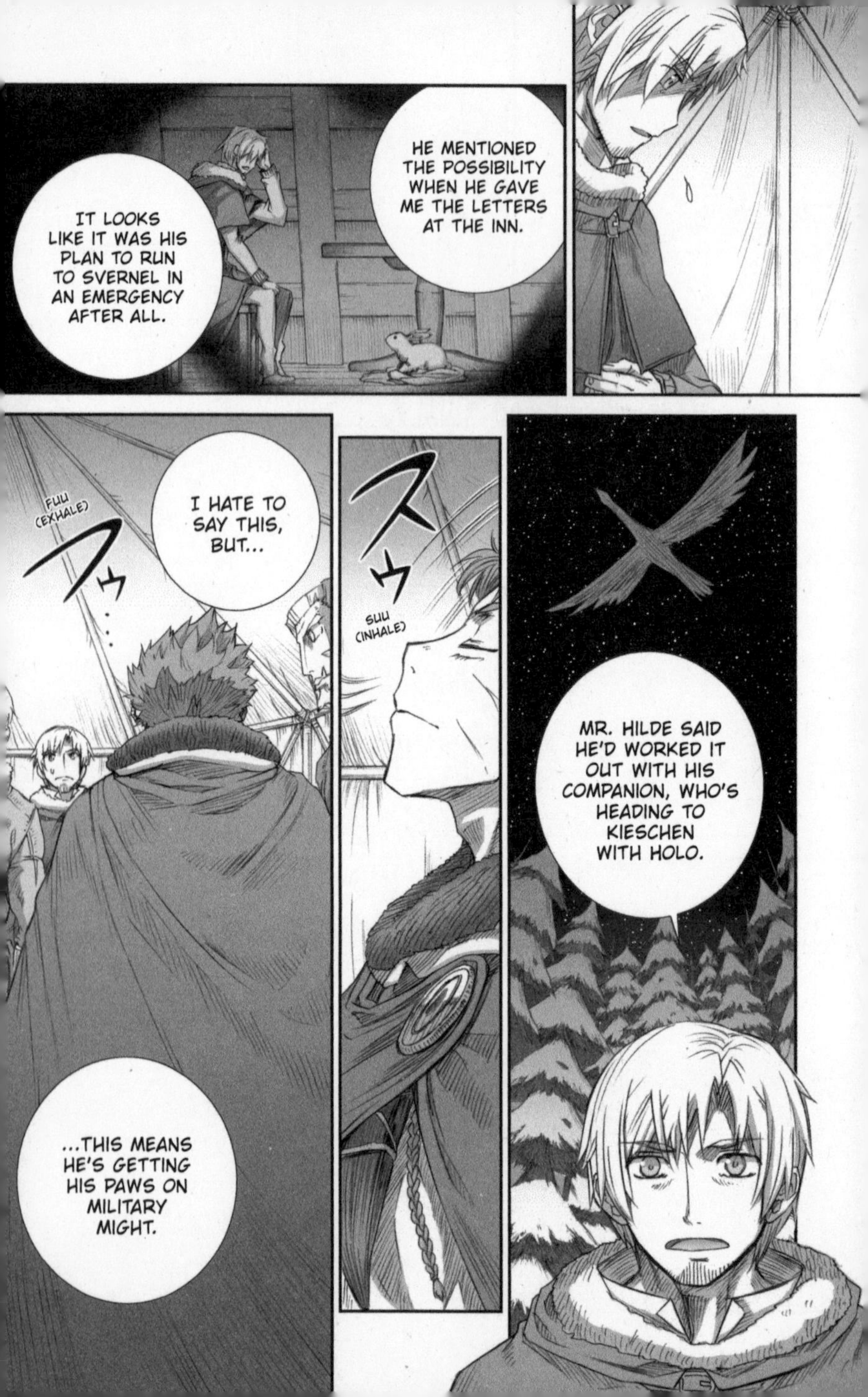
HE MENTIONED THE POSSIBILITY WHEN HE GAVE ME THE LETTERS AT THE INN.
IT LOOKS LIKE IT WAS HIS PLAN TO RUN TO SVERNEL IN AN EMERGENCY AFTER ALL.
MR. HILDE SAID HE'D WORKED IT OUT WITH HIS COMPANION, WHO'S HEADING TO KIESCHEN WITH HOLO.
スゥ
SUU (INHALE)
I HATE TO SAY THIS, BUT...
フゥ
FUU (EXHALE)
...THIS MEANS HE'S GETTING HIS PAWS ON MILITARY MIGHT.

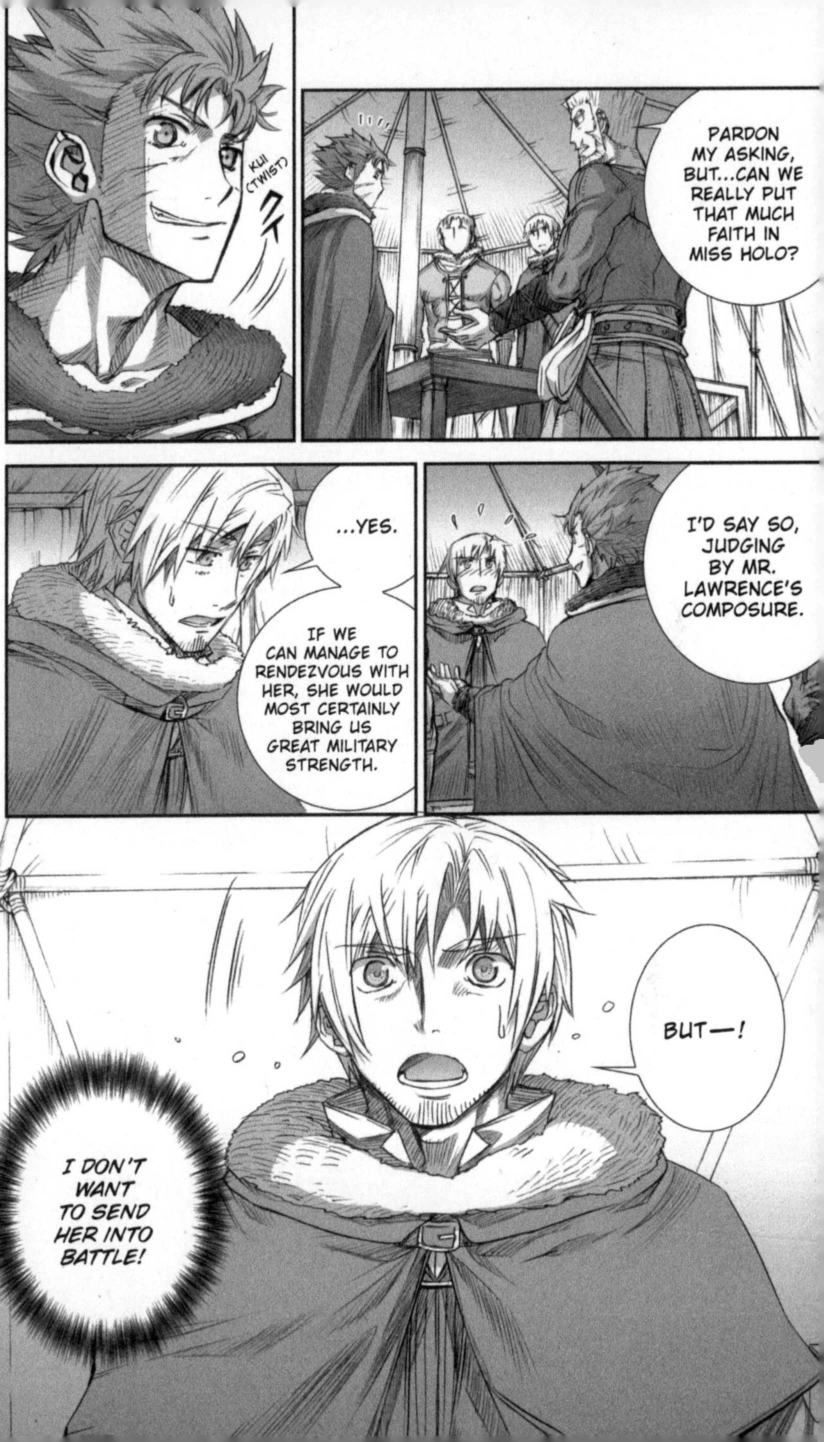
PARDON MY ASKING, BUT...CAN WE REALLY PUT THAT MUCH FAITH IN MISS HOLO?
KUI (TWIST)
I'D SAY SO, JUDGING BY MR. LAWRENCE'S COMPOSURE.
...YES.
IF WE CAN MANAGE TO RENDEZVOUS WITH HER, SHE WOULD MOST CERTAINLY BRING US GREAT MILITARY STRENGTH.
BUT—!
I DON'T WANT TO SEND HER INTO BATTLE!

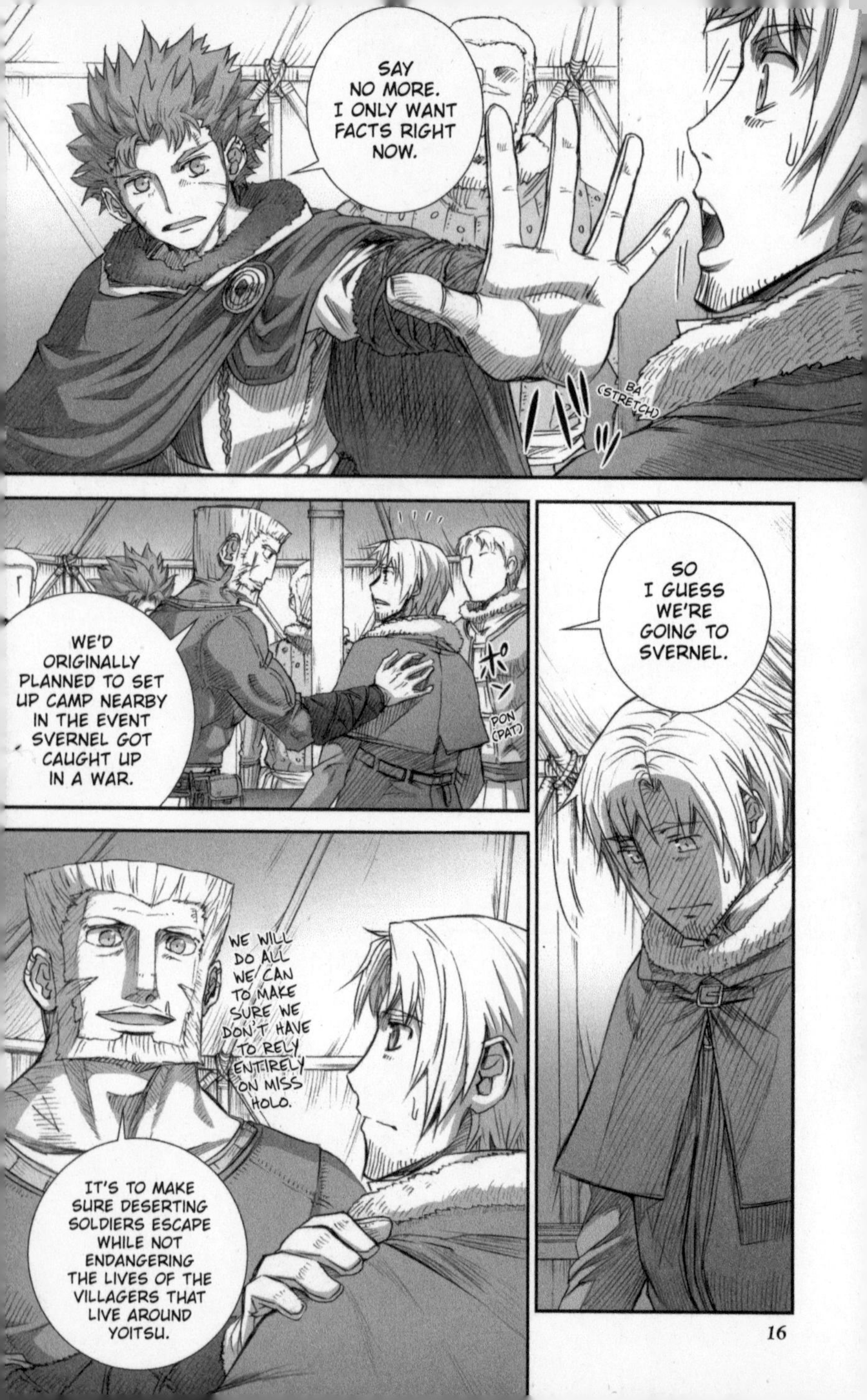
SAY NO MORE. I ONLY WANT FACTS RIGHT NOW.
BA (STRETCH)
SO I GUESS WE'RE GOING TO SVERNEL.
WE'D ORIGINALLY PLANNED TO SET UP CAMP NEARBY IN THE EVENT SVERNEL GOT CAUGHT UP IN A WAR.
PON (PAT)
WE WILL DO ALL WE CAN TO MAKE SURE WE DON'T HAVE TO RELY ENTIRELY ON MISS HOLO.
IT'S TO MAKE SURE DESERTING SOLDIERS ESCAPE WHILE NOT ENDANGERING THE LIVES OF THE VILLAGERS THAT LIVE AROUND YOITSU.

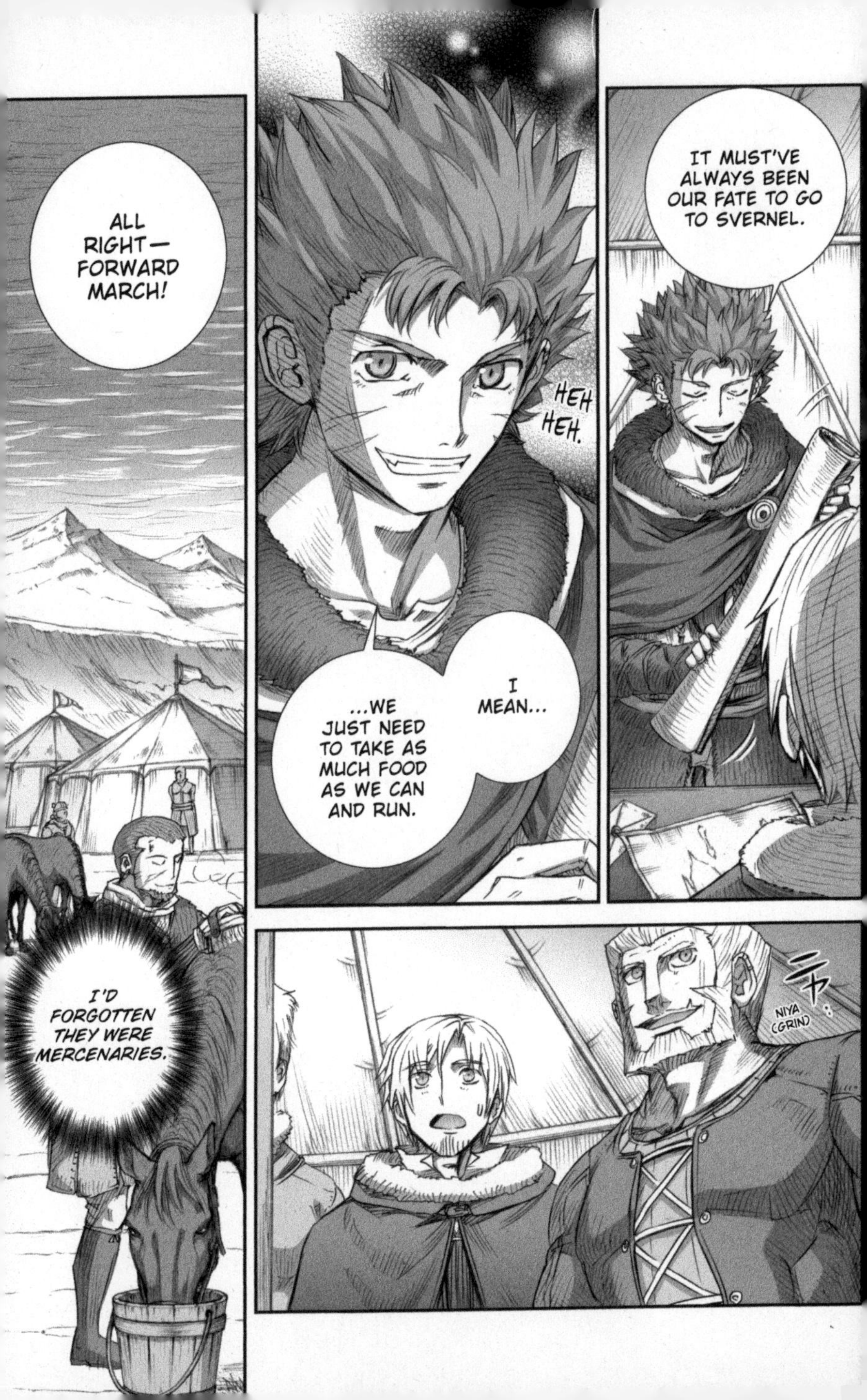
IT MUST'VE ALWAYS BEEN OUR FATE TO GO TO SVERNEL.
HEH HEH.
I MEAN...
...WE JUST NEED TO TAKE AS MUCH FOOD AS WE CAN AND RUN.
ニヤ
NIYA (GRIN)
ALL RIGHT— FORWARD MARCH!
I'D FORGOTTEN THEY WERE MERCENARIES.

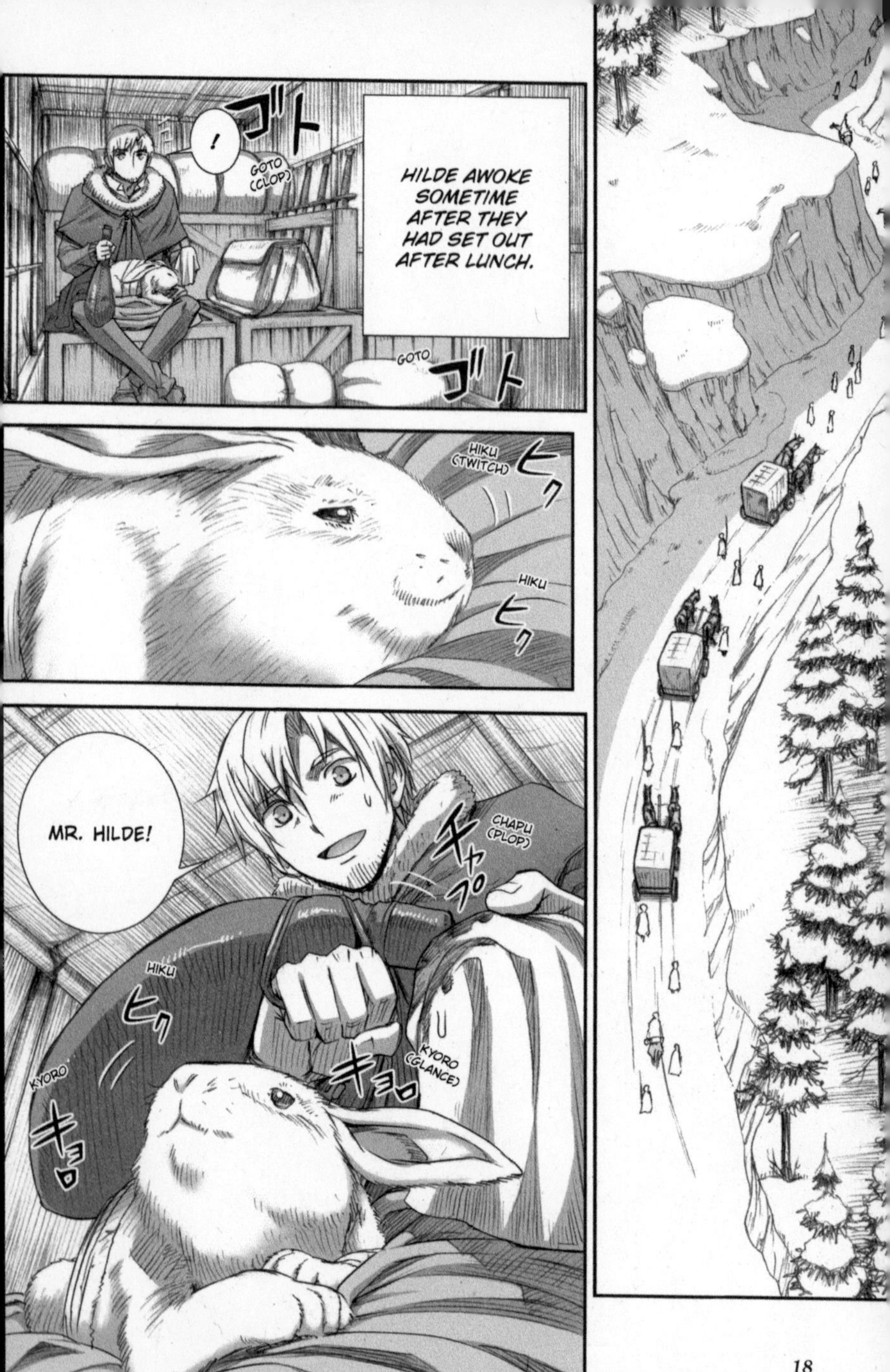

HILDE AWOKE SOMETIME AFTER THEY HAD SET OUT AFTER LUNCH.
ゴト
GOTO (CLOP)
!
ゴト
GOTO
ヒク
HIKU (TWITCH)
ヒク
HIKU
チャプ
CHAPU (PLOP)
MR. HILDE!
キョロ
KYORO (GLANCE)
ヒク
HIKU
キョロ
KYORO

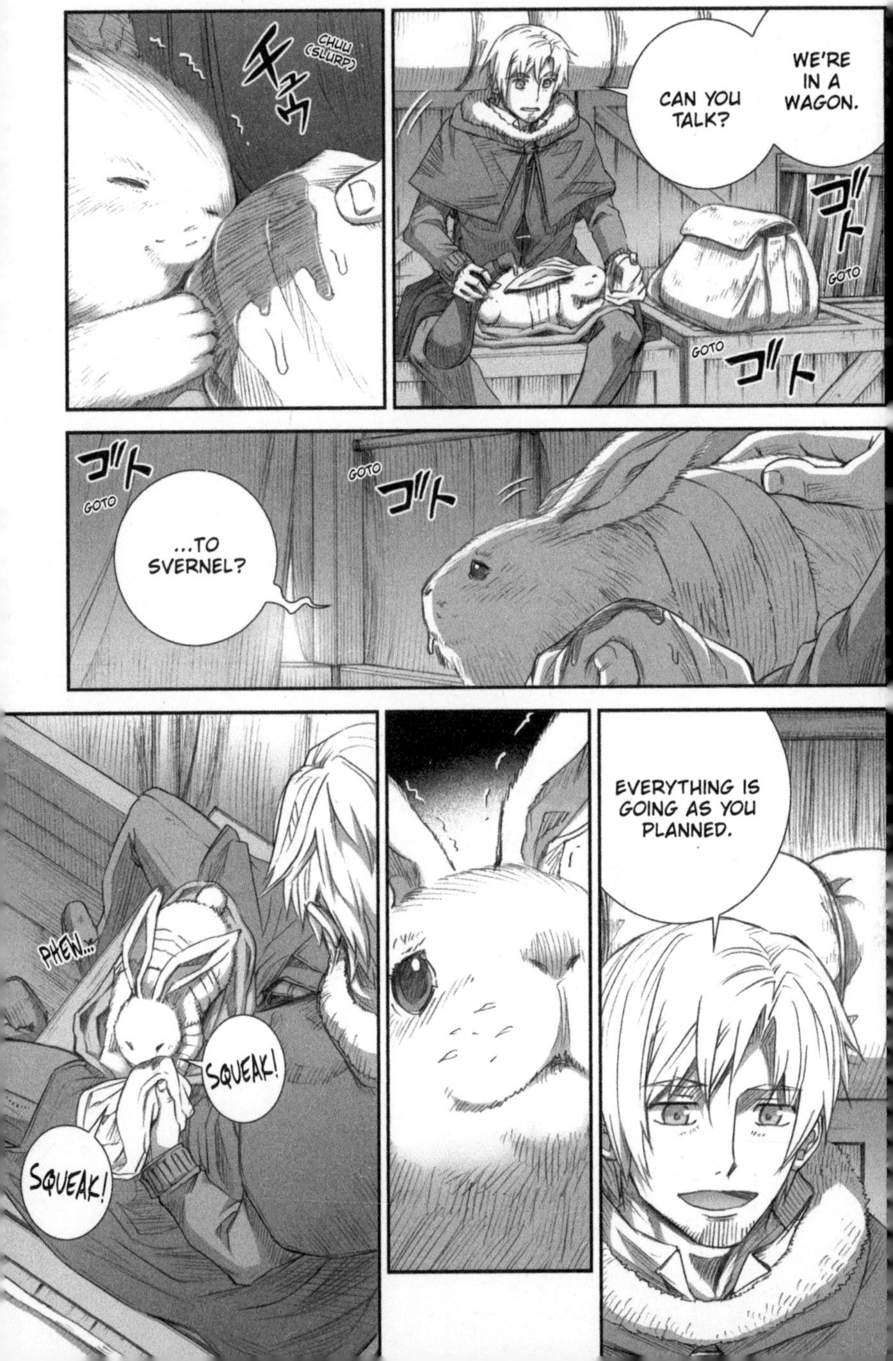
WE'RE IN A WAGON.
CAN YOU TALK?
GOTO
GOTO
CHUU (SLURP)
GOTO
...TO SVERNEL?
GOTO
EVERYTHING IS GOING AS YOU PLANNED.
PHEW...
SQUEAK!
SQUEAK!

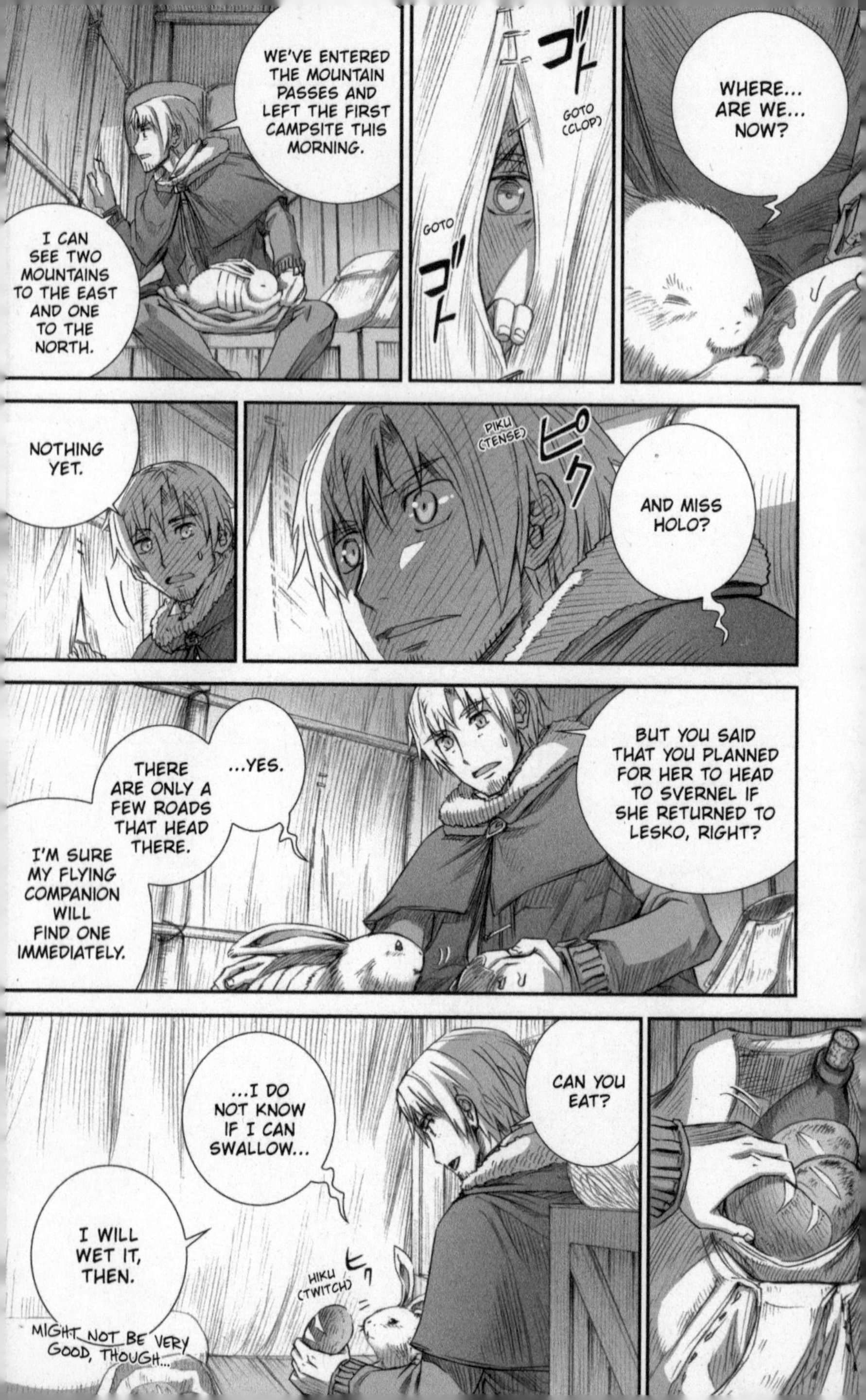
WHERE... ARE WE... NOW?
ゴト
GOTO (CLOP)
GOTO
ゴト
WE'VE ENTERED THE MOUNTAIN PASSES AND LEFT THE FIRST CAMPSITE THIS MORNING.
I CAN SEE TWO MOUNTAINS TO THE EAST AND ONE TO THE NORTH.
ピク
PIKU (TENSE)
AND MISS HOLO?
NOTHING YET.
BUT YOU SAID THAT YOU PLANNED FOR HER TO HEAD TO SVERNEL IF SHE RETURNED TO LESKO, RIGHT?
...YES.
THERE ARE ONLY A FEW ROADS THAT HEAD THERE.
I'M SURE MY FLYING COMPANION WILL FIND ONE IMMEDIATELY.
CAN YOU EAT?
...I DO NOT KNOW IF I CAN SWALLOW...
I WILL WET IT, THEN.
ヒク
HIKU (TWITCH)
MIGHT NOT BE VERY GOOD, THOUGH...

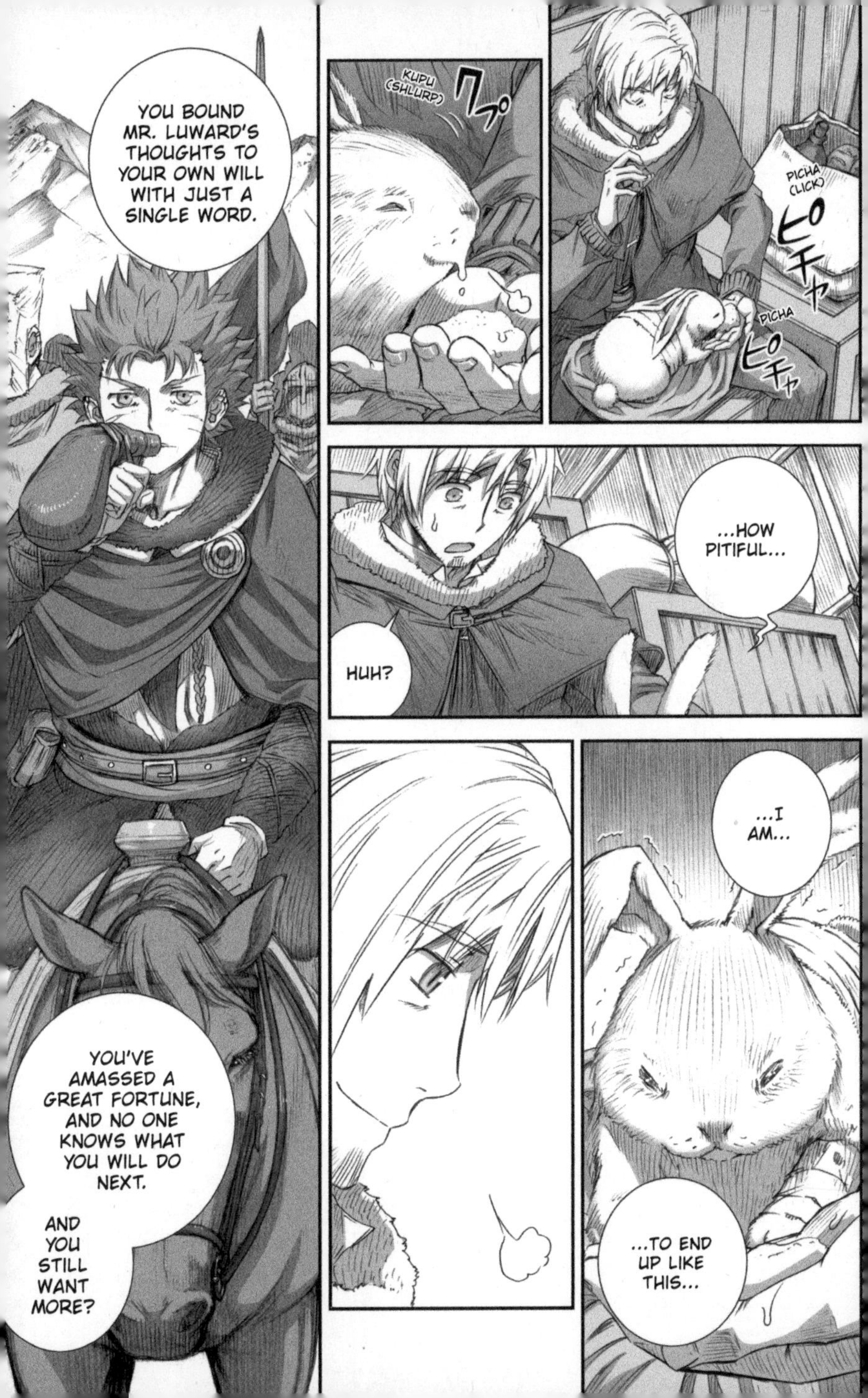
PICHA (LICK)
ピチャ
PICHA
ピチャ
KUPU (SHLURP)
クプ
...HOW PITIFUL...
HUH?
...I AM...
...TO END UP LIKE THIS...
YOU BOUND MR. LUWARD'S THOUGHTS TO YOUR OWN WILL WITH JUST A SINGLE WORD.
YOU'VE AMASSED A GREAT FORTUNE, AND NO ONE KNOWS WHAT YOU WILL DO NEXT.
AND YOU STILL WANT MORE?

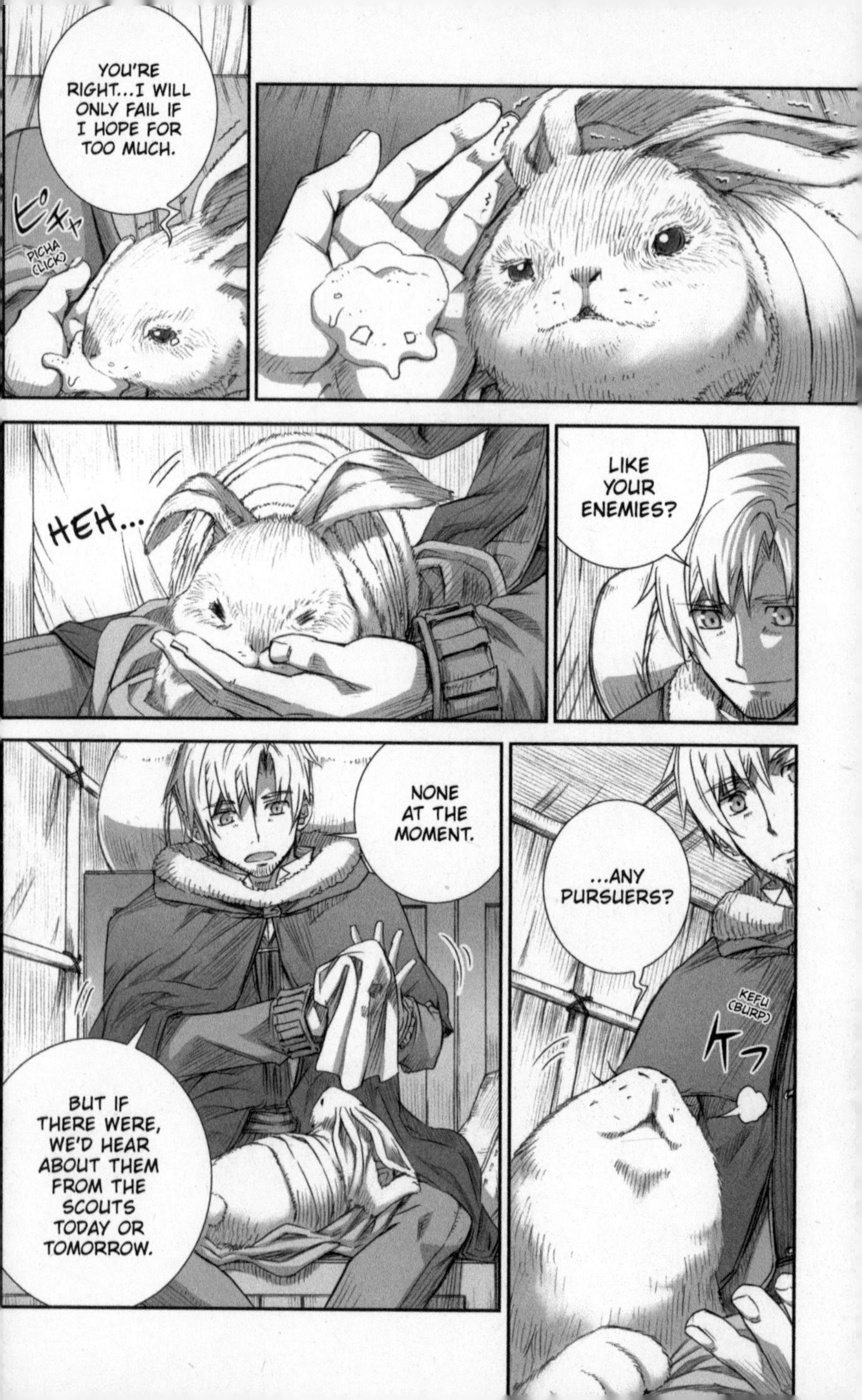

YOU'RE RIGHT...I WILL ONLY FAIL IF I HOPE FOR TOO MUCH.
ピチャ
PICHA (LICK)
LIKE YOUR ENEMIES?
HEH...
...ANY PURSUERS?
KEFU (BURP)
NONE AT THE MOMENT.
BUT IF THERE WERE, WE'D HEAR ABOUT THEM FROM THE SCOUTS TODAY OR TOMORROW.

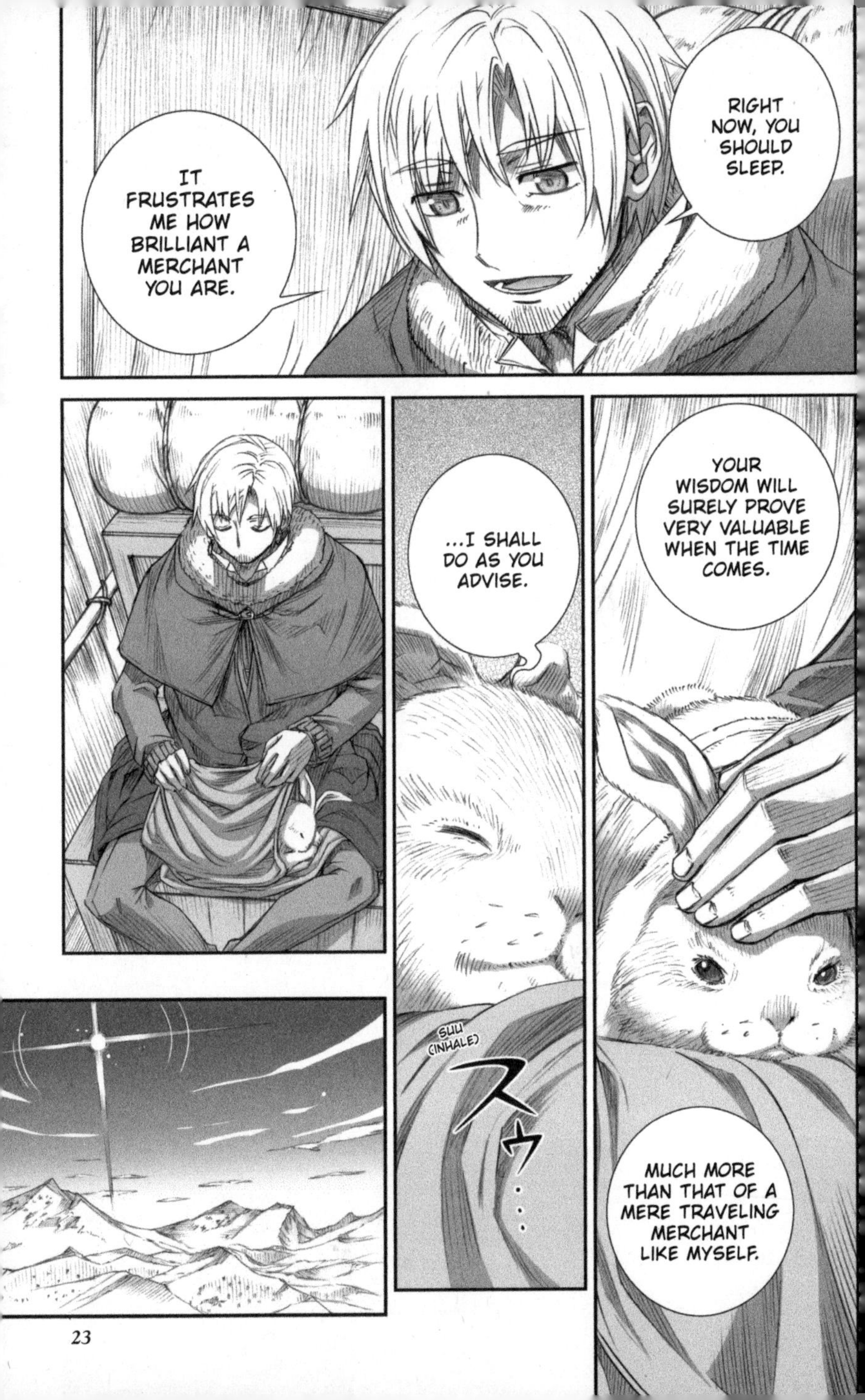
RIGHT NOW, YOU SHOULD SLEEP.
IT FRUSTRATES ME HOW BRILLIANT A MERCHANT YOU ARE.
YOUR WISDOM WILL SURELY PROVE VERY VALUABLE WHEN THE TIME COMES.
MUCH MORE THAN THAT OF A MERE TRAVELING MERCHANT LIKE MYSELF.
...I SHALL DO AS YOU ADVISE.
SUU (INHALE)
スゥ...

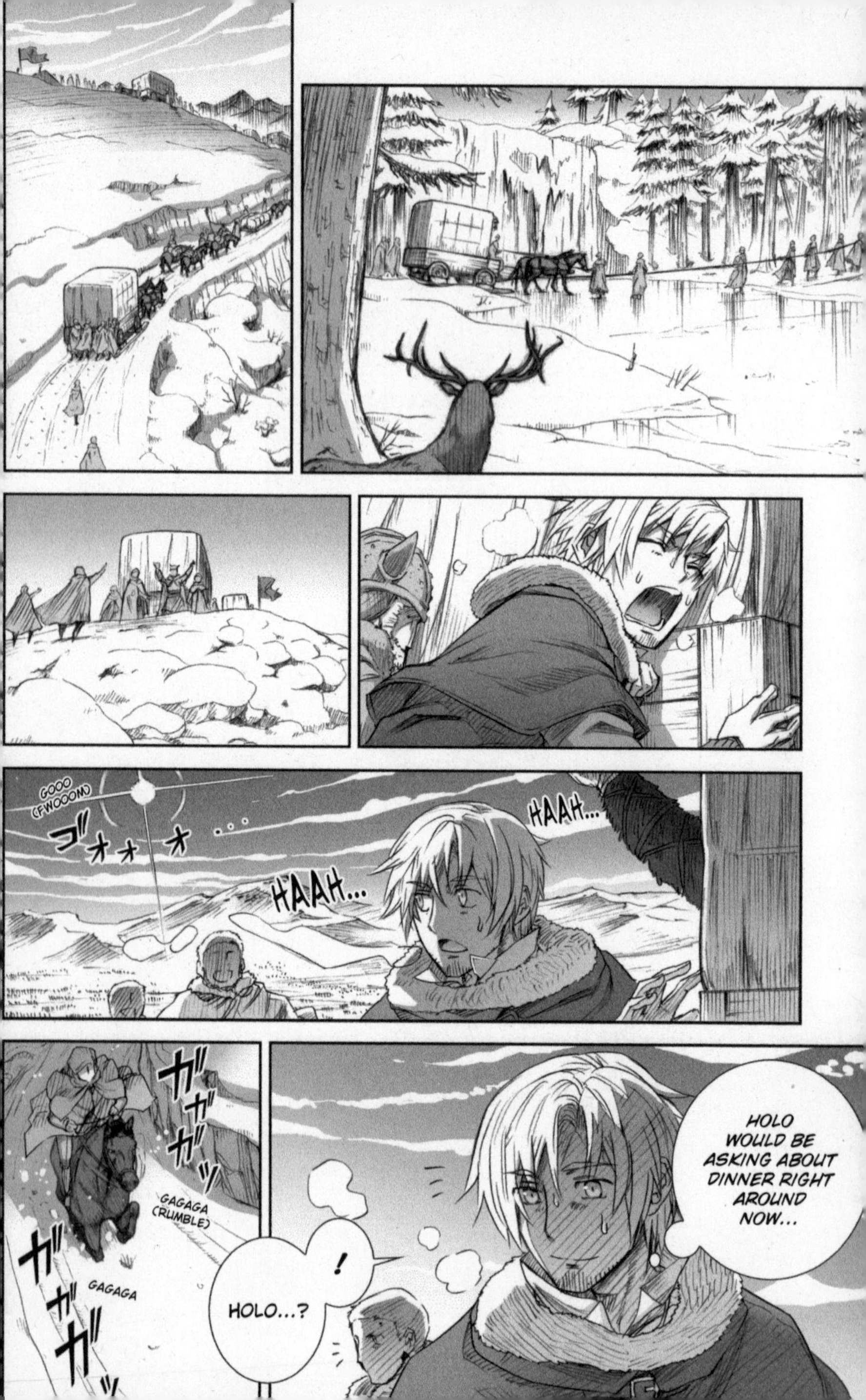
HAAH...
ゴォォォ
GOOO (FWOOOM)
HAAH...
HOLO WOULD BE ASKING ABOUT DINNER RIGHT AROUND NOW...
!
HOLO...?
ガガガッ
GAGAGA (RUMBLE)
ガガガ
GAGAGA

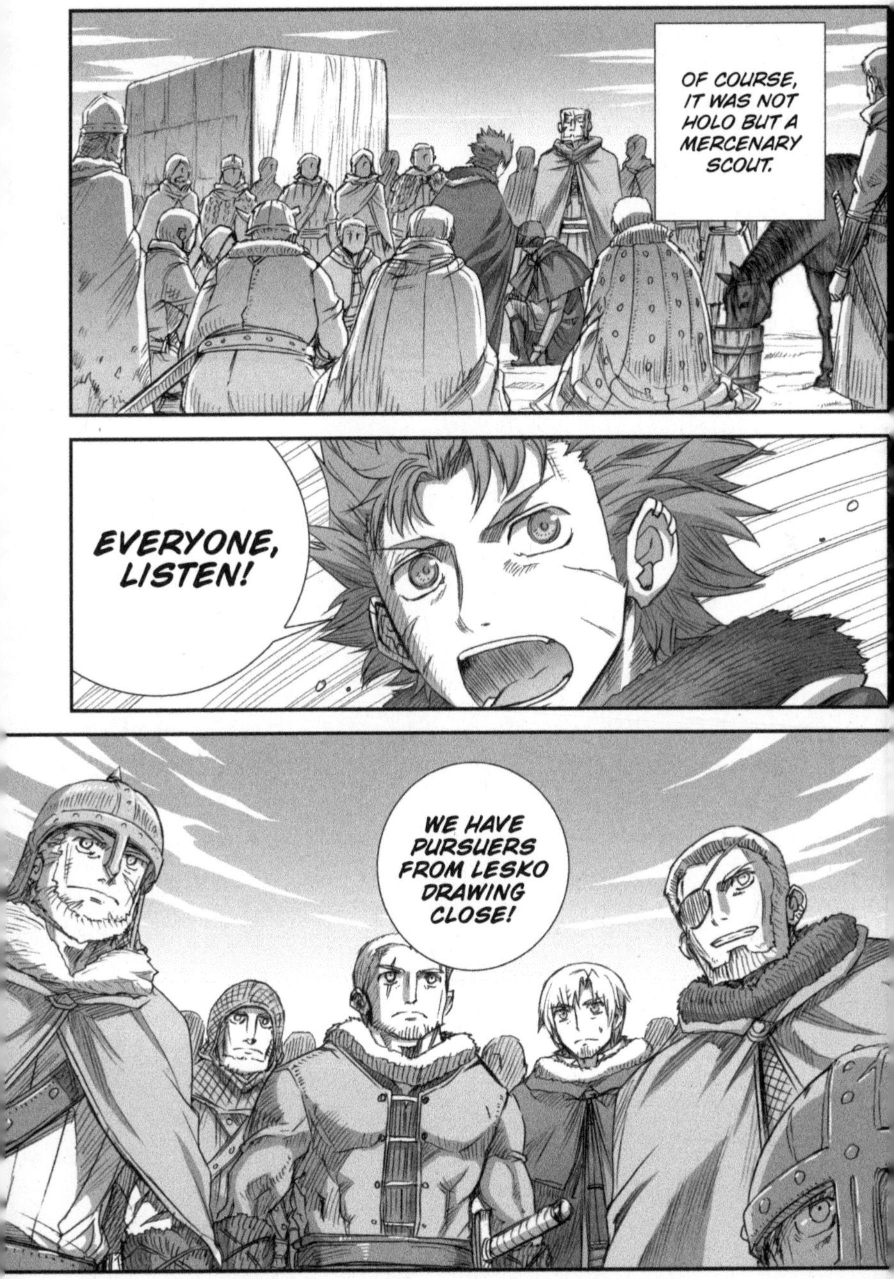
OF COURSE, IT WAS NOT HOLO BUT A MERCENARY SCOUT.
EVERYONE, LISTEN!
WE HAVE PURSUERS FROM LESKO DRAWING CLOSE!

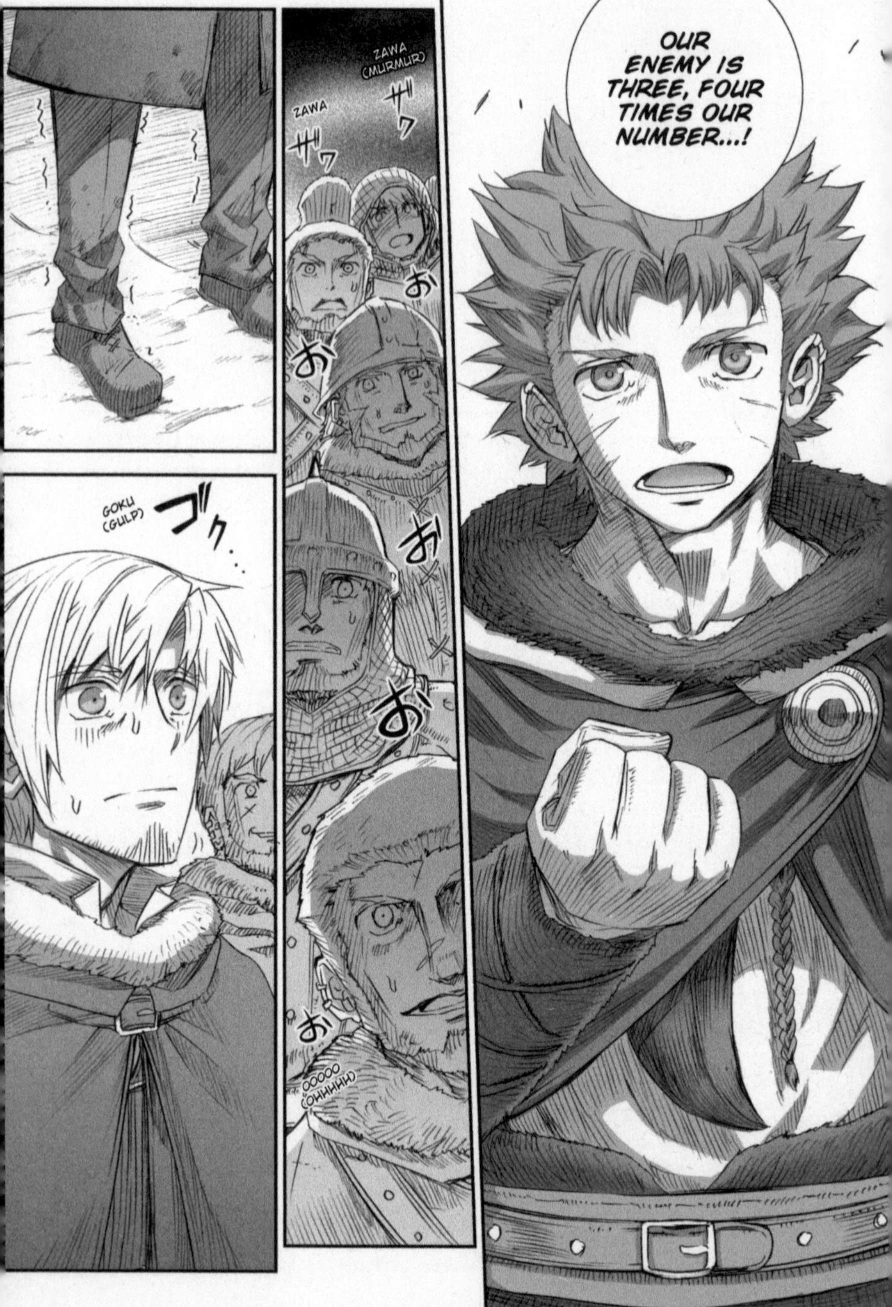
OUR ENEMY IS THREE, FOUR TIMES OUR NUMBER...!
ザワ
ZAWA (MURMUR)
ザワ
ZAWA
お
お
お
お
お
OOOOO (OHHHHH)
ゴク…
GOKU (GULP)

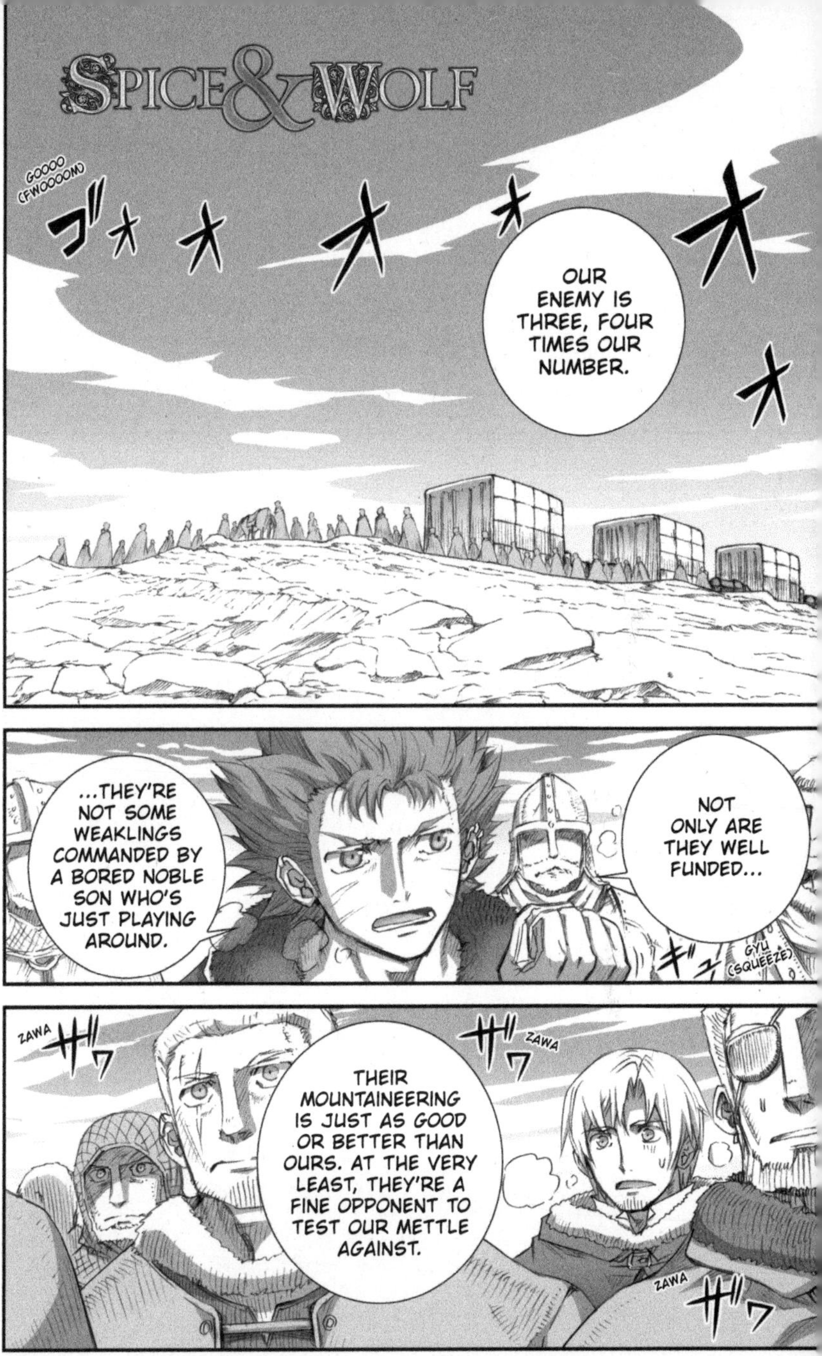
SPICE & WOLF
GOOOO (FWOOOOM)
ゴォォォォォォ
OUR ENEMY IS THREE, FOUR TIMES OUR NUMBER.
NOT ONLY ARE THEY WELL FUNDED...
GYU (SQUEEZE)
ギュ
...THEY'RE NOT SOME WEAKLINGS COMMANDED BY A BORED NOBLE SON WHO'S JUST PLAYING AROUND.
ZAWA
ザワ
THEIR MOUNTAINEERING IS JUST AS GOOD OR BETTER THAN OURS. AT THE VERY LEAST, THEY'RE A FINE OPPONENT TO TEST OUR METTLE AGAINST.
ZAWA
ザワ
ZAWA
ザワ

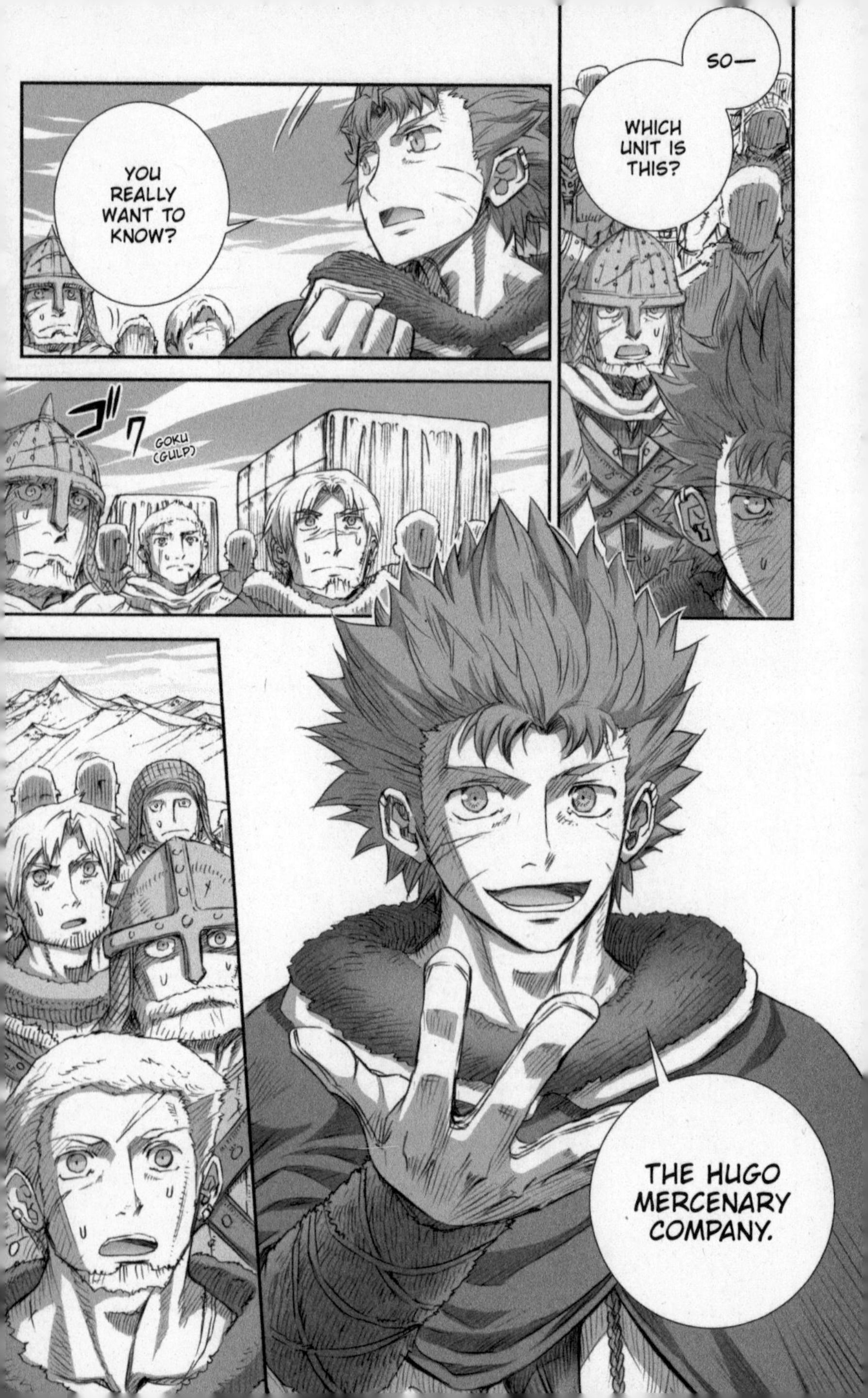
SO—
WHICH UNIT IS THIS?
YOU REALLY WANT TO KNOW?
ゴク
GOKU (GULP)
THE HUGO MERCENARY COMPANY.

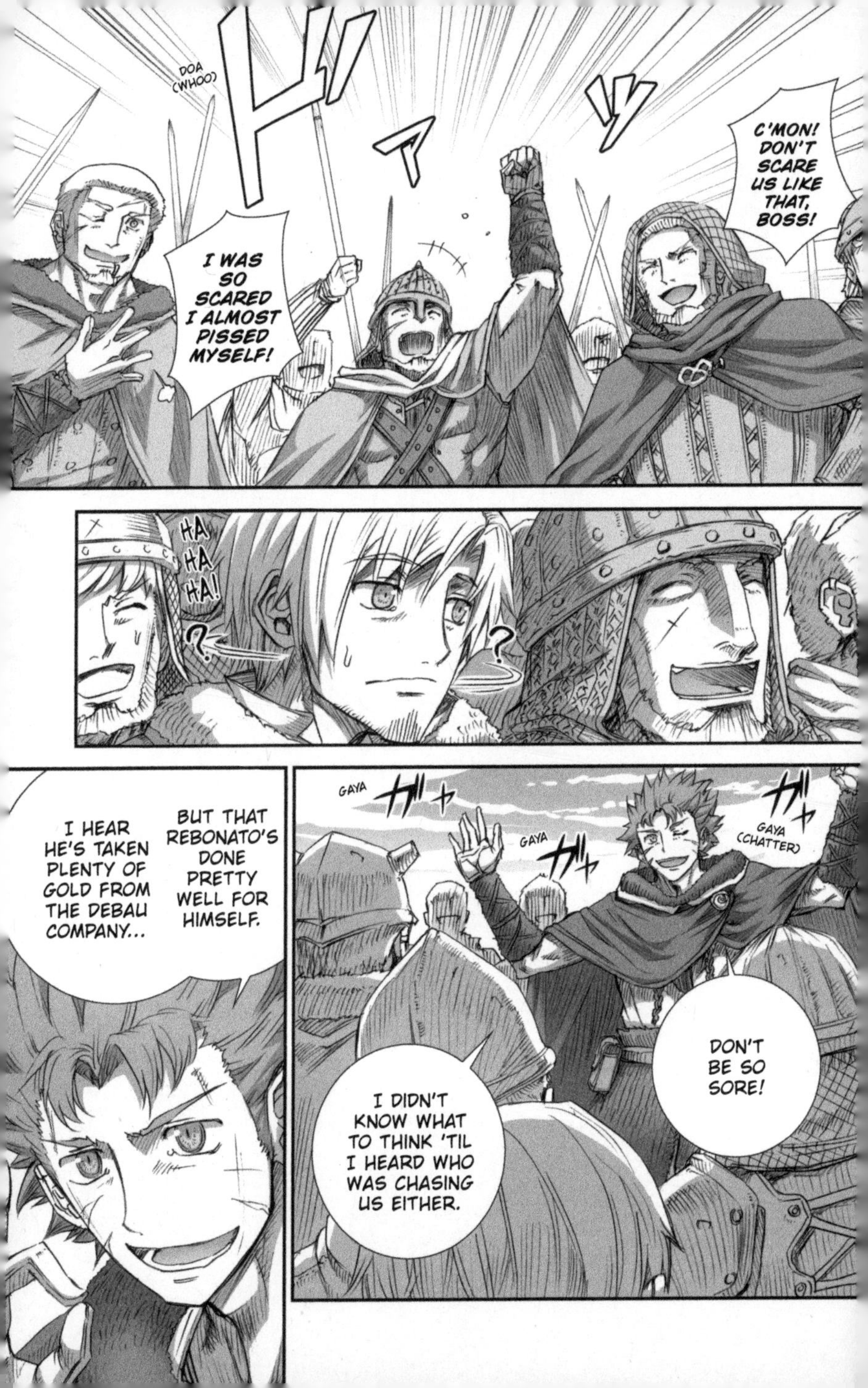
C'MON! DON'T SCARE US LIKE THAT, BOSS!
DOA (WHOO)
I WAS SO SCARED I ALMOST PISSED MYSELF!
HA HA HA!
GAYA (CHATTER)
GAYA
GAYA
DON'T BE SO SORE!
I DIDN'T KNOW WHAT TO THINK 'TIL I HEARD WHO WAS CHASING US EITHER.
BUT THAT REBONATO'S DONE PRETTY WELL FOR HIMSELF.
I HEAR HE'S TAKEN PLENTY OF GOLD FROM THE DEBAU COMPANY...

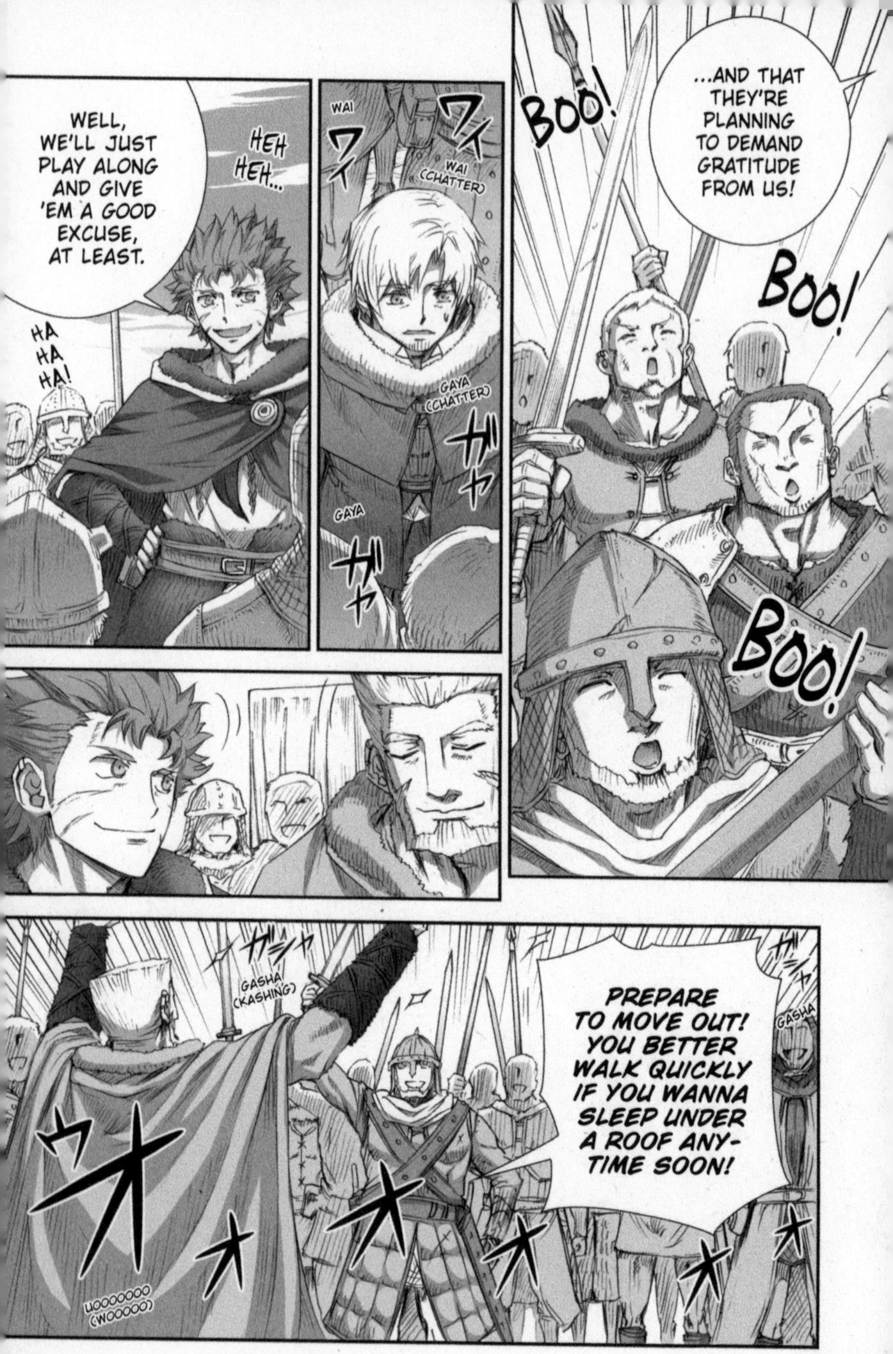
...AND THAT THEY'RE PLANNING TO DEMAND GRATITUDE FROM US!
BOO!
BOO!
BOO!
WAI
WAI (CHATTER)
GAYA (CHATTER)
GAYA
WELL, WE'LL JUST PLAY ALONG AND GIVE 'EM A GOOD EXCUSE, AT LEAST.
HEH HEH...
HA HA HA!
GASHA
PREPARE TO MOVE OUT! YOU BETTER WALK QUICKLY IF YOU WANNA SLEEP UNDER A ROOF ANY-TIME SOON!
GASHA (KASHING)
UOOOOOOO (WOOOOO)

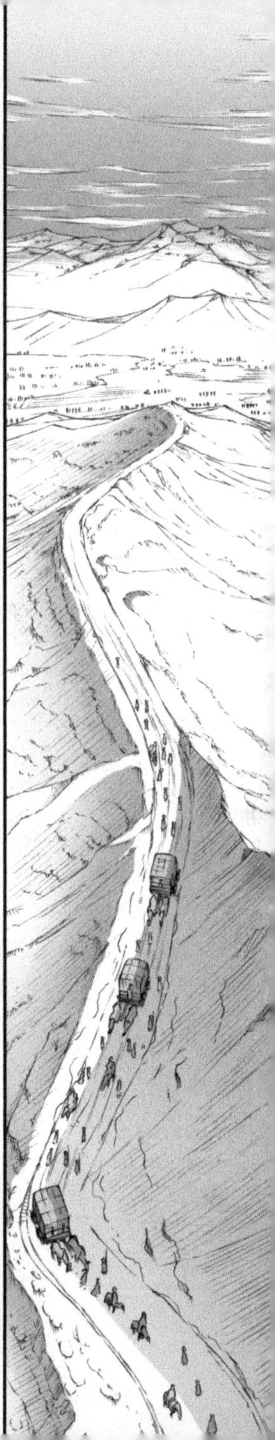

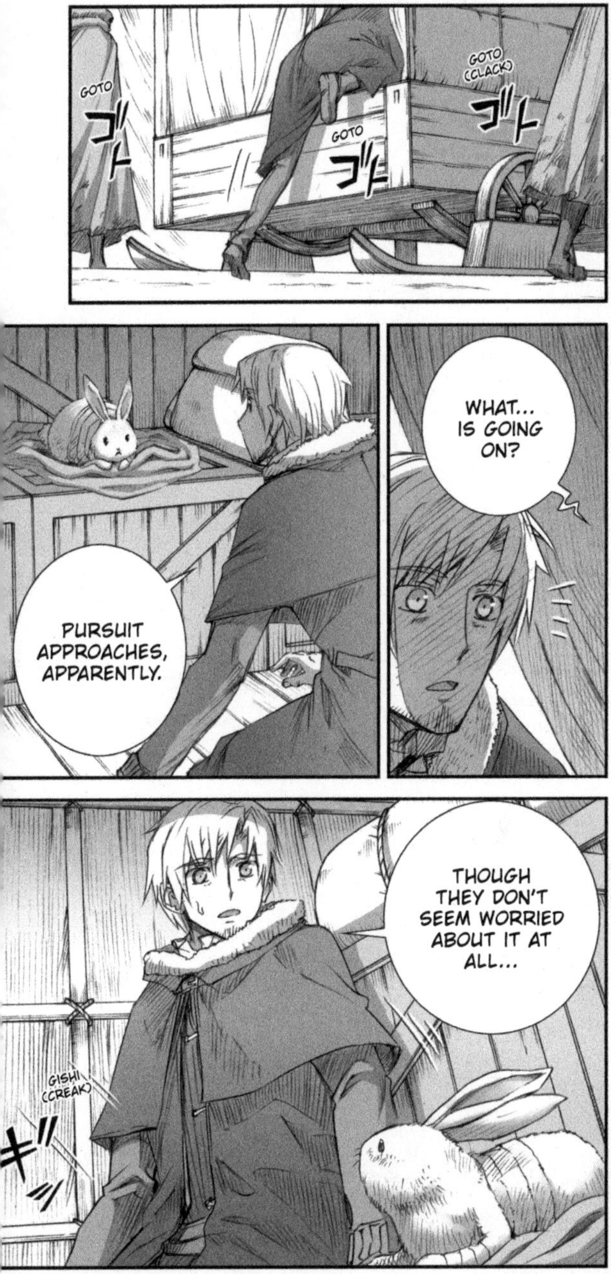
GOTO (CLACK)
GOTO
GOTO
WHAT... IS GOING ON?
PURSUIT APPROACHES, APPARENTLY.
THOUGH THEY DON'T SEEM WORRIED ABOUT IT AT ALL...
GISHI (CREAK)

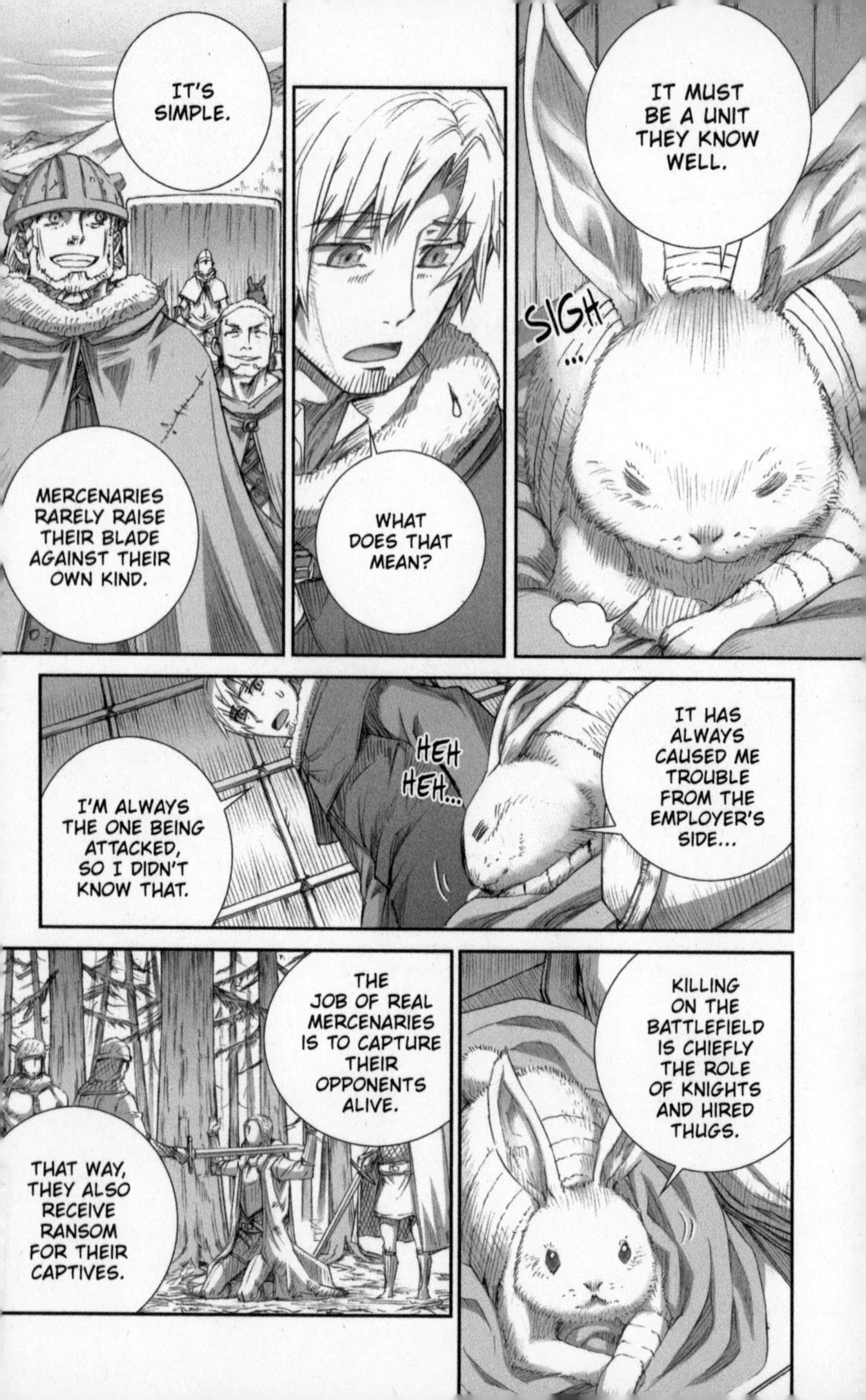
IT MUST BE A UNIT THEY KNOW WELL.
SIGH...
WHAT DOES THAT MEAN?
IT'S SIMPLE.
MERCENARIES RARELY RAISE THEIR BLADE AGAINST THEIR OWN KIND.
IT HAS ALWAYS CAUSED ME TROUBLE FROM THE EMPLOYER'S SIDE...
HEH HEH...
I'M ALWAYS THE ONE BEING ATTACKED, SO I DIDN'T KNOW THAT.
KILLING ON THE BATTLEFIELD IS CHIEFLY THE ROLE OF KNIGHTS AND HIRED THUGS.
THE JOB OF REAL MERCENARIES IS TO CAPTURE THEIR OPPONENTS ALIVE.
THAT WAY, THEY ALSO RECEIVE RANSOM FOR THEIR CAPTIVES.

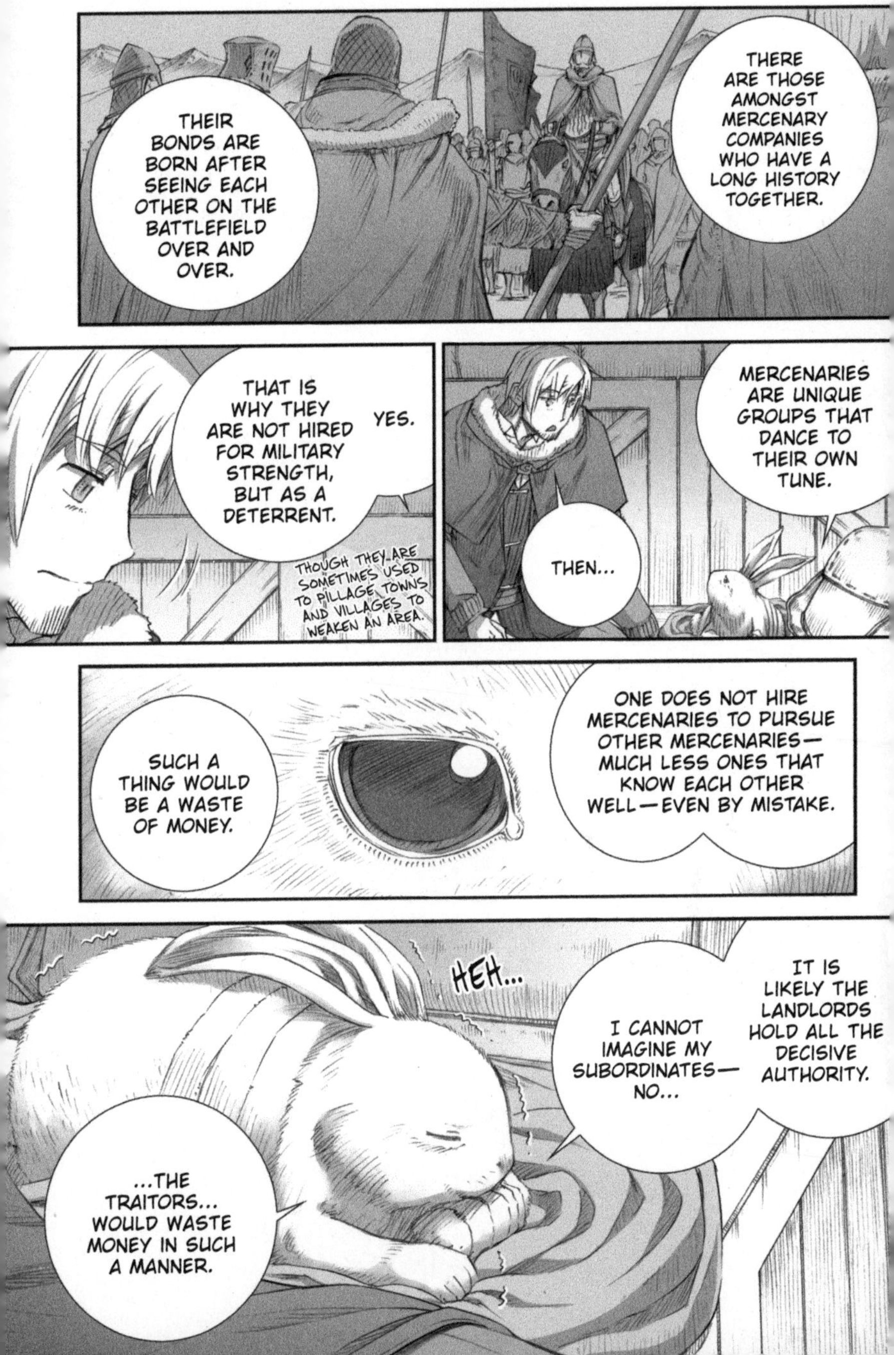
THERE ARE THOSE AMONGST MERCENARY COMPANIES WHO HAVE A LONG HISTORY TOGETHER.
THEIR BONDS ARE BORN AFTER SEEING EACH OTHER ON THE BATTLEFIELD OVER AND OVER.
MERCENARIES ARE UNIQUE GROUPS THAT DANCE TO THEIR OWN TUNE.
THEN...
YES.
THAT IS WHY THEY ARE NOT HIRED FOR MILITARY STRENGTH, BUT AS A DETERRENT.
THOUGH THEY ARE SOMETIMES USED TO PILLAGE TOWNS AND VILLAGES TO WEAKEN AN AREA.
ONE DOES NOT HIRE MERCENARIES TO PURSUE OTHER MERCENARIES—MUCH LESS ONES THAT KNOW EACH OTHER WELL—EVEN BY MISTAKE.
SUCH A THING WOULD BE A WASTE OF MONEY.
IT IS LIKELY THE LANDLORDS HOLD ALL THE DECISIVE AUTHORITY.
HEH...
I CANNOT IMAGINE MY SUBORDINATES—NO...
...THE TRAITORS... WOULD WASTE MONEY IN SUCH A MANNER.

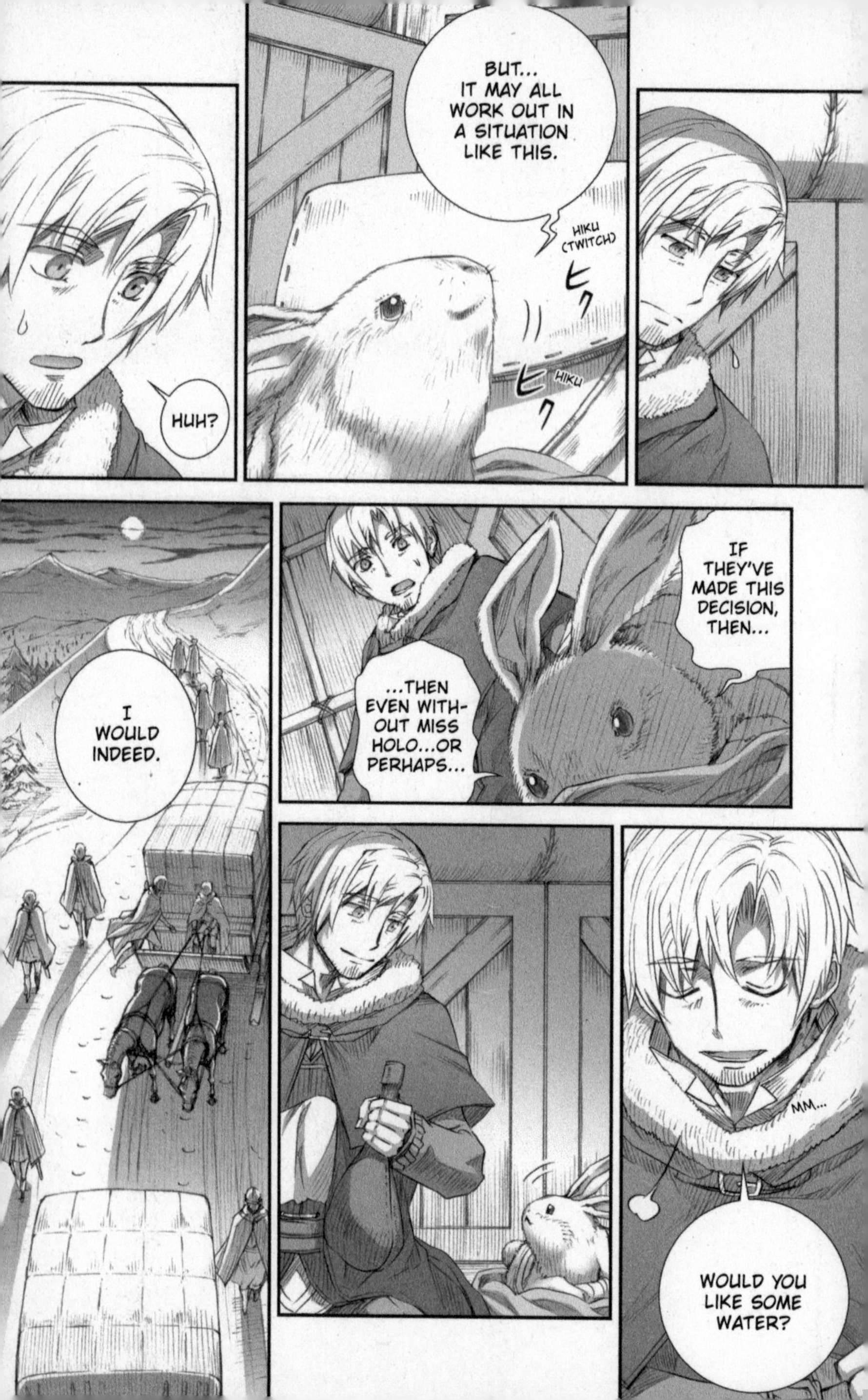
BUT... IT MAY ALL WORK OUT IN A SITUATION LIKE THIS.
HIKU (TWITCH)
HIKU
HUH?
IF THEY'VE MADE THIS DECISION, THEN...
...THEN EVEN WITH-OUT MISS HOLO...OR PERHAPS...
MM...
WOULD YOU LIKE SOME WATER?
I WOULD INDEED.

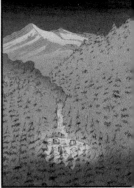

READY!!

BY AFTERNOON THE FOLLOWING DAY, THE HUGO MERCENARY COMPANY— THE PURSUERS FROM THE DEBAU COMPANY— FINALLY CAUGHT UP TO THE MYURI MERCENARY COMPANY.

SHIELDS!

AIM ...!!

ARCHERS ...!

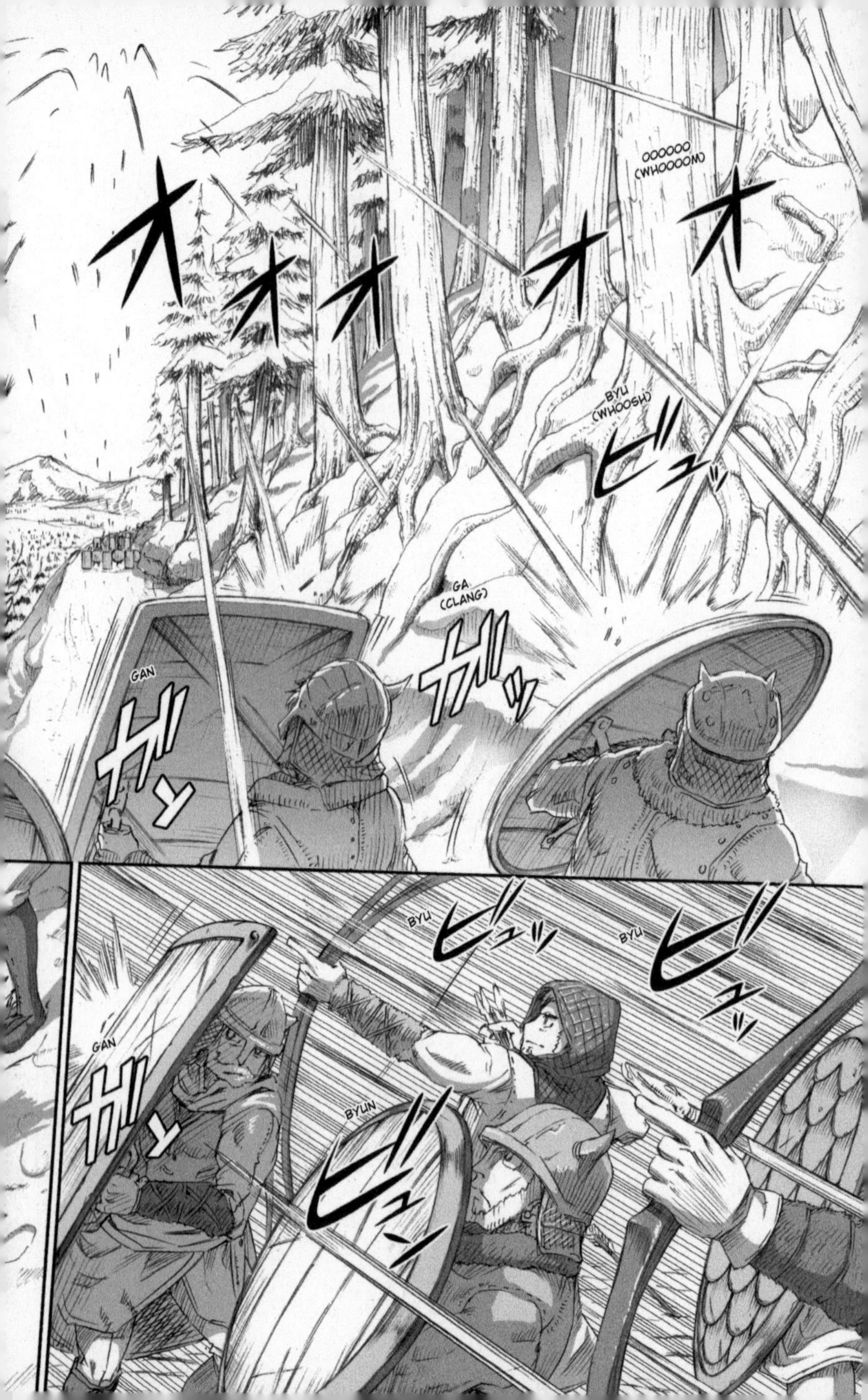
OOOOOO (WHOOOOM)
BYU (WHOOSH)
GA (CLANG)
GAN
BYU
BYU
BYUN
GAN

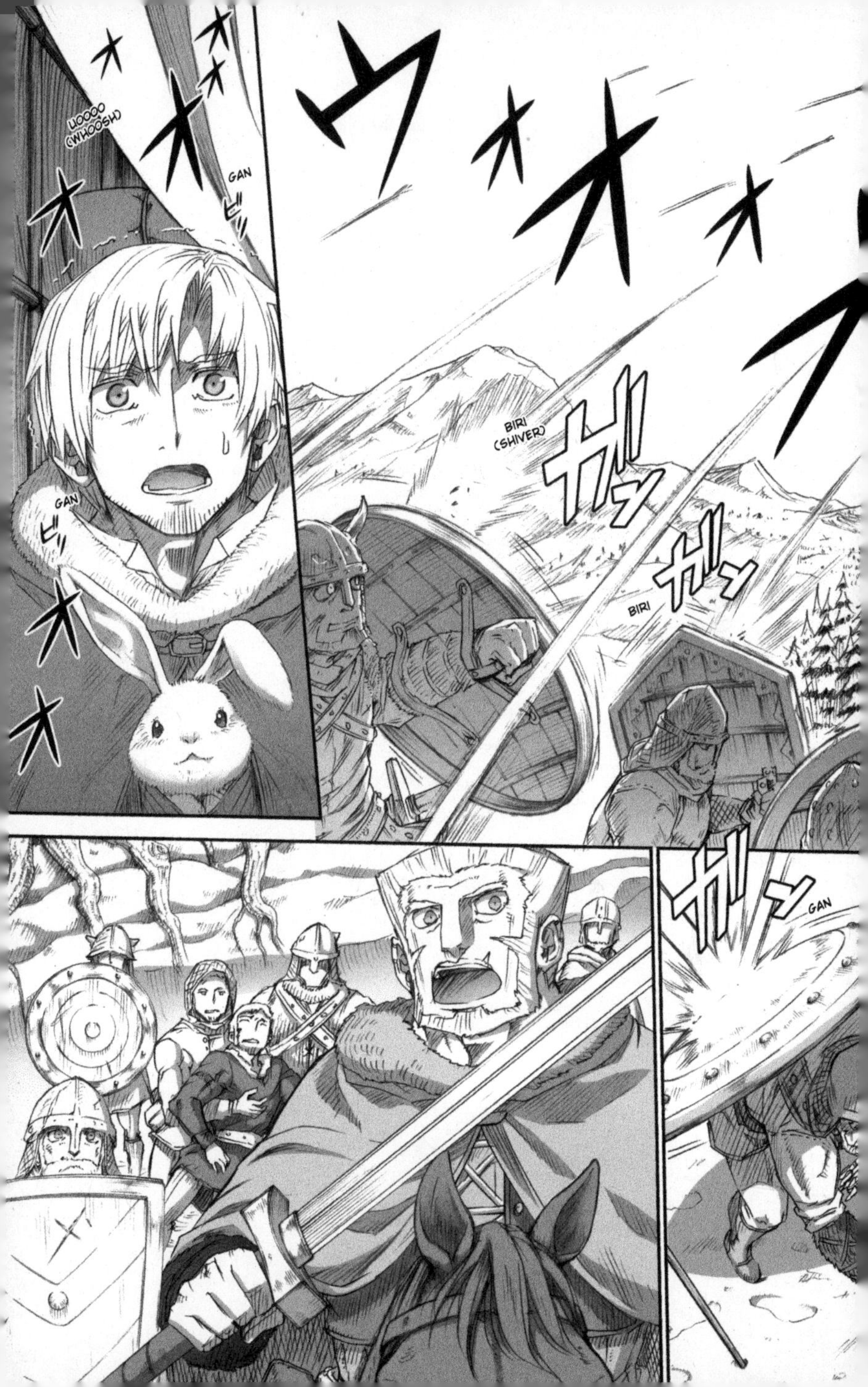
UOOOO (WHOOSH)
BIRI (SHIVER)
BIRI
GAN
GAN
GAN

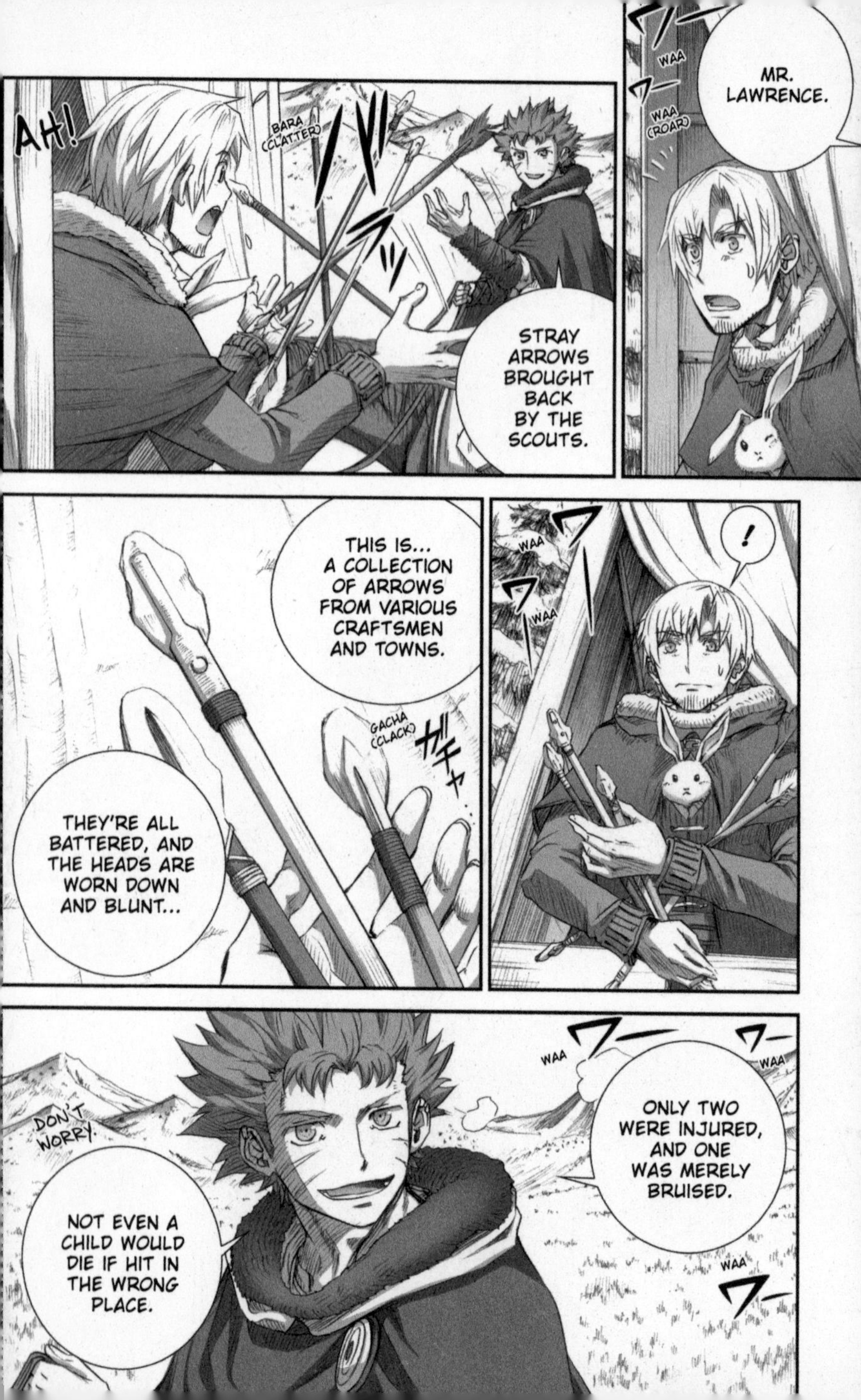
WAA
WAA (ROAR)
MR. LAWRENCE.
AH!
BARA (CLATTER)
STRAY ARROWS BROUGHT BACK BY THE SCOUTS.
WAA
WAA
!
THIS IS... A COLLECTION OF ARROWS FROM VARIOUS CRAFTSMEN AND TOWNS.
GACHA (CLACK)
THEY'RE ALL BATTERED, AND THE HEADS ARE WORN DOWN AND BLUNT...
WAA
WAA
ONLY TWO WERE INJURED, AND ONE WAS MERELY BRUISED.
DON'T WORRY.
NOT EVEN A CHILD WOULD DIE IF HIT IN THE WRONG PLACE.
WAA

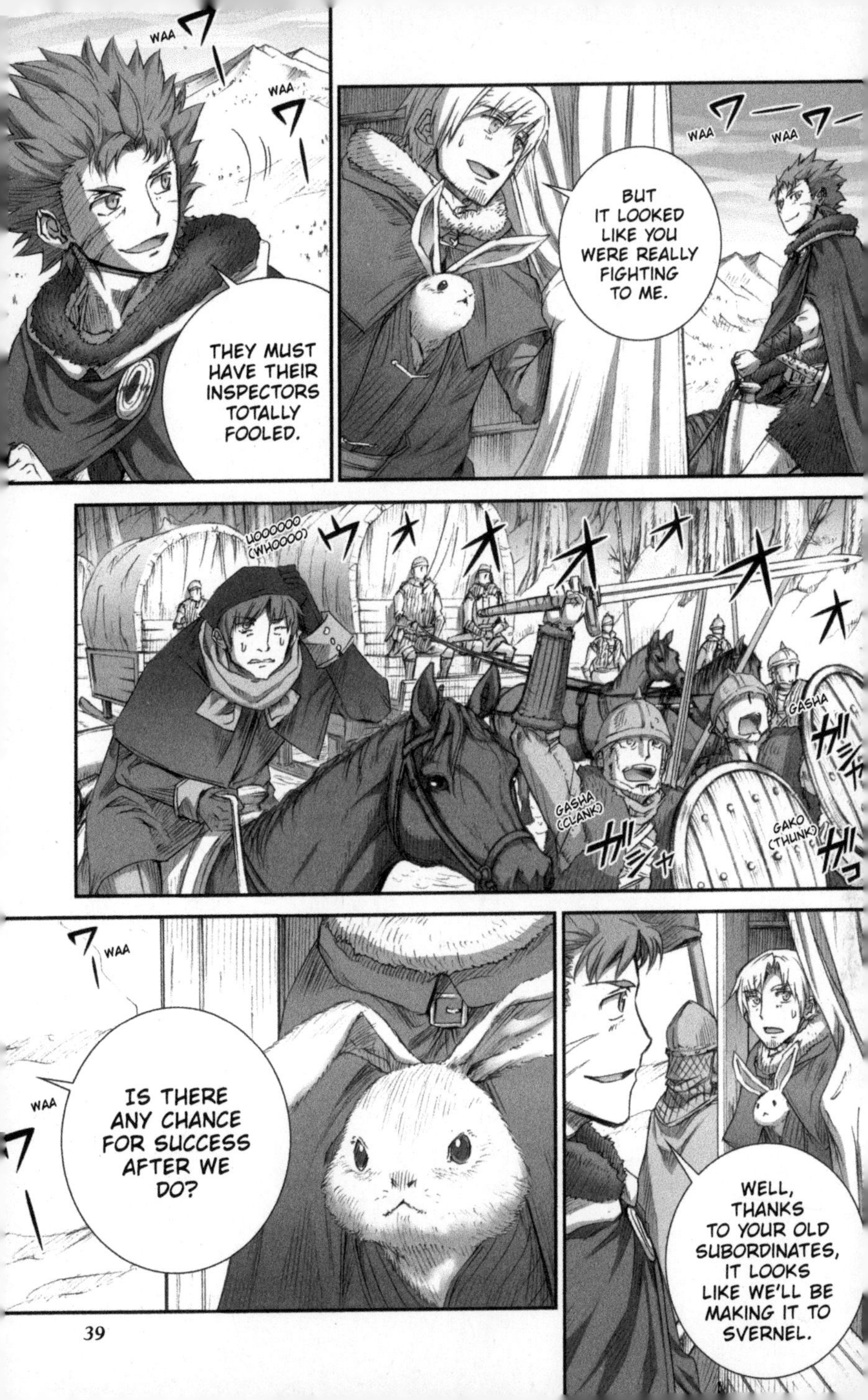
WAA
WAA
BUT IT LOOKED LIKE YOU WERE REALLY FIGHTING TO ME.
WAA
WAA
THEY MUST HAVE THEIR INSPECTORS TOTALLY FOOLED.
UOOOOOO (WHOOOO)
GASHA
GAKO (THUNK)
GASHA (CLANK)
WELL, THANKS TO YOUR OLD SUBORDINATES, IT LOOKS LIKE WE'LL BE MAKING IT TO SVERNEL.
WAA
IS THERE ANY CHANCE FOR SUCCESS AFTER WE DO?
WAA

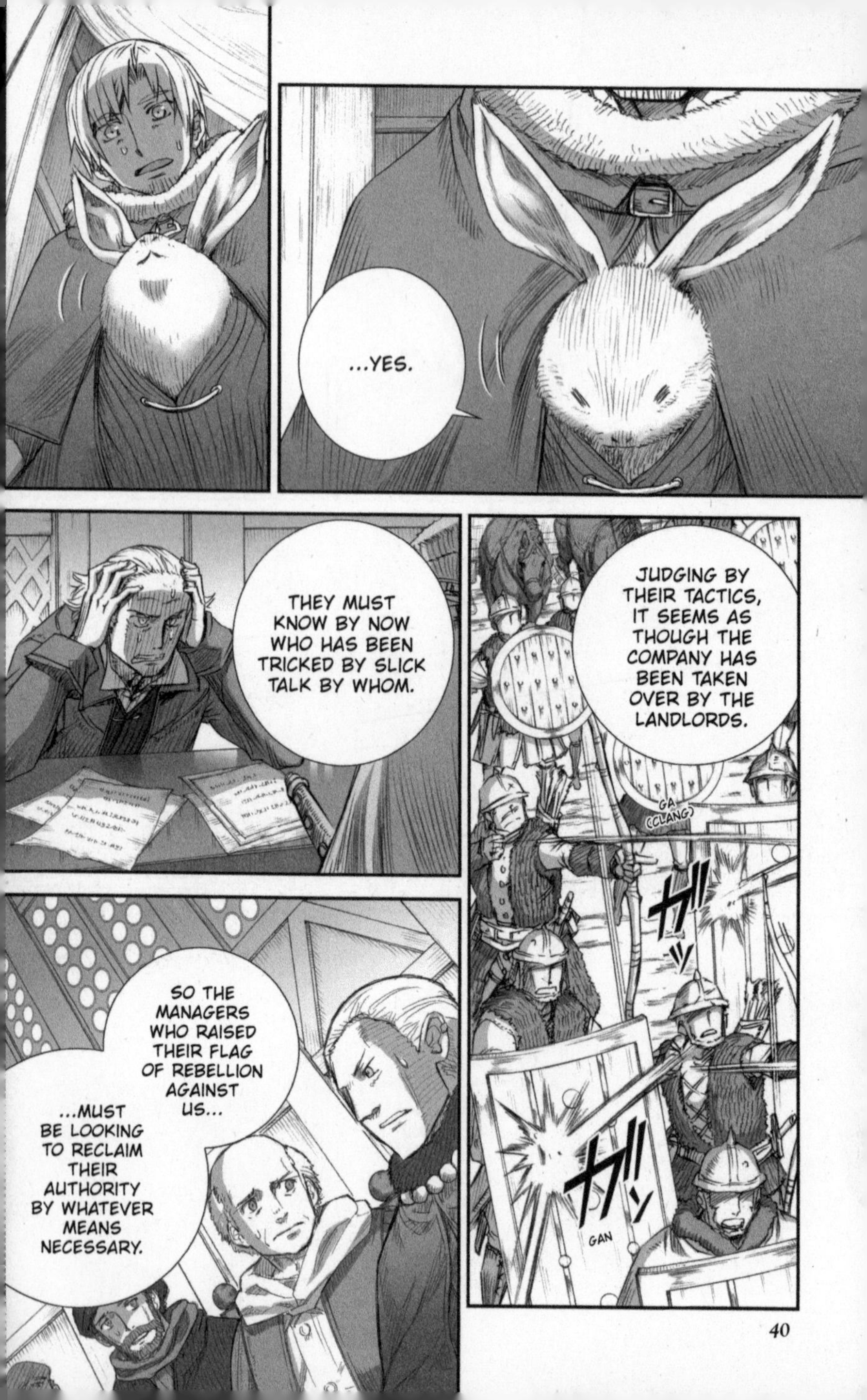
...YES.
JUDGING BY THEIR TACTICS, IT SEEMS AS THOUGH THE COMPANY HAS BEEN TAKEN OVER BY THE LANDLORDS.
GA (CLANG)
ガッ
ガン
GAN
THEY MUST KNOW BY NOW WHO HAS BEEN TRICKED BY SLICK TALK BY WHOM.
SO THE MANAGERS WHO RAISED THEIR FLAG OF REBELLION AGAINST US...
...MUST BE LOOKING TO RECLAIM THEIR AUTHORITY BY WHATEVER MEANS NECESSARY.

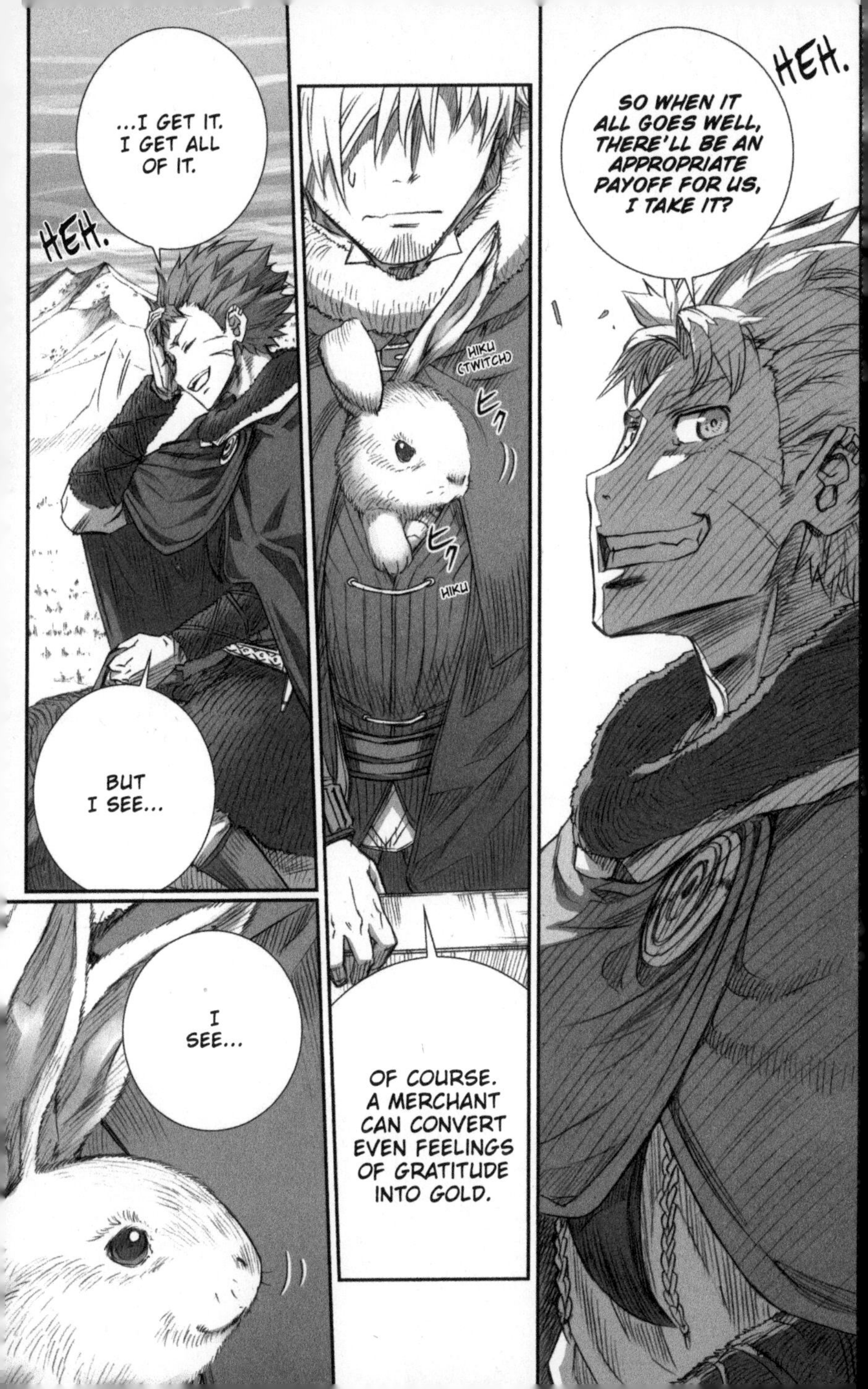
HEH.
SO WHEN IT ALL GOES WELL, THERE'LL BE AN APPROPRIATE PAYOFF FOR US, I TAKE IT?
HIKU (TWITCH)
ヒク
ヒク
HIKU
OF COURSE. A MERCHANT CAN CONVERT EVEN FEELINGS OF GRATITUDE INTO GOLD.
...I GET IT. I GET ALL OF IT.
HEH.
BUT I SEE...
I SEE...

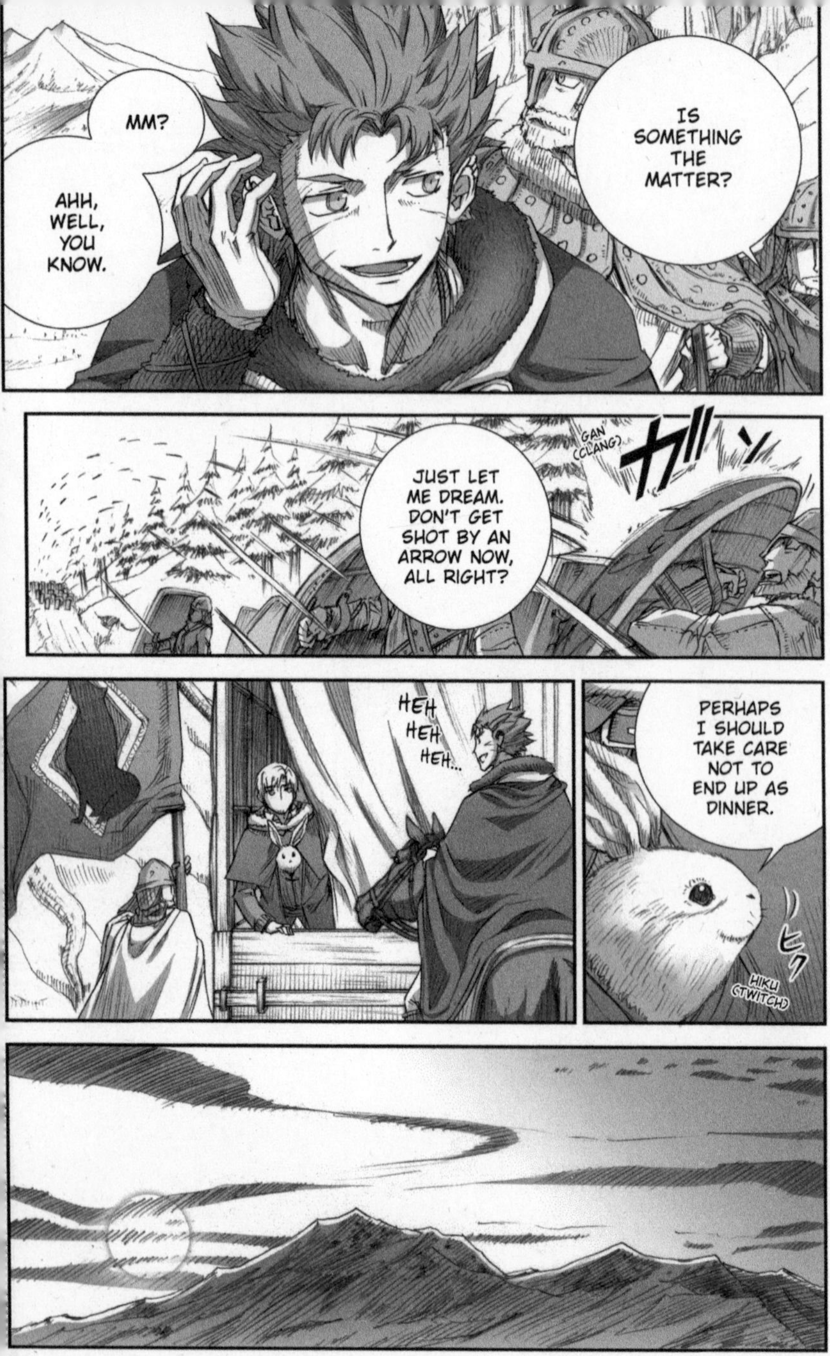
IS SOMETHING THE MATTER?
MM?
AHH, WELL, YOU KNOW.
GAN (CLANG)
JUST LET ME DREAM. DON'T GET SHOT BY AN ARROW NOW, ALL RIGHT?
PERHAPS I SHOULD TAKE CARE NOT TO END UP AS DINNER.
HIKU (TWITCH)
HEH HEH HEH...

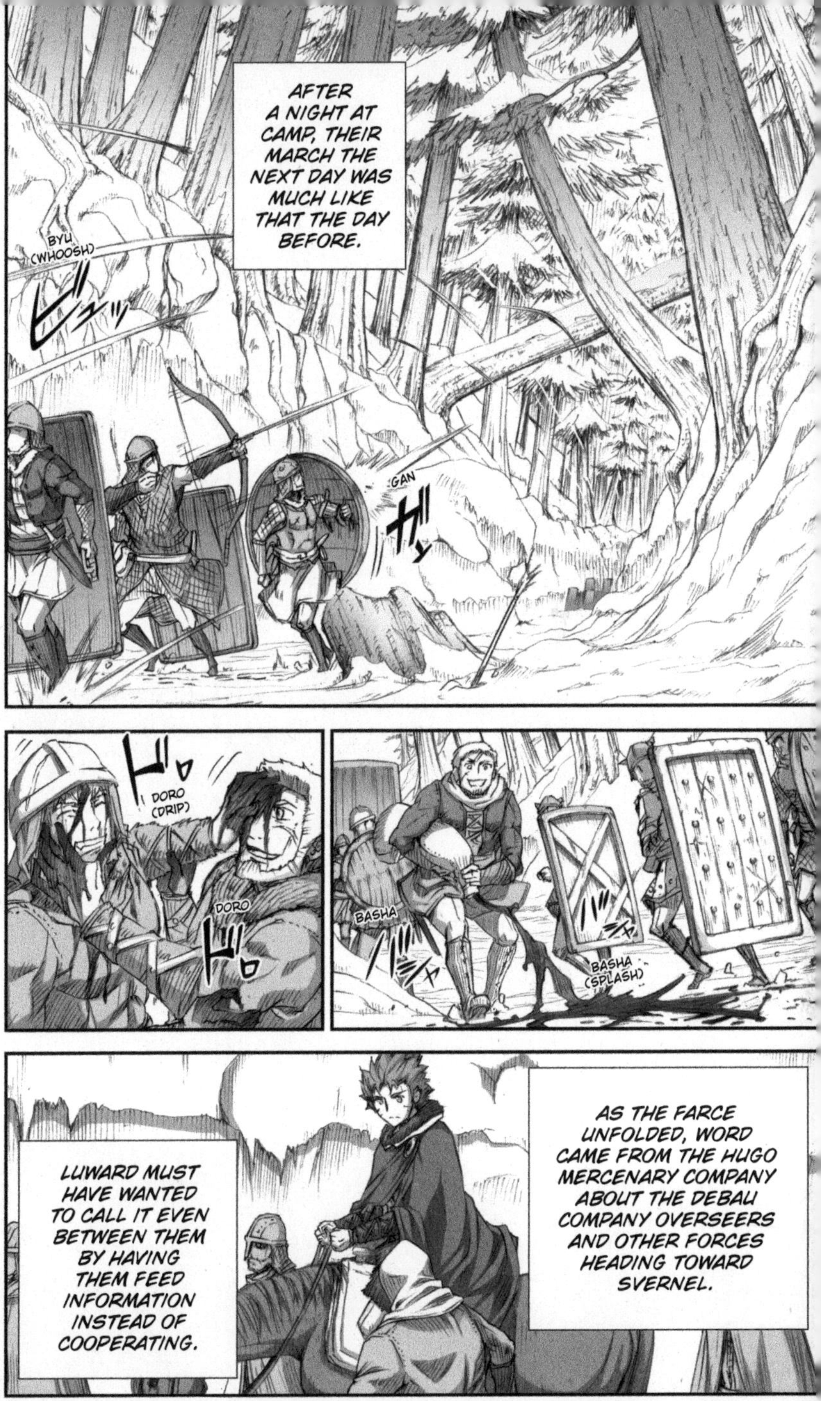
AFTER A NIGHT AT CAMP, THEIR MARCH THE NEXT DAY WAS MUCH LIKE THAT THE DAY BEFORE.
BYU (WHOOSH)
GAN
BASHA
BASHA (SPLASH)
DORO (DRIP)
DORO
AS THE FARCE UNFOLDED, WORD CAME FROM THE HUGO MERCENARY COMPANY ABOUT THE DEBAU COMPANY OVERSEERS AND OTHER FORCES HEADING TOWARD SVERNEL.
LUWARD MUST HAVE WANTED TO CALL IT EVEN BETWEEN THEM BY HAVING THEM FEED INFORMATION INSTEAD OF COOPERATING.

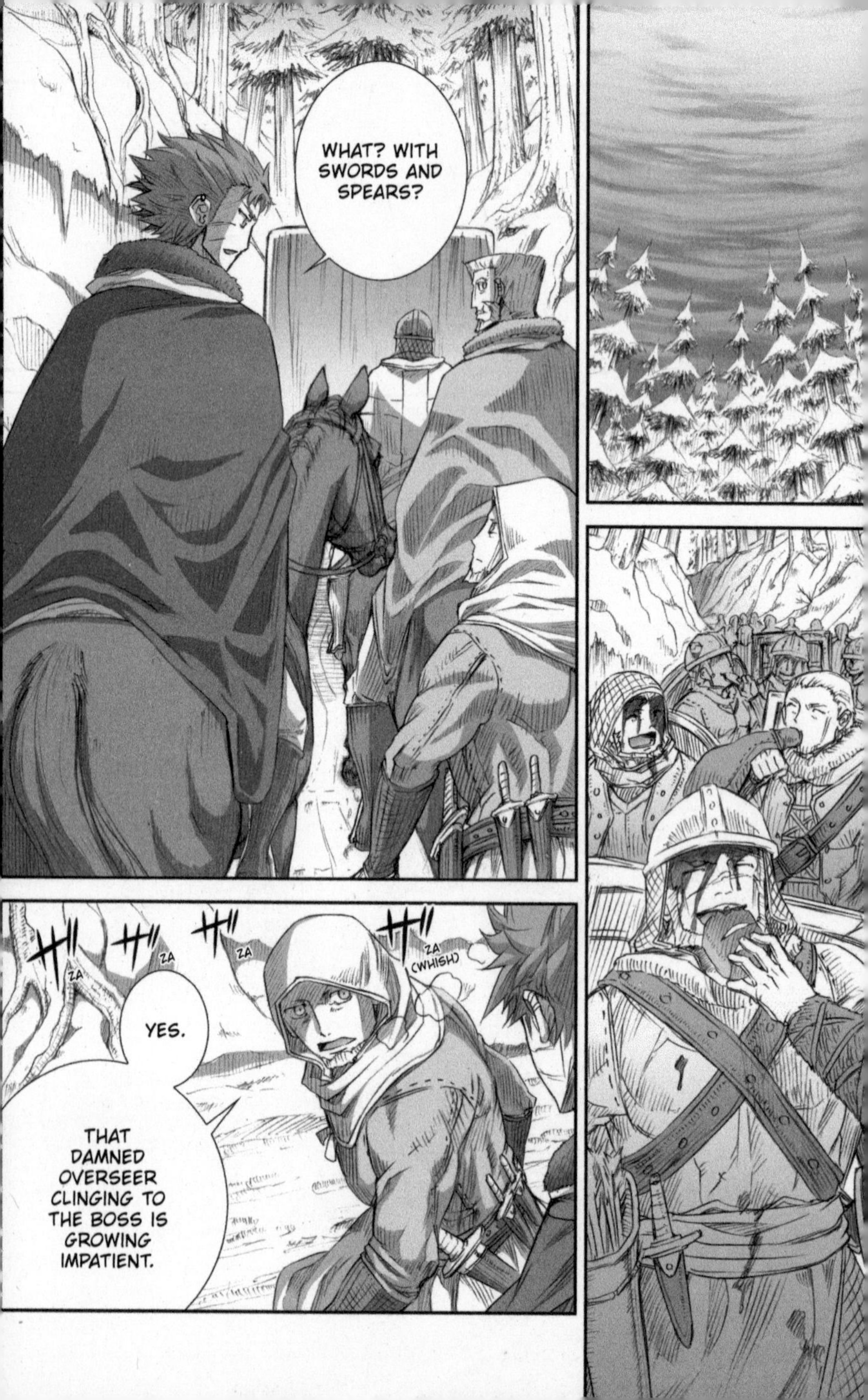
WHAT? WITH SWORDS AND SPEARS?
ZA ZA ZA ZA (WHISH)
YES.
THAT DAMNED OVERSEER CLINGING TO THE BOSS IS GROWING IMPATIENT.

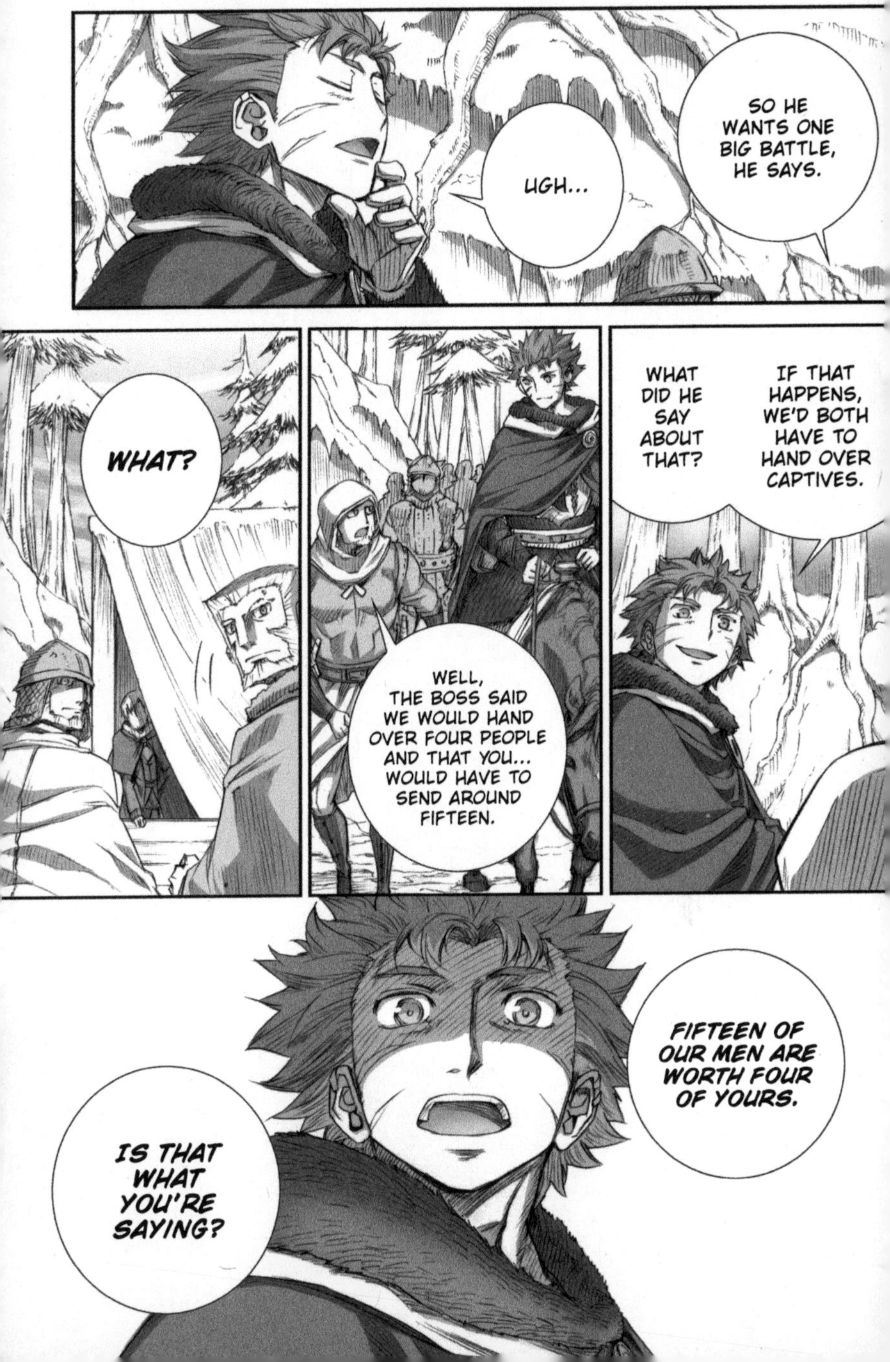
SO HE WANTS ONE BIG BATTLE, HE SAYS.
UGH...
IF THAT HAPPENS, WE'D BOTH HAVE TO HAND OVER CAPTIVES.
WHAT DID HE SAY ABOUT THAT?
WELL, THE BOSS SAID WE WOULD HAND OVER FOUR PEOPLE AND THAT YOU... WOULD HAVE TO SEND AROUND FIFTEEN.
WHAT?
FIFTEEN OF OUR MEN ARE WORTH FOUR OF YOURS.
IS THAT WHAT YOU'RE SAYING?

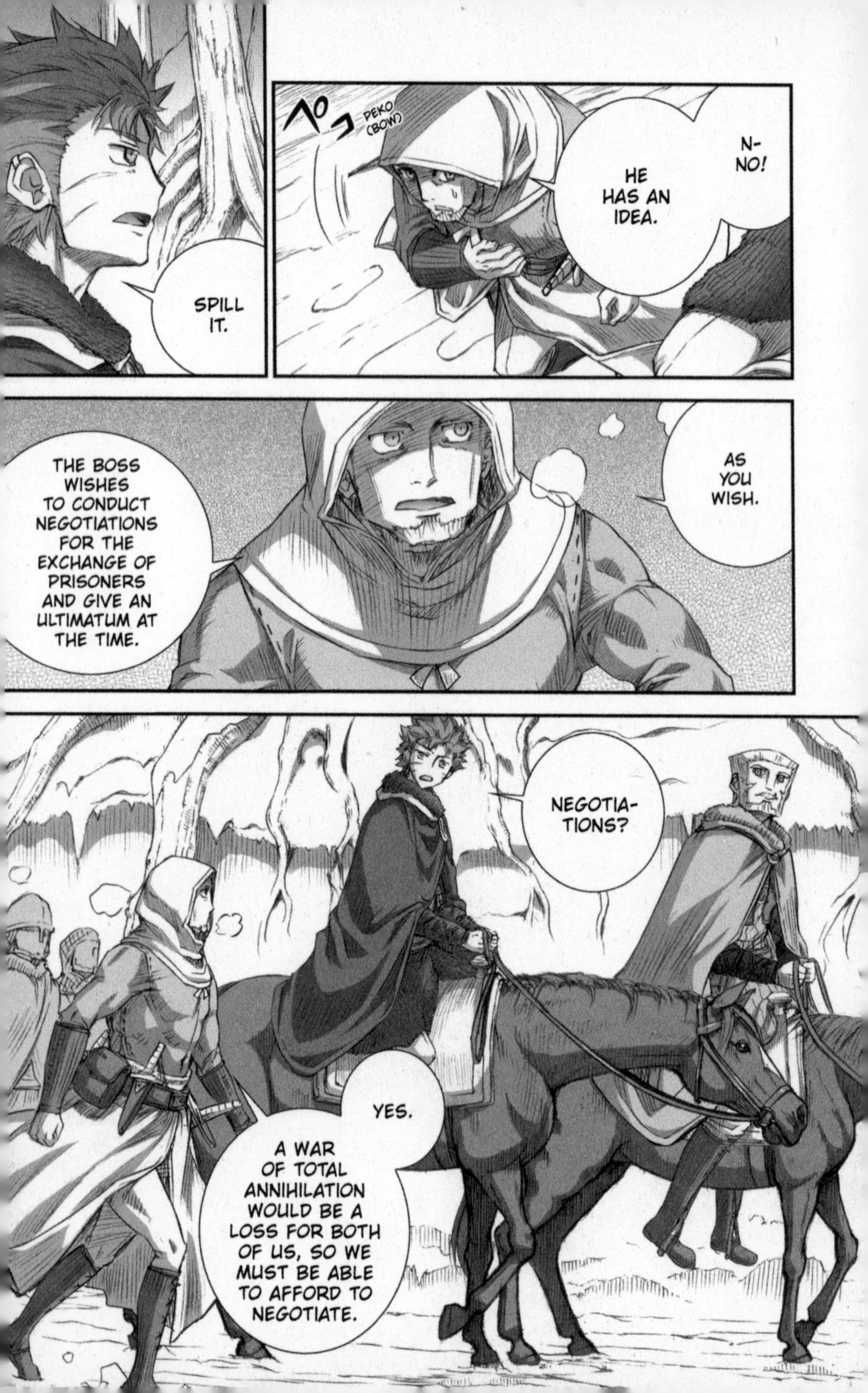
ペコ
PEKO (BOW)
N- NO!
HE HAS AN IDEA.
SPILL IT.
AS YOU WISH.
THE BOSS WISHES TO CONDUCT NEGOTIATIONS FOR THE EXCHANGE OF PRISONERS AND GIVE AN ULTIMATUM AT THE TIME.
NEGOTIATIONS?
YES.
A WAR OF TOTAL ANNIHILATION WOULD BE A LOSS FOR BOTH OF US, SO WE MUST BE ABLE TO AFFORD TO NEGOTIATE.

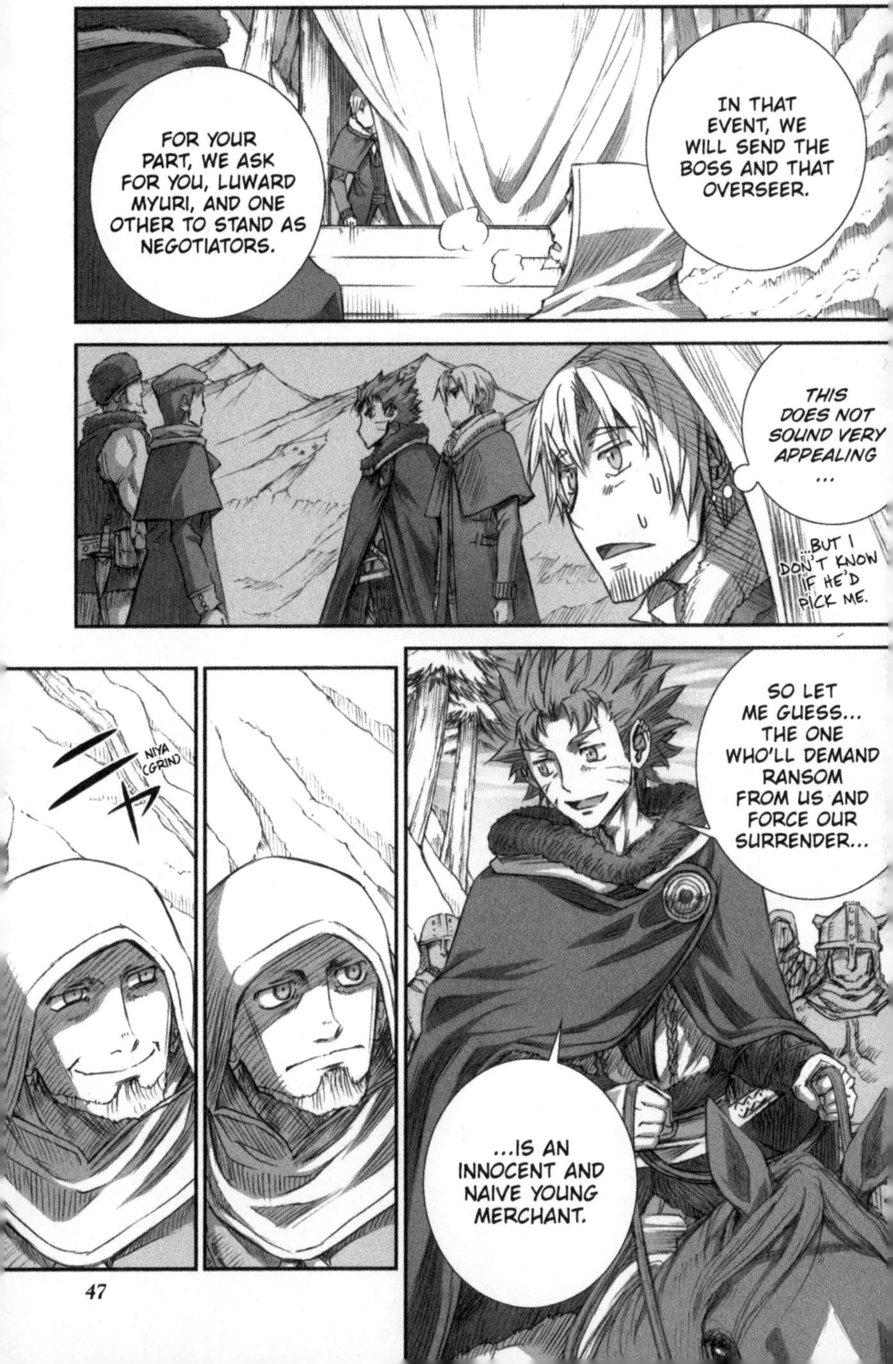
IN THAT EVENT, WE WILL SEND THE BOSS AND THAT OVERSEER.
FOR YOUR PART, WE ASK FOR YOU, LUWARD MYURI, AND ONE OTHER TO STAND AS NEGOTIATORS.
THIS DOES NOT SOUND VERY APPEALING ...
...BUT I DON'T KNOW IF HE'D PICK ME.
SO LET ME GUESS... THE ONE WHO'LL DEMAND RANSOM FROM US AND FORCE OUR SURRENDER...
...IS AN INNOCENT AND NAIVE YOUNG MERCHANT.
NIYA (GRIN)

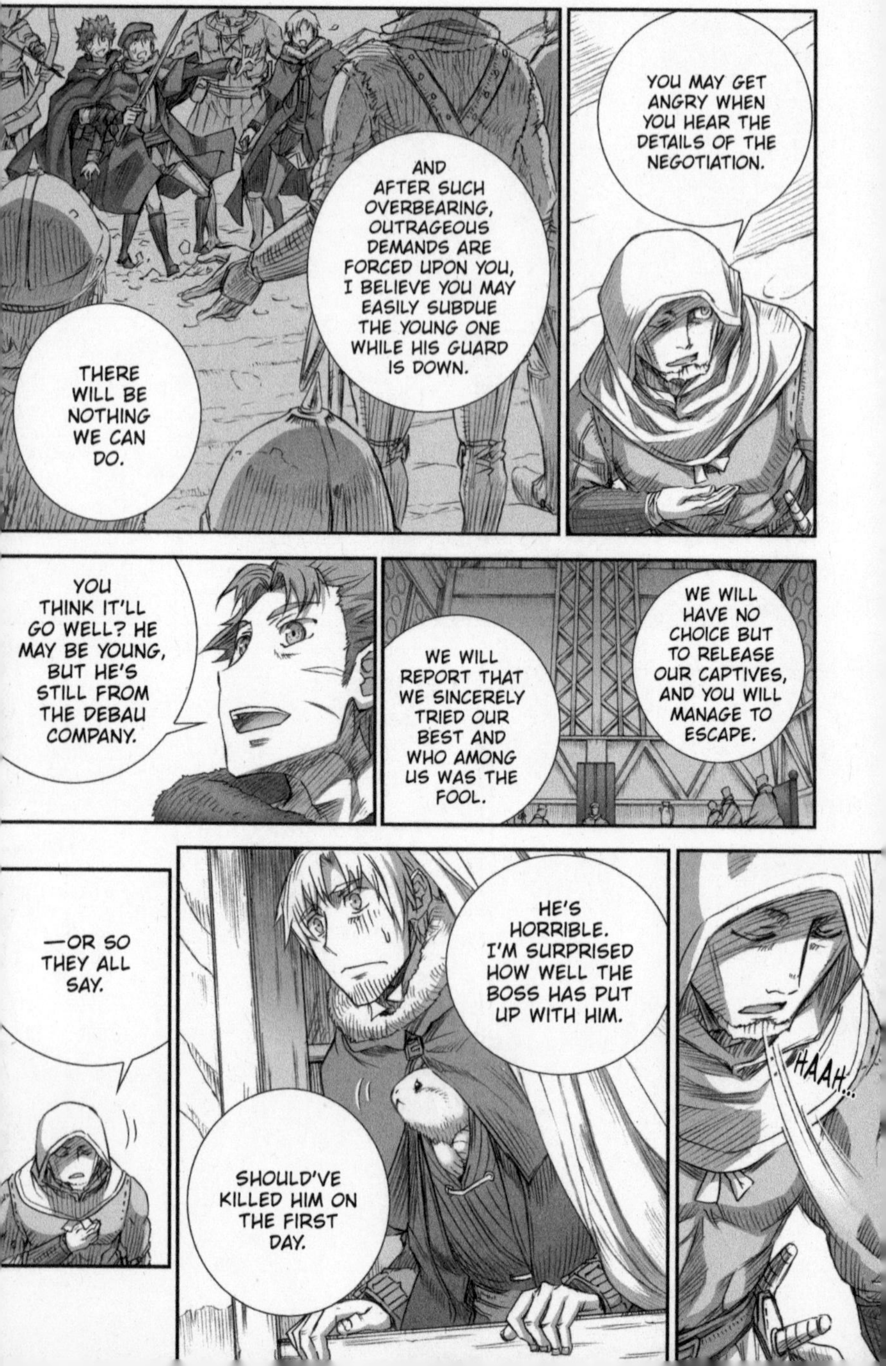
YOU MAY GET ANGRY WHEN YOU HEAR THE DETAILS OF THE NEGOTIATION.
AND AFTER SUCH OVERBEARING, OUTRAGEOUS DEMANDS ARE FORCED UPON YOU, I BELIEVE YOU MAY EASILY SUBDUE THE YOUNG ONE WHILE HIS GUARD IS DOWN.
THERE WILL BE NOTHING WE CAN DO.
WE WILL HAVE NO CHOICE BUT TO RELEASE OUR CAPTIVES, AND YOU WILL MANAGE TO ESCAPE.
WE WILL REPORT THAT WE SINCERELY TRIED OUR BEST AND WHO AMONG US WAS THE FOOL.
YOU THINK IT'LL GO WELL? HE MAY BE YOUNG, BUT HE'S STILL FROM THE DEBAU COMPANY.
HAAAH...
HE'S HORRIBLE. I'M SURPRISED HOW WELL THE BOSS HAS PUT UP WITH HIM.
SHOULD'VE KILLED HIM ON THE FIRST DAY.
—OR SO THEY ALL SAY.

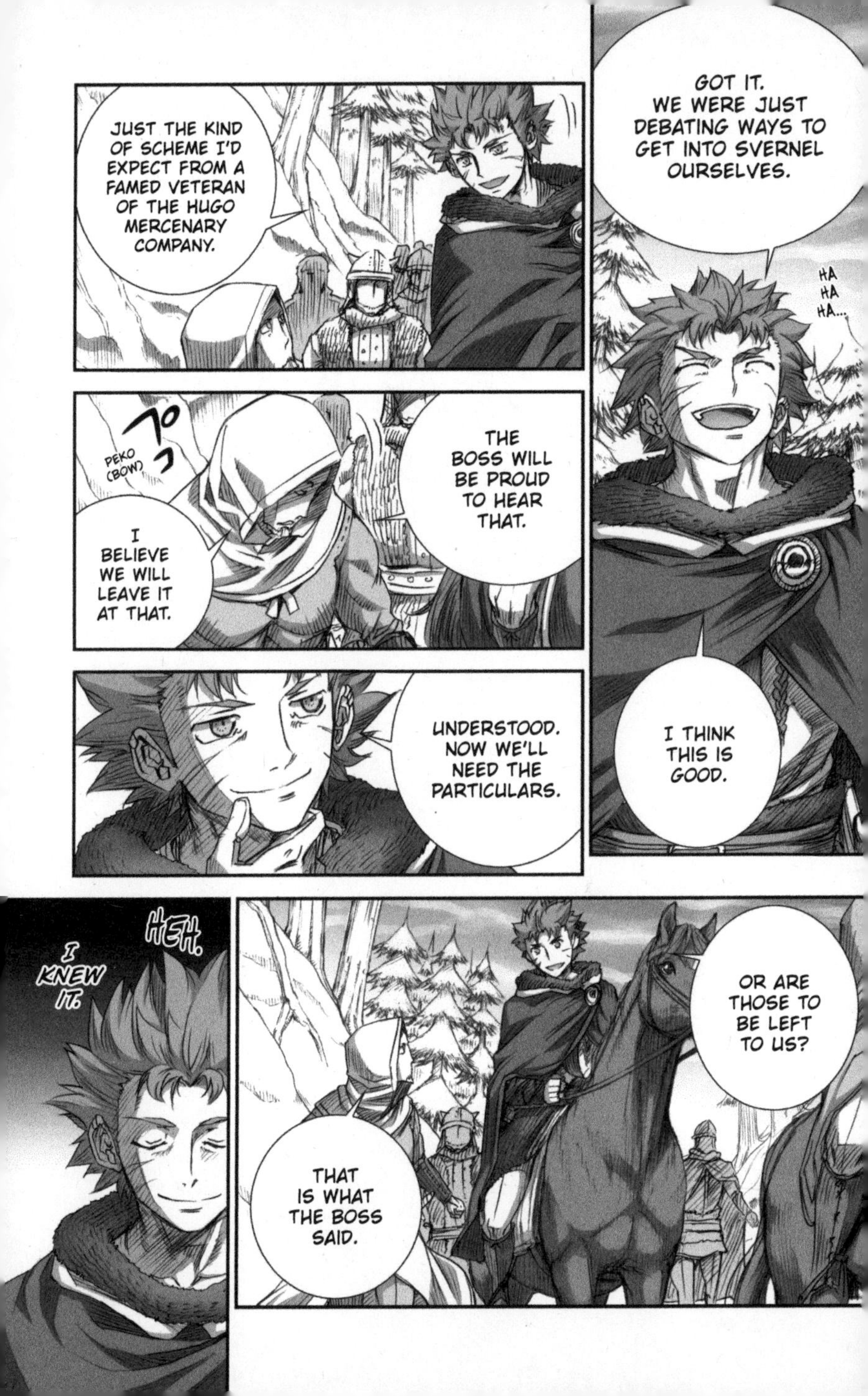
GOT IT. WE WERE JUST DEBATING WAYS TO GET INTO SVERNEL OURSELVES.
HA HA HA...
I THINK THIS IS GOOD.
JUST THE KIND OF SCHEME I'D EXPECT FROM A FAMED VETERAN OF THE HUGO MERCENARY COMPANY.
THE BOSS WILL BE PROUD TO HEAR THAT.
ペコ
PEKO (BOW)
I BELIEVE WE WILL LEAVE IT AT THAT.
UNDERSTOOD. NOW WE'LL NEED THE PARTICULARS.
OR ARE THOSE TO BE LEFT TO US?
THAT IS WHAT THE BOSS SAID.
HEH.
I KNEW IT.

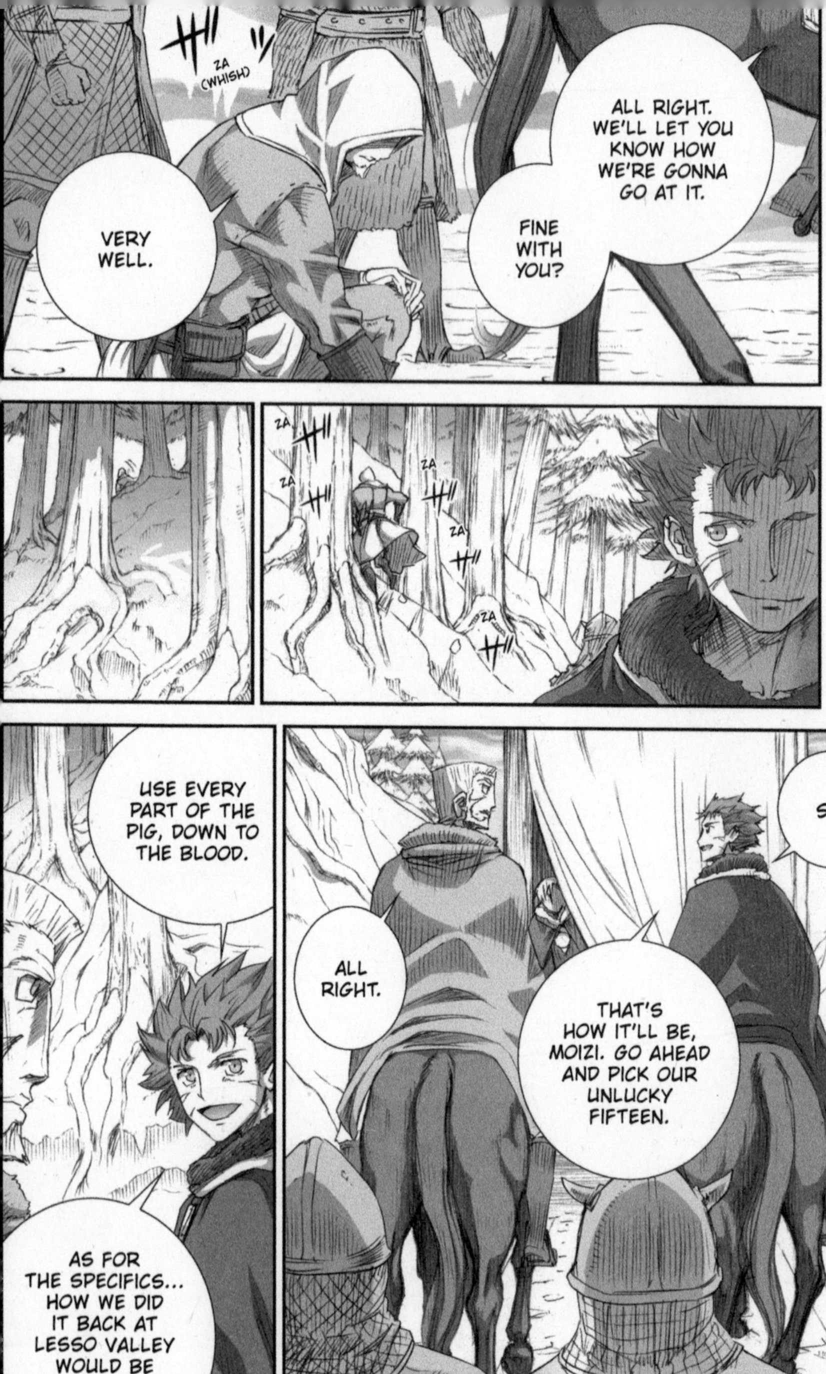
ALL RIGHT. WE'LL LET YOU KNOW HOW WE'RE GONNA GO AT IT.
FINE WITH YOU?
ZA (WHISH)
VERY WELL.
ZA
ZA
ZA
ZA
ZA
SO.
THAT'S HOW IT'LL BE, MOIZI. GO AHEAD AND PICK OUR UNLUCKY FIFTEEN.
ALL RIGHT.
USE EVERY PART OF THE PIG, DOWN TO THE BLOOD.
AS FOR THE SPECIFICS... HOW WE DID IT BACK AT LESSO VALLEY WOULD BE FINE.

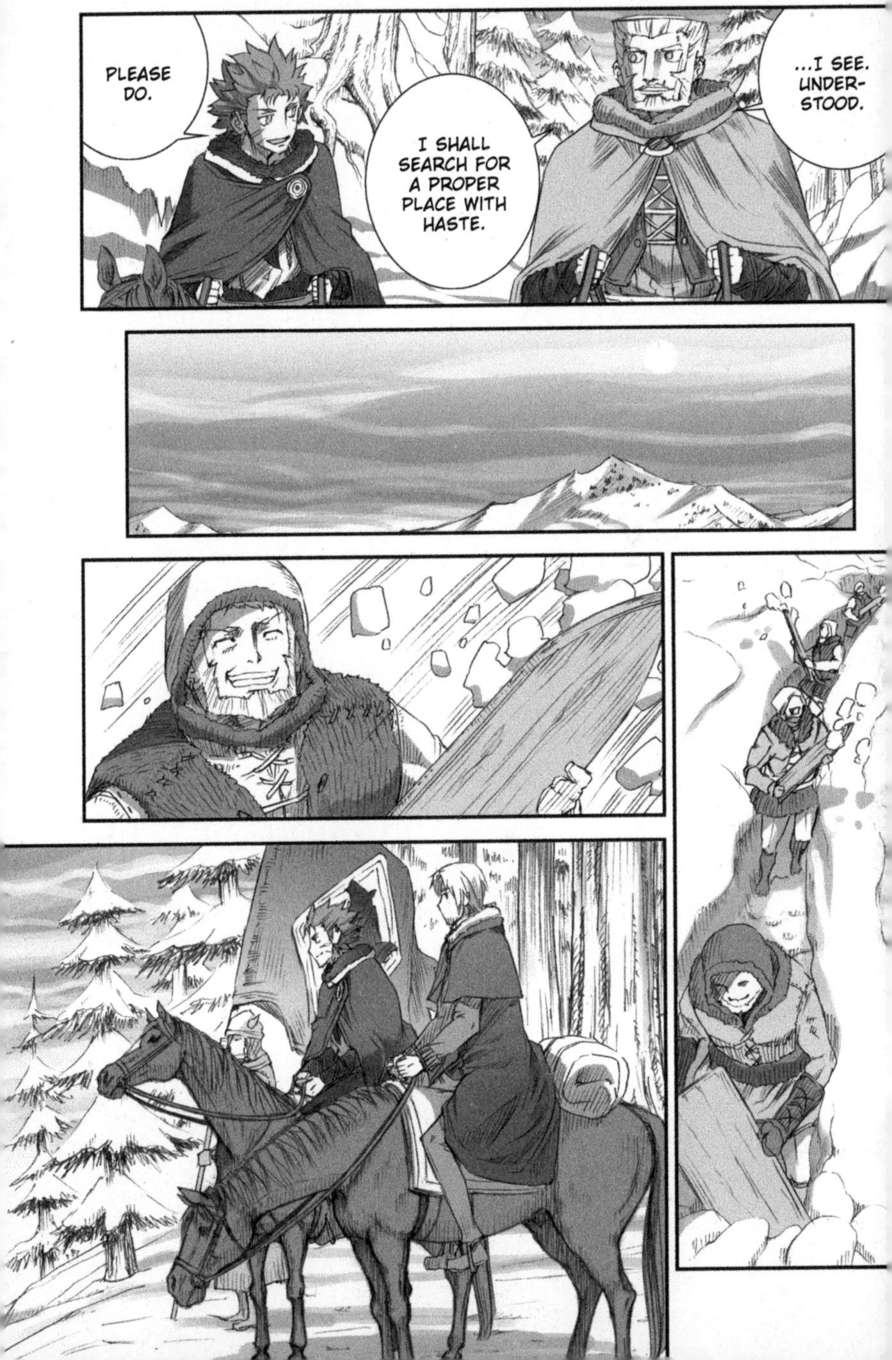
...I SEE. UNDERSTOOD.
I SHALL SEARCH FOR A PROPER PLACE WITH HASTE.
PLEASE DO.

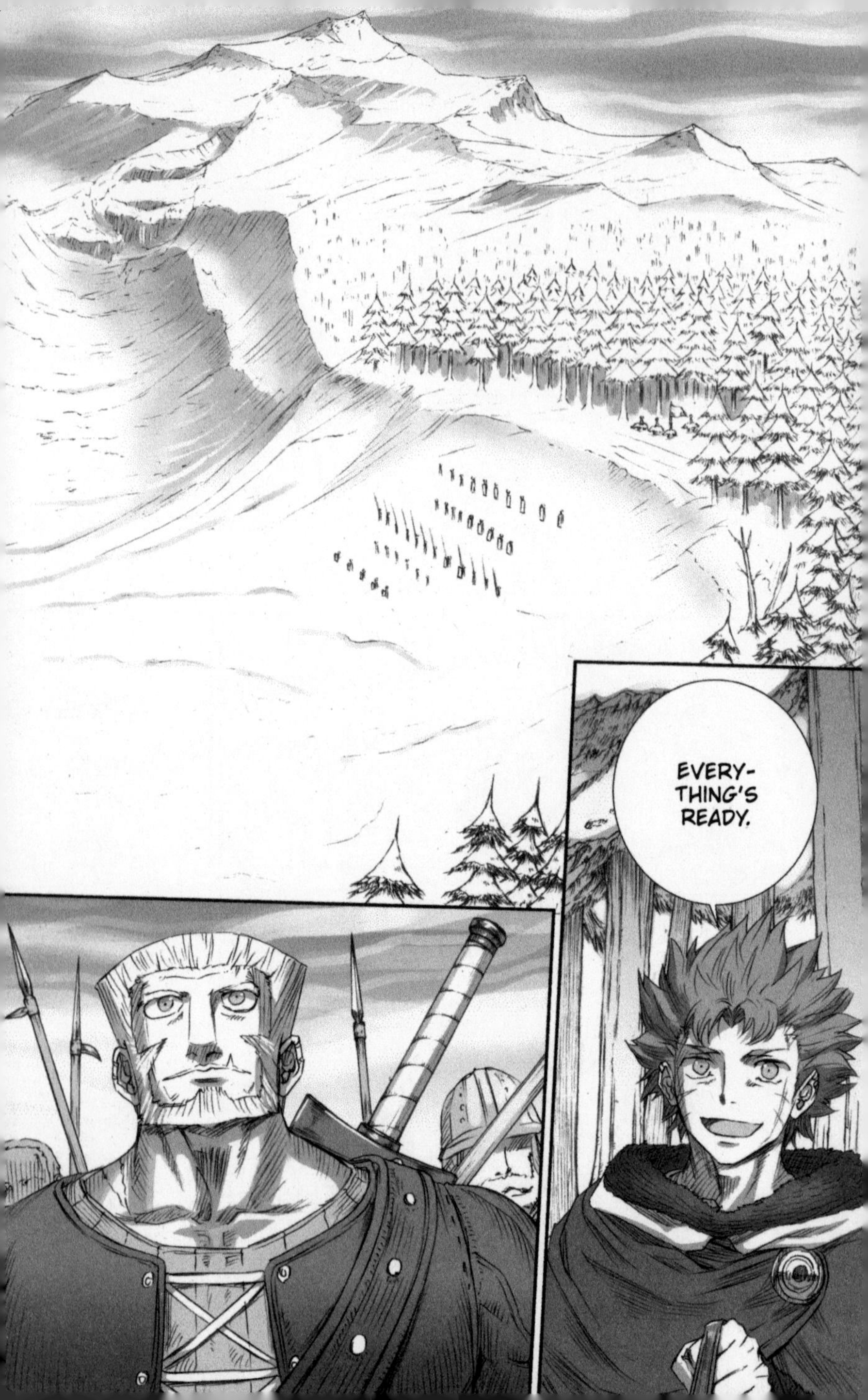
EVERY-
THING'S
READY.

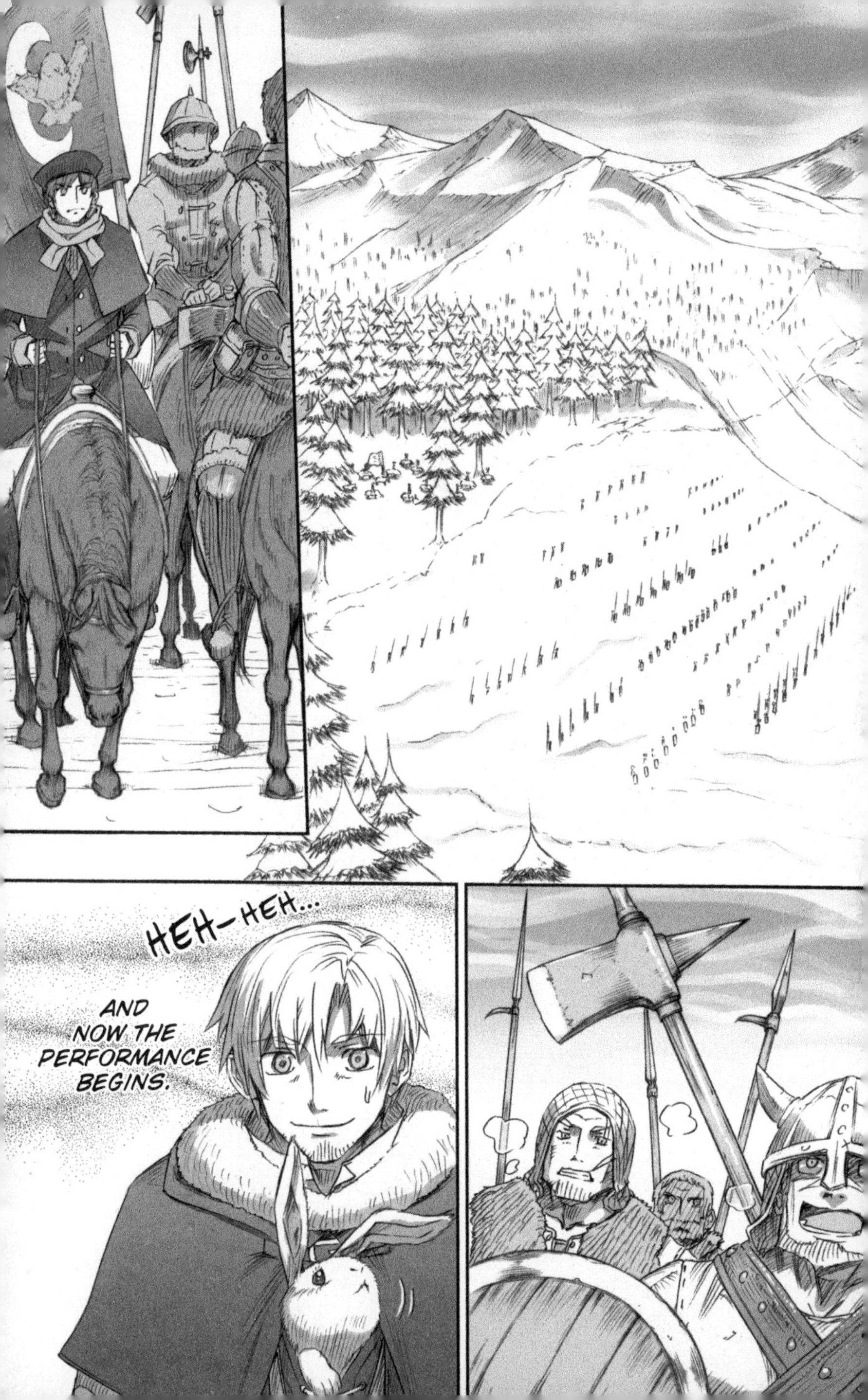
HEH-HEH...
AND NOW THE PERFORMANCE BEGINS.

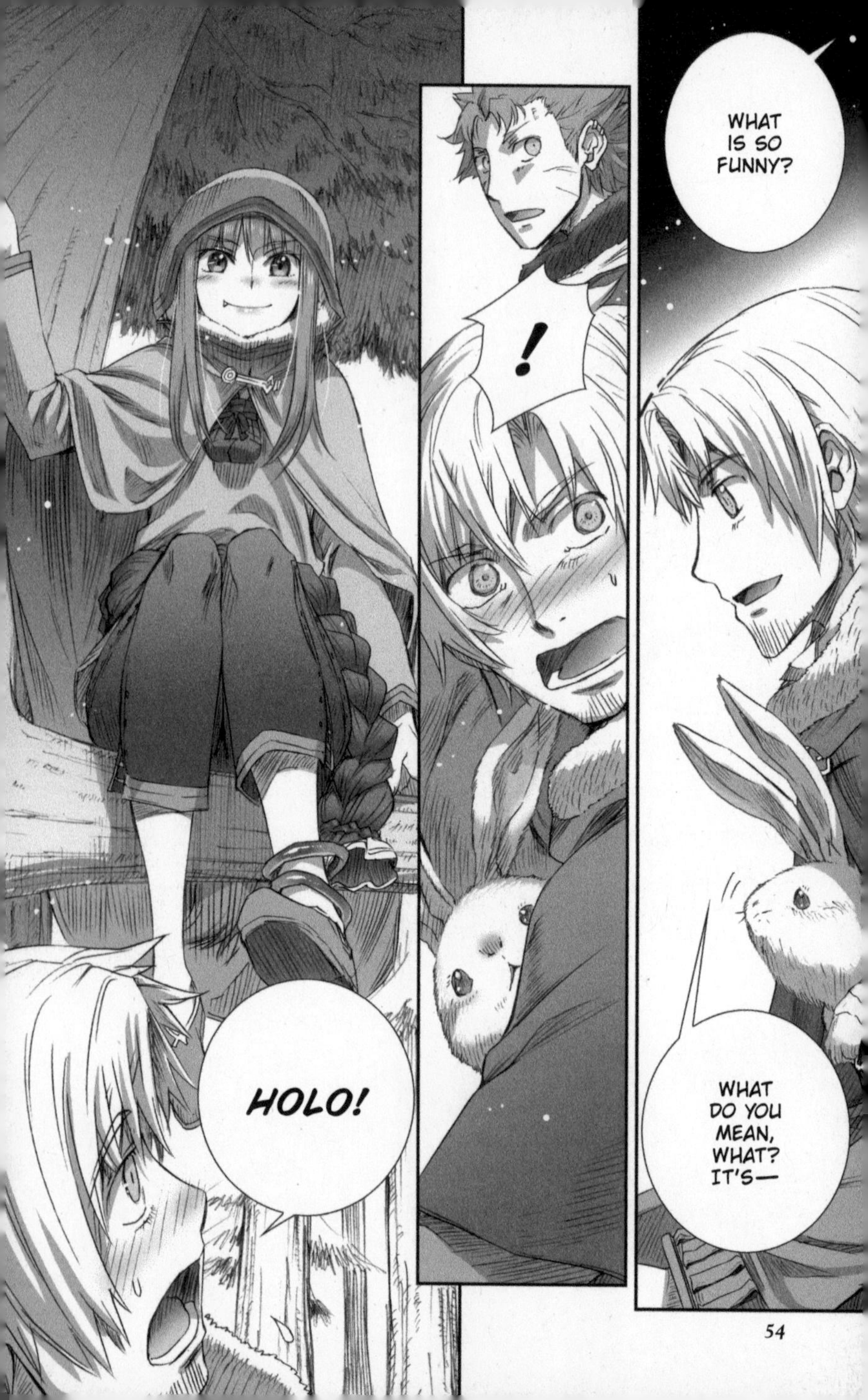
WHAT IS SO FUNNY?
WHAT DO YOU MEAN, WHAT? IT'S—
!
HOLO!

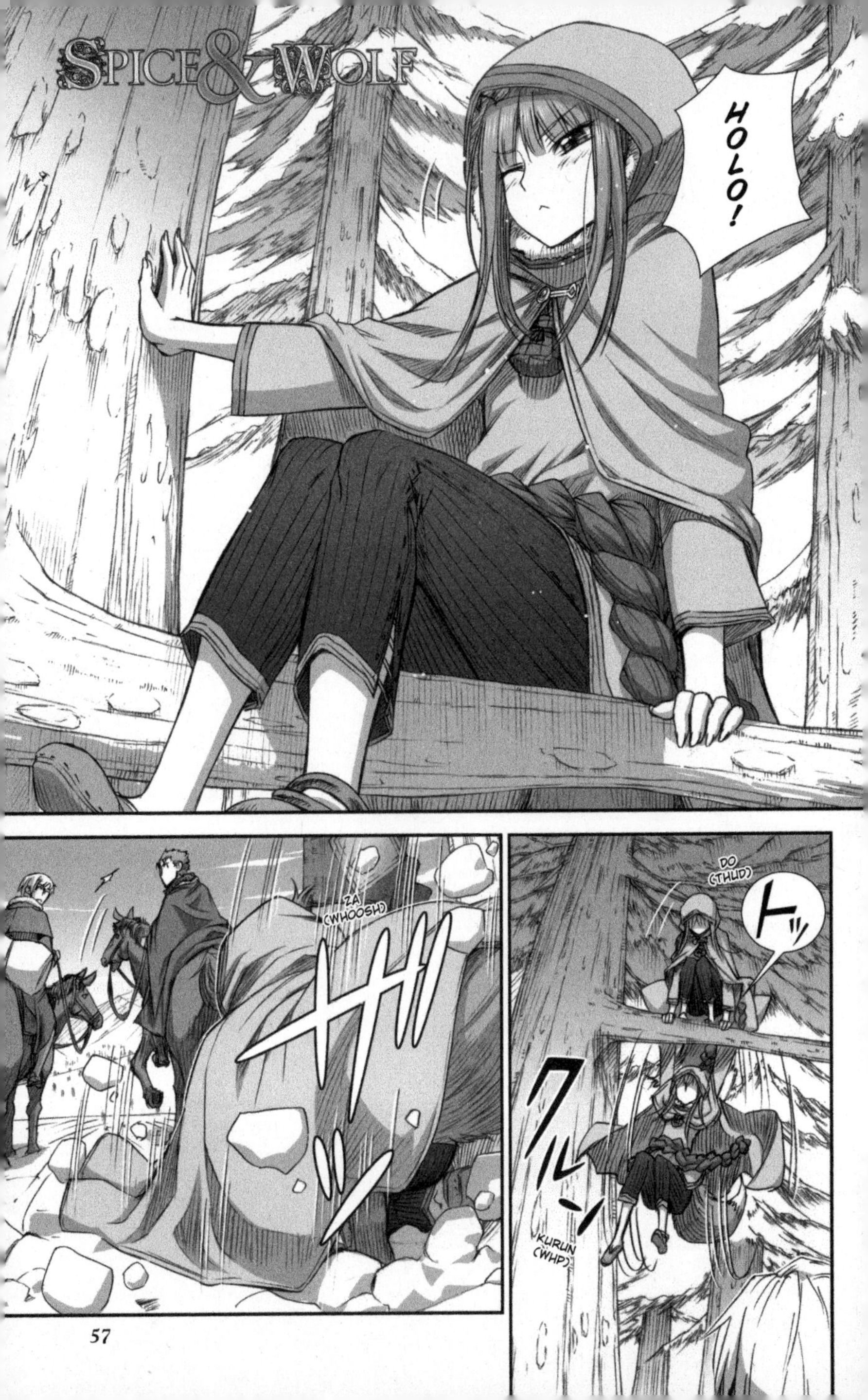
SPICE & WOLF
HOLO!
DO (THUD)
トッ
クルーン
KURUN (WHP)
ZA (WHOOSH)
ザッ

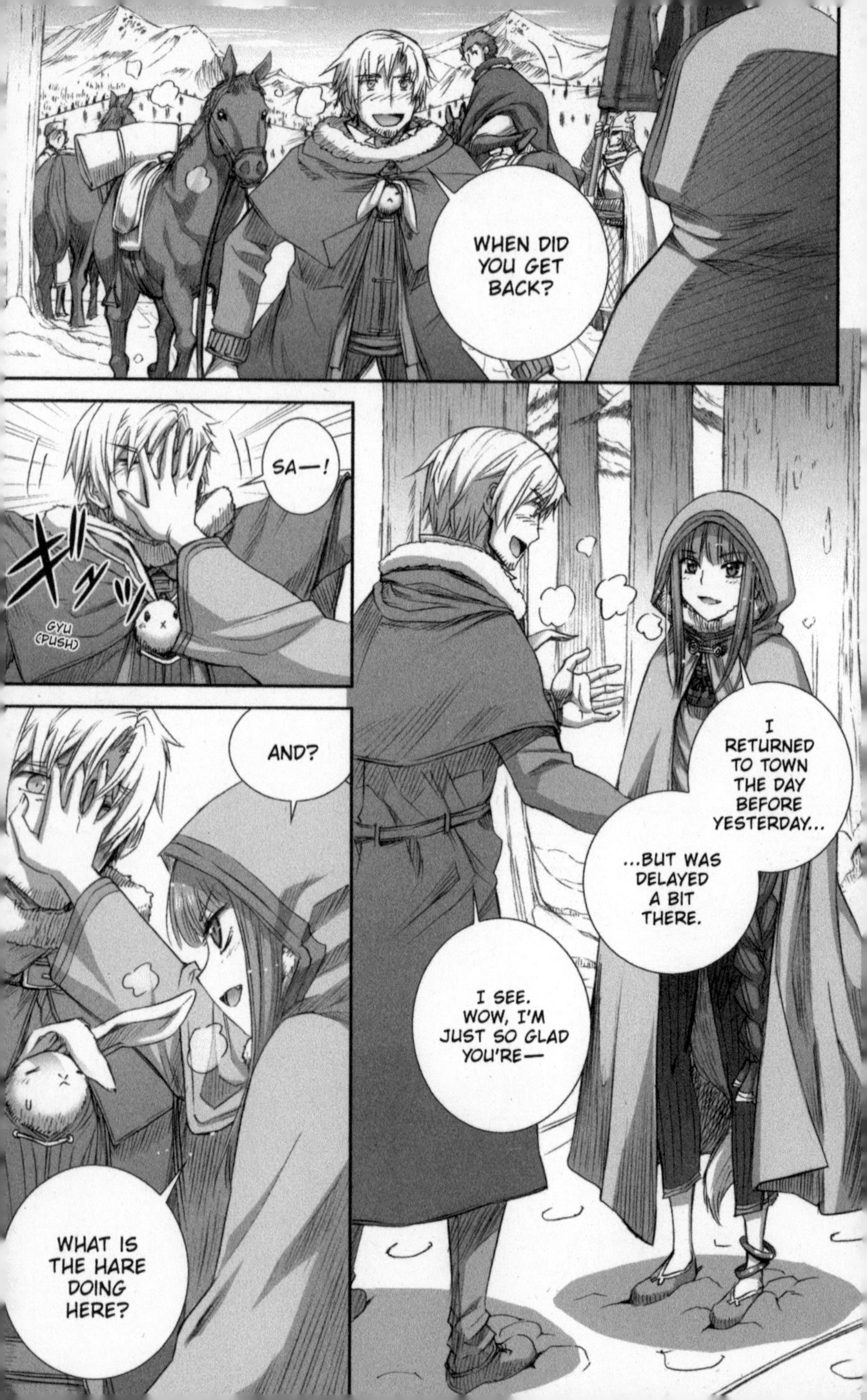
WHEN DID YOU GET BACK?
I RETURNED TO TOWN THE DAY BEFORE YESTERDAY...
...BUT WAS DELAYED A BIT THERE.
I SEE. WOW, I'M JUST SO GLAD YOU'RE—
SA—!
GYU (PUSH)
AND?
WHAT IS THE HARE DOING HERE?

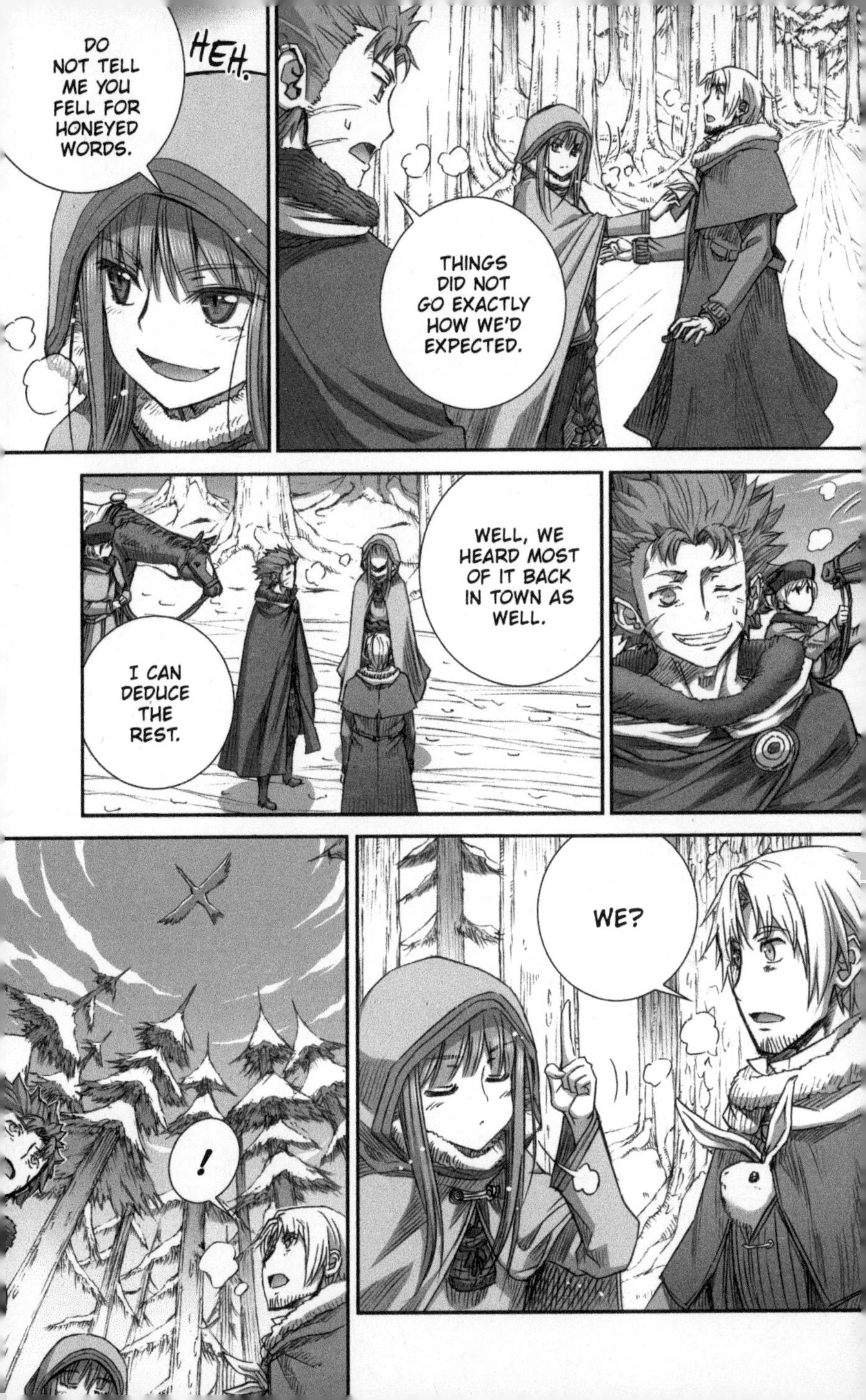
THINGS DID NOT GO EXACTLY HOW WE'D EXPECTED.
HEH.
DO NOT TELL ME YOU FELL FOR HONEYED WORDS.
WELL, WE HEARD MOST OF IT BACK IN TOWN AS WELL.
I CAN DEDUCE THE REST.
WE?
!

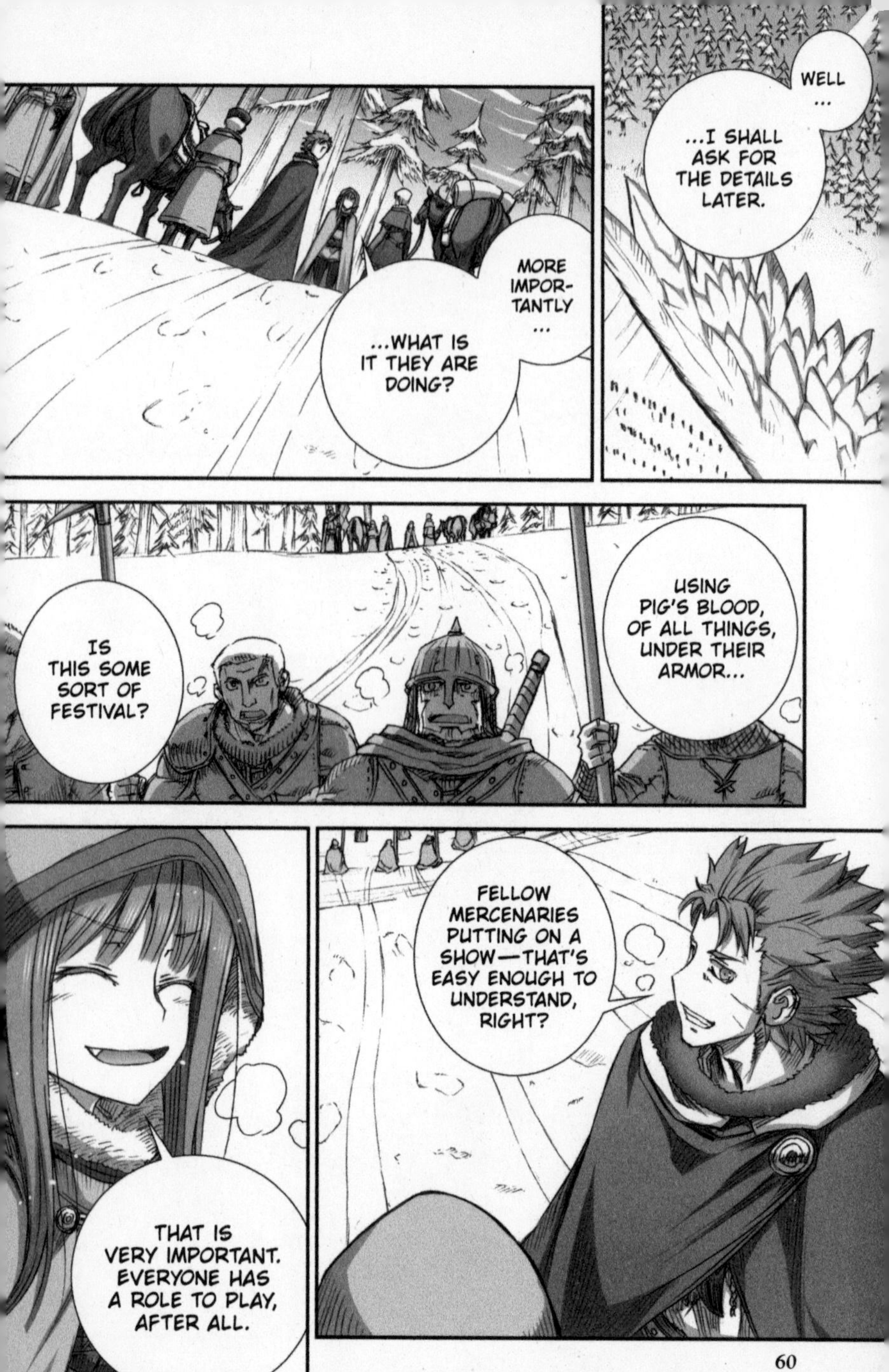
WELL ...
...I SHALL ASK FOR THE DETAILS LATER.
MORE IMPOR-TANTLY ...
...WHAT IS IT THEY ARE DOING?
USING PIG'S BLOOD, OF ALL THINGS, UNDER THEIR ARMOR...
IS THIS SOME SORT OF FESTIVAL?
FELLOW MERCENARIES PUTTING ON A SHOW—THAT'S EASY ENOUGH TO UNDERSTAND, RIGHT?
THAT IS VERY IMPORTANT. EVERYONE HAS A ROLE TO PLAY, AFTER ALL.

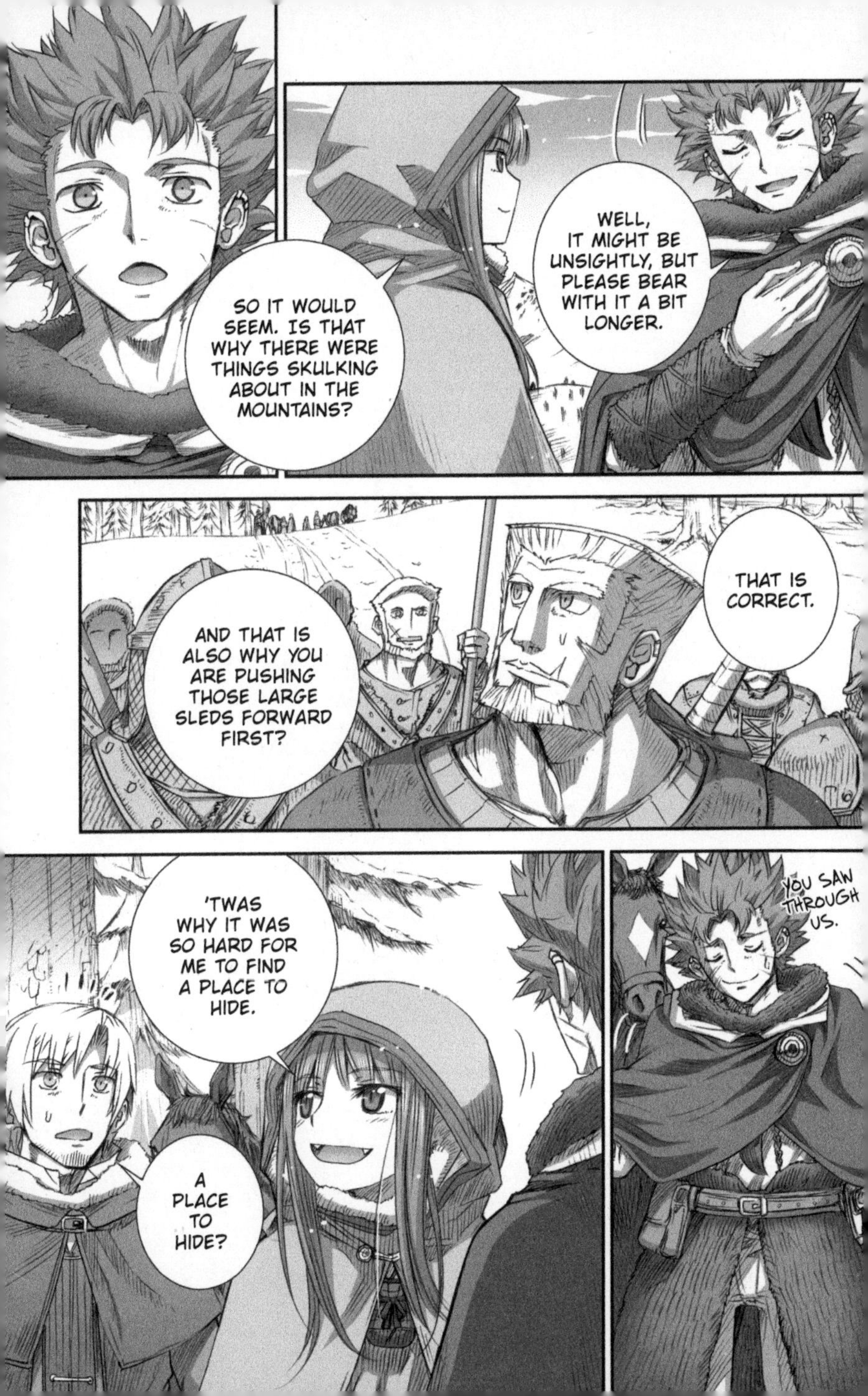
WELL, IT MIGHT BE UNSIGHTLY, BUT PLEASE BEAR WITH IT A BIT LONGER.
SO IT WOULD SEEM. IS THAT WHY THERE WERE THINGS SKULKING ABOUT IN THE MOUNTAINS?
AND THAT IS ALSO WHY YOU ARE PUSHING THOSE LARGE SLEDS FORWARD FIRST?
THAT IS CORRECT.
YOU SAW THROUGH US.
'TWAS WHY IT WAS SO HARD FOR ME TO FIND A PLACE TO HIDE.
A PLACE TO HIDE?

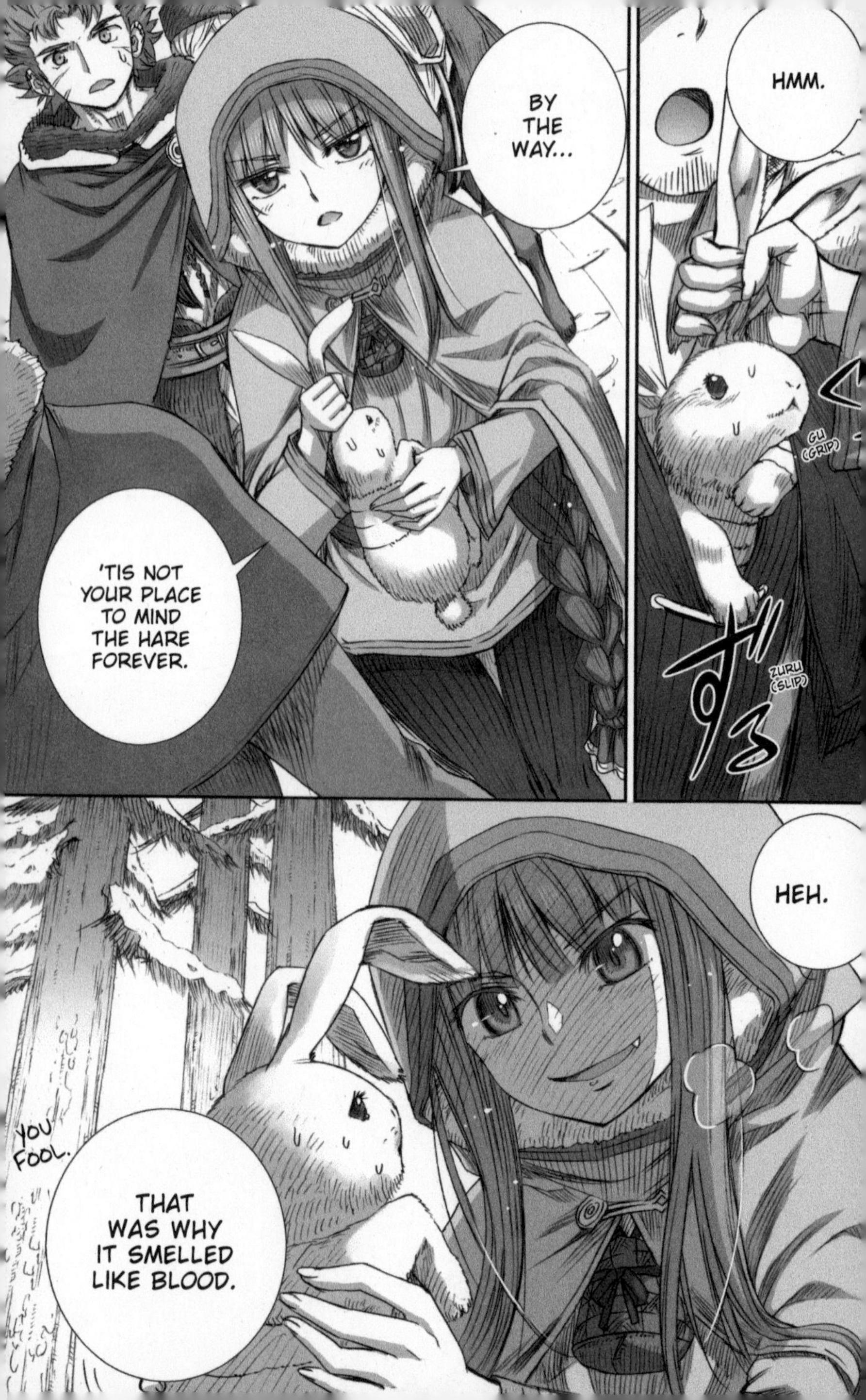
HMM.
GU (GRIP)
ZURU (SLIP)
BY THE WAY...
'TIS NOT YOUR PLACE TO MIND THE HARE FOREVER.
HEH.
YOU FOOL.
THAT WAS WHY IT SMELLED LIKE BLOOD.

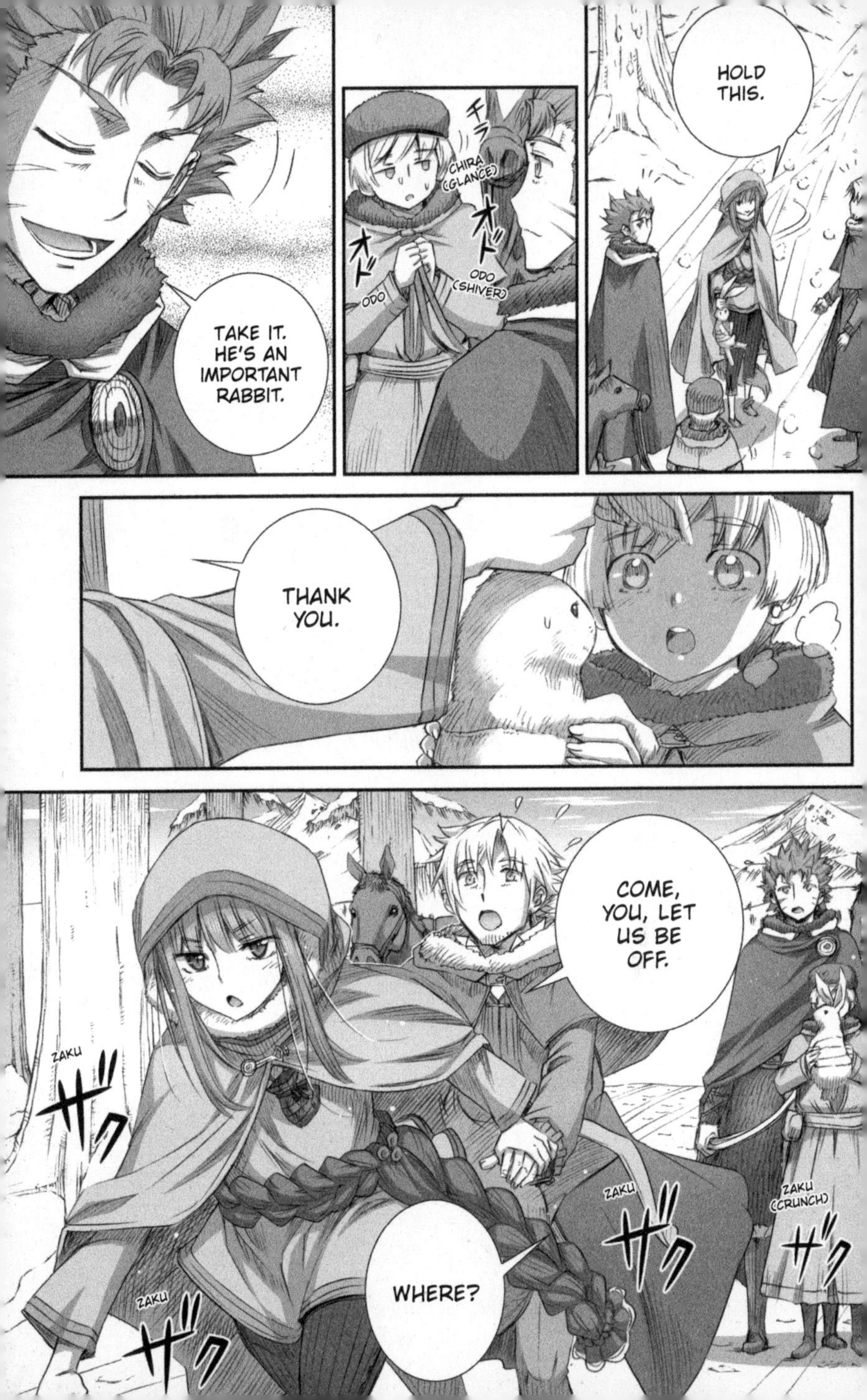
HOLD THIS.
チラ
CHIRA (GLANCE)
オド
ODO (SHIVER)
オド
ODO
TAKE IT. HE'S AN IMPORTANT RABBIT.
THANK YOU.
COME, YOU, LET US BE OFF.
ザク
ZAKU (CRUNCH)
ザク
ZAKU
WHERE?
ザク
ZAKU
ザク
ZAKU

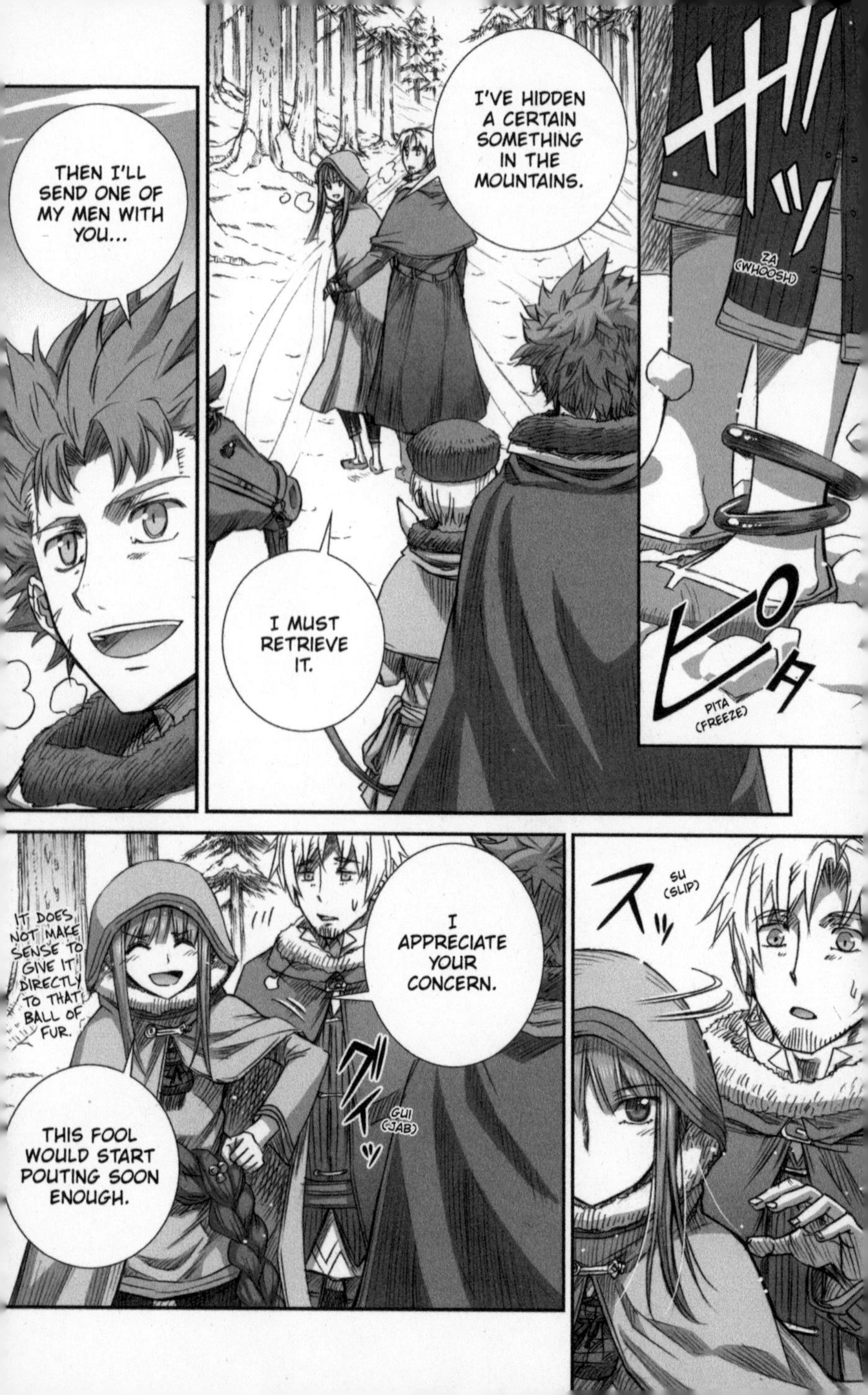
ZA (WHOOSH)
PITA (FREEZE)
I'VE HIDDEN A CERTAIN SOMETHING IN THE MOUNTAINS.
I MUST RETRIEVE IT.
THEN I'LL SEND ONE OF MY MEN WITH YOU...
SU (SLIP)
I APPRECIATE YOUR CONCERN.
GUI (JAB)
IT DOES NOT MAKE SENSE TO GIVE IT DIRECTLY TO THAT BALL OF FUR.
THIS FOOL WOULD START POUTING SOON ENOUGH.

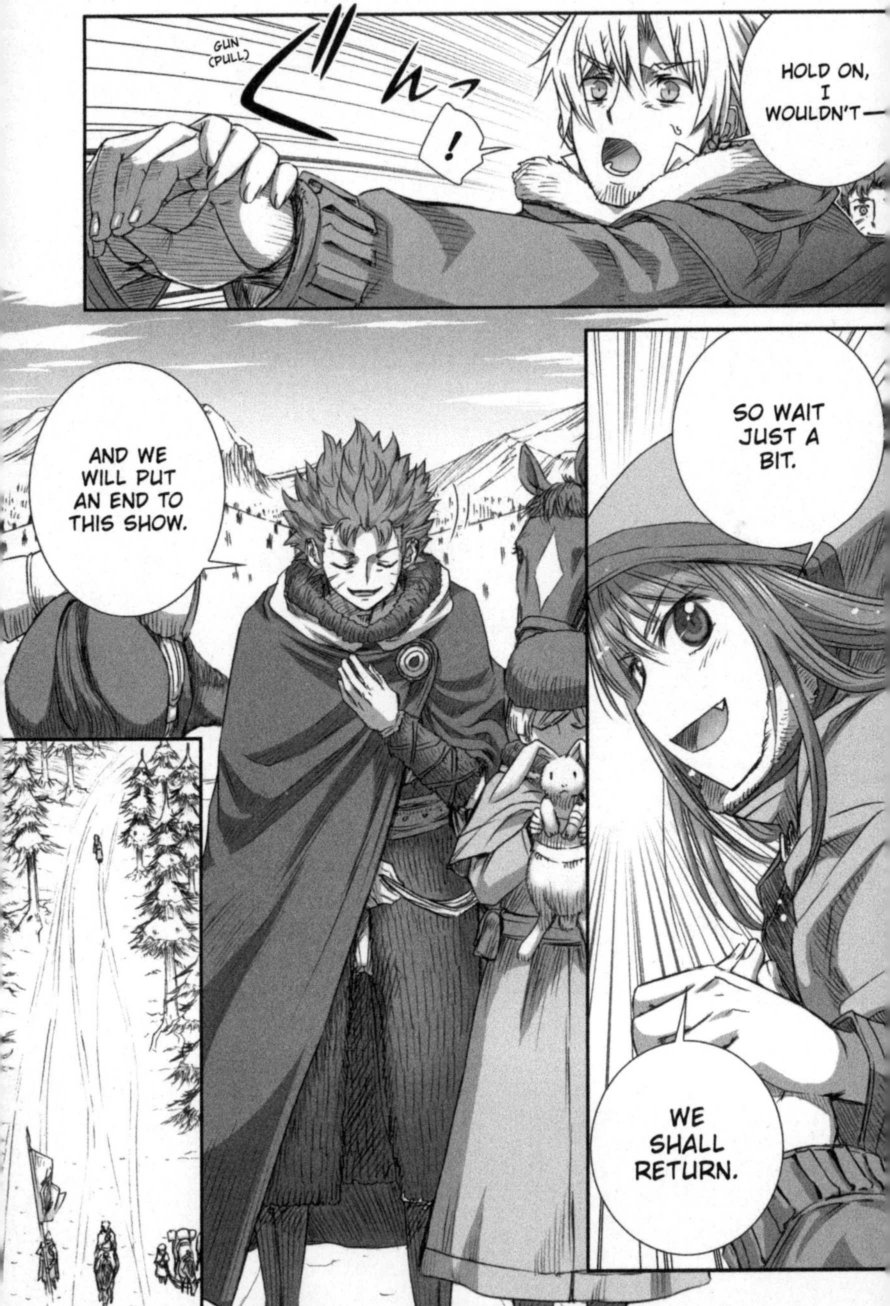
HOLD ON, I WOULDN'T—
GUN (PULL)
!
SO WAIT JUST A BIT.
WE SHALL RETURN.
AND WE WILL PUT AN END TO THIS SHOW.

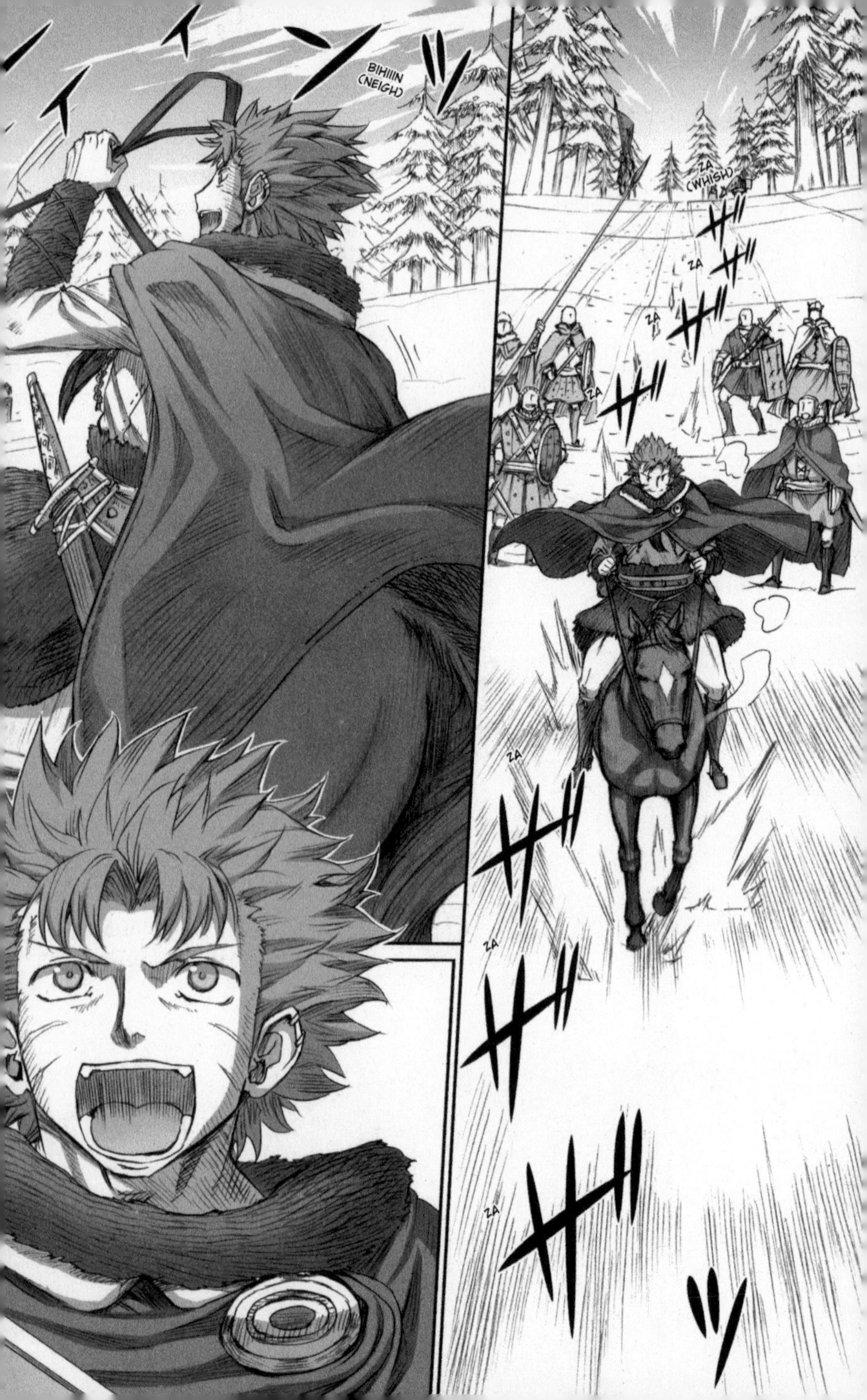
ZA (WHISH)
ZA
ZA
ZA
ZA
ZA
ZA
BIHIIIN (NEIGH)

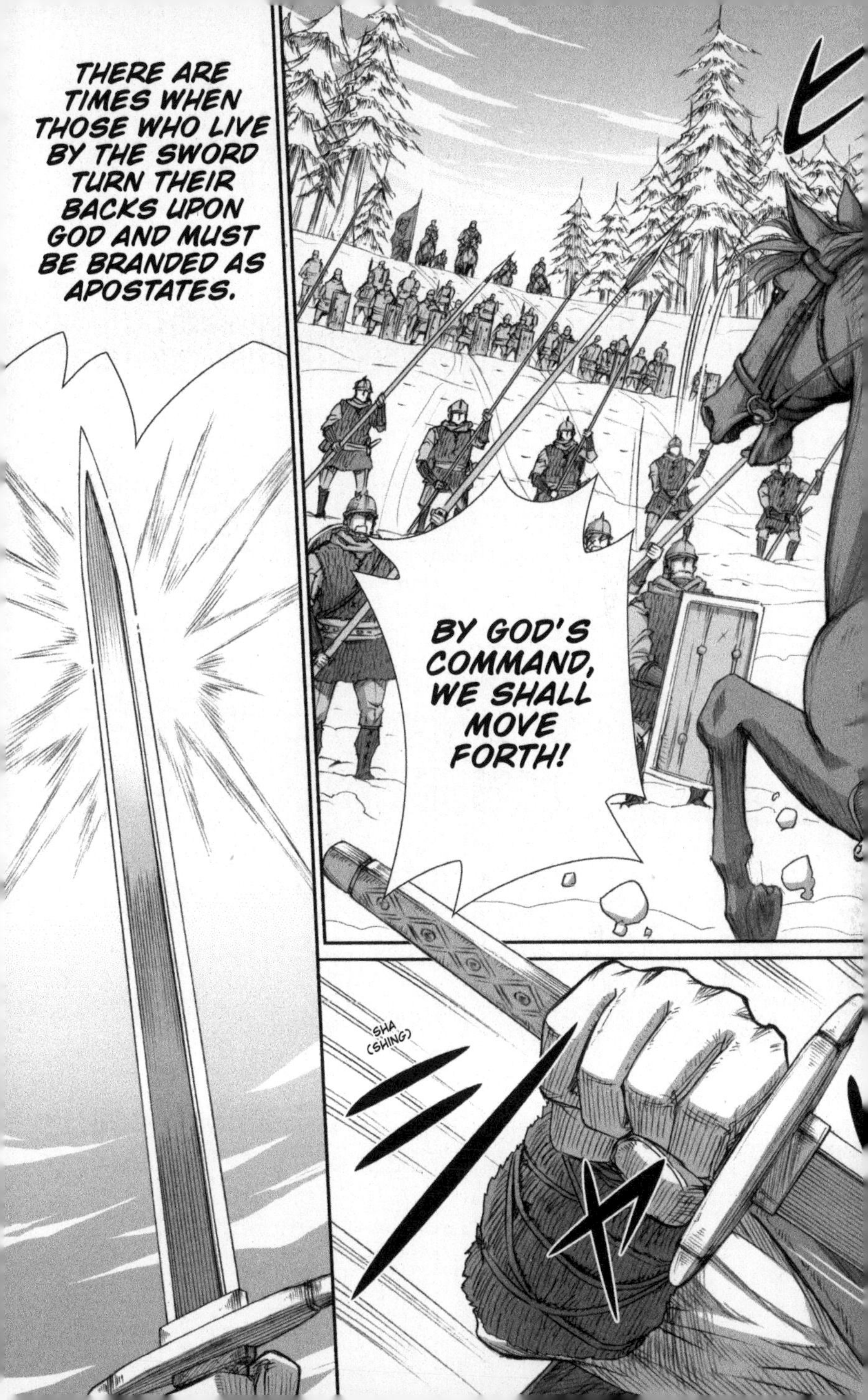
BY GOD'S COMMAND, WE SHALL MOVE FORTH!
SHA (SHING)
THERE ARE TIMES WHEN THOSE WHO LIVE BY THE SWORD TURN THEIR BACKS UPON GOD AND MUST BE BRANDED AS APOSTATES.

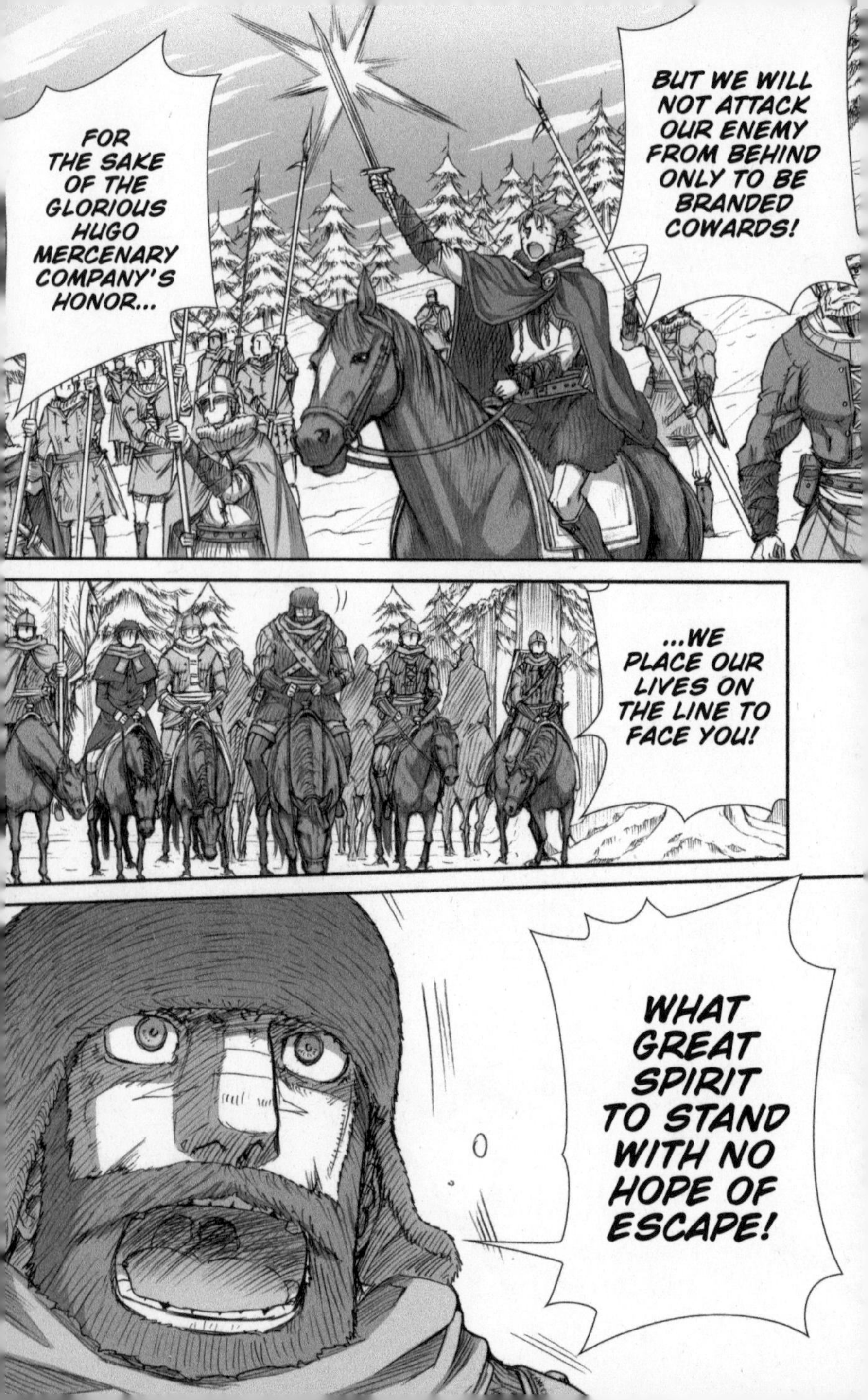
BUT WE WILL NOT ATTACK OUR ENEMY FROM BEHIND ONLY TO BE BRANDED COWARDS!
FOR THE SAKE OF THE GLORIOUS HUGO MERCENARY COMPANY'S HONOR...
...WE PLACE OUR LIVES ON THE LINE TO FACE YOU!
WHAT GREAT SPIRIT TO STAND WITH NO HOPE OF ESCAPE!

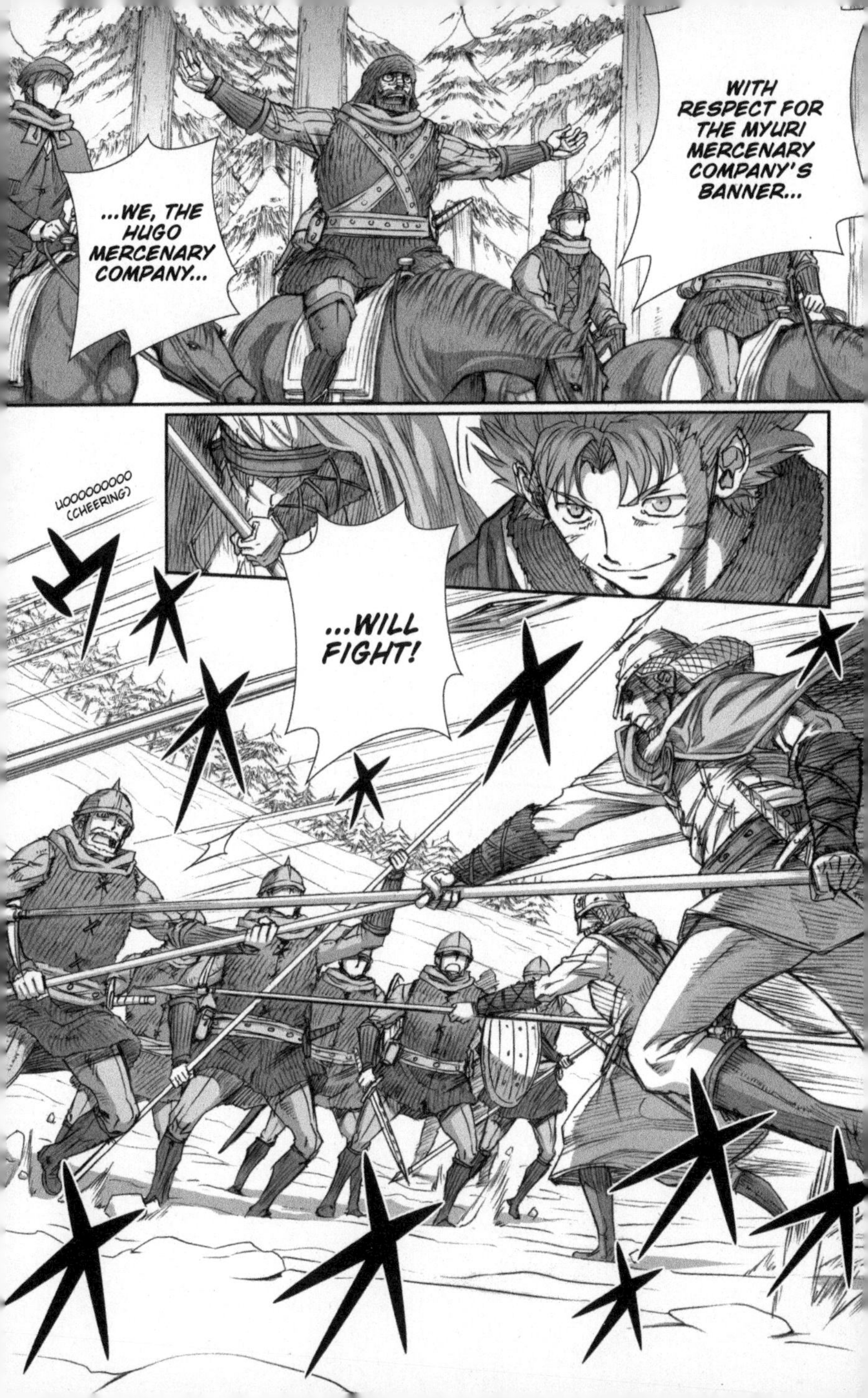

WITH RESPECT FOR THE MYURI MERCENARY COMPANY'S BANNER...
...WE, THE HUGO MERCENARY COMPANY...
...WILL FIGHT!
UOOOOOOOOO (CHEERING)

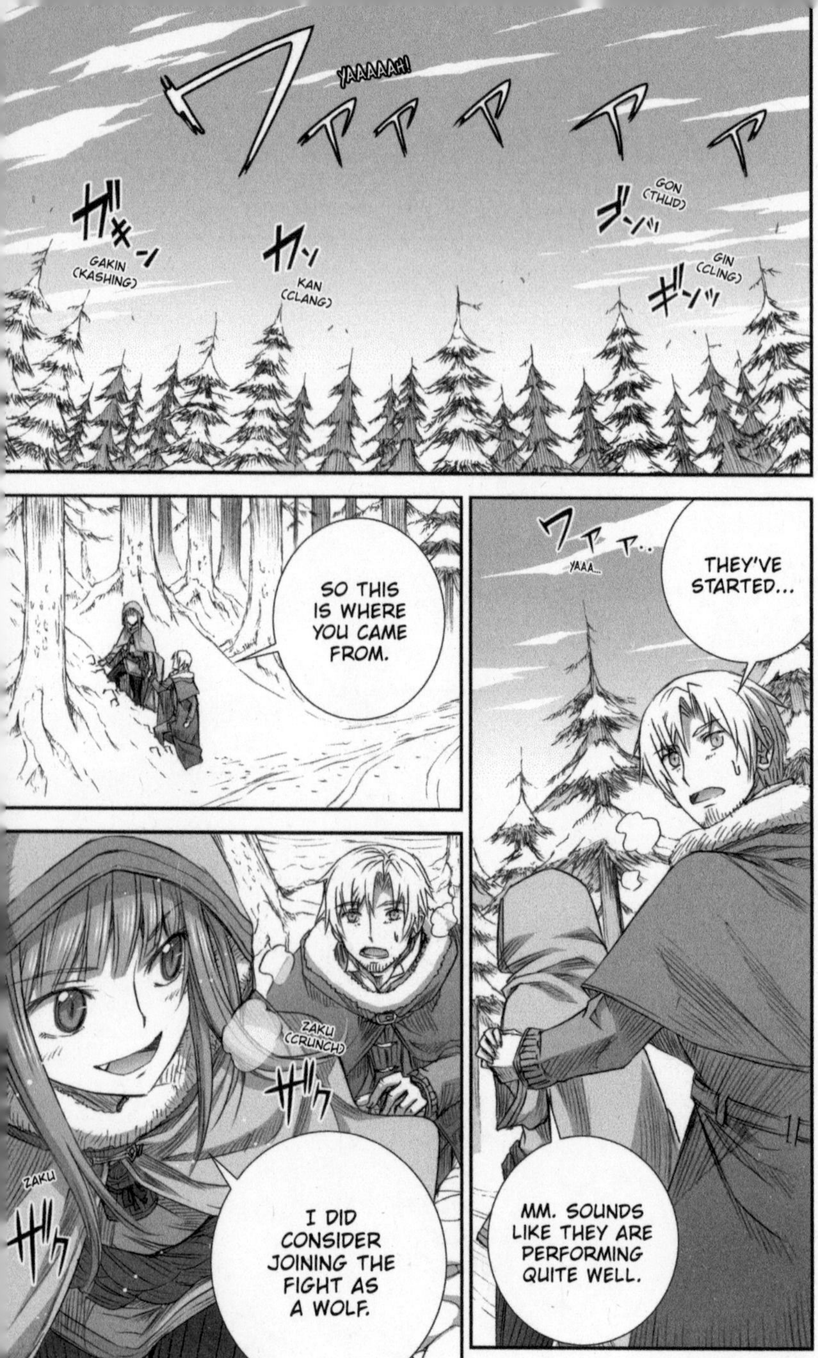
YAAAAAH!
GON (THUD)
GIN (CLING)
KAN (CLANG)
GAKIN (KASHING)
YAAA...
THEY'VE STARTED...
MM. SOUNDS LIKE THEY ARE PERFORMING QUITE WELL.
SO THIS IS WHERE YOU CAME FROM.
ZAKU (CRUNCH)
I DID CONSIDER JOINING THE FIGHT AS A WOLF.
ZAKU

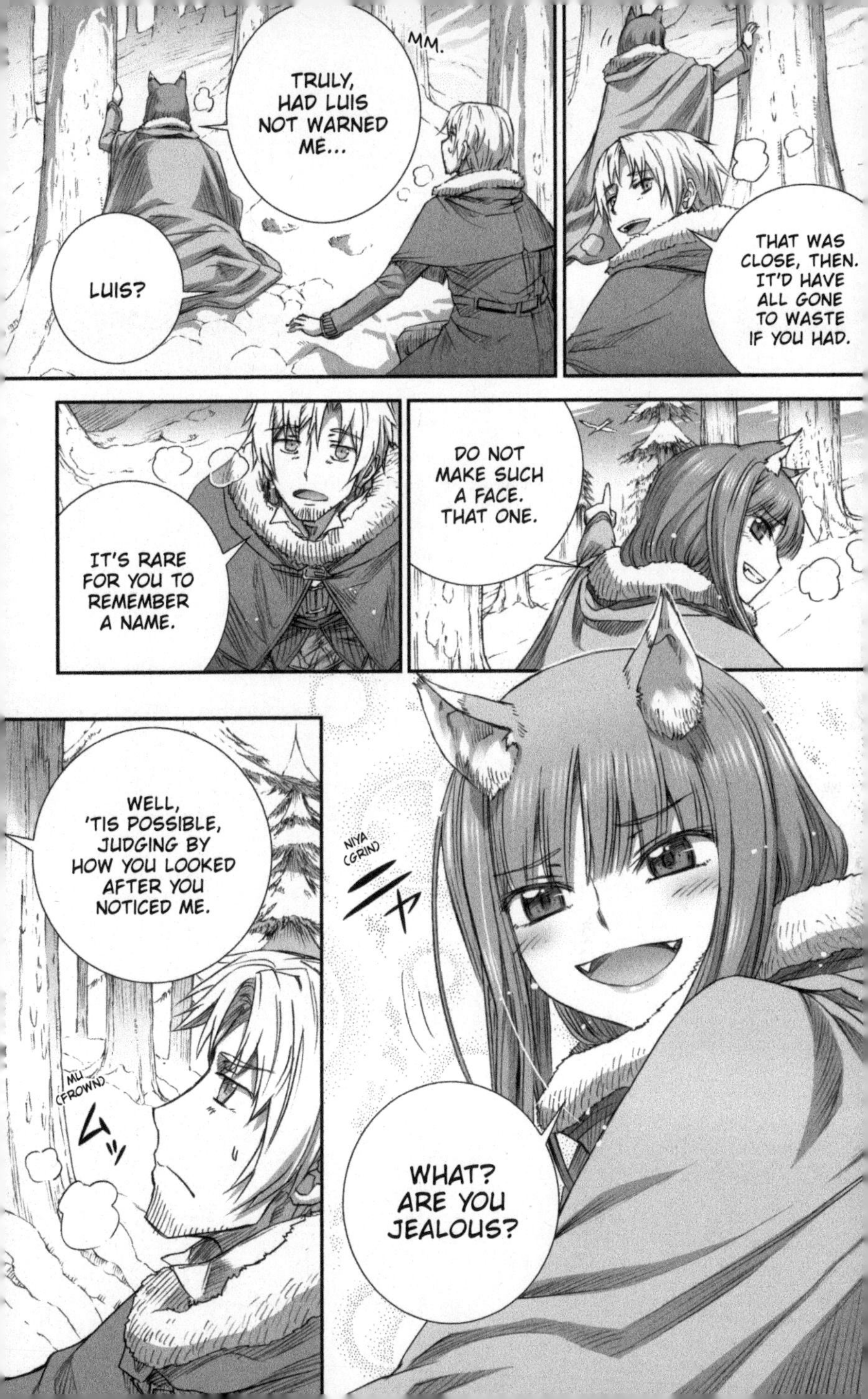
THAT WAS CLOSE, THEN. IT'D HAVE ALL GONE TO WASTE IF YOU HAD.
MM.
TRULY, HAD LUIS NOT WARNED ME...
LUIS?
DO NOT MAKE SUCH A FACE. THAT ONE.
IT'S RARE FOR YOU TO REMEMBER A NAME.
NIYA (GRIN)
ニヤ
WHAT? ARE YOU JEALOUS?
WELL, 'TIS POSSIBLE, JUDGING BY HOW YOU LOOKED AFTER YOU NOTICED ME.
MU (FROWN)
ムッ

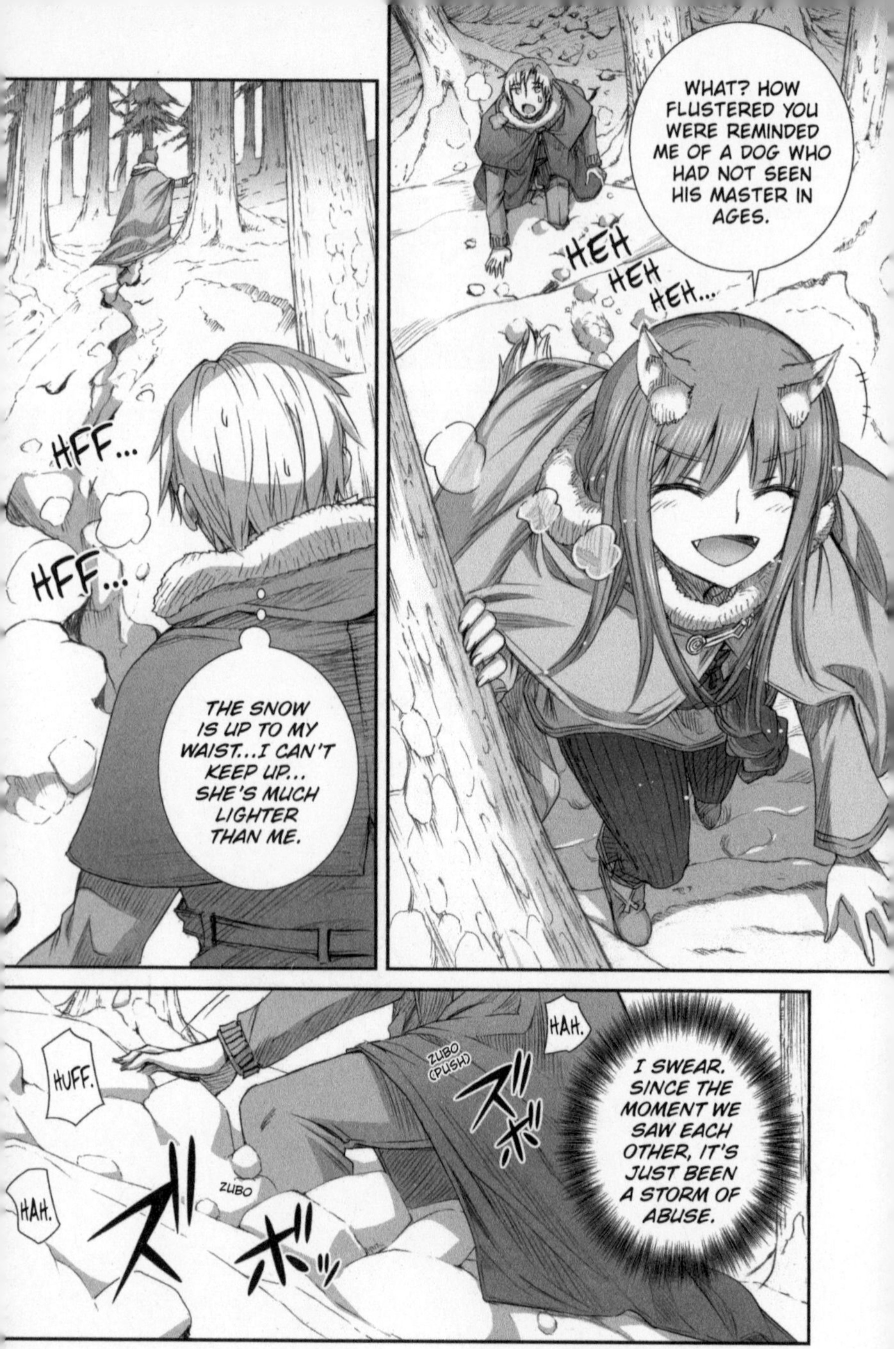
WHAT? HOW FLUSTERED YOU WERE REMINDED ME OF A DOG WHO HAD NOT SEEN HIS MASTER IN AGES.
HEH HEH HEH...
HFF...
HFF...
THE SNOW IS UP TO MY WAIST...I CAN'T KEEP UP... SHE'S MUCH LIGHTER THAN ME.
HAH.
I SWEAR. SINCE THE MOMENT WE SAW EACH OTHER, IT'S JUST BEEN A STORM OF ABUSE.
ZUBO (PUSH)
ズボ
HUFF.
ZUBO
ズボッ
HAH.

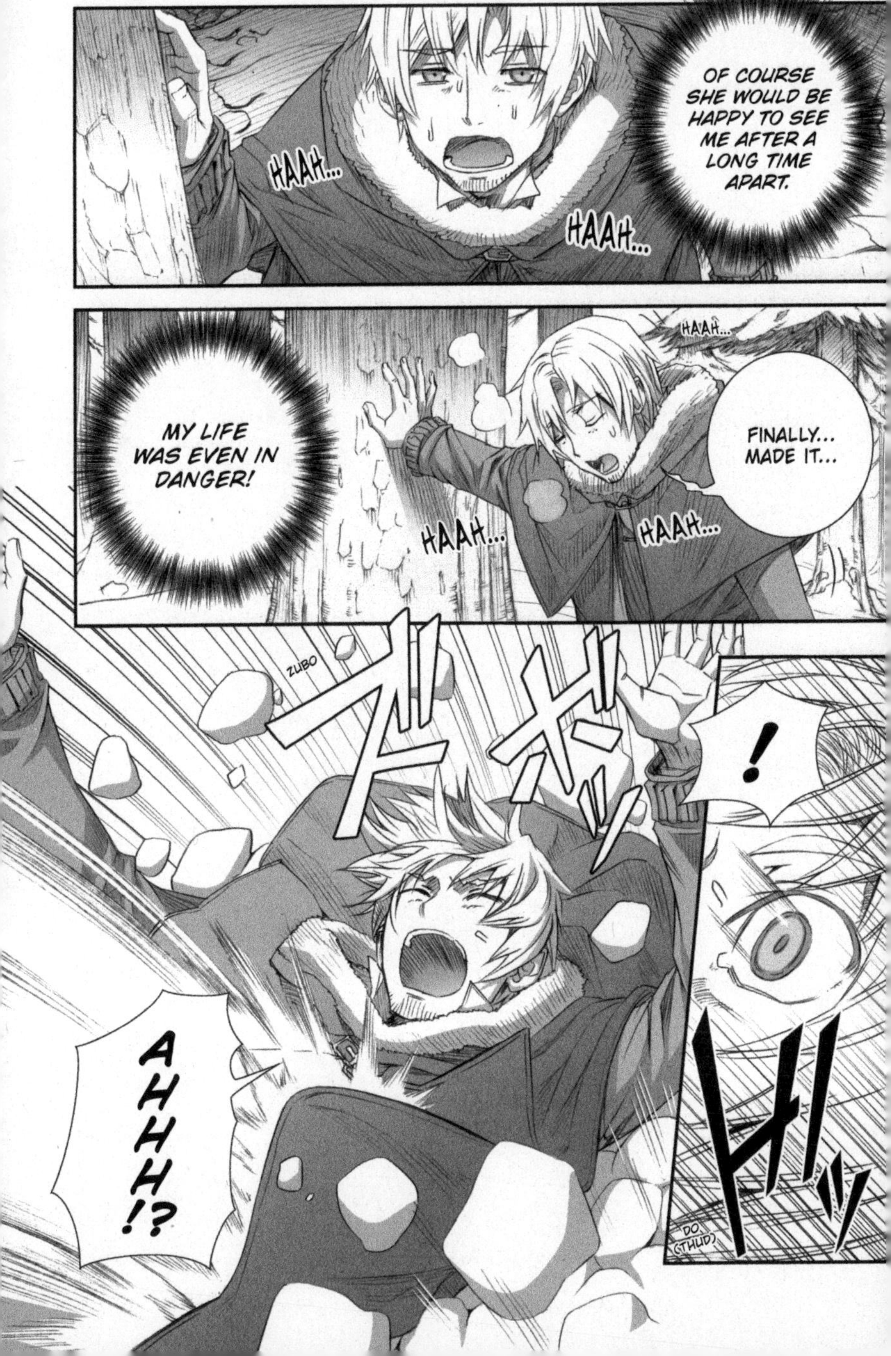
OF COURSE SHE WOULD BE HAPPY TO SEE ME AFTER A LONG TIME APART.
HAAH...
HAAH...
HAAH...
FINALLY... MADE IT...
HAAH...
HAAH...
MY LIFE WAS EVEN IN DANGER!
!
DO (THUD)
ZUBO
AHHHH!?

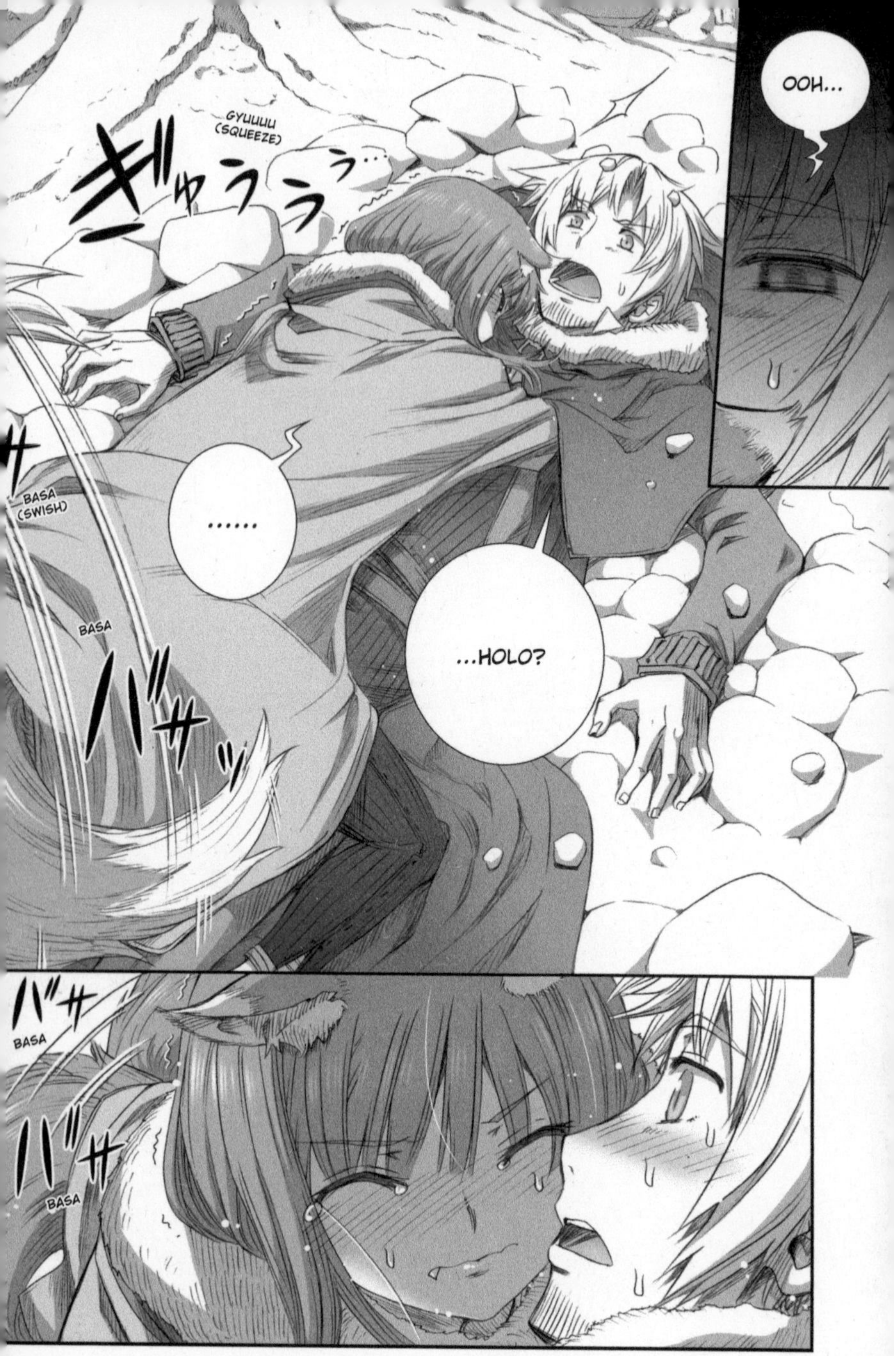
OOH...
GYUUUU (SQUEEZE)
......
...HOLO?
BASA (SWISH)
BASA
BASA
BASA

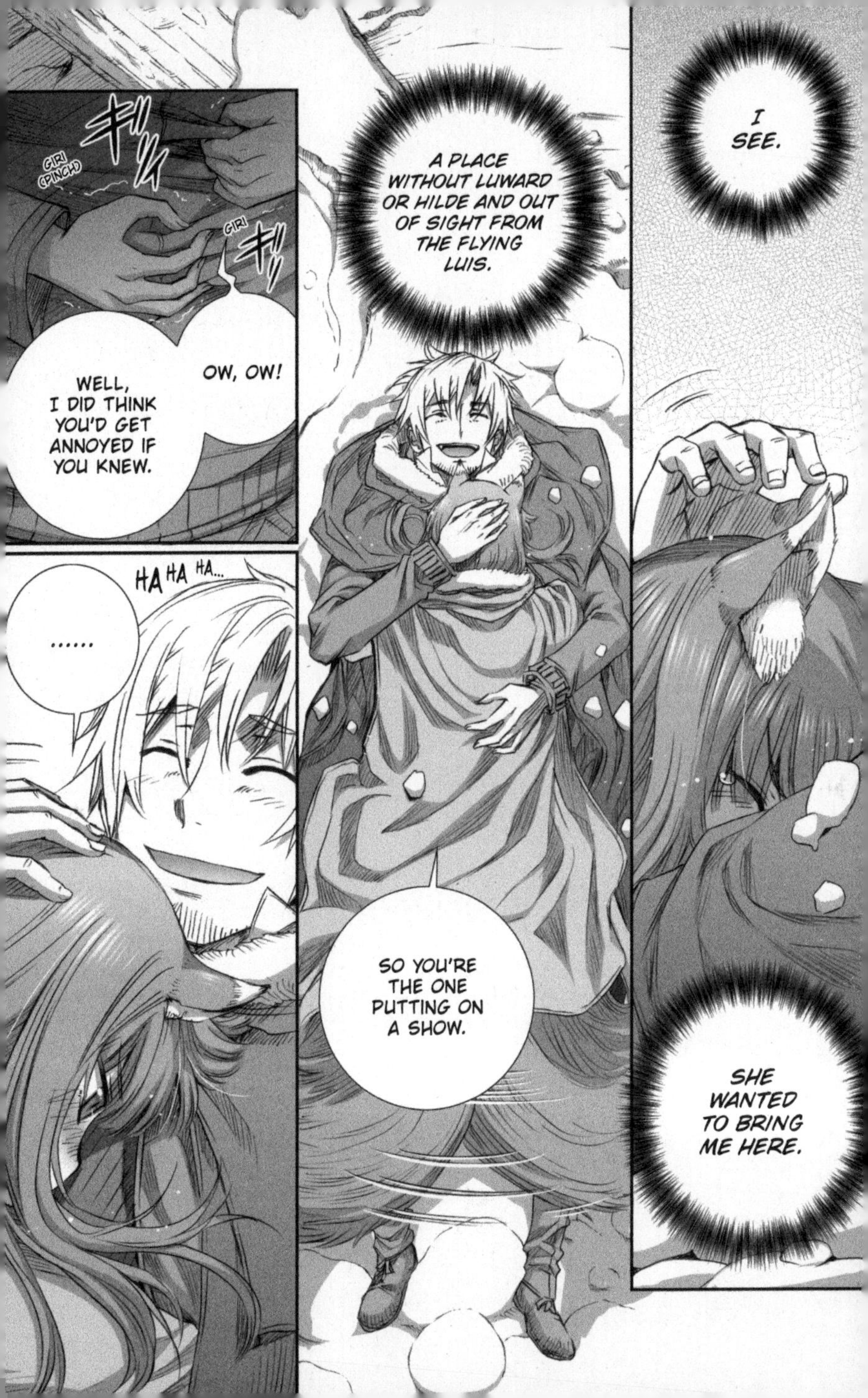
I SEE.
SHE WANTED TO BRING ME HERE.
A PLACE WITHOUT LUWARD OR HILDE AND OUT OF SIGHT FROM THE FLYING LUIS.
SO YOU'RE THE ONE PUTTING ON A SHOW.
GIRI (PINCH)
GIRI
OW, OW!
WELL, I DID THINK YOU'D GET ANNOYED IF YOU KNEW.
HA HA HA...
......

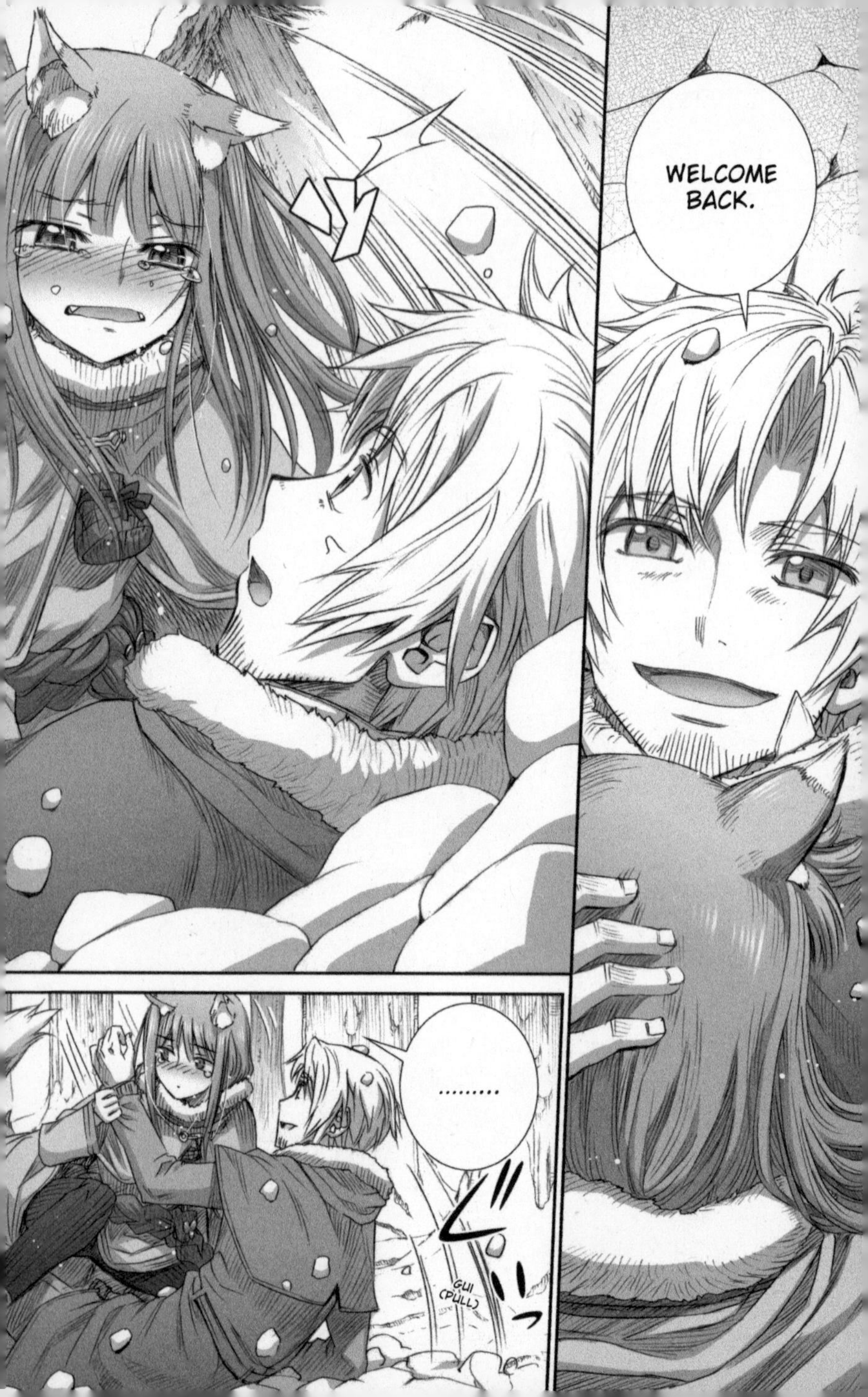
WELCOME BACK.
....
GUI (PULL)

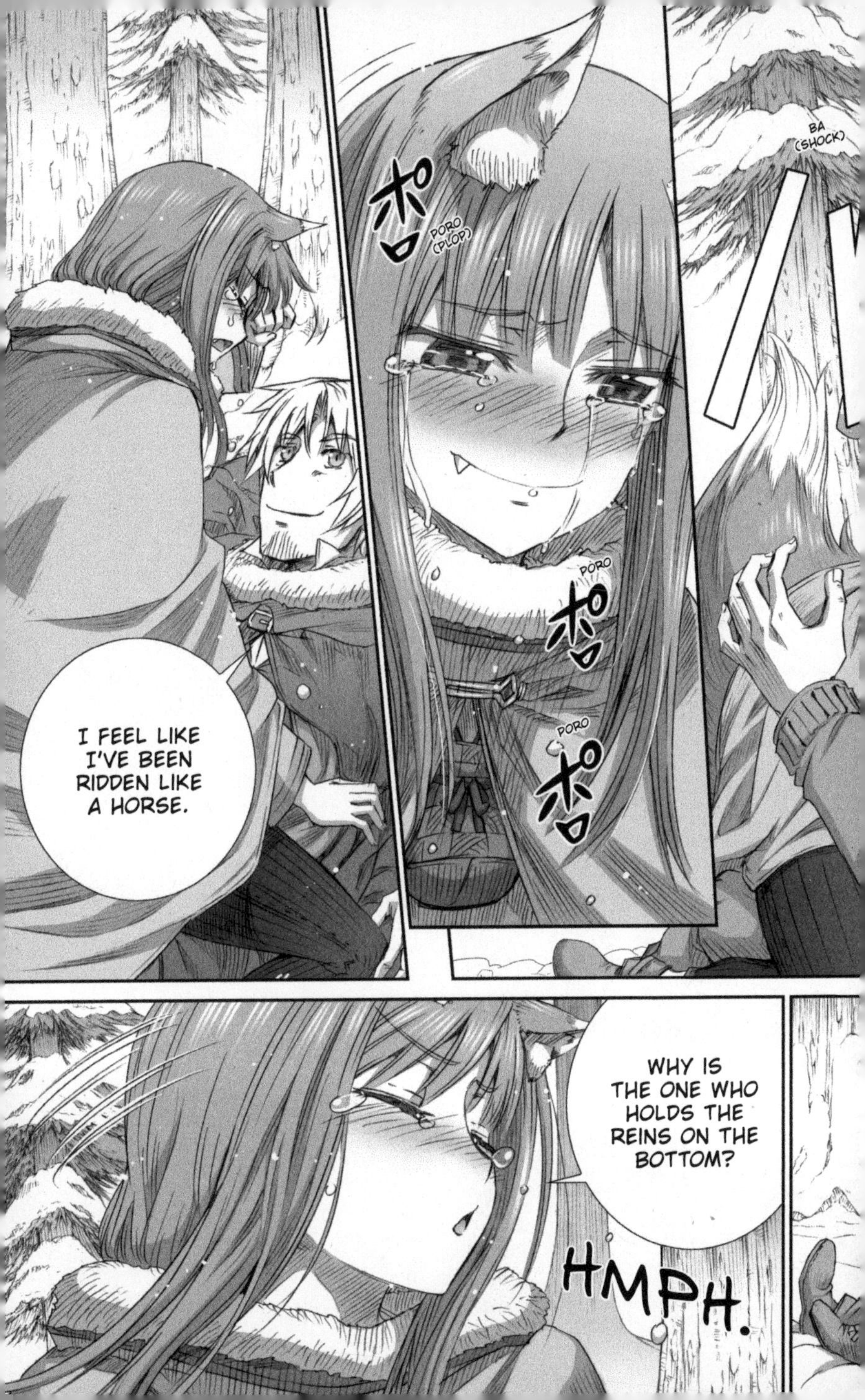
BA (SHOCK)
PORO (PLOP)
PORO
PORO
I FEEL LIKE I'VE BEEN RIDDEN LIKE A HORSE.
WHY IS THE ONE WHO HOLDS THE REINS ON THE BOTTOM?
HMPH.

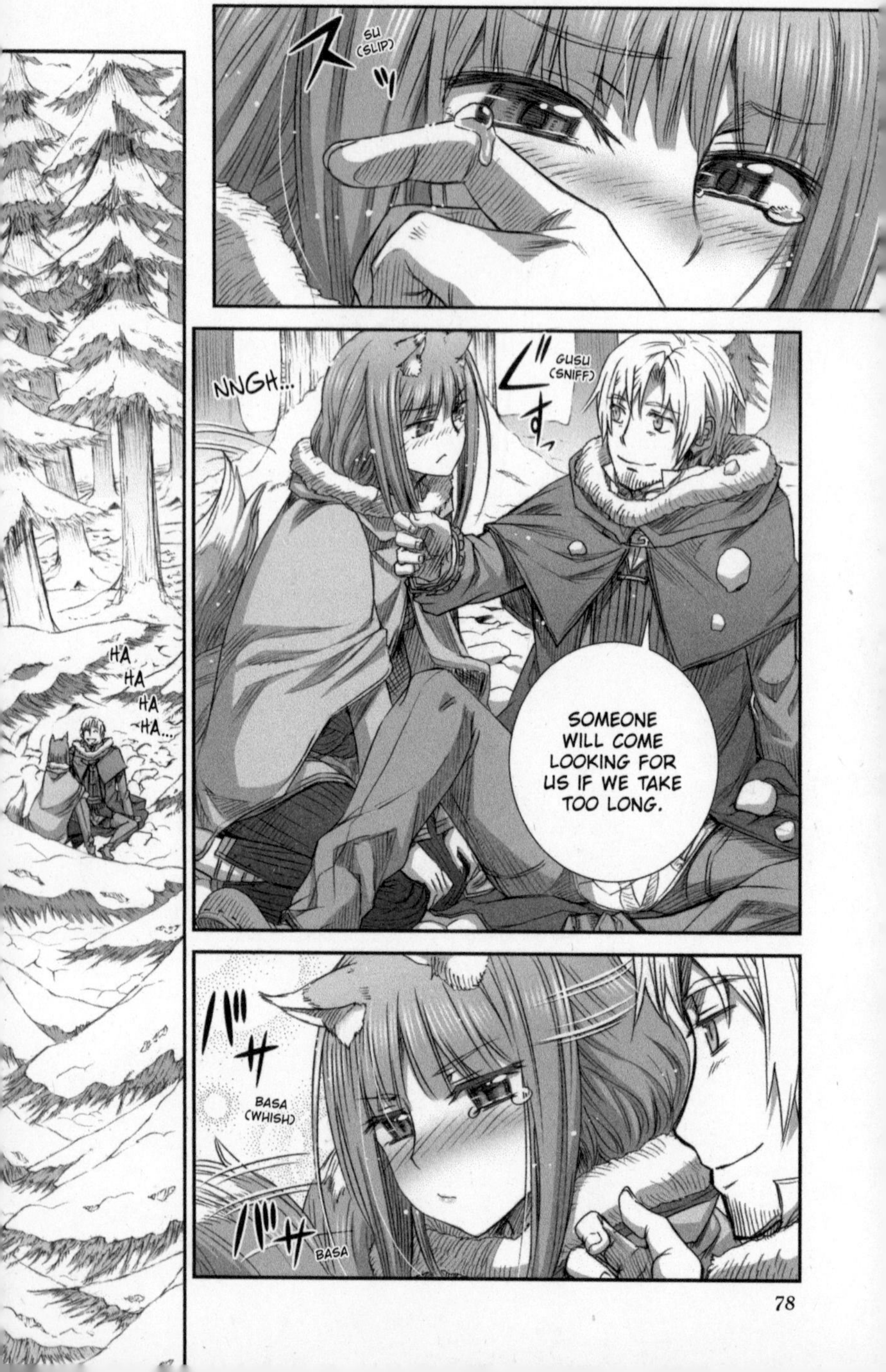
SU (SLIP)
GUSU (SNIFF)
NNGH...
SOMEONE WILL COME LOOKING FOR US IF WE TAKE TOO LONG.
BASA (WHISH)
BASA
HA HA HA HA...

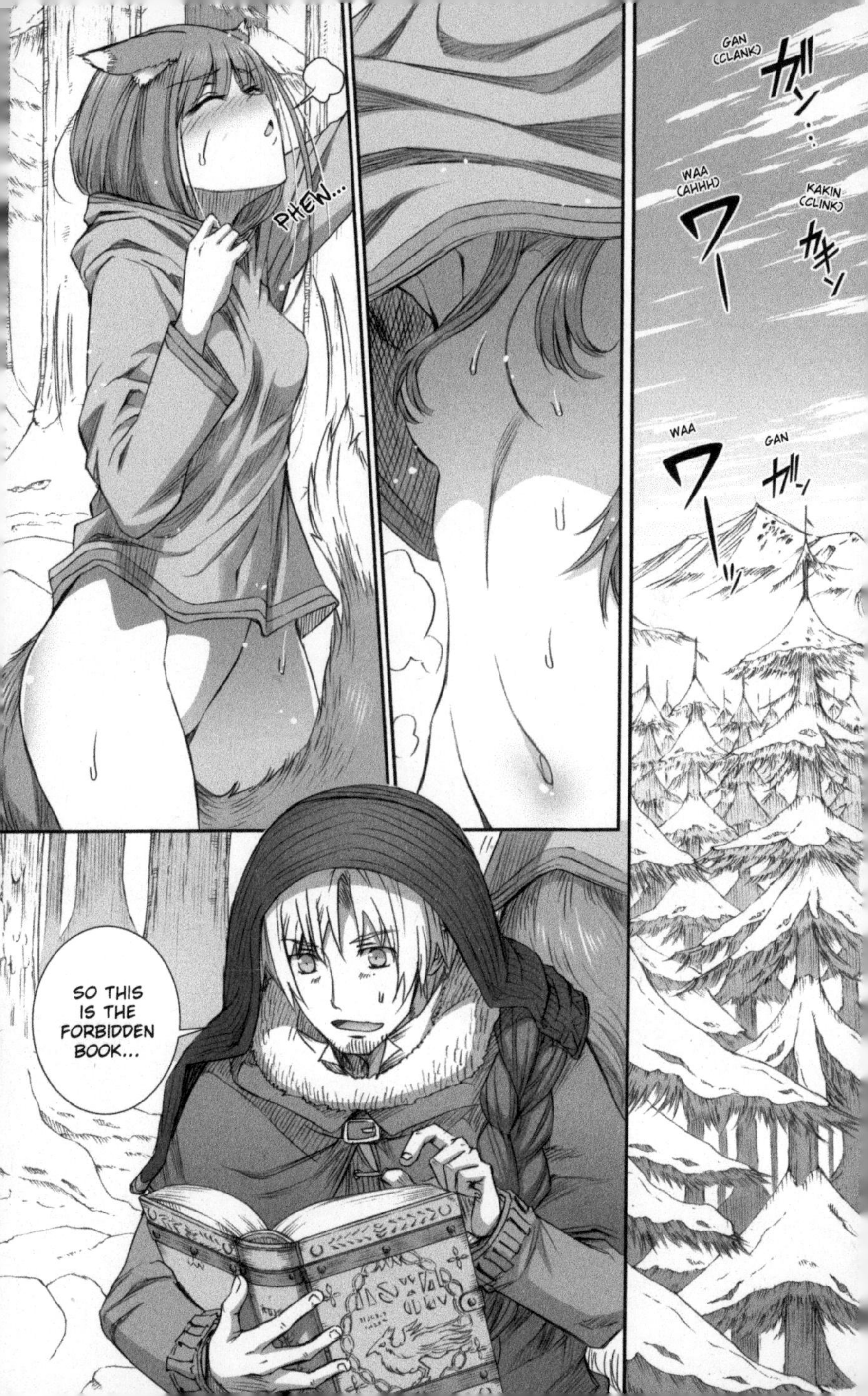
GAN (CLANK)
ガン・・・
KAKIN (CLINK)
カキン
WAA (AHHH)
ワー
GAN
ガン
WAA
ワーッ
PHEW...
SO THIS IS THE FORBIDDEN BOOK...

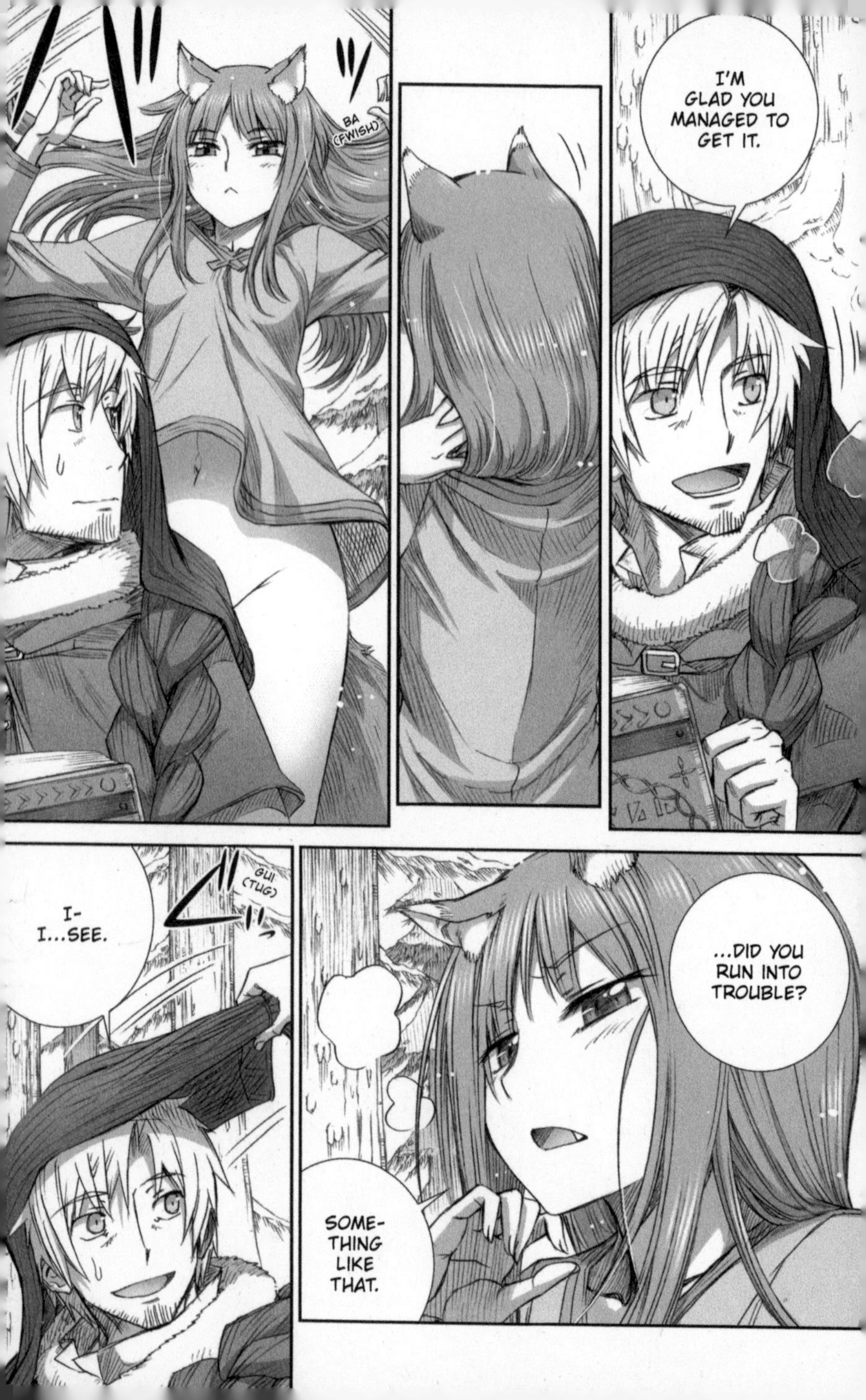
I'M GLAD YOU MANAGED TO GET IT.
BA (FWISH)
...DID YOU RUN INTO TROUBLE?
SOME-THING LIKE THAT.
GUI (TUG)
I- I...SEE.

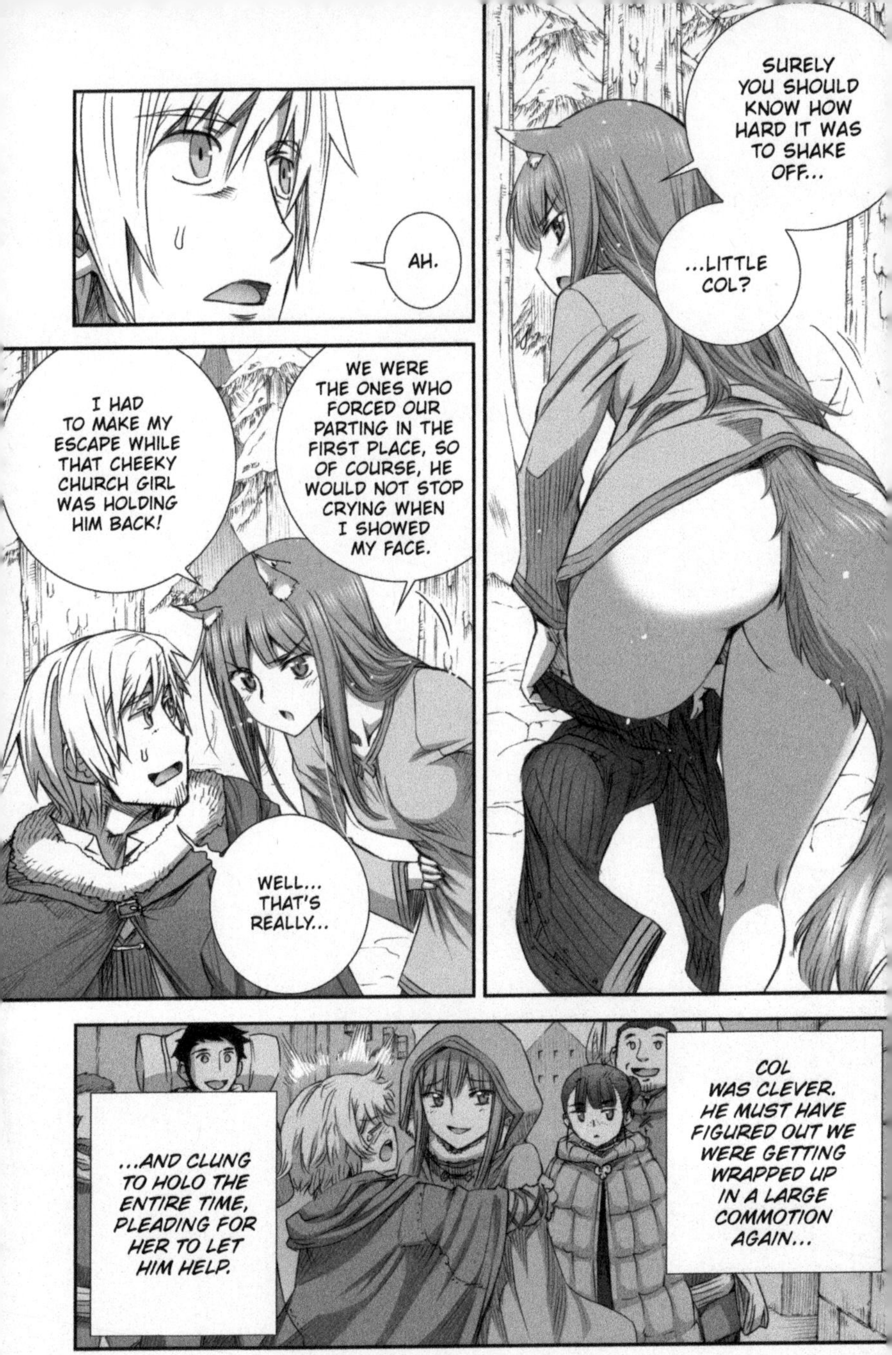
SURELY YOU SHOULD KNOW HOW HARD IT WAS TO SHAKE OFF...
...LITTLE COL?
AH.
WE WERE THE ONES WHO FORCED OUR PARTING IN THE FIRST PLACE, SO OF COURSE, HE WOULD NOT STOP CRYING WHEN I SHOWED MY FACE.
I HAD TO MAKE MY ESCAPE WHILE THAT CHEEKY CHURCH GIRL WAS HOLDING HIM BACK!
WELL... THAT'S REALLY...
COL WAS CLEVER. HE MUST HAVE FIGURED OUT WE WERE GETTING WRAPPED UP IN A LARGE COMMOTION AGAIN...
...AND CLUNG TO HOLO THE ENTIRE TIME, PLEADING FOR HER TO LET HIM HELP.

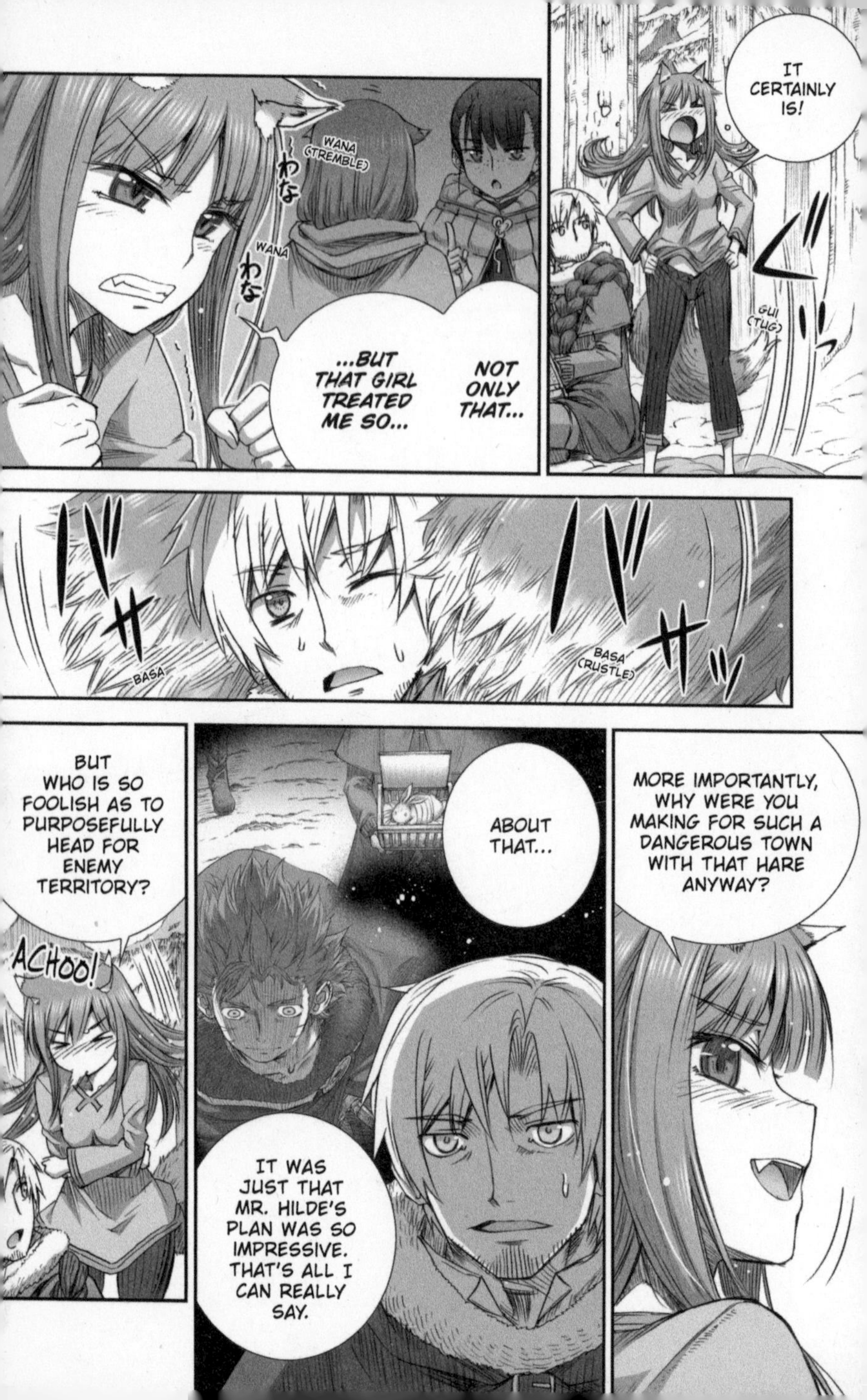
IT CERTAINLY IS!
GUI (TUG)
WANA (TREMBLE)
WANA
NOT ONLY THAT...
...BUT THAT GIRL TREATED ME SO...
BASA (RUSTLE)
BASA
MORE IMPORTANTLY, WHY WERE YOU MAKING FOR SUCH A DANGEROUS TOWN WITH THAT HARE ANYWAY?
ABOUT THAT...
IT WAS JUST THAT MR. HILDE'S PLAN WAS SO IMPRESSIVE. THAT'S ALL I CAN REALLY SAY.
BUT WHO IS SO FOOLISH AS TO PURPOSEFULLY HEAD FOR ENEMY TERRITORY?
ACHOO!

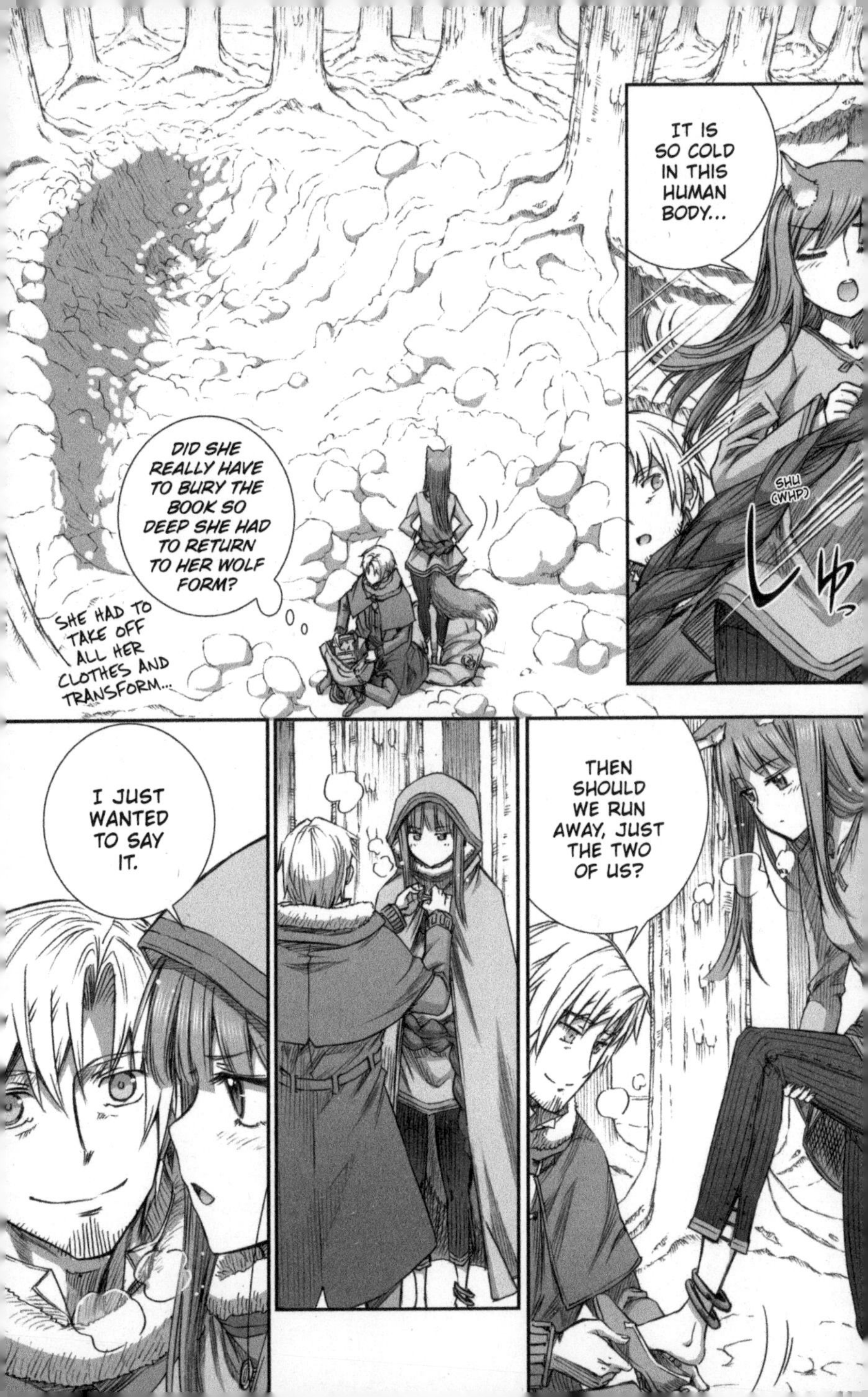
IT IS SO COLD IN THIS HUMAN BODY...
SHU (WHP)
しゅっ
DID SHE REALLY HAVE TO BURY THE BOOK SO DEEP SHE HAD TO RETURN TO HER WOLF FORM?
SHE HAD TO TAKE OFF ALL HER CLOTHES AND TRANSFORM...
THEN SHOULD WE RUN AWAY, JUST THE TWO OF US?
I JUST WANTED TO SAY IT.

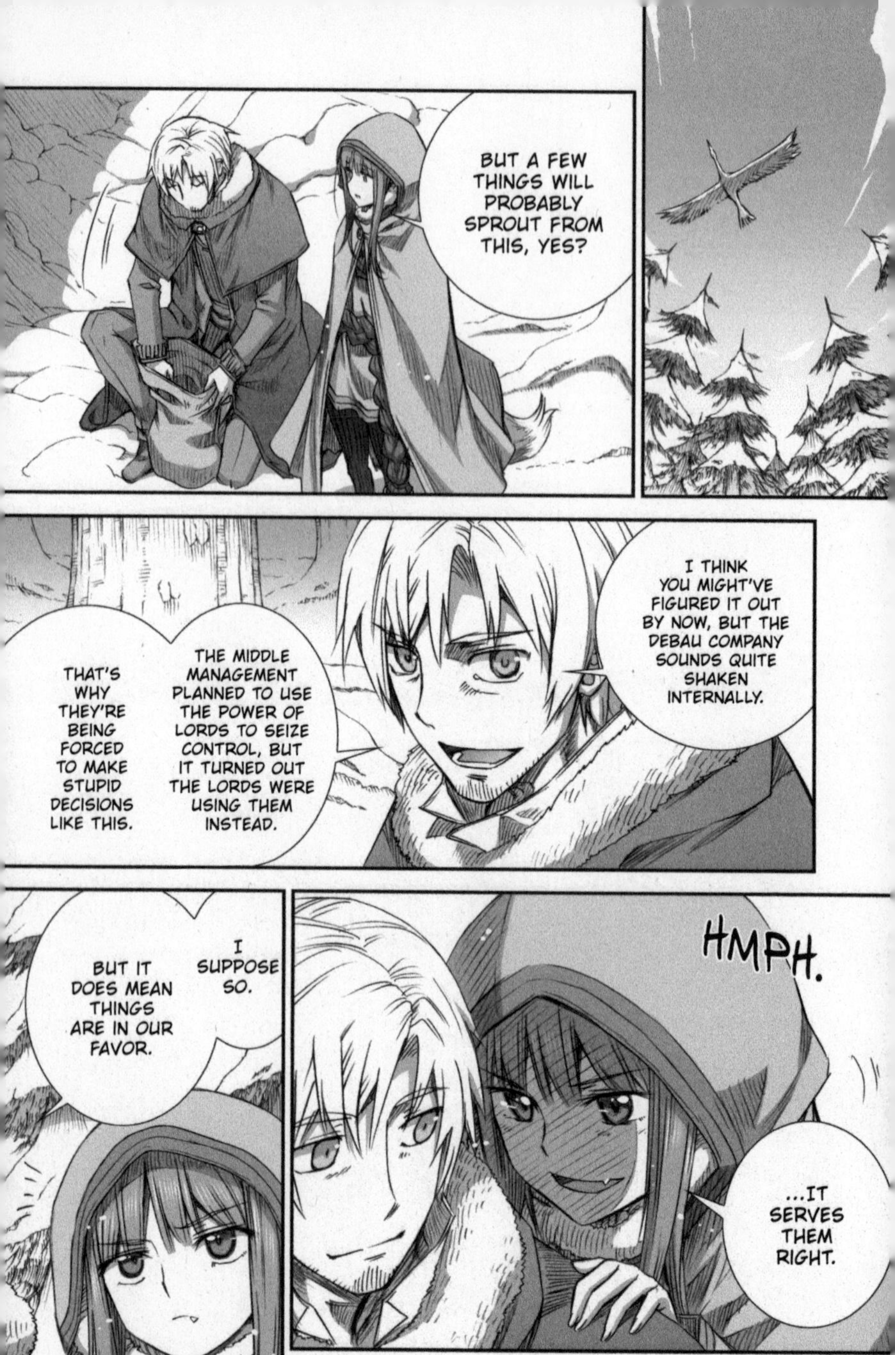
BUT A FEW THINGS WILL PROBABLY SPROUT FROM THIS, YES?
I THINK YOU MIGHT'VE FIGURED IT OUT BY NOW, BUT THE DEBAU COMPANY SOUNDS QUITE SHAKEN INTERNALLY.
THE MIDDLE MANAGEMENT PLANNED TO USE THE POWER OF LORDS TO SEIZE CONTROL, BUT IT TURNED OUT THE LORDS WERE USING THEM INSTEAD.
THAT'S WHY THEY'RE BEING FORCED TO MAKE STUPID DECISIONS LIKE THIS.
HMPH.
...IT SERVES THEM RIGHT.
I SUPPOSE SO.
BUT IT DOES MEAN THINGS ARE IN OUR FAVOR.

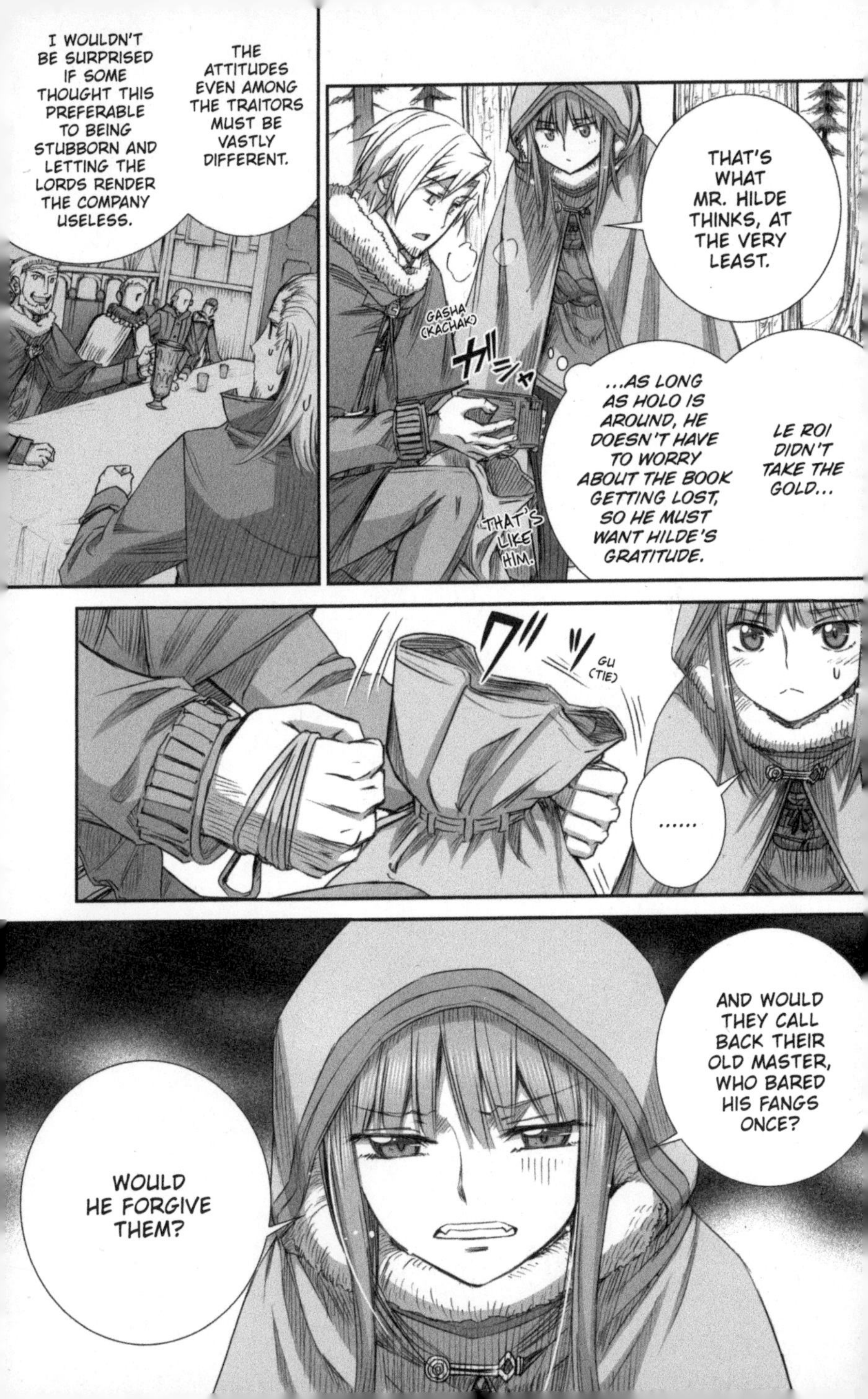
THAT'S WHAT MR. HILDE THINKS, AT THE VERY LEAST.
LE ROI DIDN'T TAKE THE GOLD...
...AS LONG AS HOLO IS AROUND, HE DOESN'T HAVE TO WORRY ABOUT THE BOOK GETTING LOST, SO HE MUST WANT HILDE'S GRATITUDE.
ガシャ
GASHA (KACHAK)
THAT'S LIKE HIM.
THE ATTITUDES EVEN AMONG THE TRAITORS MUST BE VASTLY DIFFERENT.
I WOULDN'T BE SURPRISED IF SOME THOUGHT THIS PREFERABLE TO BEING STUBBORN AND LETTING THE LORDS RENDER THE COMPANY USELESS.
グッ
GU (TIE)
......
AND WOULD THEY CALL BACK THEIR OLD MASTER, WHO BARED HIS FANGS ONCE?
WOULD HE FORGIVE THEM?

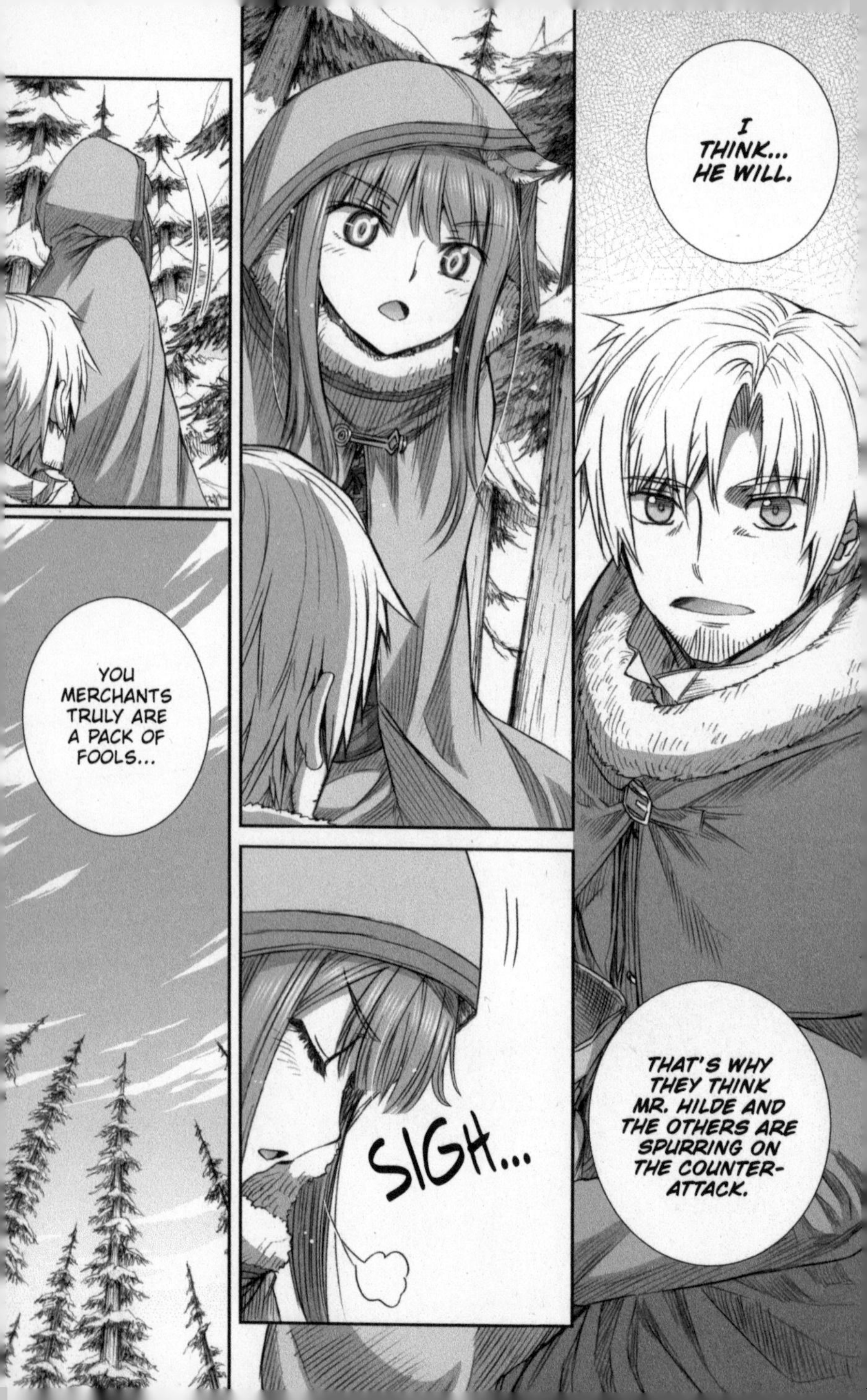
I THINK... HE WILL.
THAT'S WHY THEY THINK MR. HILDE AND THE OTHERS ARE SPURRING ON THE COUNTER-ATTACK.
SIGH...
YOU MERCHANTS TRULY ARE A PACK OF FOOLS...

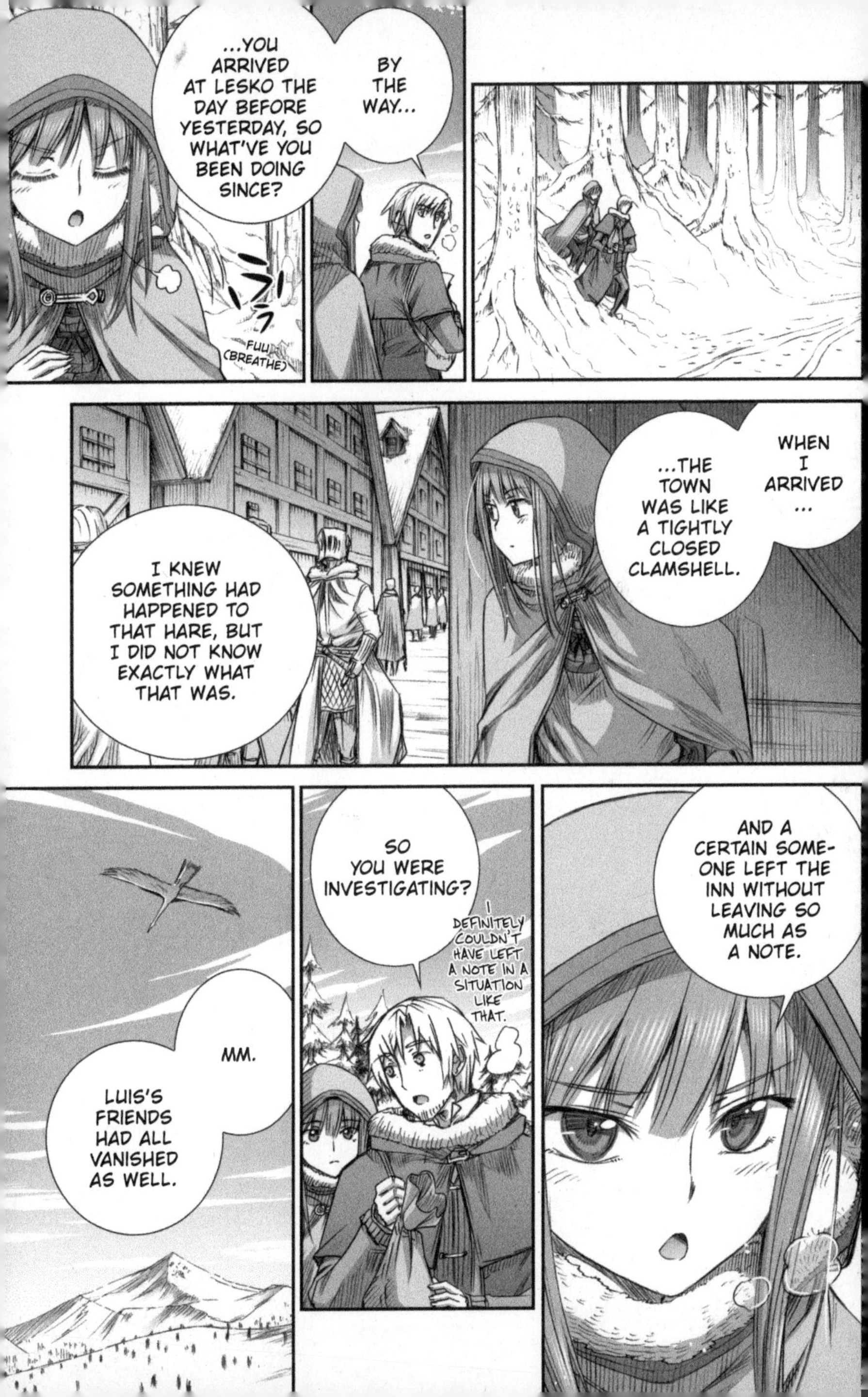
BY THE WAY...
...YOU ARRIVED AT LESKO THE DAY BEFORE YESTERDAY, SO WHAT'VE YOU BEEN DOING SINCE?
FUU (BREATHE)
WHEN I ARRIVED...
...THE TOWN WAS LIKE A TIGHTLY CLOSED CLAMSHELL.
I KNEW SOMETHING HAD HAPPENED TO THAT HARE, BUT I DID NOT KNOW EXACTLY WHAT THAT WAS.
AND A CERTAIN SOME-ONE LEFT THE INN WITHOUT LEAVING SO MUCH AS A NOTE.
SO YOU WERE INVESTIGATING?
I DEFINITELY COULDN'T HAVE LEFT A NOTE IN A SITUATION LIKE THAT.
MM.
LUIS'S FRIENDS HAD ALL VANISHED AS WELL.

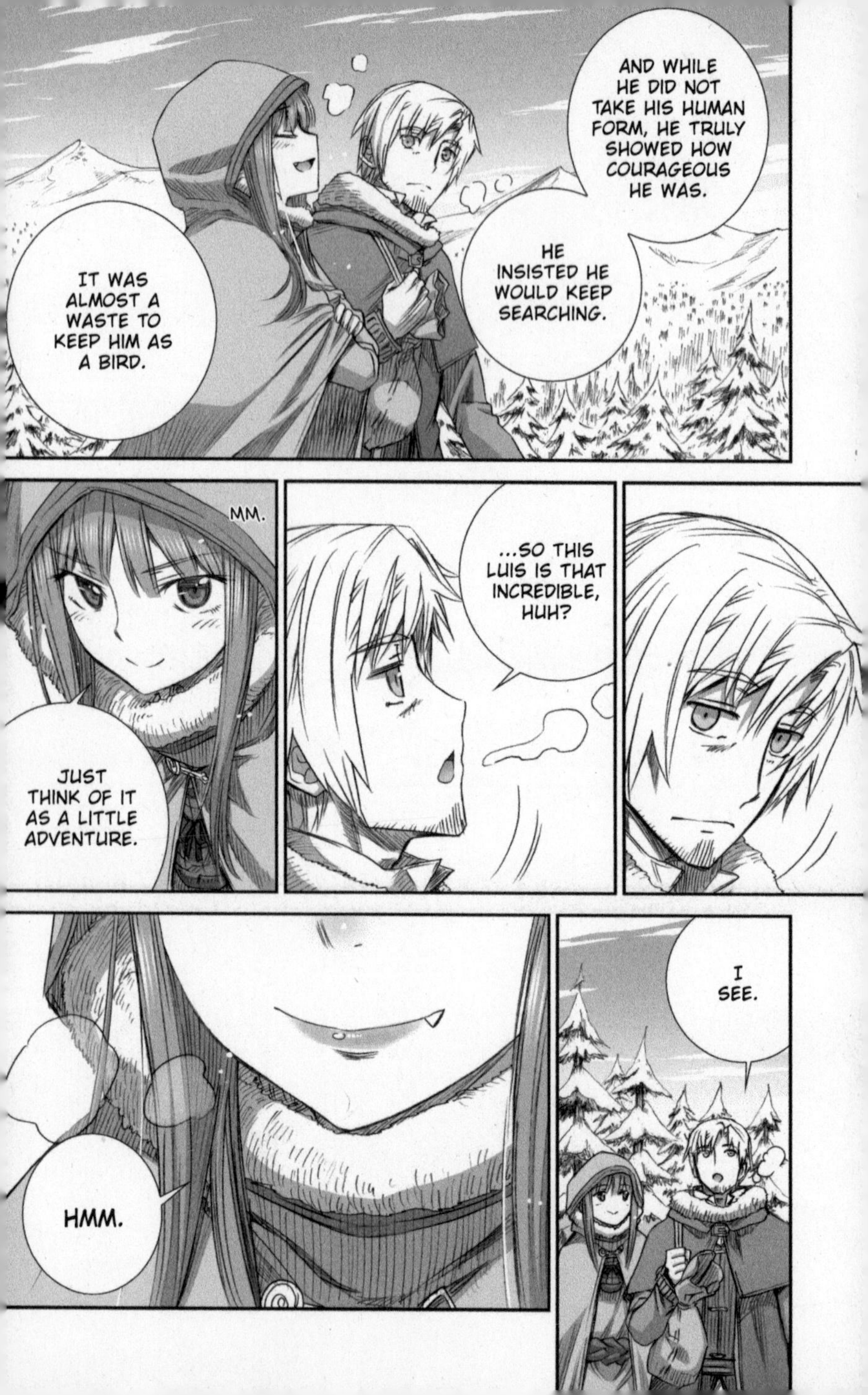
AND WHILE HE DID NOT TAKE HIS HUMAN FORM, HE TRULY SHOWED HOW COURAGEOUS HE WAS.
HE INSISTED HE WOULD KEEP SEARCHING.
IT WAS ALMOST A WASTE TO KEEP HIM AS A BIRD.
...SO THIS LUIS IS THAT INCREDIBLE, HUH?
MM.
JUST THINK OF IT AS A LITTLE ADVENTURE.
I SEE.
HMM.

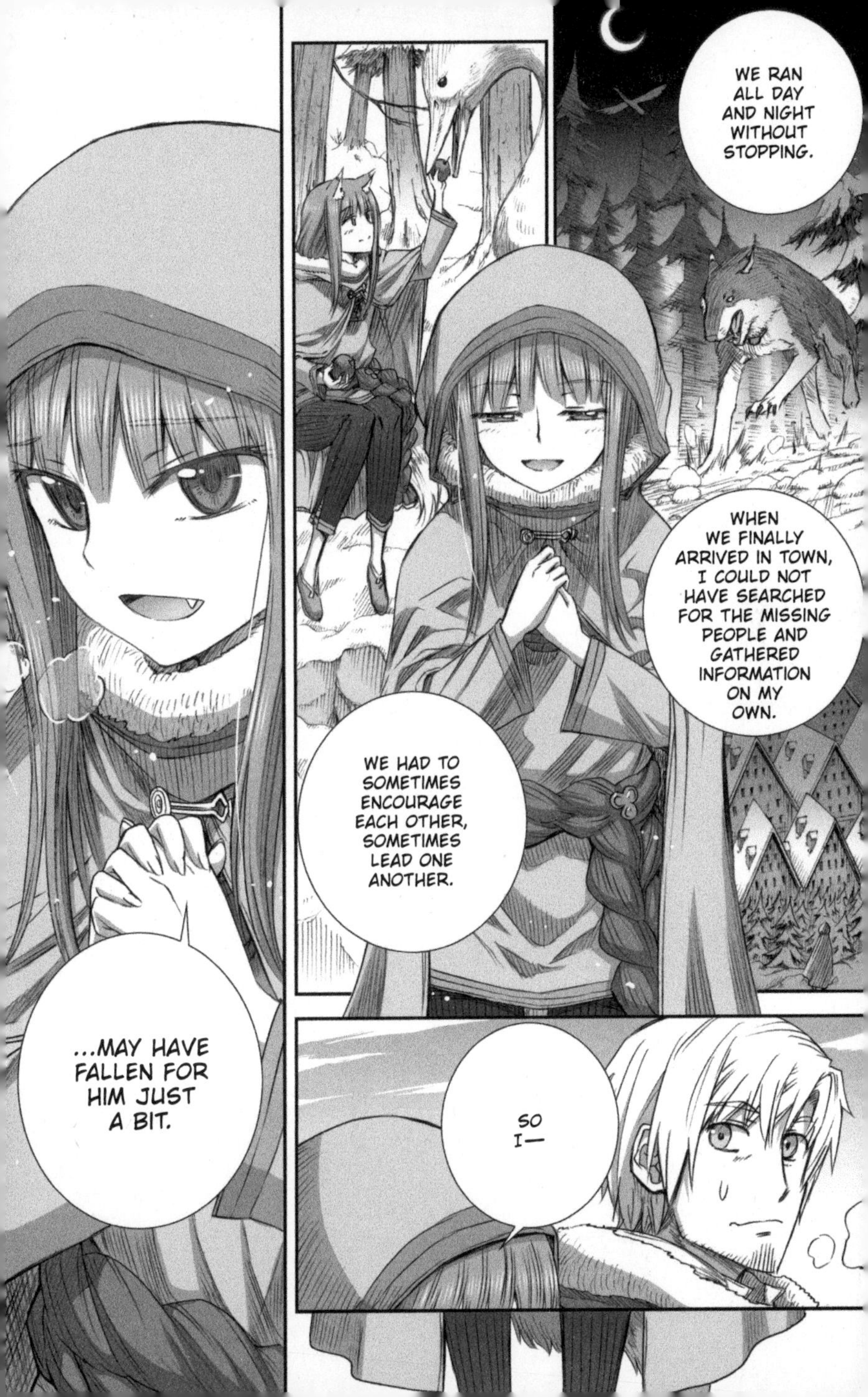

WE RAN ALL DAY AND NIGHT WITHOUT STOPPING.
WHEN WE FINALLY ARRIVED IN TOWN, I COULD NOT HAVE SEARCHED FOR THE MISSING PEOPLE AND GATHERED INFORMATION ON MY OWN.
WE HAD TO SOMETIMES ENCOURAGE EACH OTHER, SOMETIMES LEAD ONE ANOTHER.
SO I—
...MAY HAVE FALLEN FOR HIM JUST A BIT.

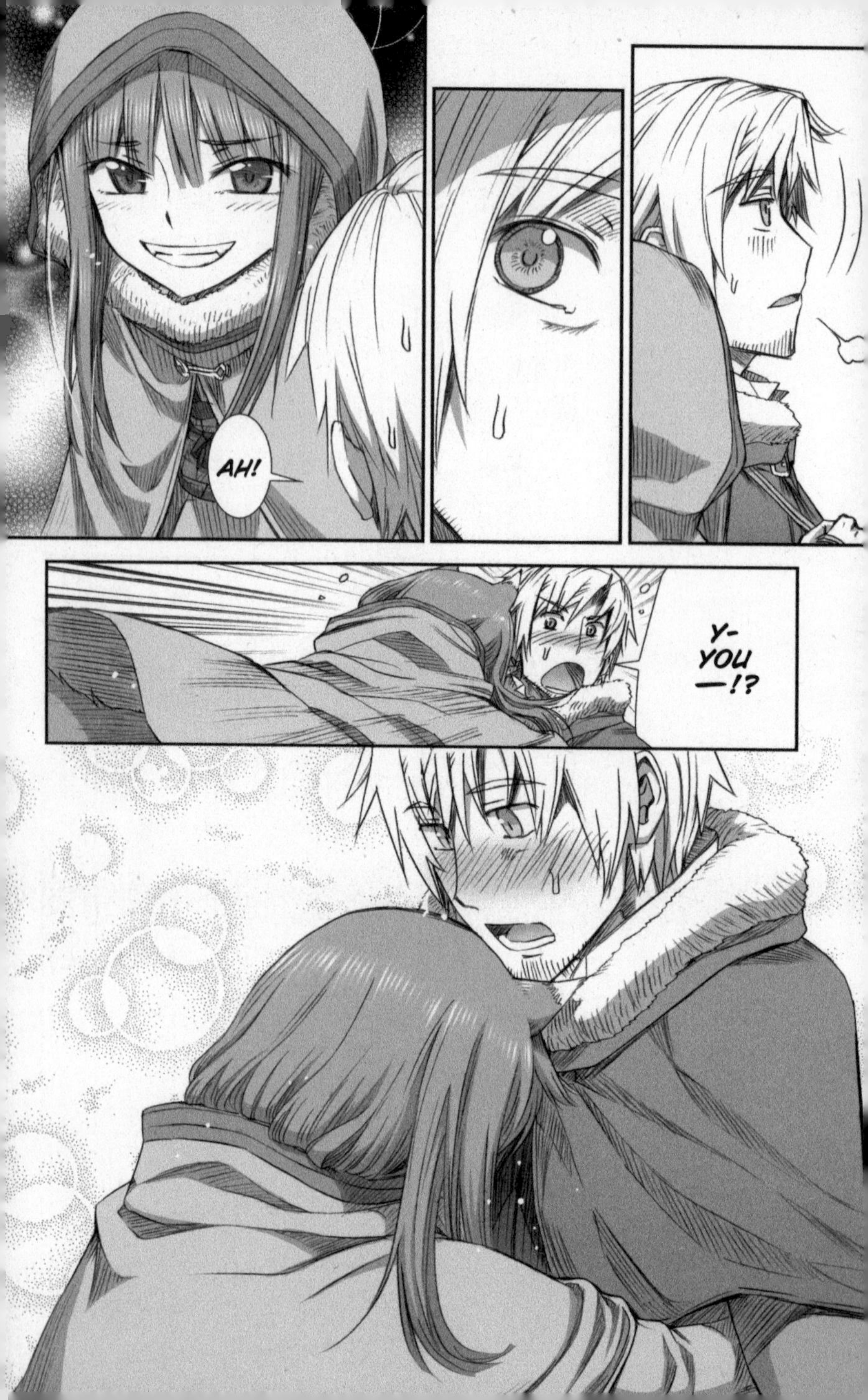
AH!
Y-YOU—!?

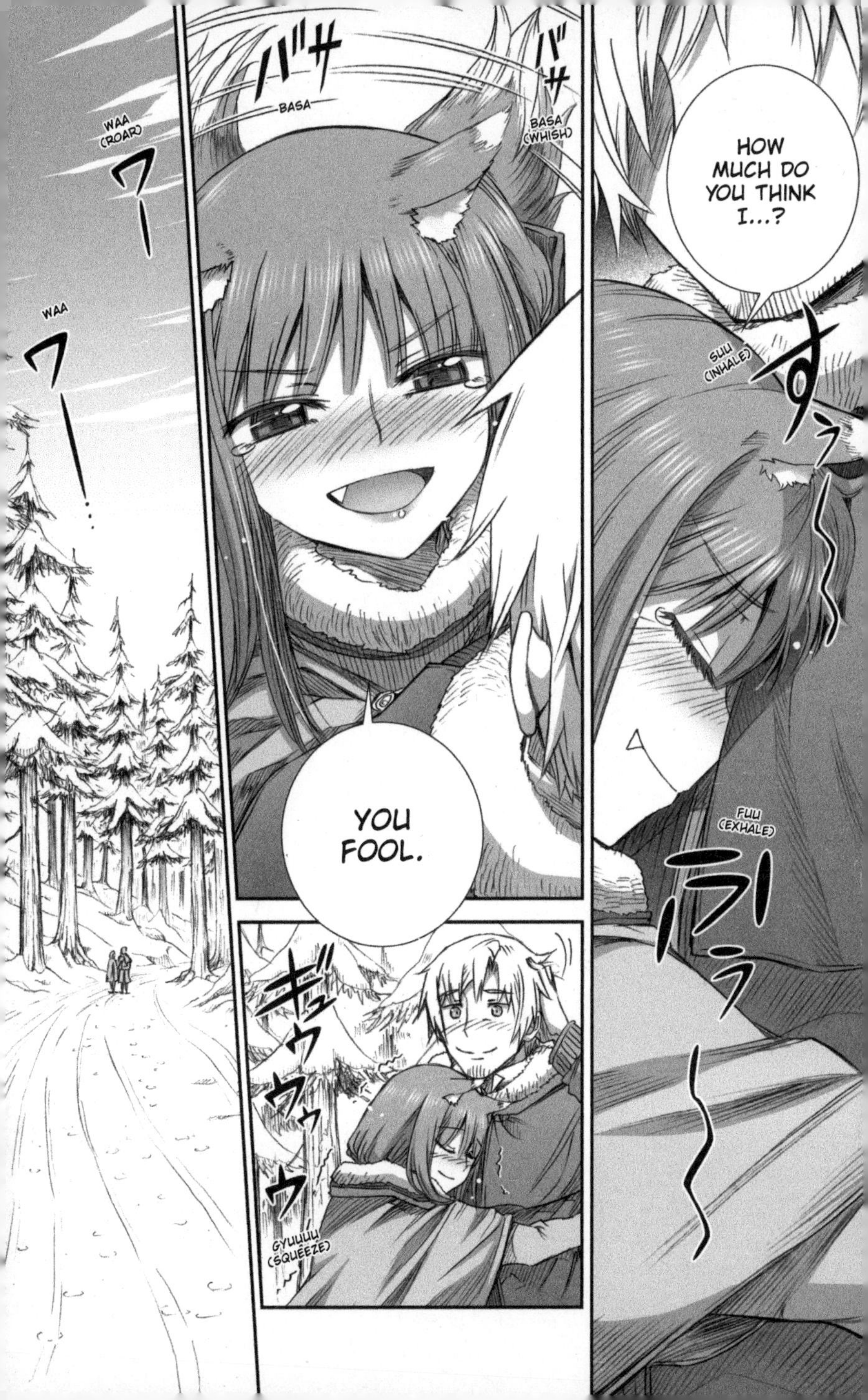

HOW MUCH DO YOU THINK I...?
SUU (INHALE)
FUU (EXHALE)
BASA (WHISH)
BASA
YOU FOOL.
GYUUUU (SQUEEZE)
WAA (ROAR)
WAA

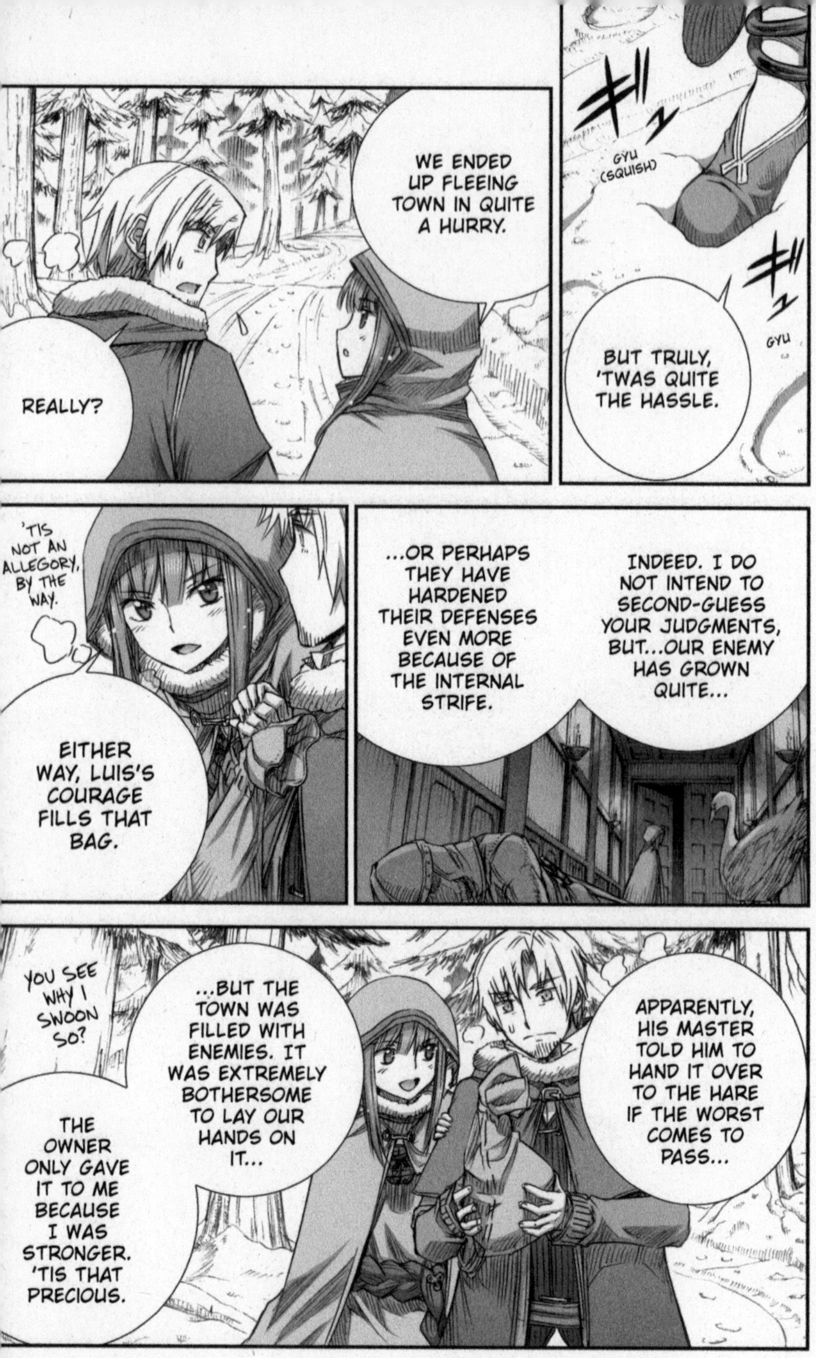
GYU (SQUISH)
GYU
BUT TRULY, 'TWAS QUITE THE HASSLE.
WE ENDED UP FLEEING TOWN IN QUITE A HURRY.
REALLY?
INDEED. I DO NOT INTEND TO SECOND-GUESS YOUR JUDGMENTS, BUT...OUR ENEMY HAS GROWN QUITE...
...OR PERHAPS THEY HAVE HARDENED THEIR DEFENSES EVEN MORE BECAUSE OF THE INTERNAL STRIFE.
'TIS NOT AN ALLEGORY, BY THE WAY.
EITHER WAY, LUIS'S COURAGE FILLS THAT BAG.
APPARENTLY, HIS MASTER TOLD HIM TO HAND IT OVER TO THE HARE IF THE WORST COMES TO PASS...
...BUT THE TOWN WAS FILLED WITH ENEMIES. IT WAS EXTREMELY BOTHERSOME TO LAY OUR HANDS ON IT...
YOU SEE WHY I SWOON SO?
THE OWNER ONLY GAVE IT TO ME BECAUSE I WAS STRONGER. 'TIS THAT PRECIOUS.

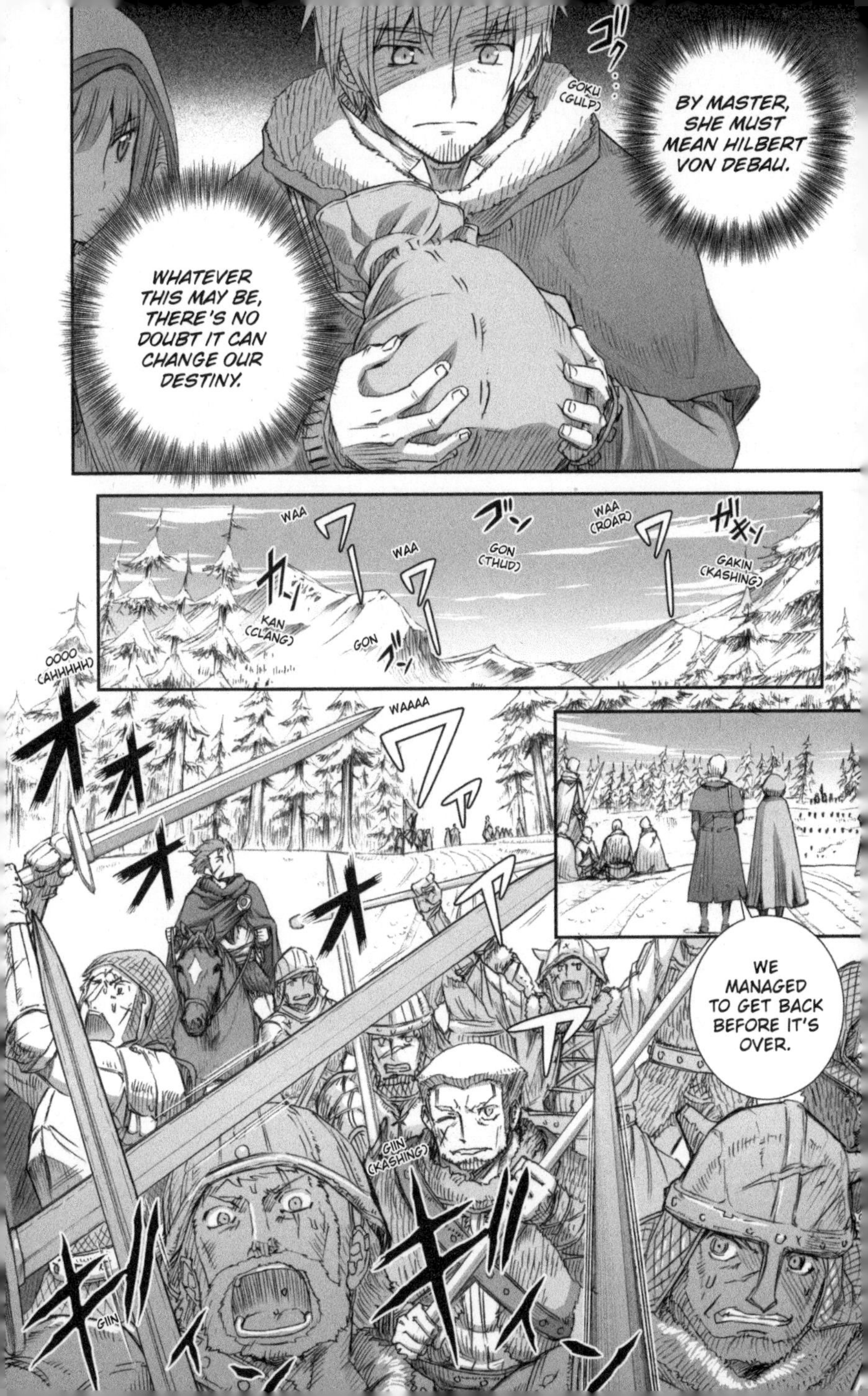
GOKU (GULP)
BY MASTER, SHE MUST MEAN HILBERT VON DEBAU.
WHATEVER THIS MAY BE, THERE'S NO DOUBT IT CAN CHANGE OUR DESTINY.
GAKIN (KASHING)
WAA (ROAR)
GON (THUD)
WAA
WAA
KAN (CLANG)
GON
WE MANAGED TO GET BACK BEFORE IT'S OVER.
OOOO (AHHHHHH)
WAAAA
GIIN (KASHING)
GIIN

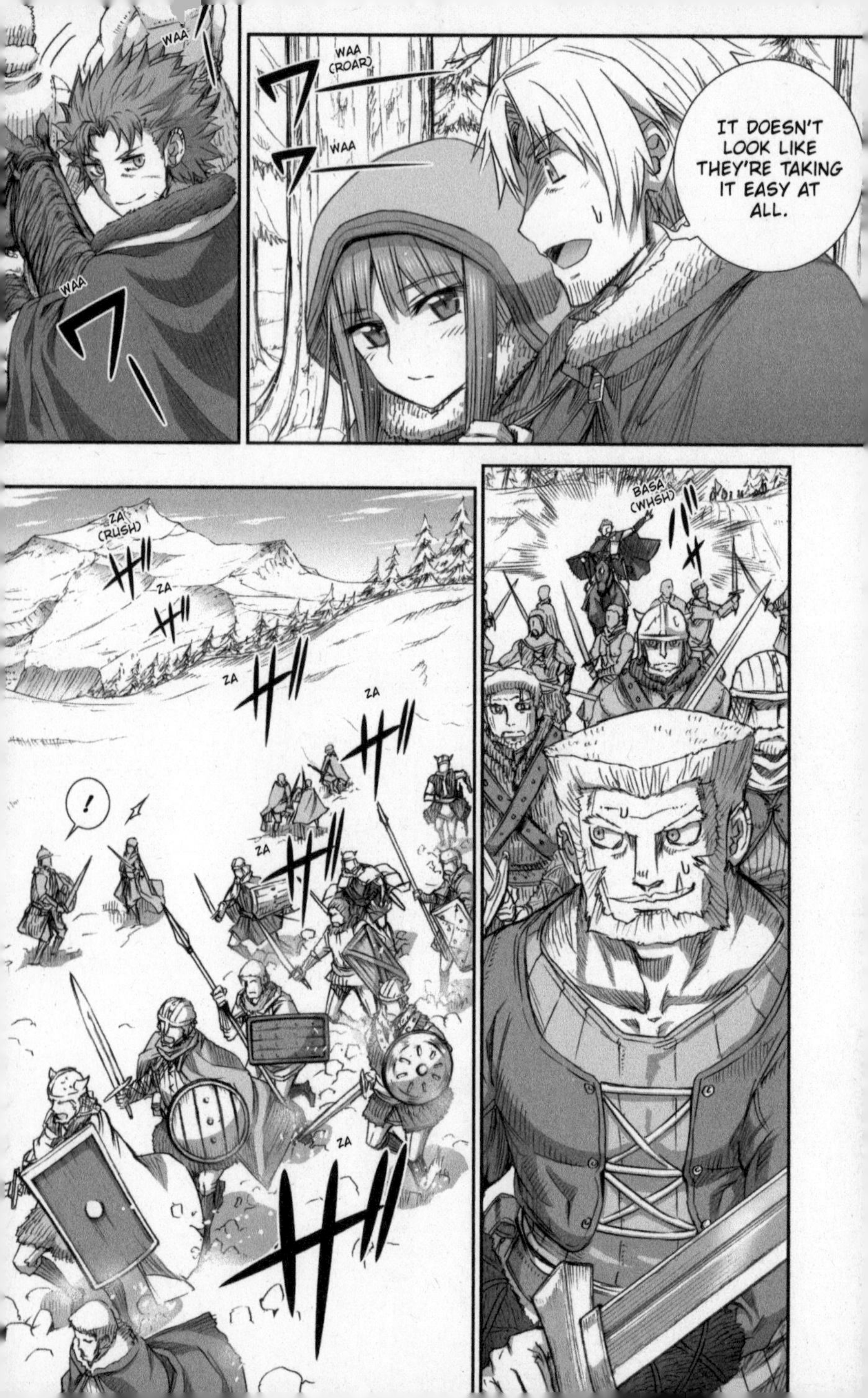
IT DOESN'T LOOK LIKE THEY'RE TAKING IT EASY AT ALL.
WAA (ROAR)
WAA
WAA
WAA
BASA (WHSH)
ZA (RUSH)
ZA
ZA
ZA
!
ZA
ZA

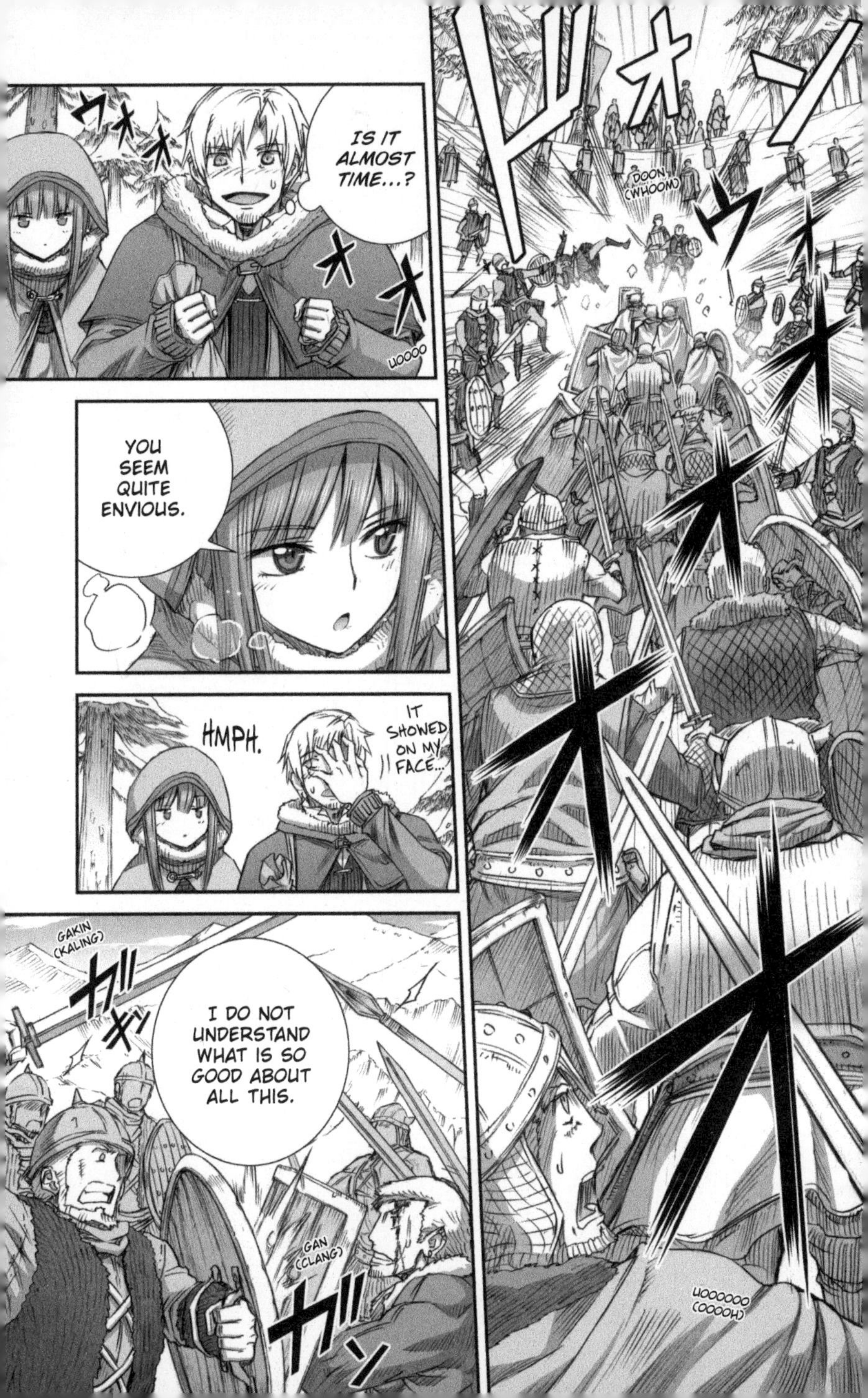
DOON (WHOOM)
UOOOOOO (OOOOH)
UOOOO
IS IT ALMOST TIME...?
YOU SEEM QUITE ENVIOUS.
IT SHOWED ON MY FACE...
HMPH.
GAKIN (KALING)
I DO NOT UNDERSTAND WHAT IS SO GOOD ABOUT ALL THIS.
GAN (CLANG)

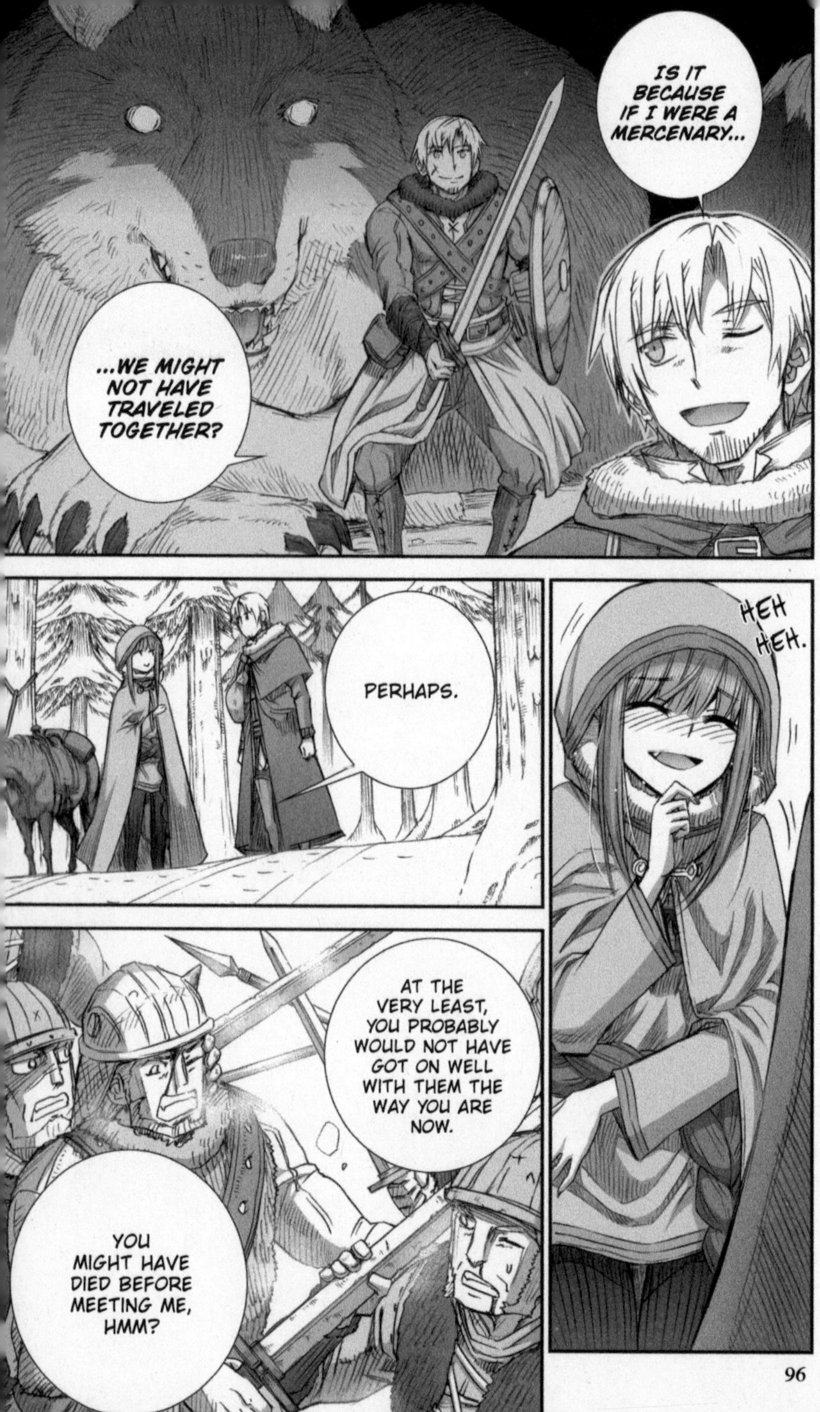
IS IT BECAUSE IF I WERE A MERCENARY...
...WE MIGHT NOT HAVE TRAVELED TOGETHER?
HEH HEH.
PERHAPS.
AT THE VERY LEAST, YOU PROBABLY WOULD NOT HAVE GOT ON WELL WITH THEM THE WAY YOU ARE NOW.
YOU MIGHT HAVE DIED BEFORE MEETING ME, HMM?

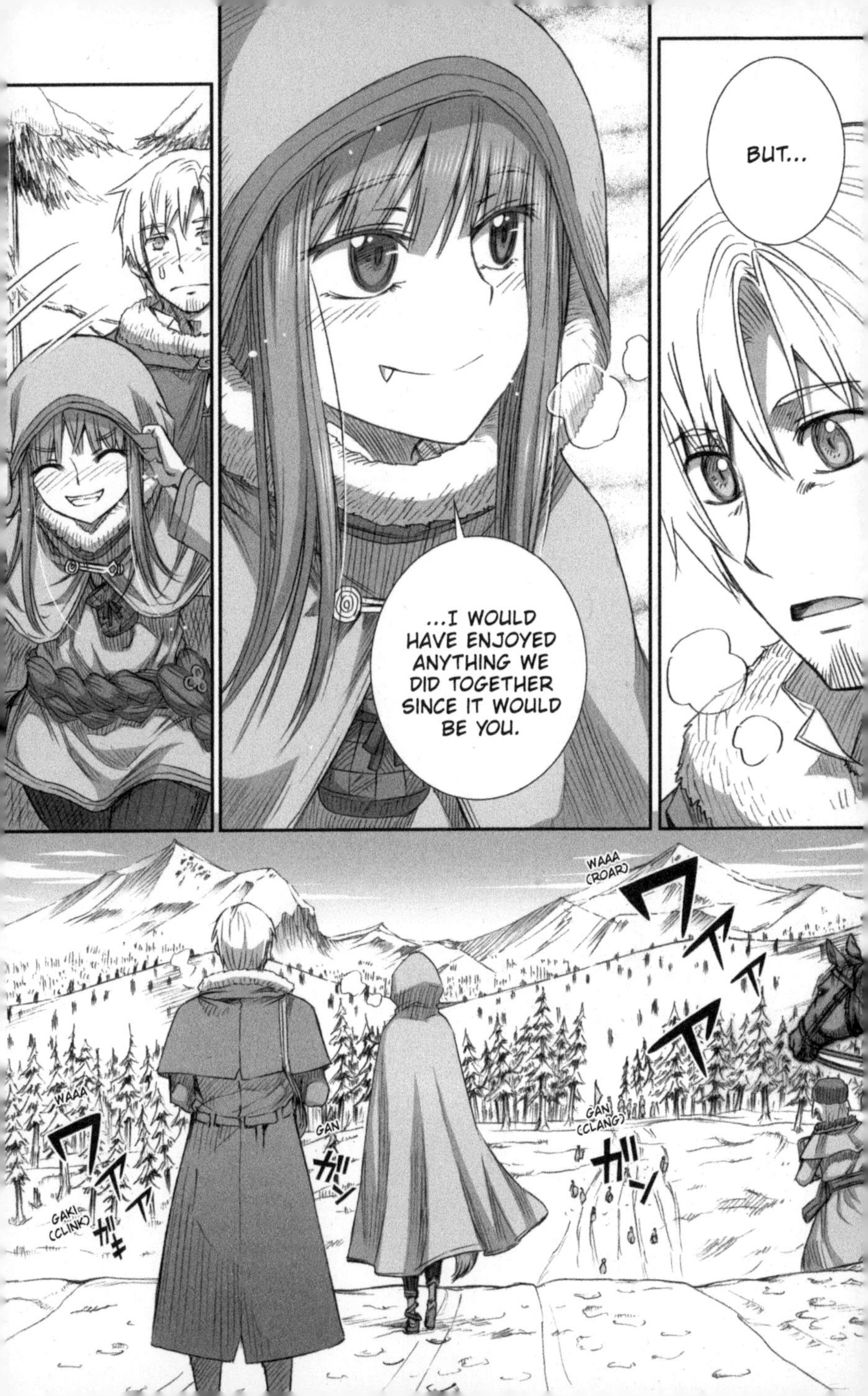
BUT...
...I WOULD HAVE ENJOYED ANYTHING WE DID TOGETHER SINCE IT WOULD BE YOU.
WAAA (ROAR)
GAN (CLANG)
GAN
WAAA
GAKI (CLINK)

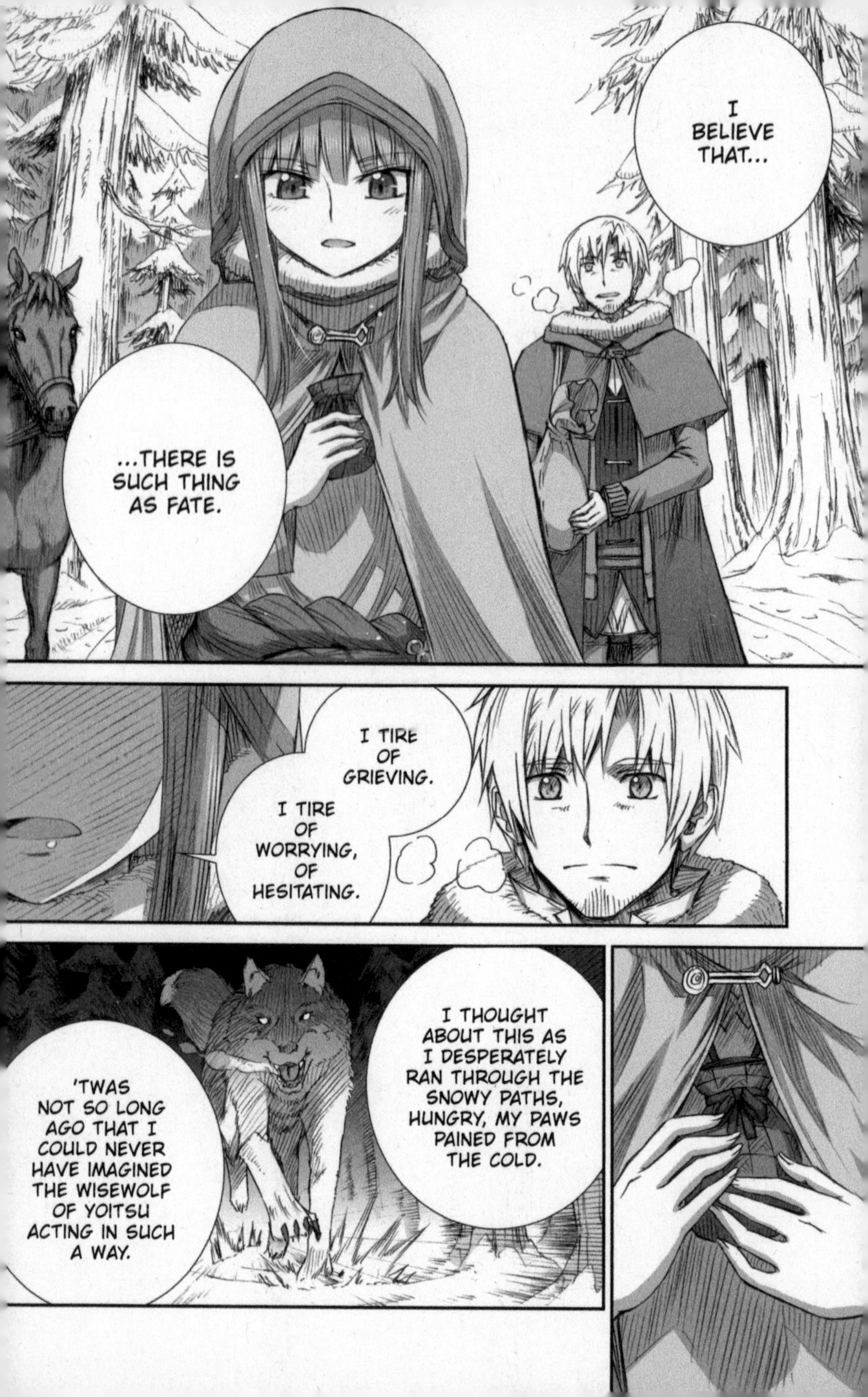
I BELIEVE THAT...
...THERE IS SUCH THING AS FATE.
I TIRE OF GRIEVING.
I TIRE OF WORRYING, OF HESITATING.
I THOUGHT ABOUT THIS AS I DESPERATELY RAN THROUGH THE SNOWY PATHS, HUNGRY, MY PAWS PAINED FROM THE COLD.
'TWAS NOT SO LONG AGO THAT I COULD NEVER HAVE IMAGINED THE WISEWOLF OF YOITSU ACTING IN SUCH A WAY.

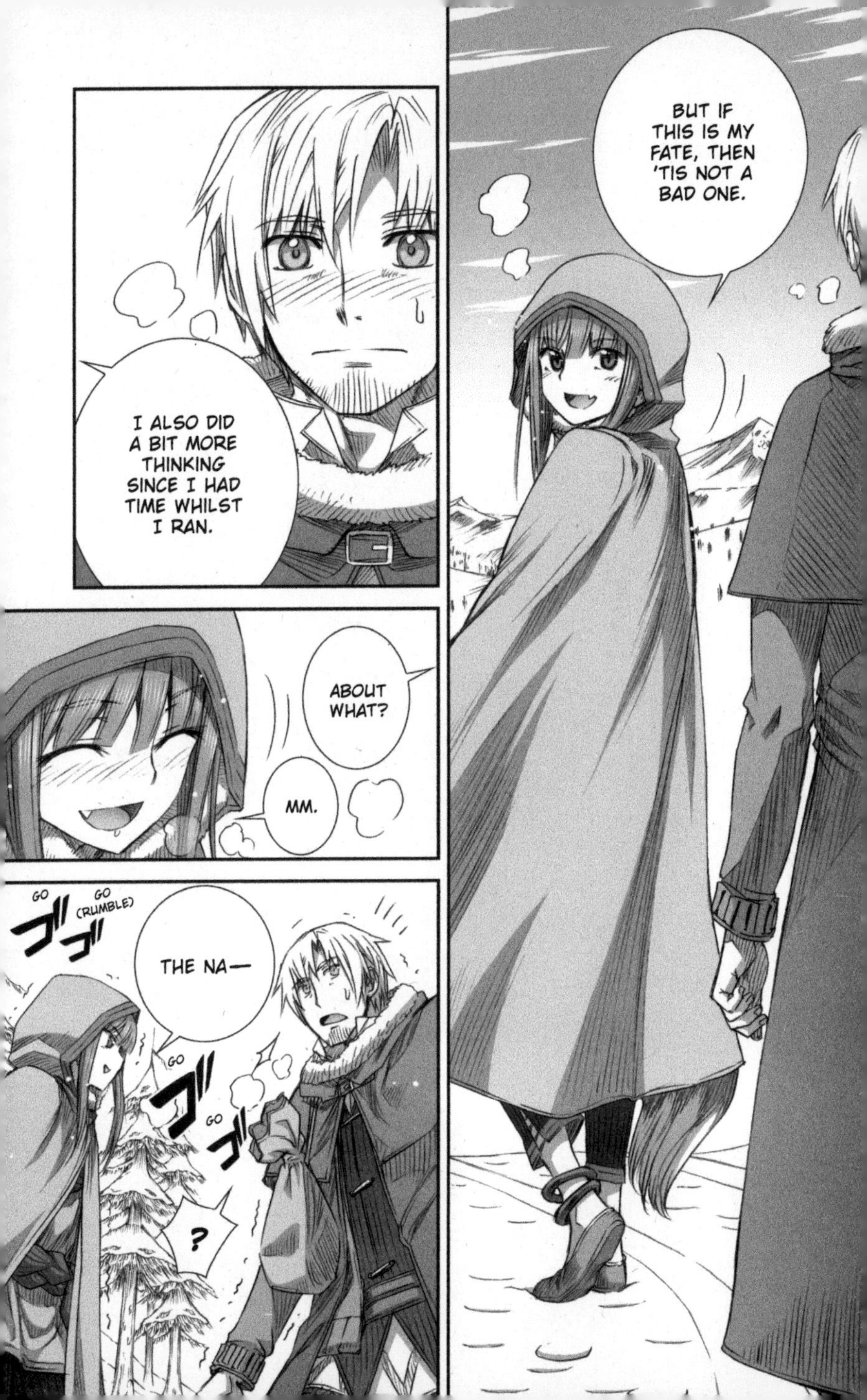
BUT IF THIS IS MY FATE, THEN 'TIS NOT A BAD ONE.
I ALSO DID A BIT MORE THINKING SINCE I HAD TIME WHILST I RAN.
ABOUT WHAT?
MM.
THE NA—
GO GO (RUMBLE)
GO GO
?

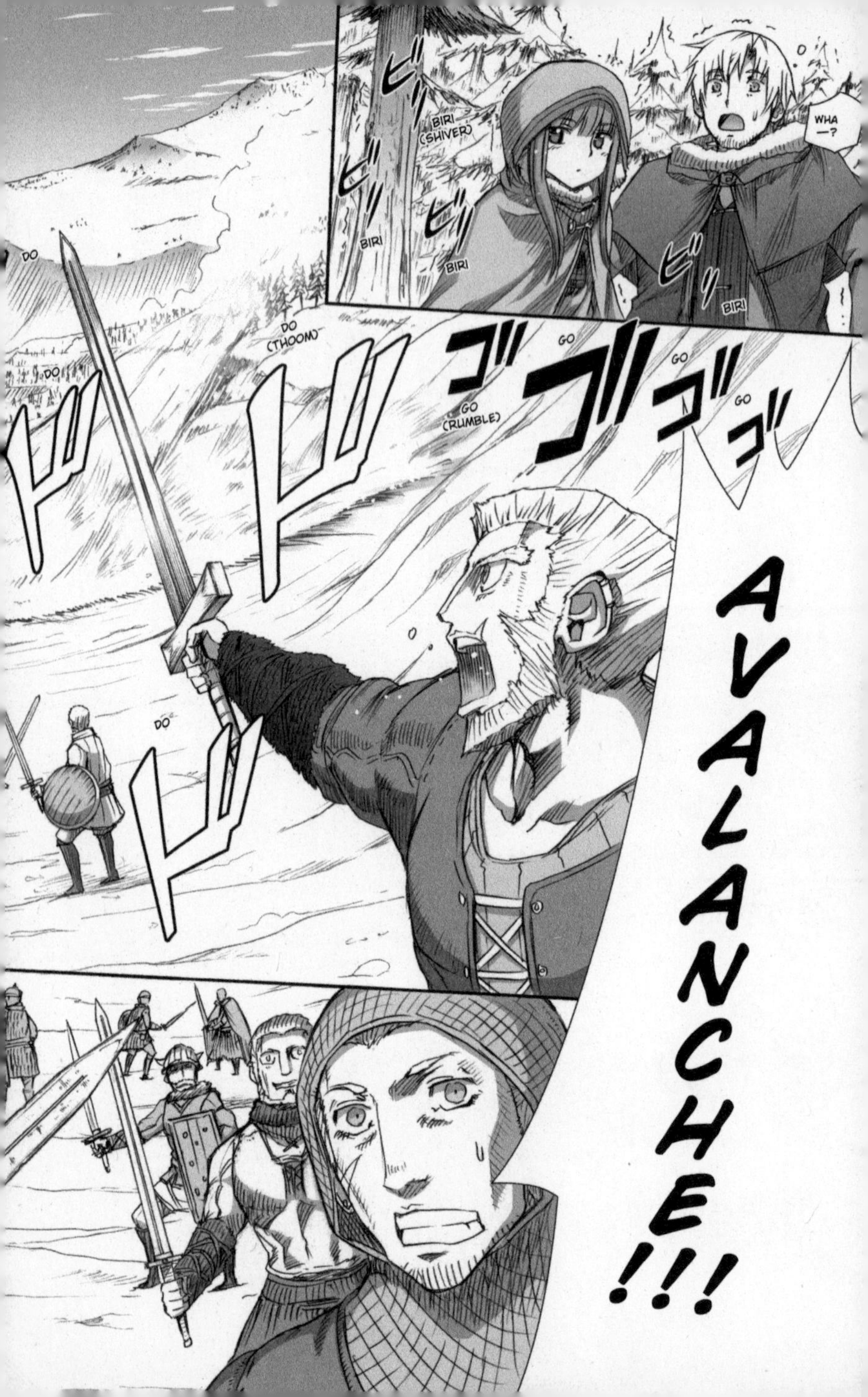
WHA —?
BIRI
BIRI
BIRI
BIRI (SHIVER)
GO
GO
GO
GO (RUMBLE)
DO (THOOM)
DO
DO
DO
AVALANCHE!!!

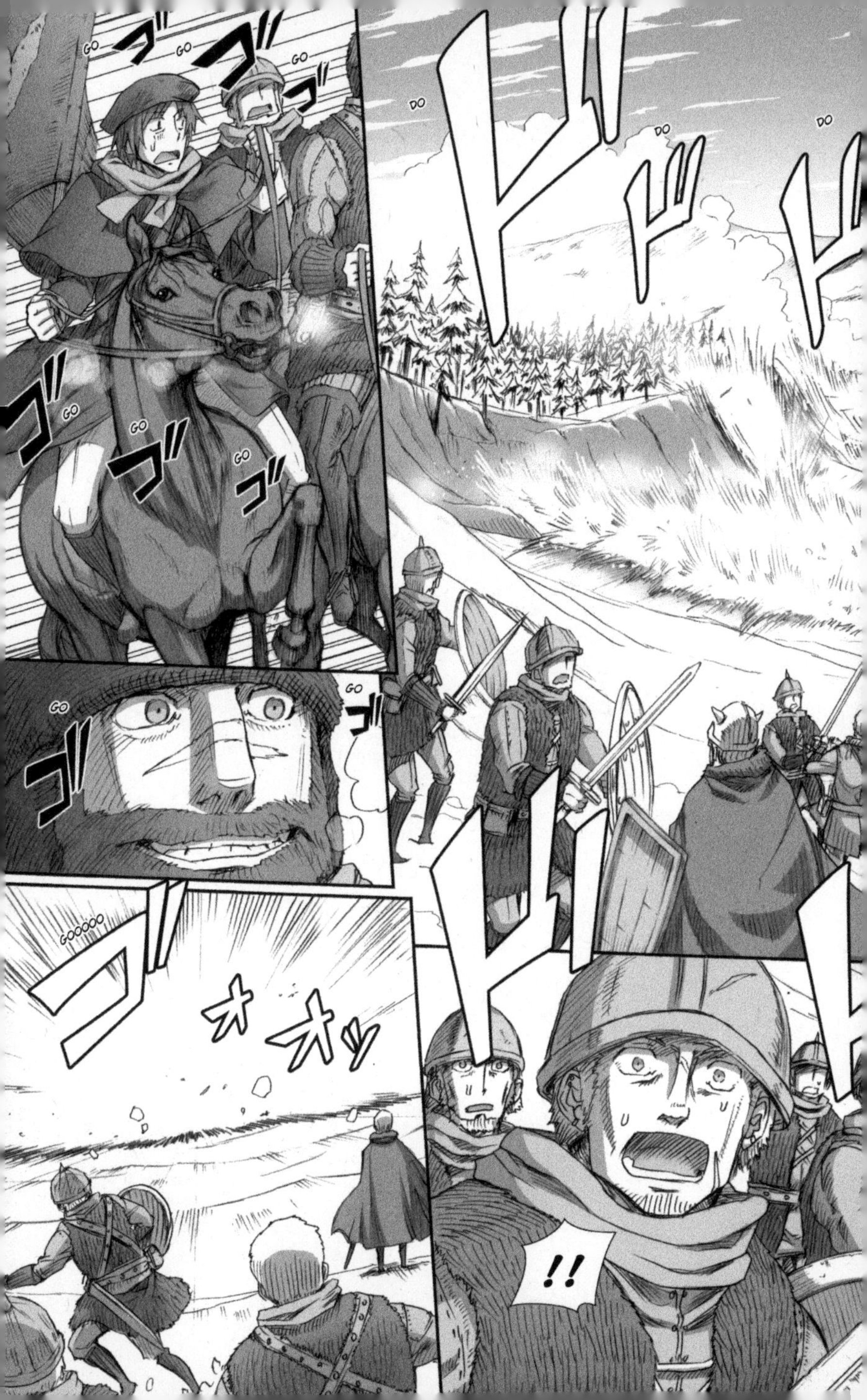
DO
DO
DO
GO
GO
GO
GO
GO
GO
GO
GO
!!
GOOOOO

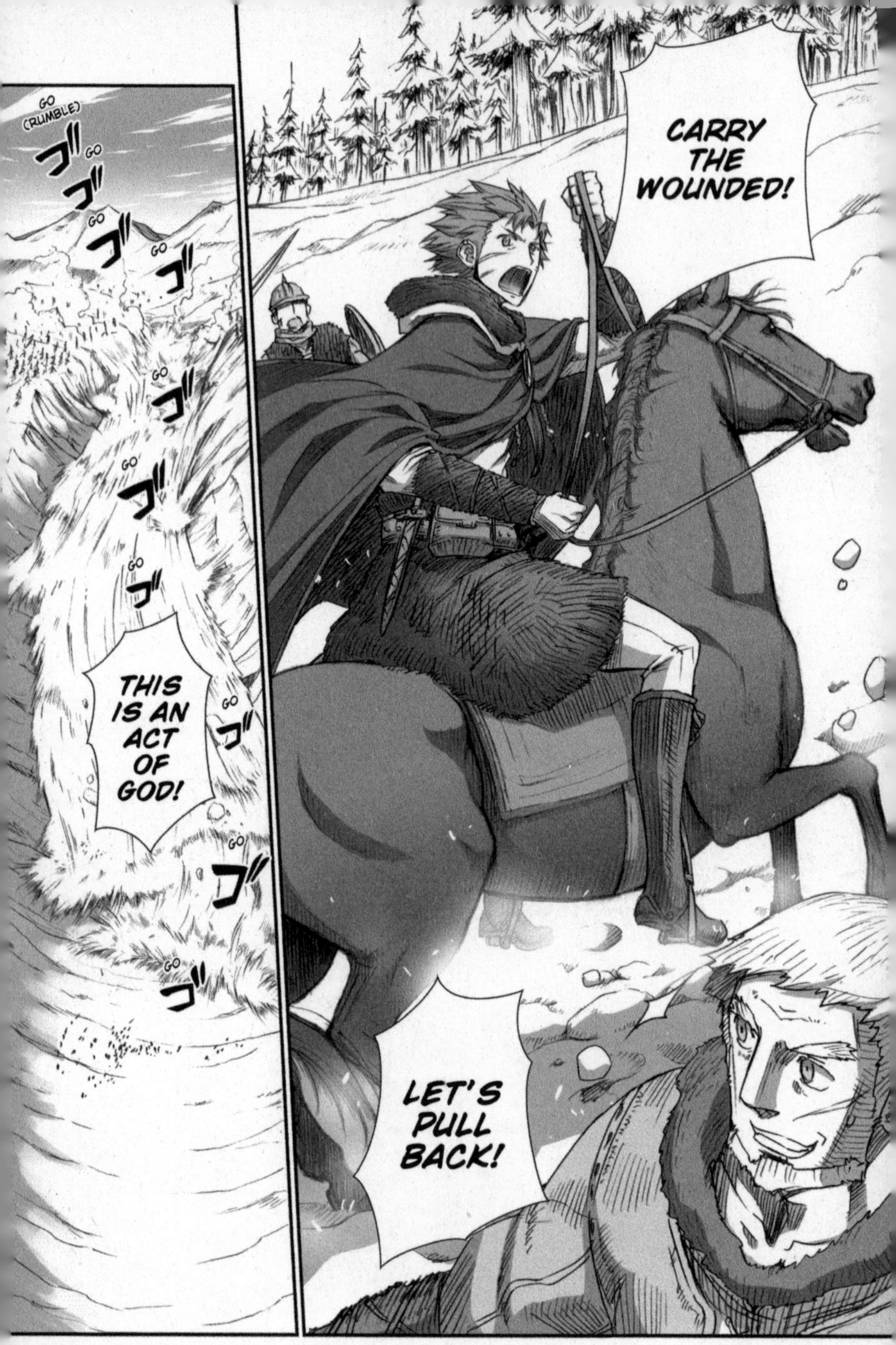
CARRY THE WOUNDED!
LET'S PULL BACK!
GO (RUMBLE)
ゴ GO ゴ GO ゴ GO ゴ GO ゴ GO ゴ GO ゴ GO ゴ GO ゴ
THIS IS AN ACT OF GOD!

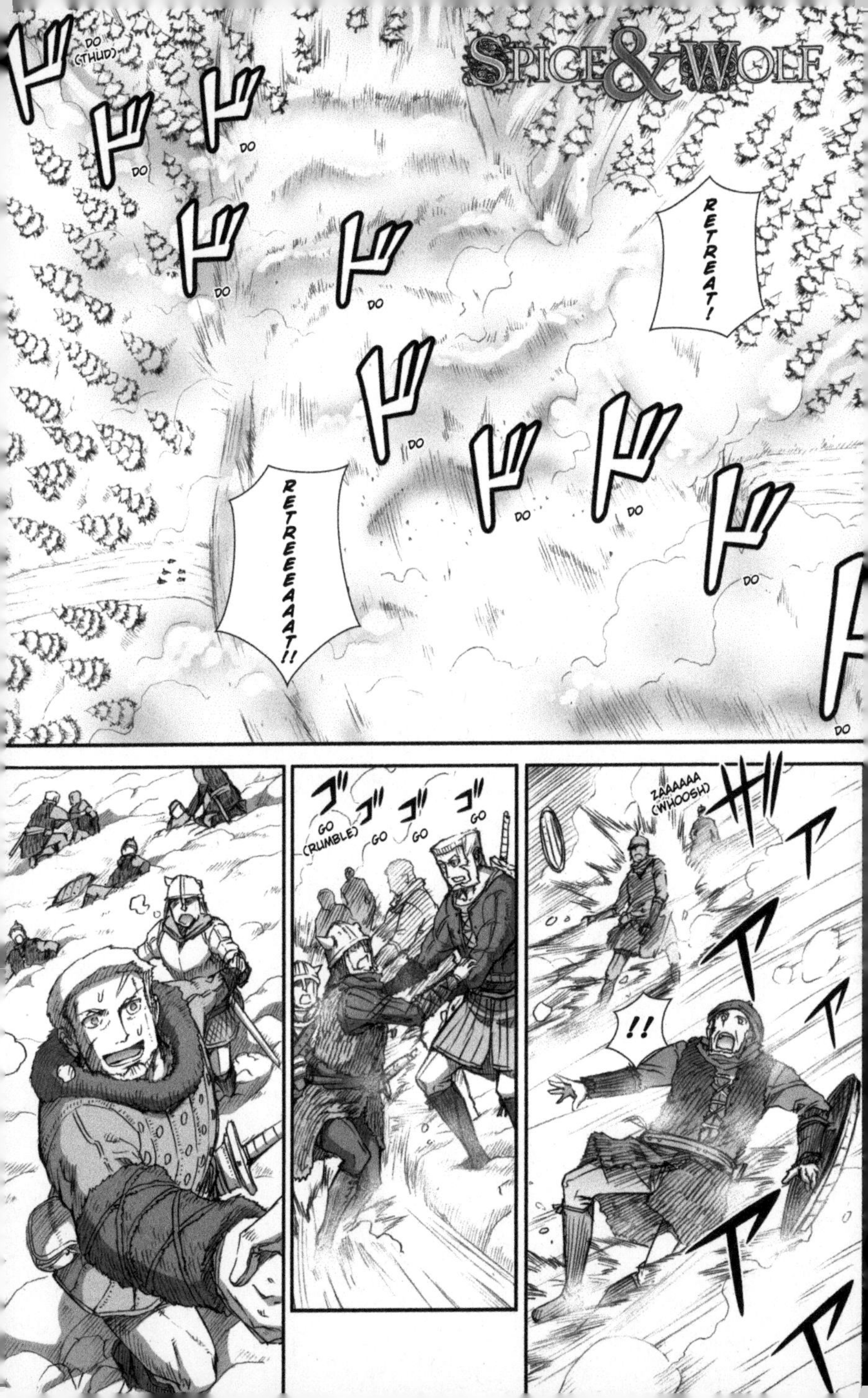
SPICE & WOLF
RETREAT!
ド DO (THUD)
ド DO
ド DO
ド DO
ド DO
ド DO
ド DO
ド DO
ド DO
ド DO
RETREEEEAAAAT!!
ザァァァァァ ZAAAAAA (WHOOSH)
!!
ゴ GO (RUMBLE)
ゴ GO
ゴ GO
ゴ GO

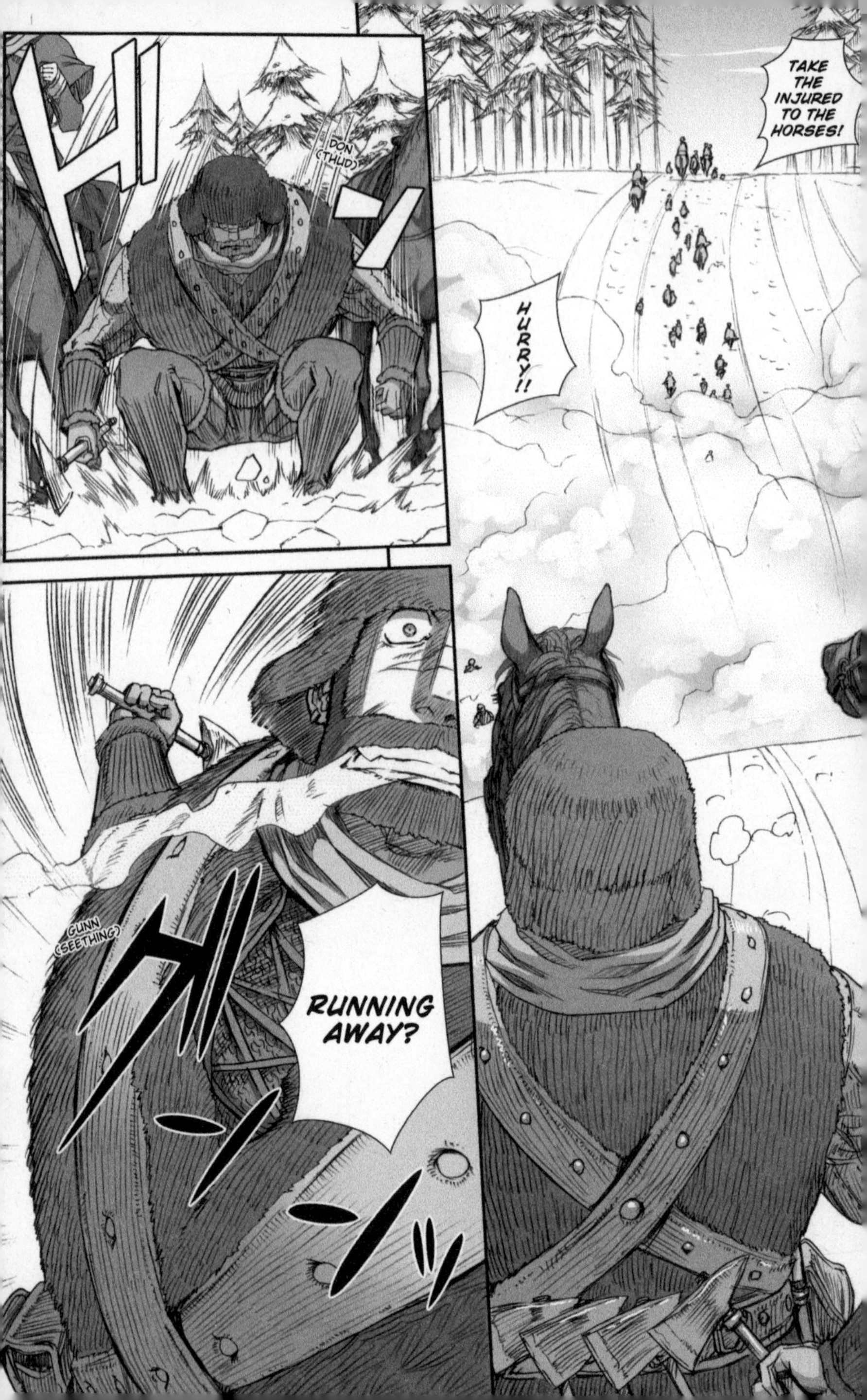
TAKE THE INJURED TO THE HORSES!
HURRY!!
DON (THUD)
GUNN (SEETHING)
RUNNING AWAY?

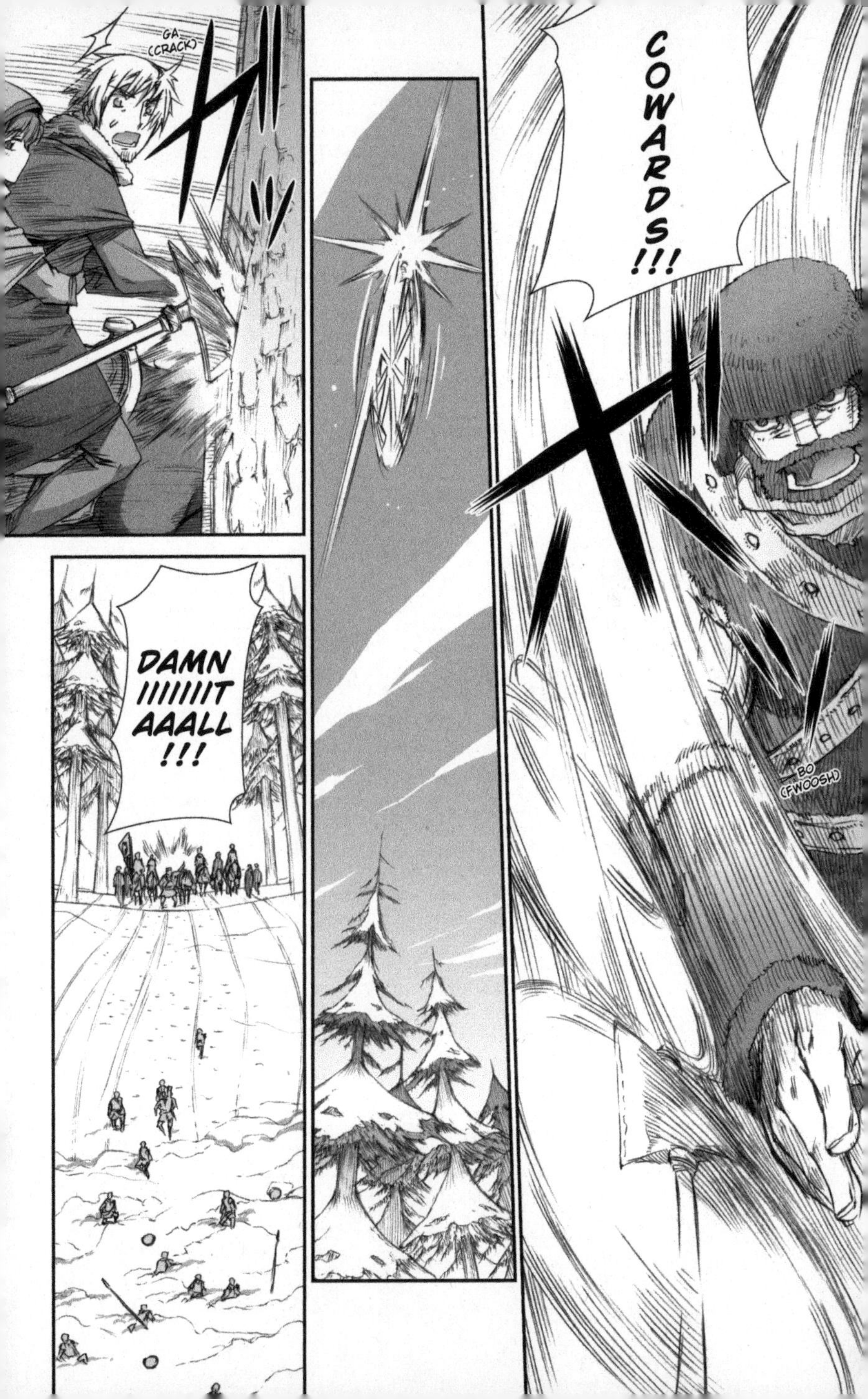
COWARDS!!!
BO (FWOOSH)
GA (CRACK)
DAMN IIIIIIIT AAALL!!!

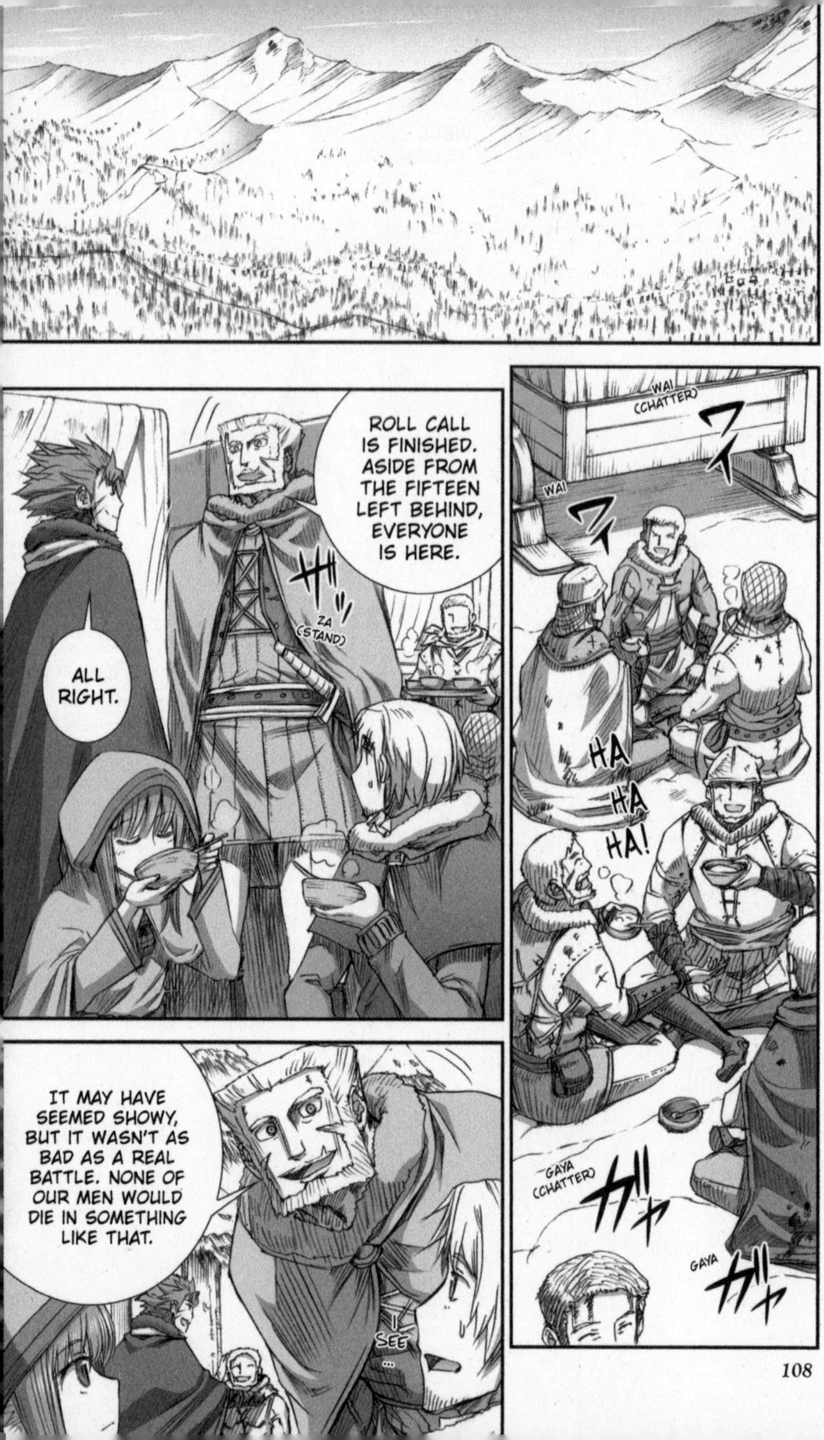
WAI (CHATTER)
WAI
HA HA HA!
GAYA (CHATTER)
GAYA
ROLL CALL IS FINISHED. ASIDE FROM THE FIFTEEN LEFT BEHIND, EVERYONE IS HERE.
ZA (STAND)
ALL RIGHT.
IT MAY HAVE SEEMED SHOWY, BUT IT WASN'T AS BAD AS A REAL BATTLE. NONE OF OUR MEN WOULD DIE IN SOMETHING LIKE THAT.
I SEE...

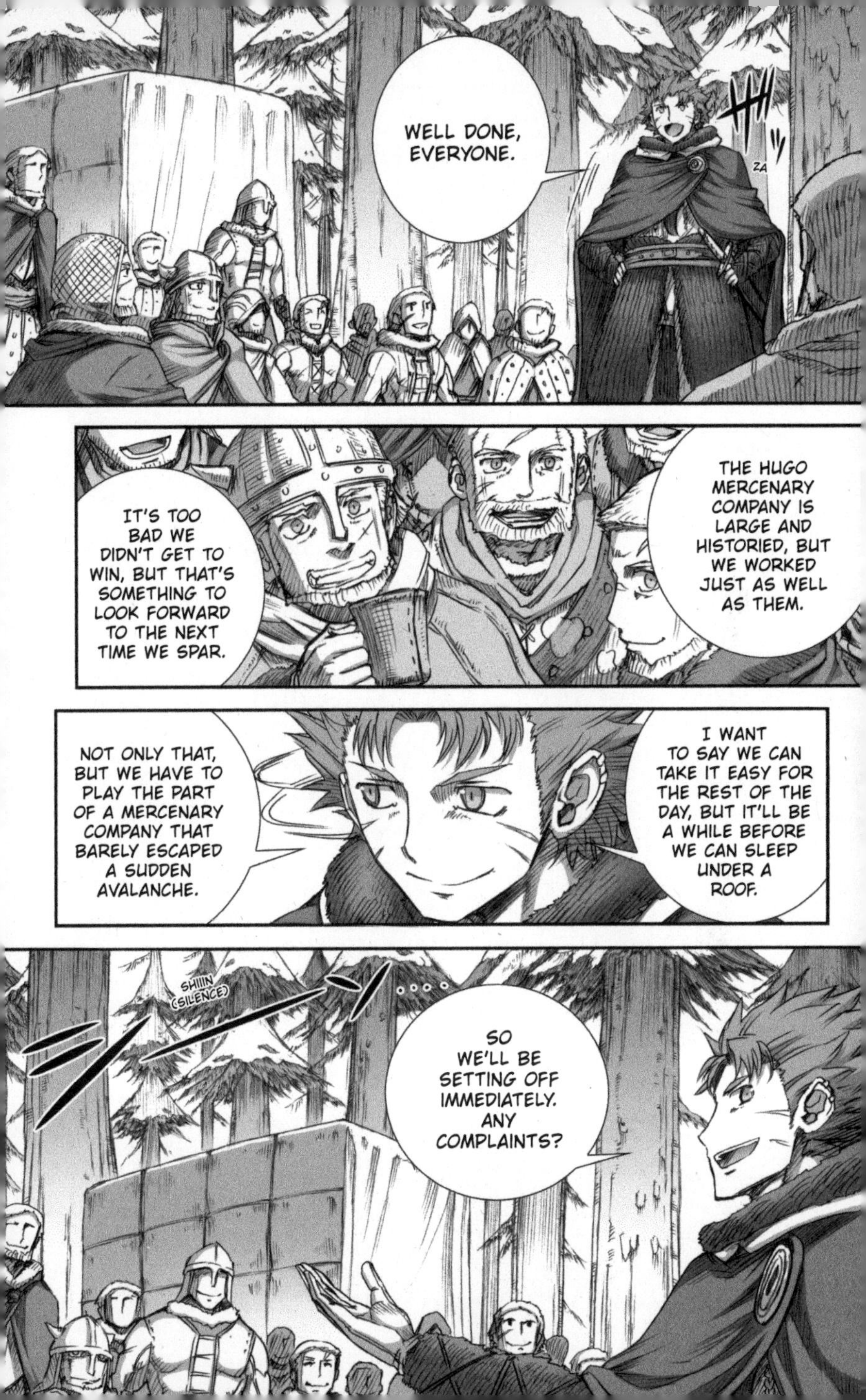
ZA
WELL DONE, EVERYONE.
THE HUGO MERCENARY COMPANY IS LARGE AND HISTORIED, BUT WE WORKED JUST AS WELL AS THEM.
IT'S TOO BAD WE DIDN'T GET TO WIN, BUT THAT'S SOMETHING TO LOOK FORWARD TO THE NEXT TIME WE SPAR.
I WANT TO SAY WE CAN TAKE IT EASY FOR THE REST OF THE DAY, BUT IT'LL BE A WHILE BEFORE WE CAN SLEEP UNDER A ROOF.
NOT ONLY THAT, BUT WE HAVE TO PLAY THE PART OF A MERCENARY COMPANY THAT BARELY ESCAPED A SUDDEN AVALANCHE.
....
SO WE'LL BE SETTING OFF IMMEDIATELY. ANY COMPLAINTS?
SHIIN (SILENCE)

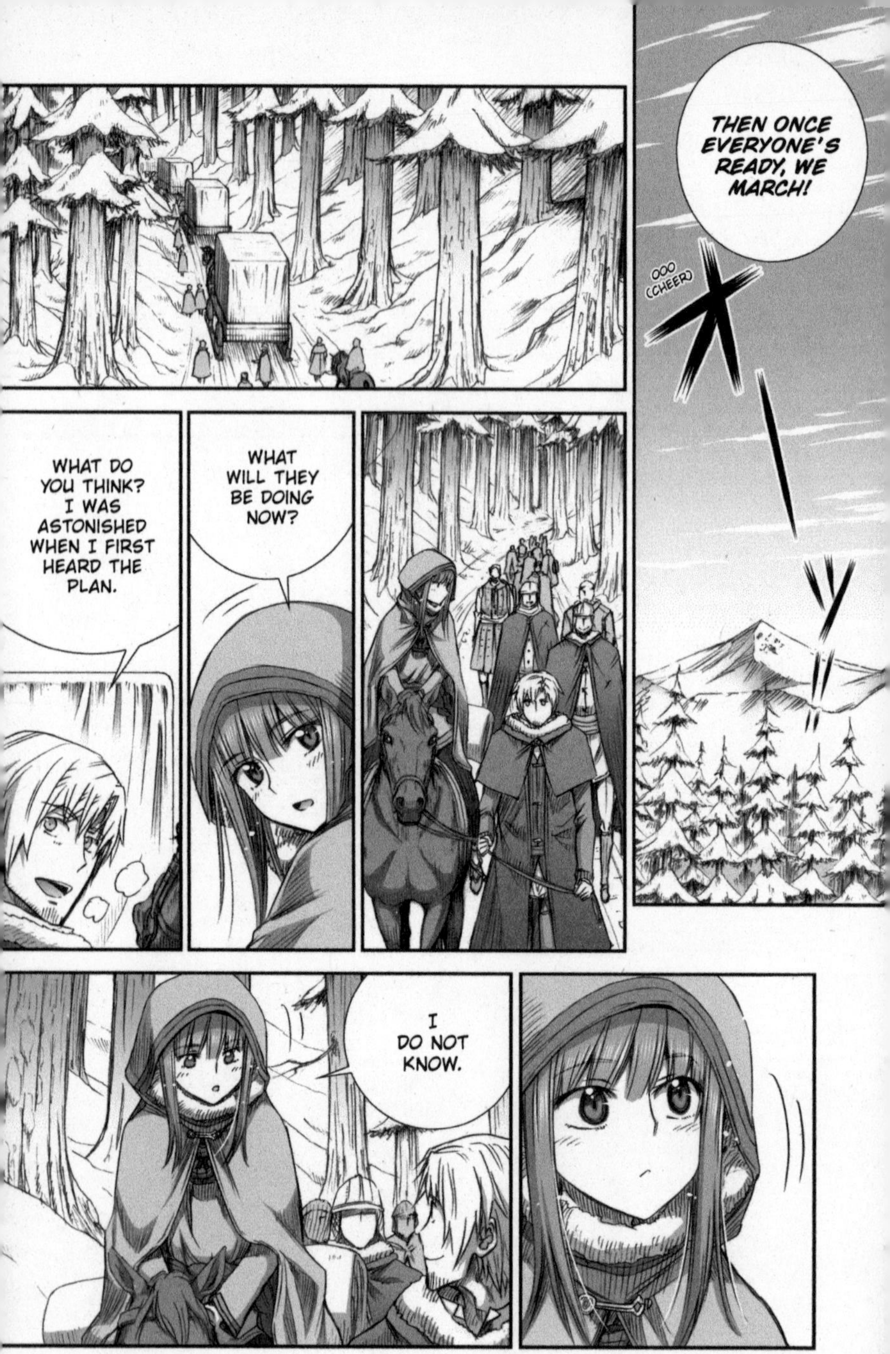
THEN ONCE EVERYONE'S READY, WE MARCH!
OOO (CHEER)
WHAT WILL THEY BE DOING NOW?
WHAT DO YOU THINK? I WAS ASTONISHED WHEN I FIRST HEARD THE PLAN.
I DO NOT KNOW.

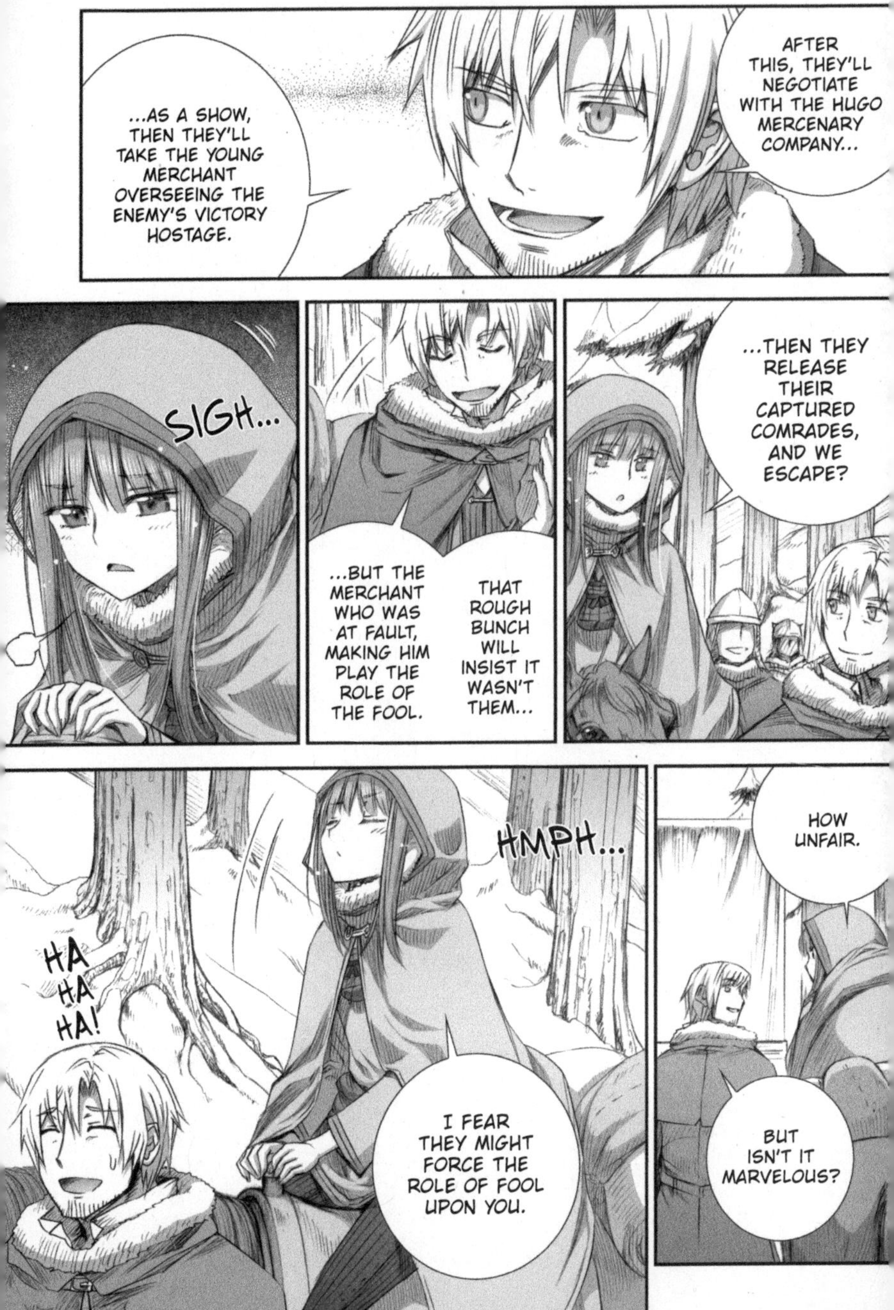
AFTER THIS, THEY'LL NEGOTIATE WITH THE HUGO MERCENARY COMPANY...
...AS A SHOW, THEN THEY'LL TAKE THE YOUNG MERCHANT OVERSEEING THE ENEMY'S VICTORY HOSTAGE.
...THEN THEY RELEASE THEIR CAPTURED COMRADES, AND WE ESCAPE?
THAT ROUGH BUNCH WILL INSIST IT WASN'T THEM...
...BUT THE MERCHANT WHO WAS AT FAULT, MAKING HIM PLAY THE ROLE OF THE FOOL.
SIGH...
HOW UNFAIR.
BUT ISN'T IT MARVELOUS?
HMPH...
I FEAR THEY MIGHT FORCE THE ROLE OF FOOL UPON YOU.
HA HA HA!

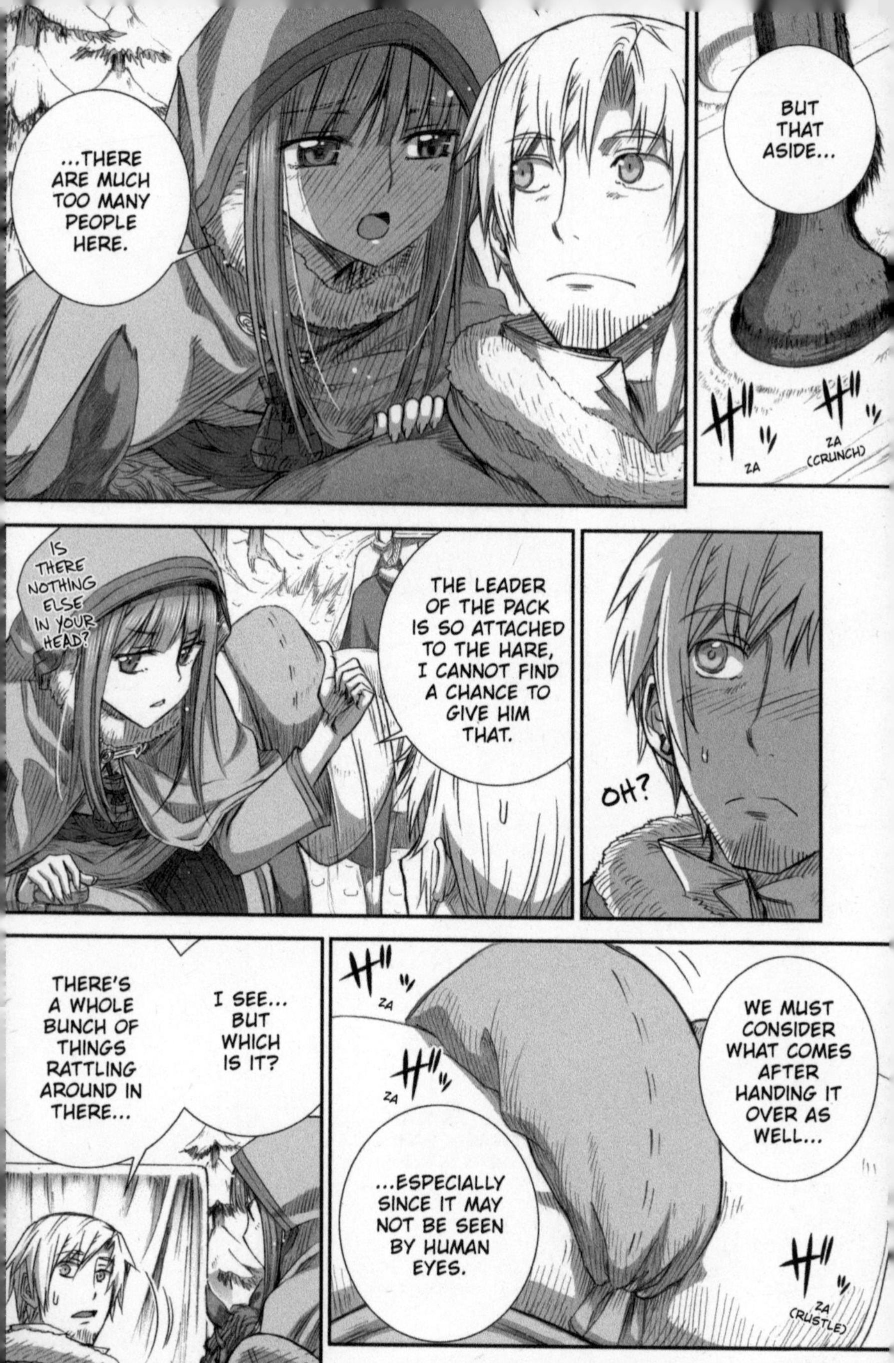
BUT THAT ASIDE...
ZA
ZA (CRUNCH)
...THERE ARE MUCH TOO MANY PEOPLE HERE.
OH?
THE LEADER OF THE PACK IS SO ATTACHED TO THE HARE, I CANNOT FIND A CHANCE TO GIVE HIM THAT.
IS THERE NOTHING ELSE IN YOUR HEAD?
ZA
ZA
WE MUST CONSIDER WHAT COMES AFTER HANDING IT OVER AS WELL...
...ESPECIALLY SINCE IT MAY NOT BE SEEN BY HUMAN EYES.
ZA (RUSTLE)
I SEE... BUT WHICH IS IT?
THERE'S A WHOLE BUNCH OF THINGS RATTLING AROUND IN THERE...

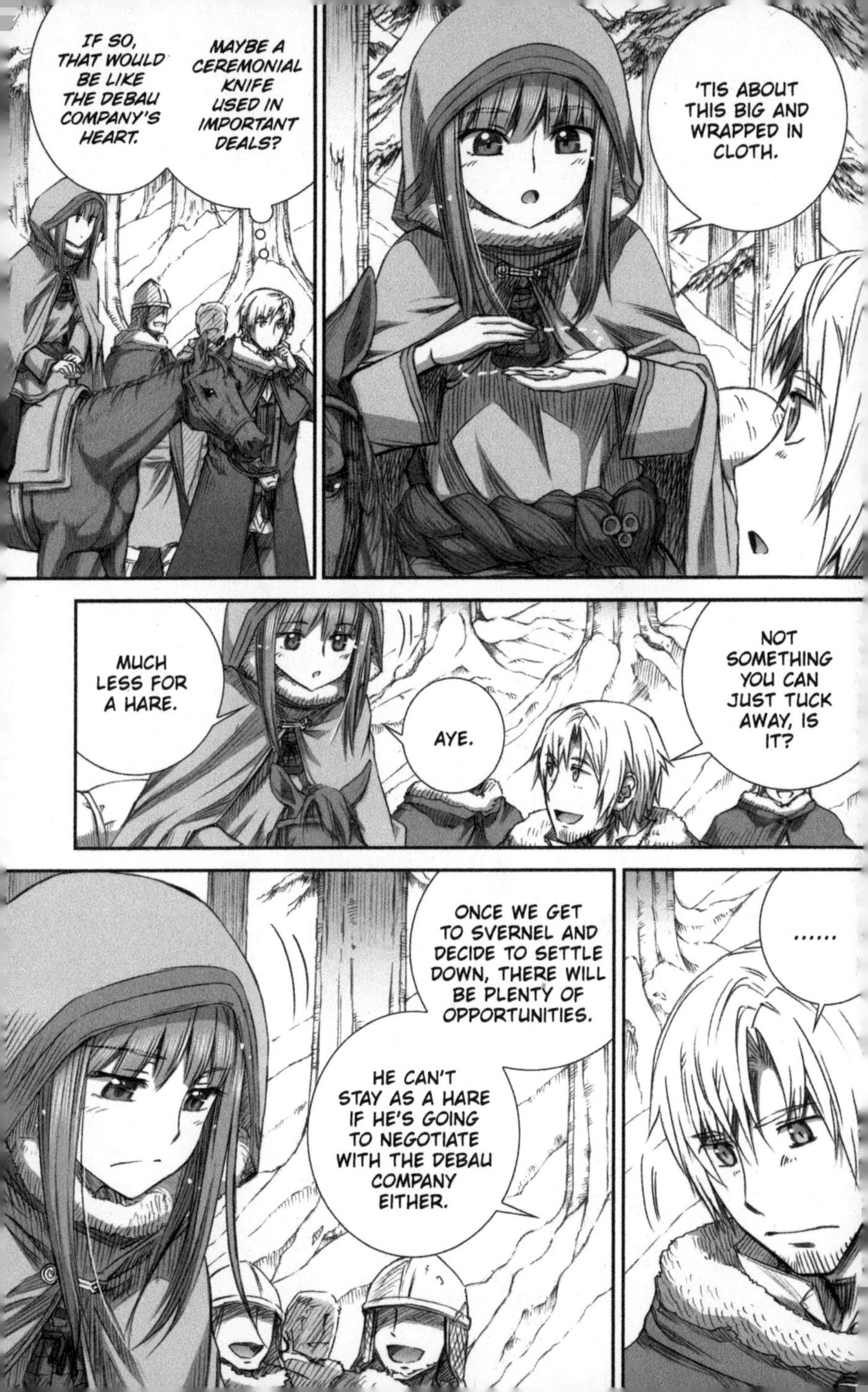
'TIS ABOUT THIS BIG AND WRAPPED IN CLOTH.
MAYBE A CEREMONIAL KNIFE USED IN IMPORTANT DEALS?
IF SO, THAT WOULD BE LIKE THE DEBAU COMPANY'S HEART.
NOT SOMETHING YOU CAN JUST TUCK AWAY, IS IT?
AYE.
MUCH LESS FOR A HARE.
......
ONCE WE GET TO SVERNEL AND DECIDE TO SETTLE DOWN, THERE WILL BE PLENTY OF OPPORTUNITIES.
HE CAN'T STAY AS A HARE IF HE'S GOING TO NEGOTIATE WITH THE DEBAU COMPANY EITHER.

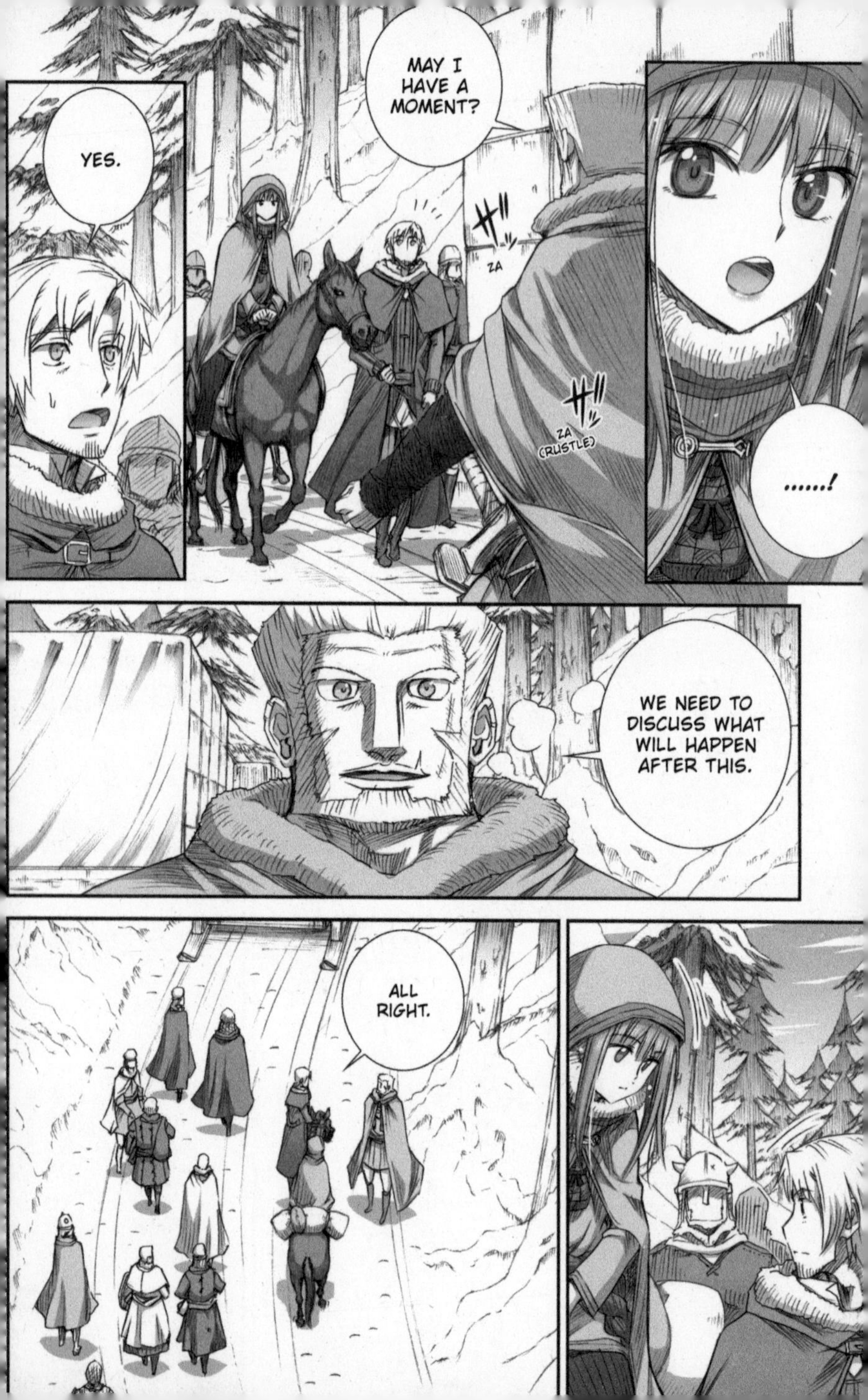
MAY I HAVE A MOMENT?
ZA
ZA (RUSTLE)
......!
YES.
WE NEED TO DISCUSS WHAT WILL HAPPEN AFTER THIS.
ALL RIGHT.

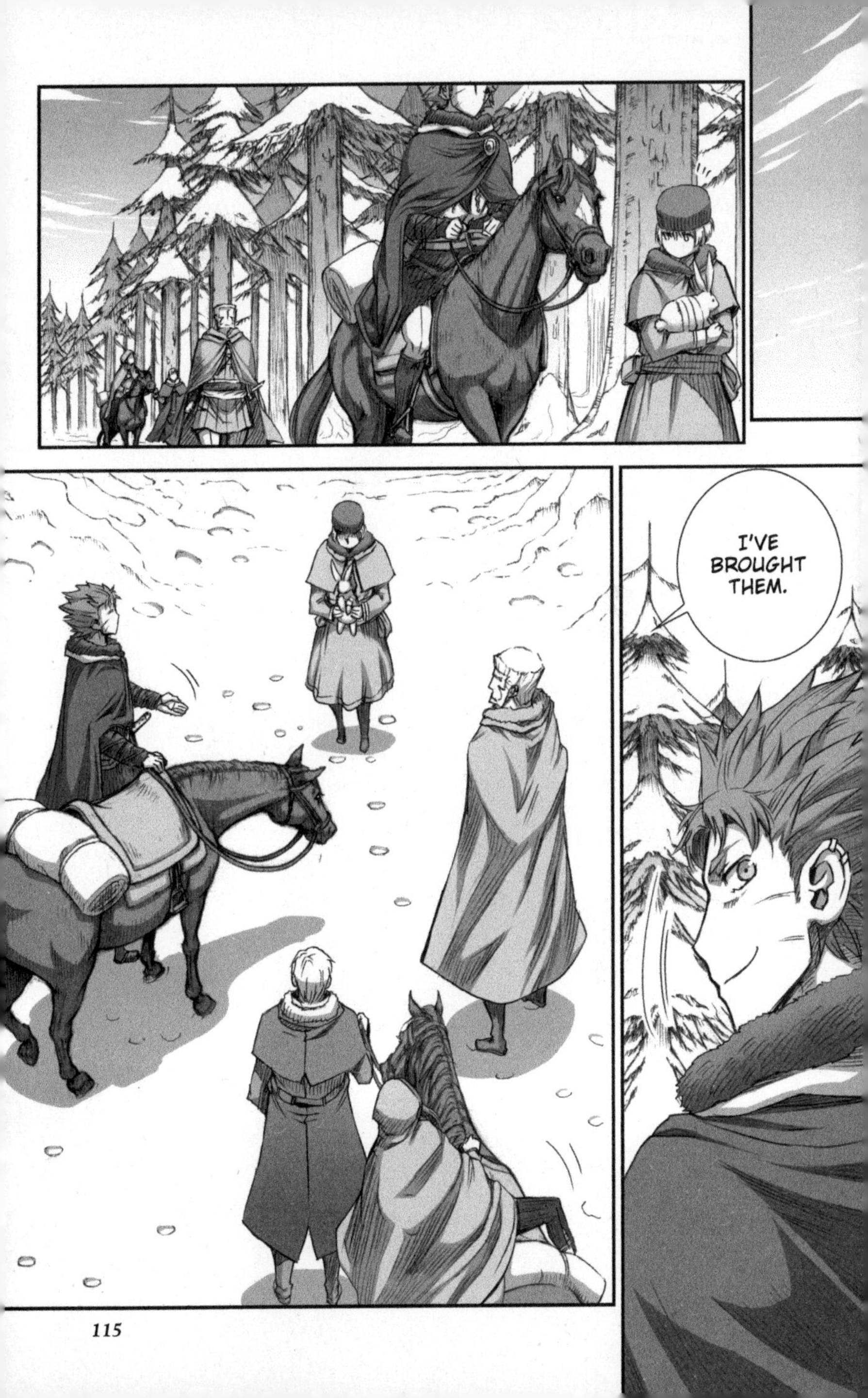
I'VE BROUGHT THEM.

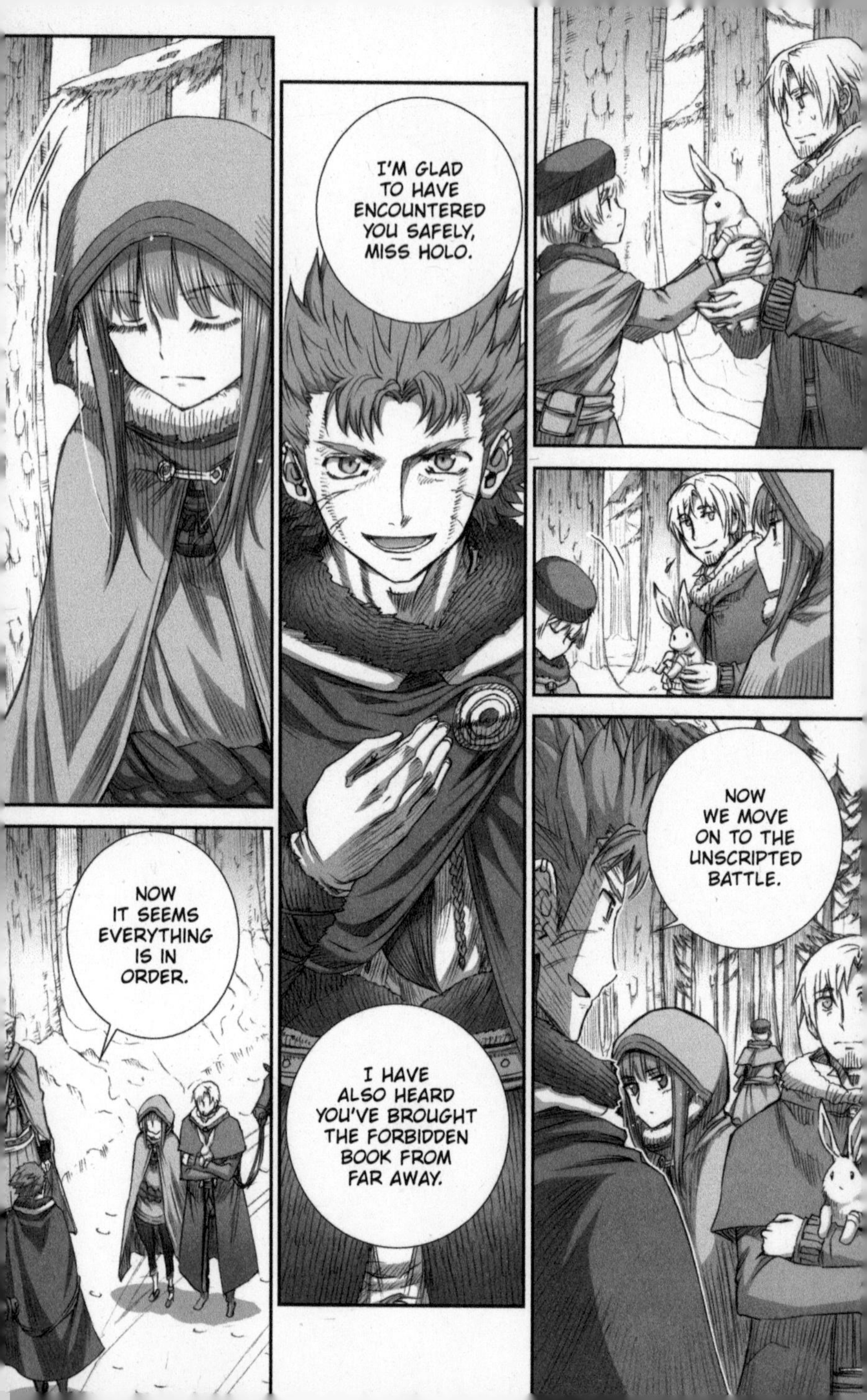
NOW WE MOVE ON TO THE UNSCRIPTED BATTLE.
I'M GLAD TO HAVE ENCOUNTERED YOU SAFELY, MISS HOLO.
I HAVE ALSO HEARD YOU'VE BROUGHT THE FORBIDDEN BOOK FROM FAR AWAY.
NOW IT SEEMS EVERYTHING IS IN ORDER.

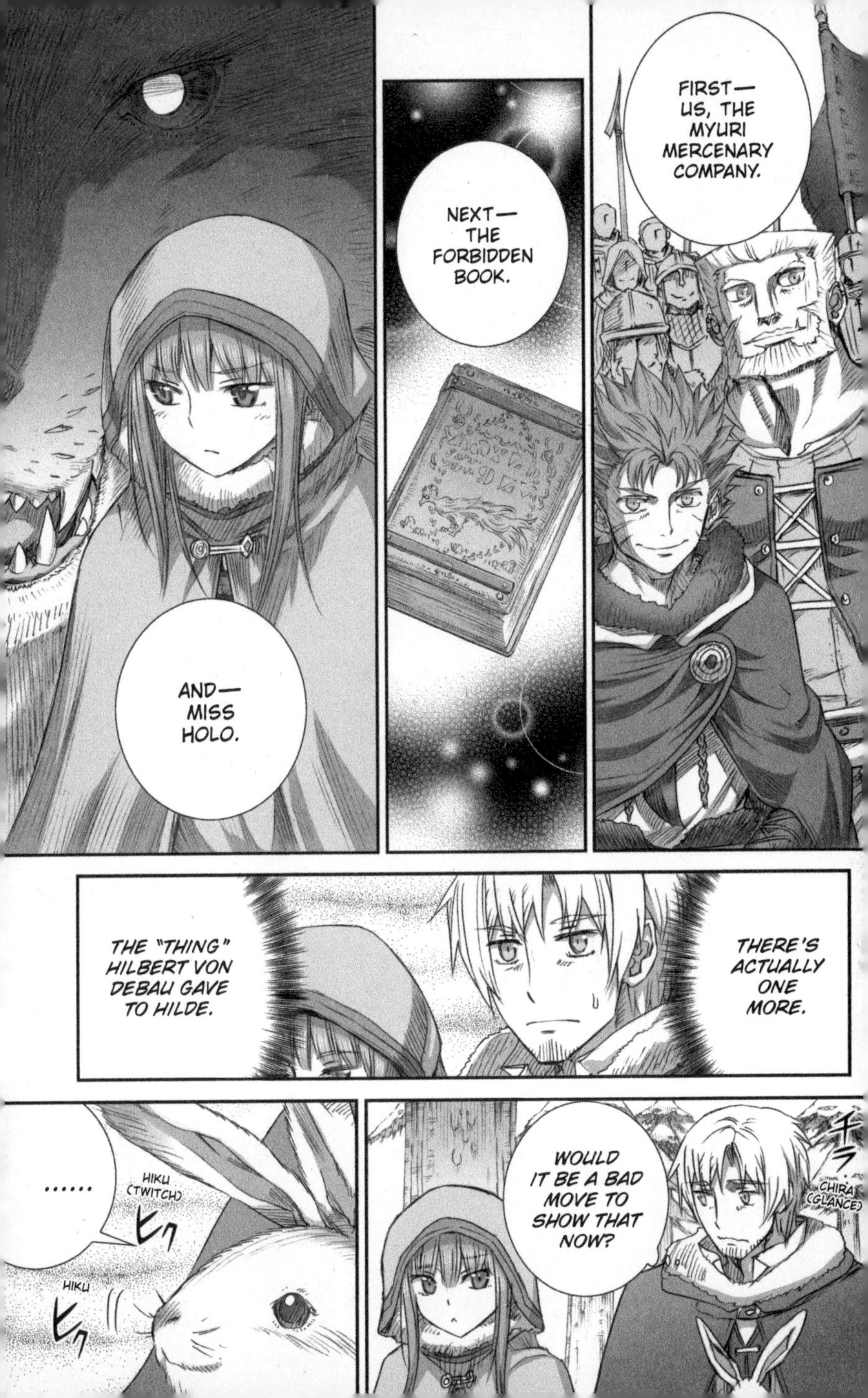
FIRST— US, THE MYURI MERCENARY COMPANY.
NEXT— THE FORBIDDEN BOOK.
AND— MISS HOLO.
THERE'S ACTUALLY ONE MORE.
THE "THING" HILBERT VON DEBAU GAVE TO HILDE.
チラ
CHIRA (GLANCE)
WOULD IT BE A BAD MOVE TO SHOW THAT NOW?
......
ヒク
HIKU (TWITCH)
ヒク
HIKU

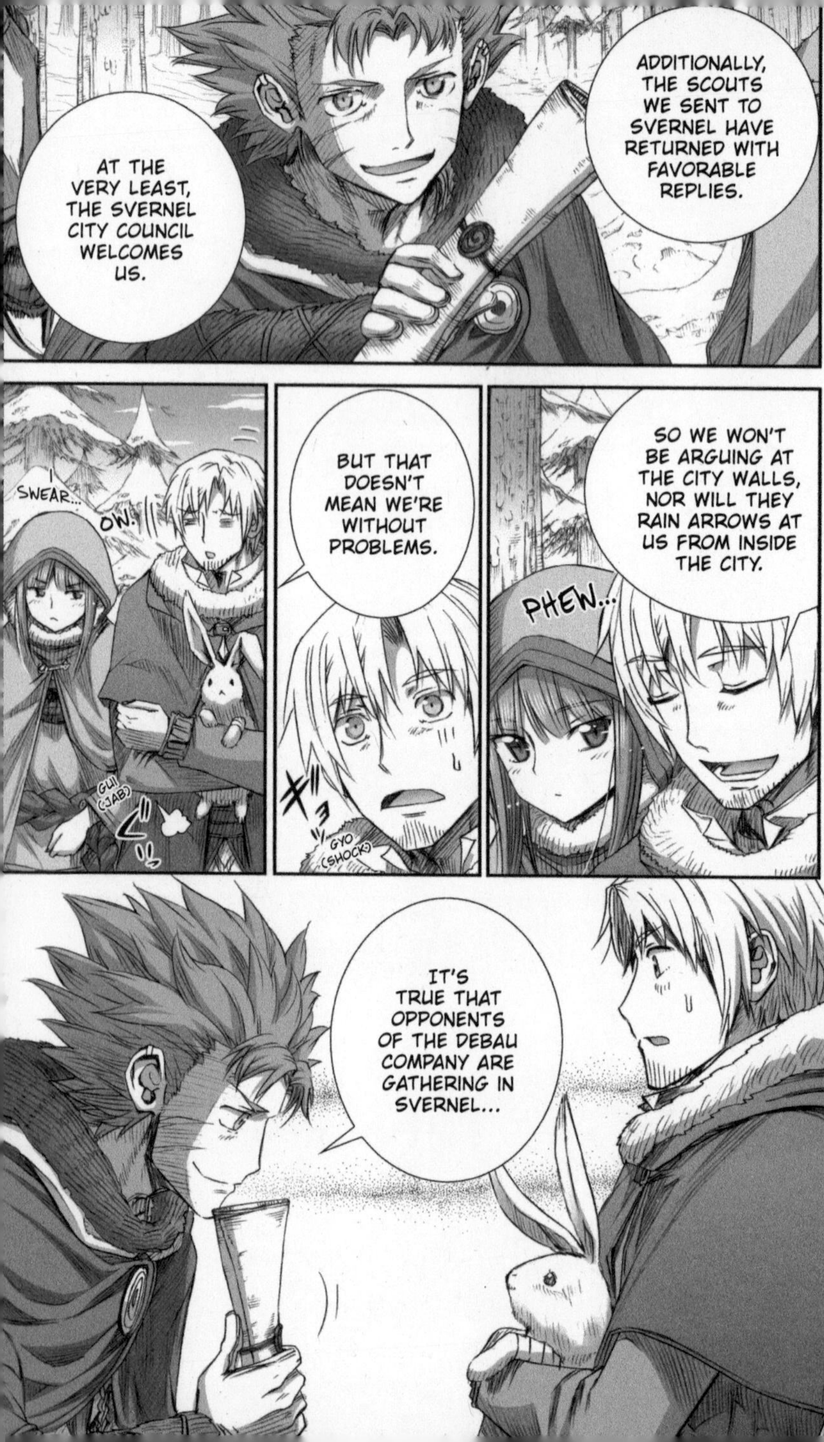

ADDITIONALLY, THE SCOUTS WE SENT TO SVERNEL HAVE RETURNED WITH FAVORABLE REPLIES.
AT THE VERY LEAST, THE SVERNEL CITY COUNCIL WELCOMES US.
SO WE WON'T BE ARGUING AT THE CITY WALLS, NOR WILL THEY RAIN ARROWS AT US FROM INSIDE THE CITY.
PHEW...
BUT THAT DOESN'T MEAN WE'RE WITHOUT PROBLEMS.
GYO (SHOCK)
I SWEAR...
OW.
GUI (JAB)
IT'S TRUE THAT OPPONENTS OF THE DEBAU COMPANY ARE GATHERING IN SVERNEL...

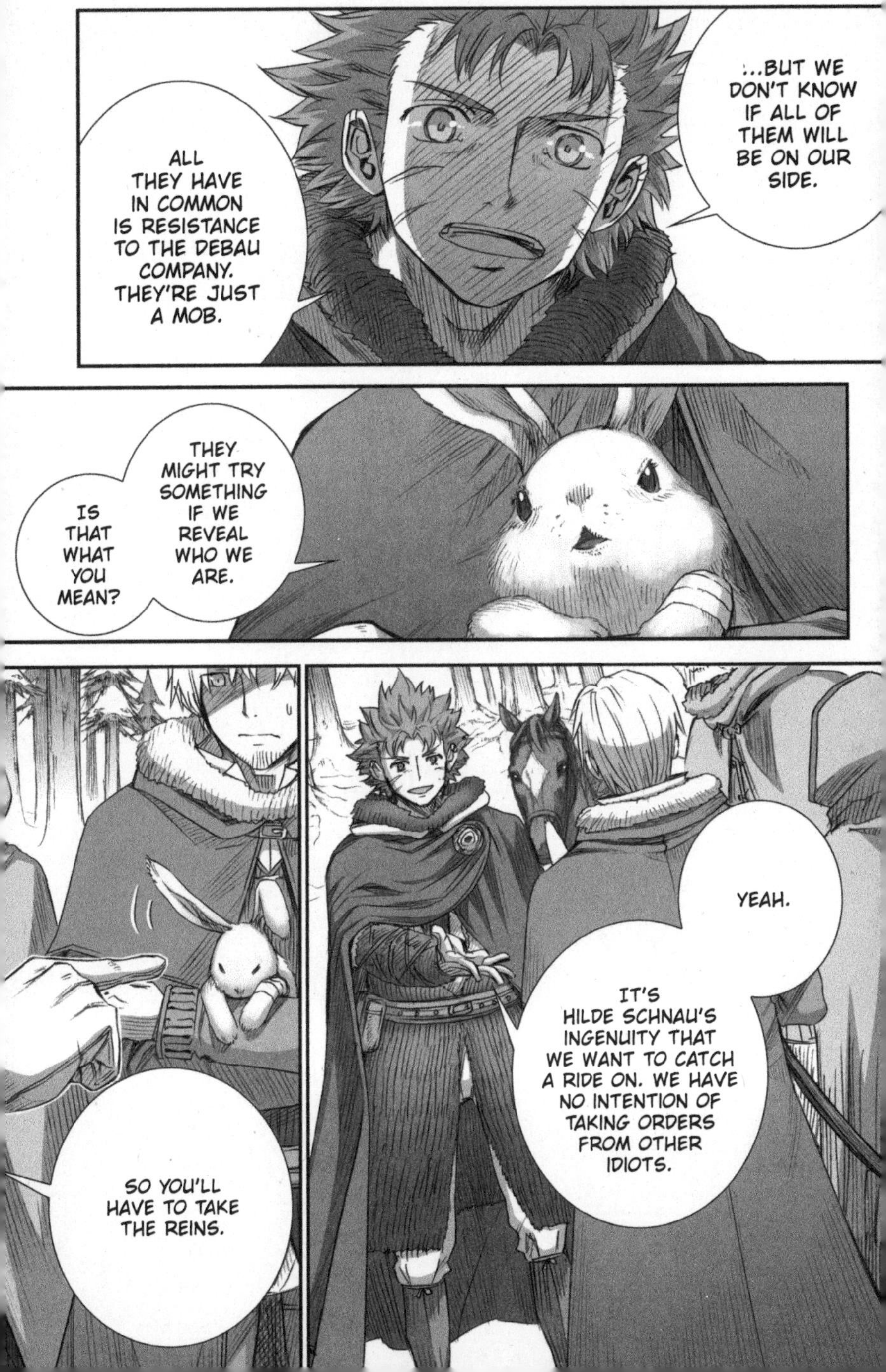
...BUT WE DON'T KNOW IF ALL OF THEM WILL BE ON OUR SIDE.
ALL THEY HAVE IN COMMON IS RESISTANCE TO THE DEBAU COMPANY. THEY'RE JUST A MOB.
THEY MIGHT TRY SOMETHING IF WE REVEAL WHO WE ARE. IS THAT WHAT YOU MEAN?
YEAH.
IT'S HILDE SCHNAU'S INGENUITY THAT WE WANT TO CATCH A RIDE ON. WE HAVE NO INTENTION OF TAKING ORDERS FROM OTHER IDIOTS.
SO YOU'LL HAVE TO TAKE THE REINS.

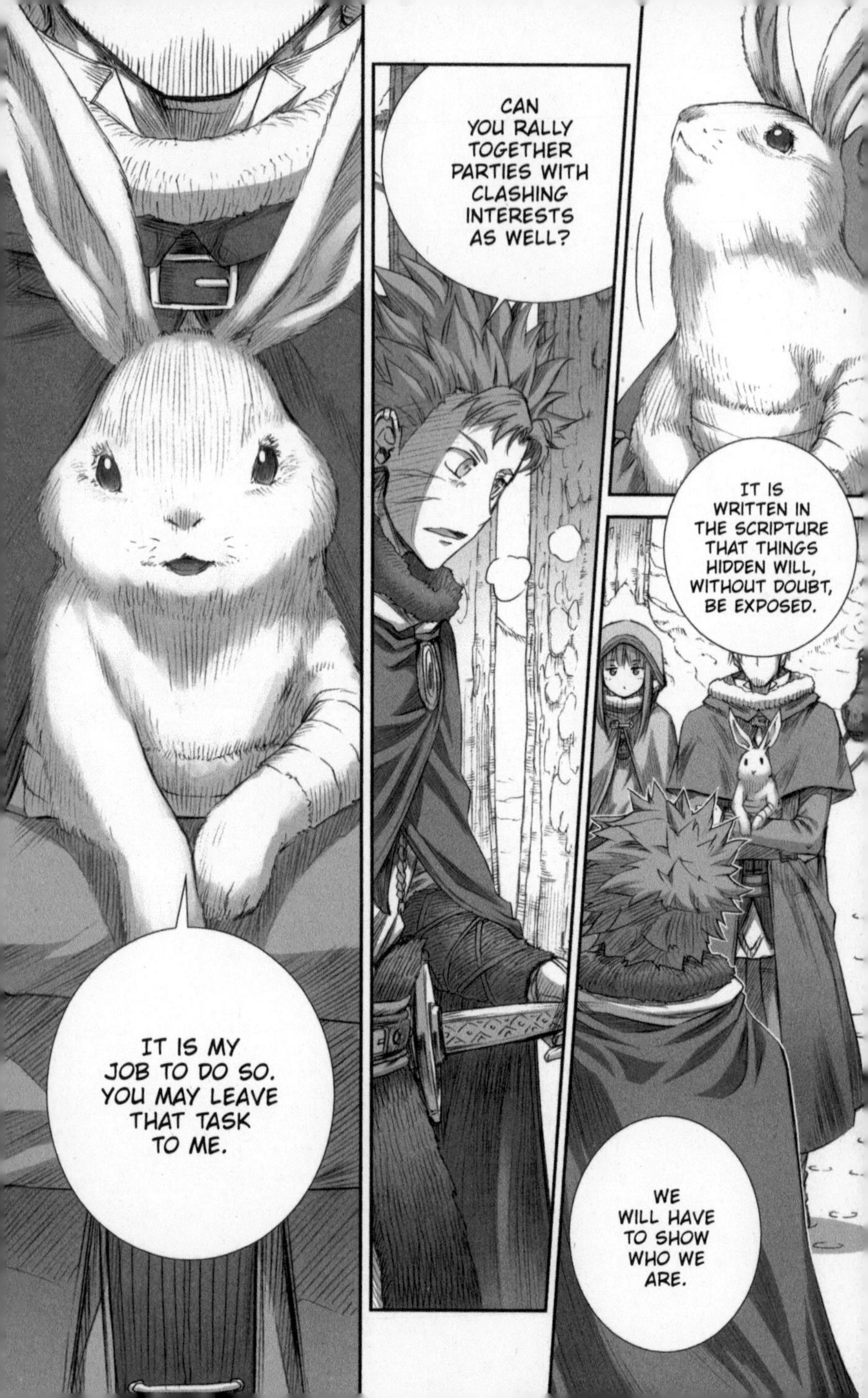
IT IS WRITTEN IN THE SCRIPTURE THAT THINGS HIDDEN WILL, WITHOUT DOUBT, BE EXPOSED.
WE WILL HAVE TO SHOW WHO WE ARE.
CAN YOU RALLY TOGETHER PARTIES WITH CLASHING INTERESTS AS WELL?
IT IS MY JOB TO DO SO. YOU MAY LEAVE THAT TASK TO ME.

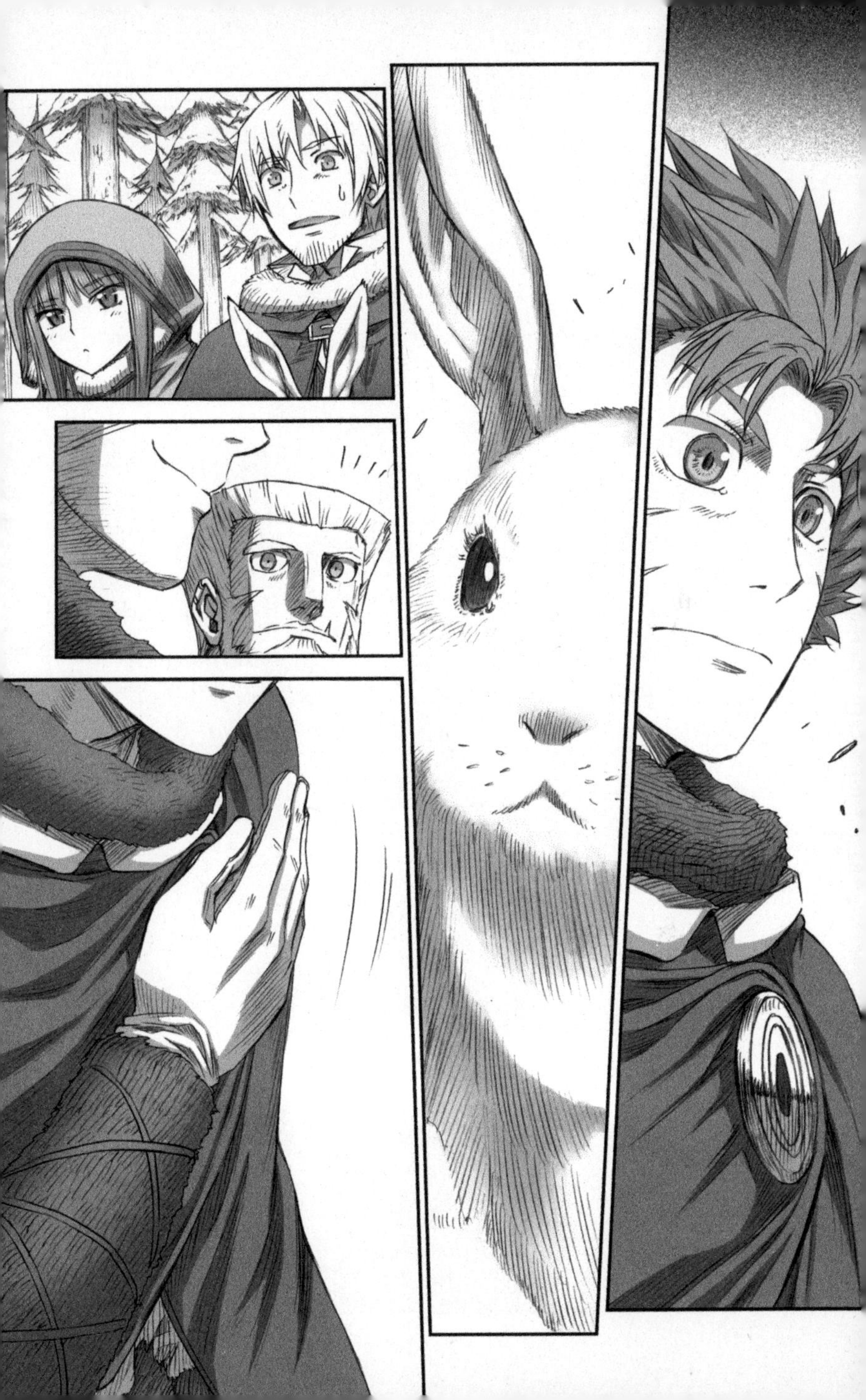

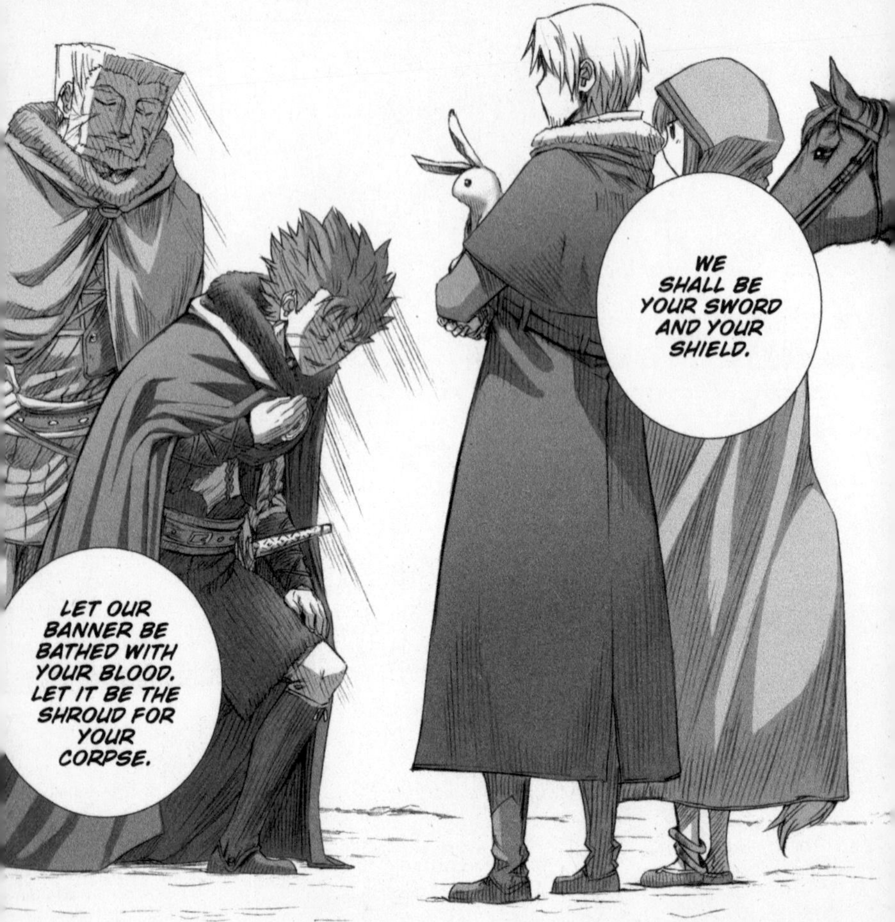
WE SHALL BE YOUR SWORD AND YOUR SHIELD.
LET OUR BANNER BE BATHED WITH YOUR BLOOD. LET IT BE THE SHROUD FOR YOUR CORPSE.

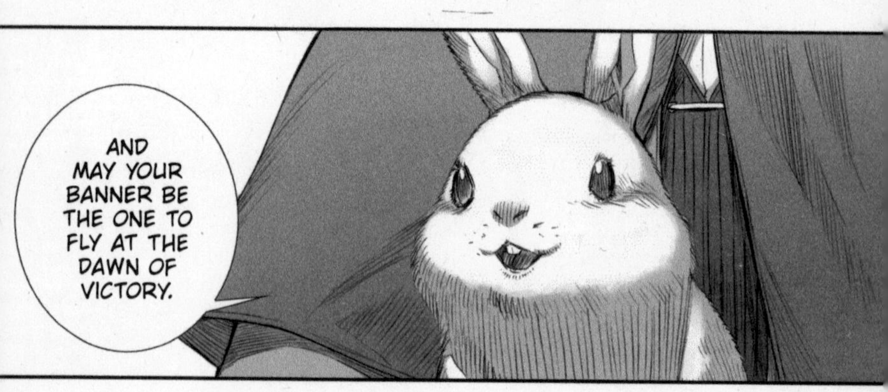
AND MAY YOUR BANNER BE THE ONE TO FLY AT THE DAWN OF VICTORY.

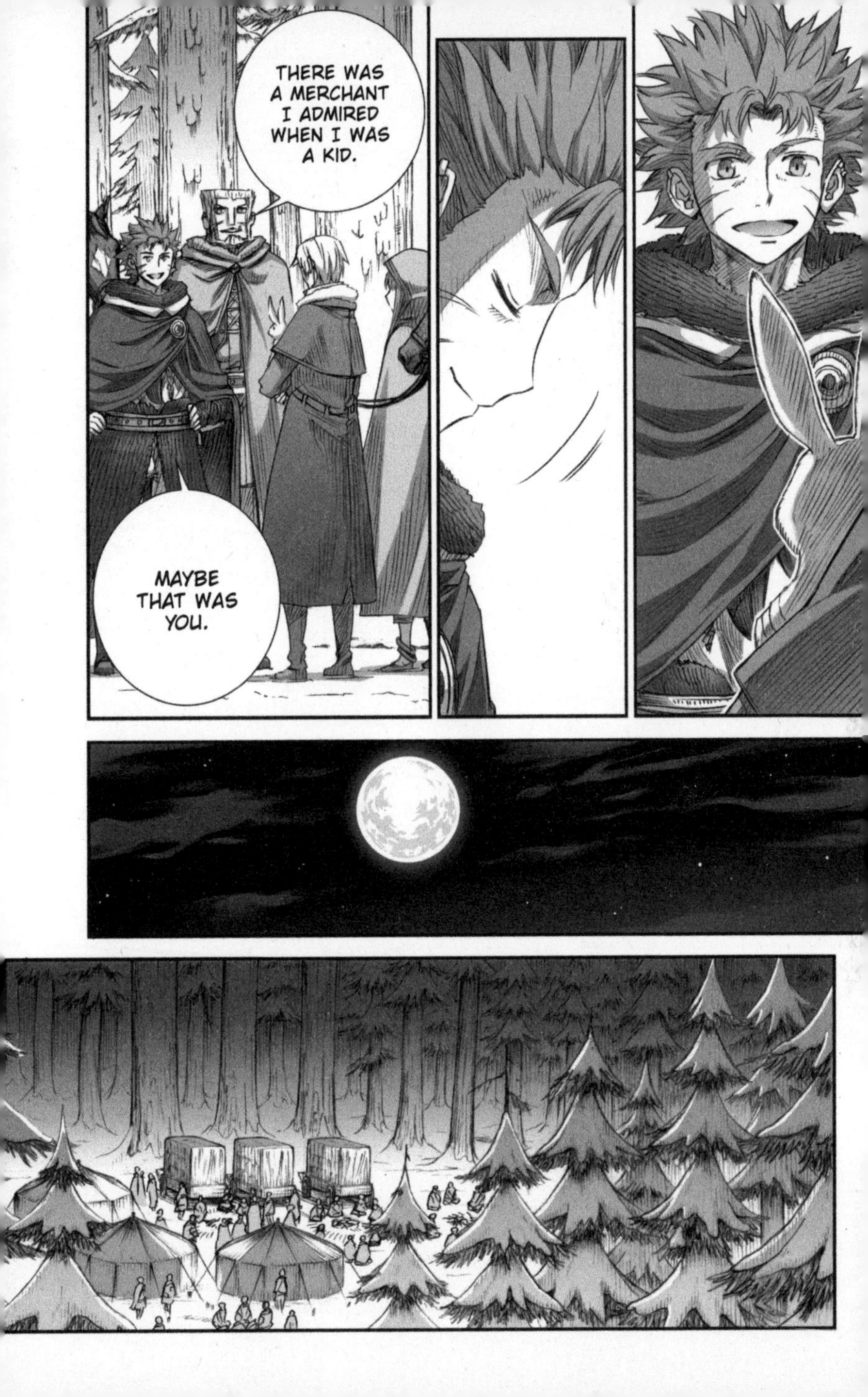
THERE WAS A MERCHANT I ADMIRED WHEN I WAS A KID.
MAYBE THAT WAS YOU.

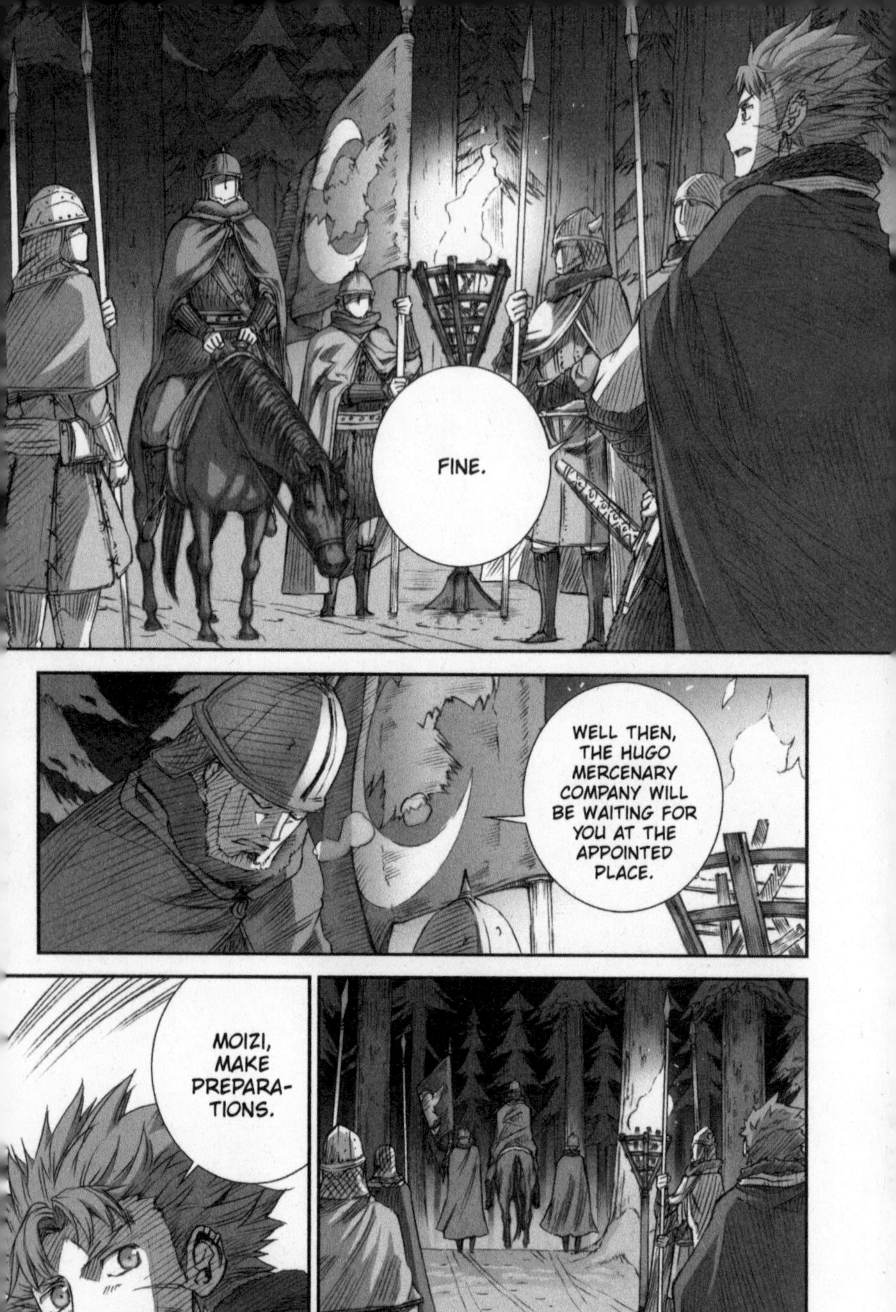
FINE.
WELL THEN, THE HUGO MERCENARY COMPANY WILL BE WAITING FOR YOU AT THE APPOINTED PLACE.
MOIZI, MAKE PREPARA-TIONS.

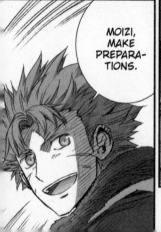

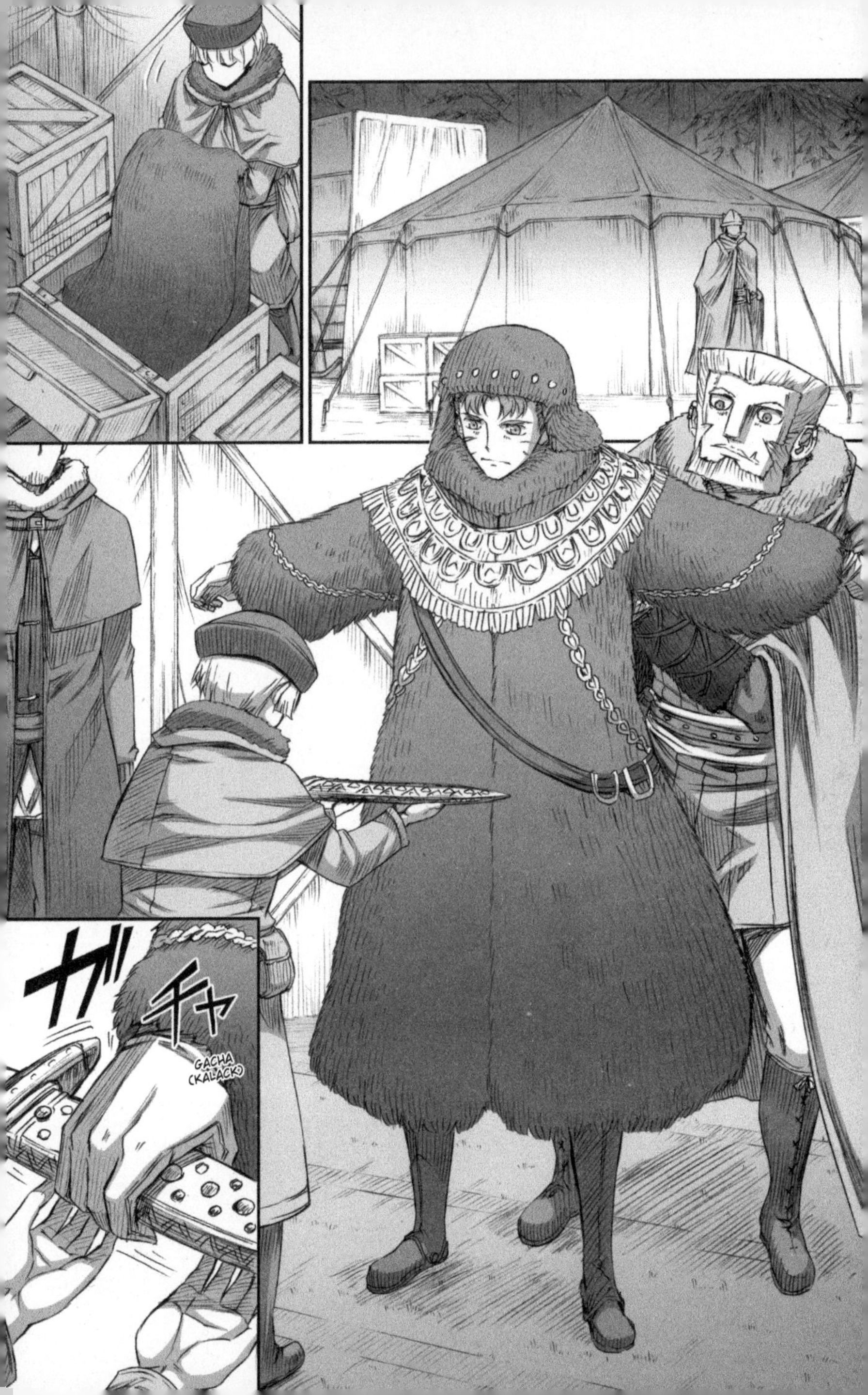
ガチャ
GACHA (KALACK)

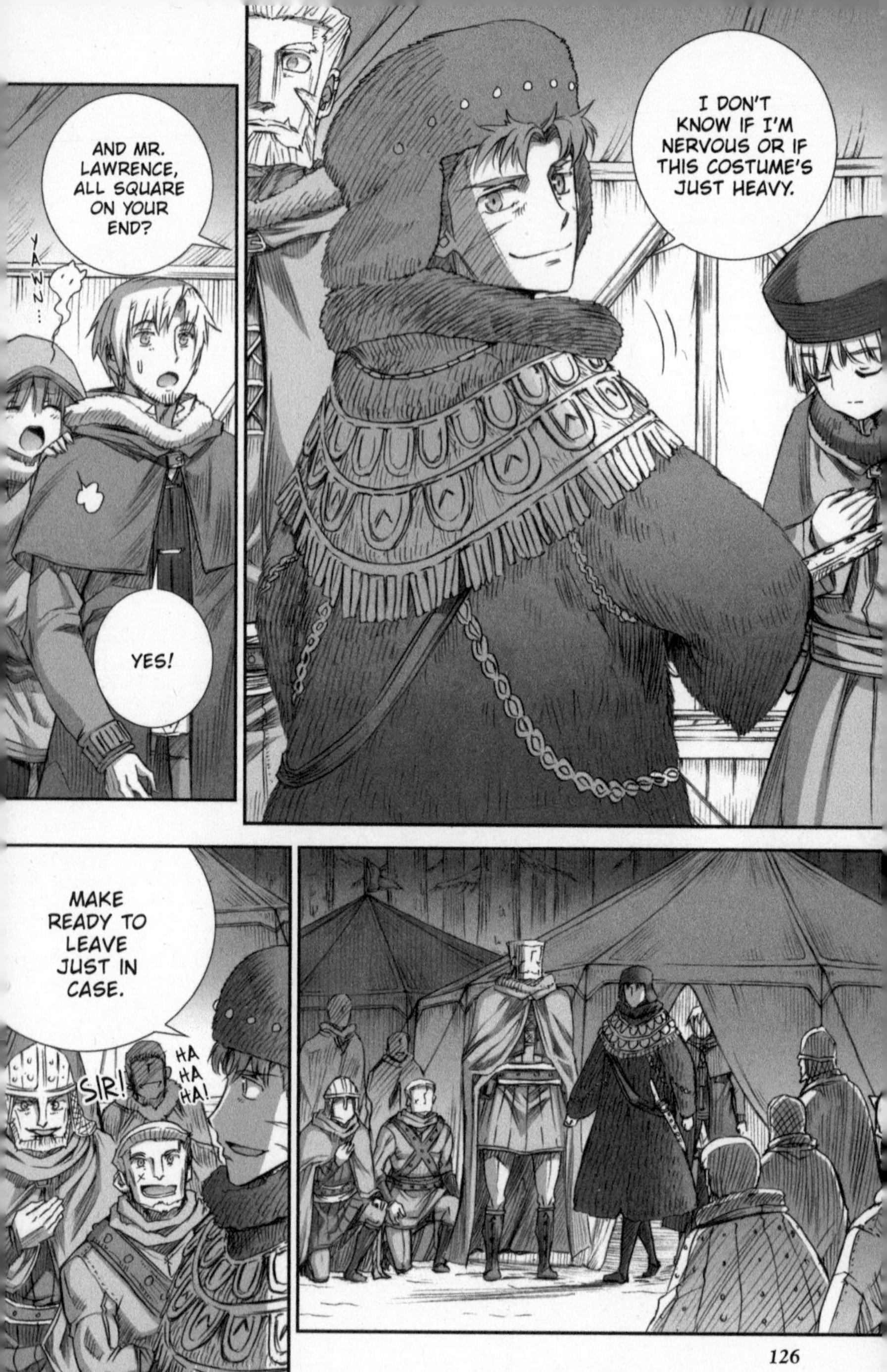
I DON'T KNOW IF I'M NERVOUS OR IF THIS COSTUME'S JUST HEAVY.
AND MR. LAWRENCE, ALL SQUARE ON YOUR END?
YAWN...
YES!
MAKE READY TO LEAVE JUST IN CASE.
SIR!
HA HA HA HA!

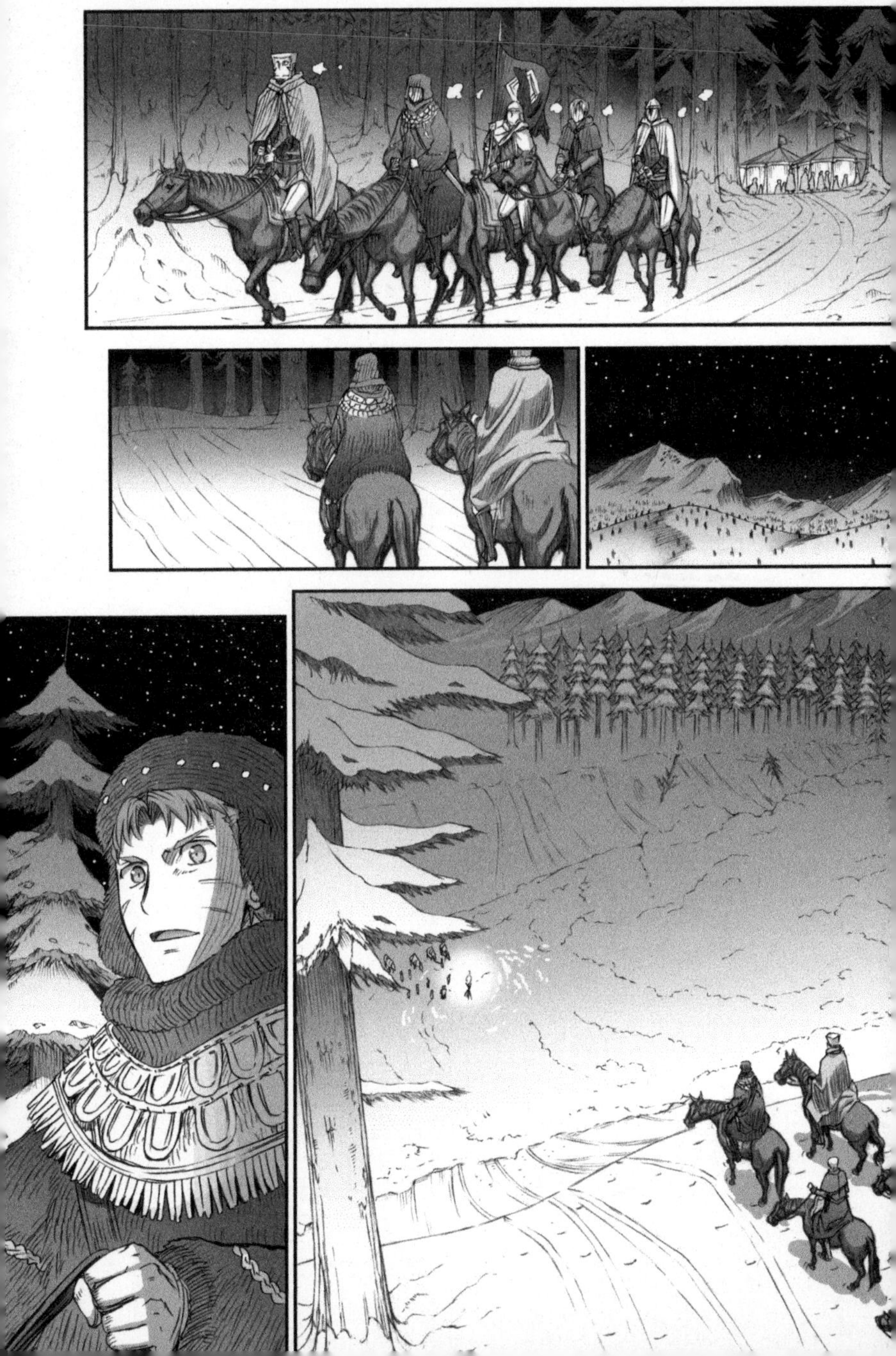

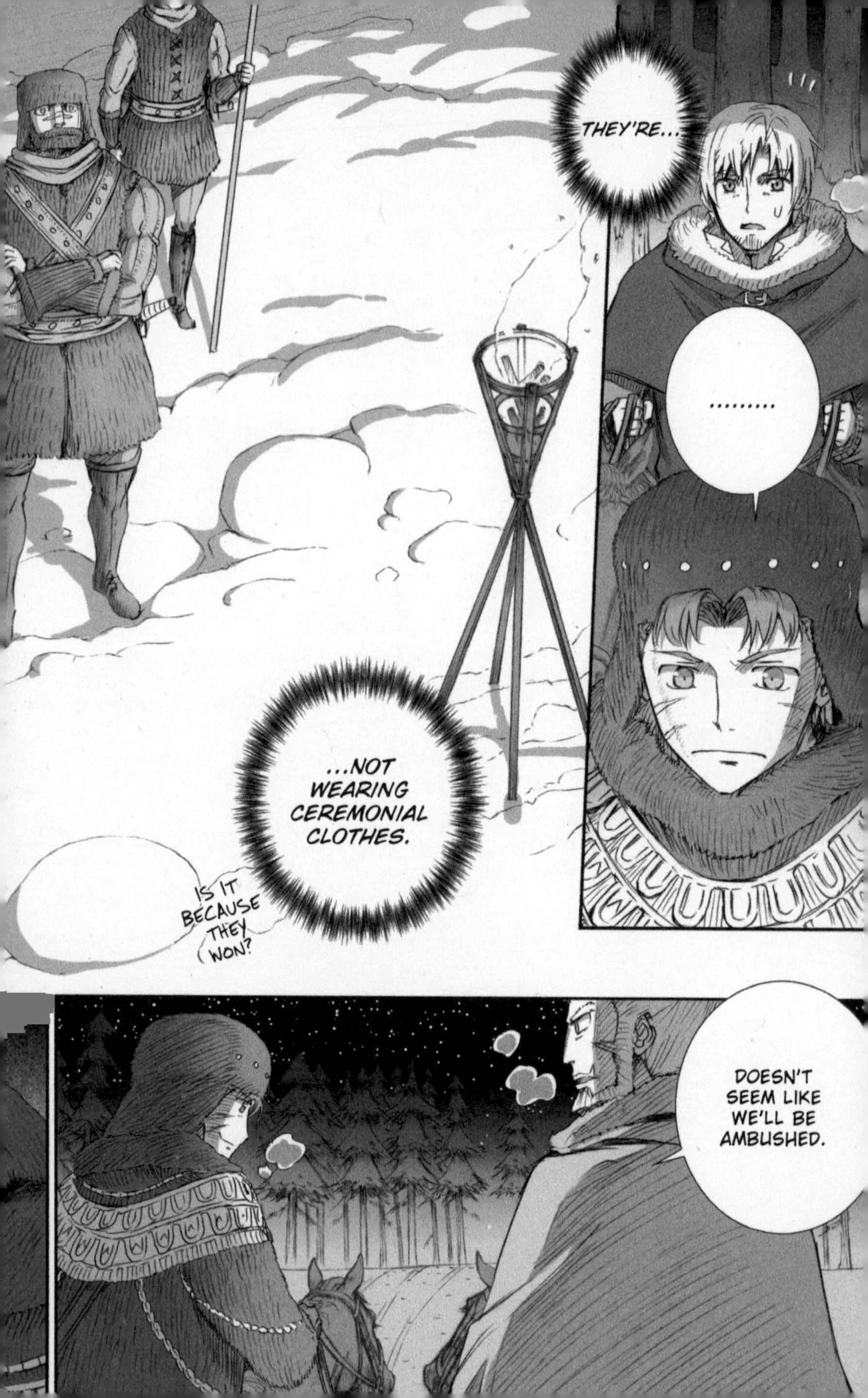
THEY'RE...
....
...NOT WEARING CEREMONIAL CLOTHES.
IS IT BECAUSE THEY WON?
DOESN'T SEEM LIKE WE'LL BE AMBUSHED.

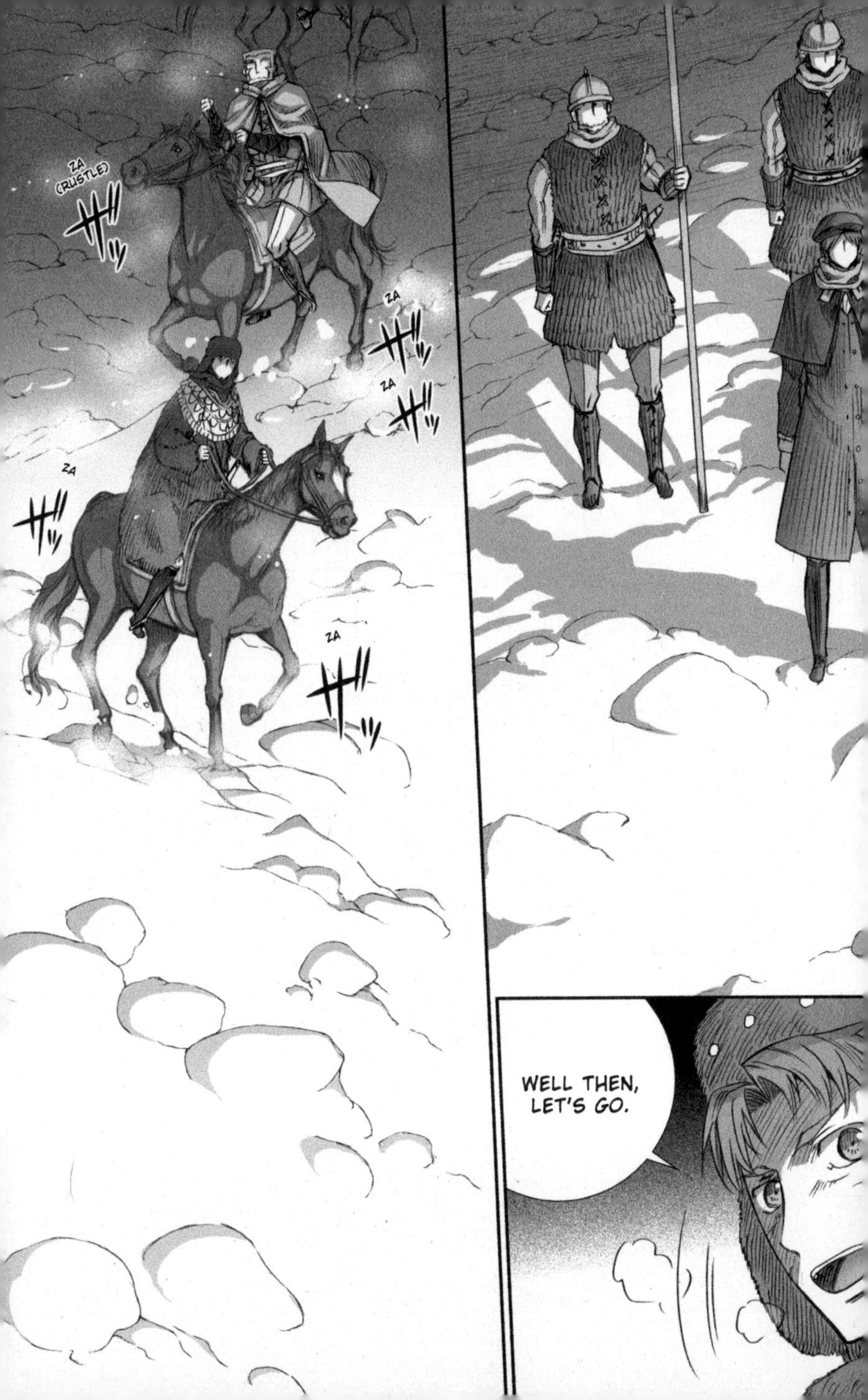
WELL THEN, LET'S GO.
ZA (RUSTLE)
ZA
ZA
ZA
ZA

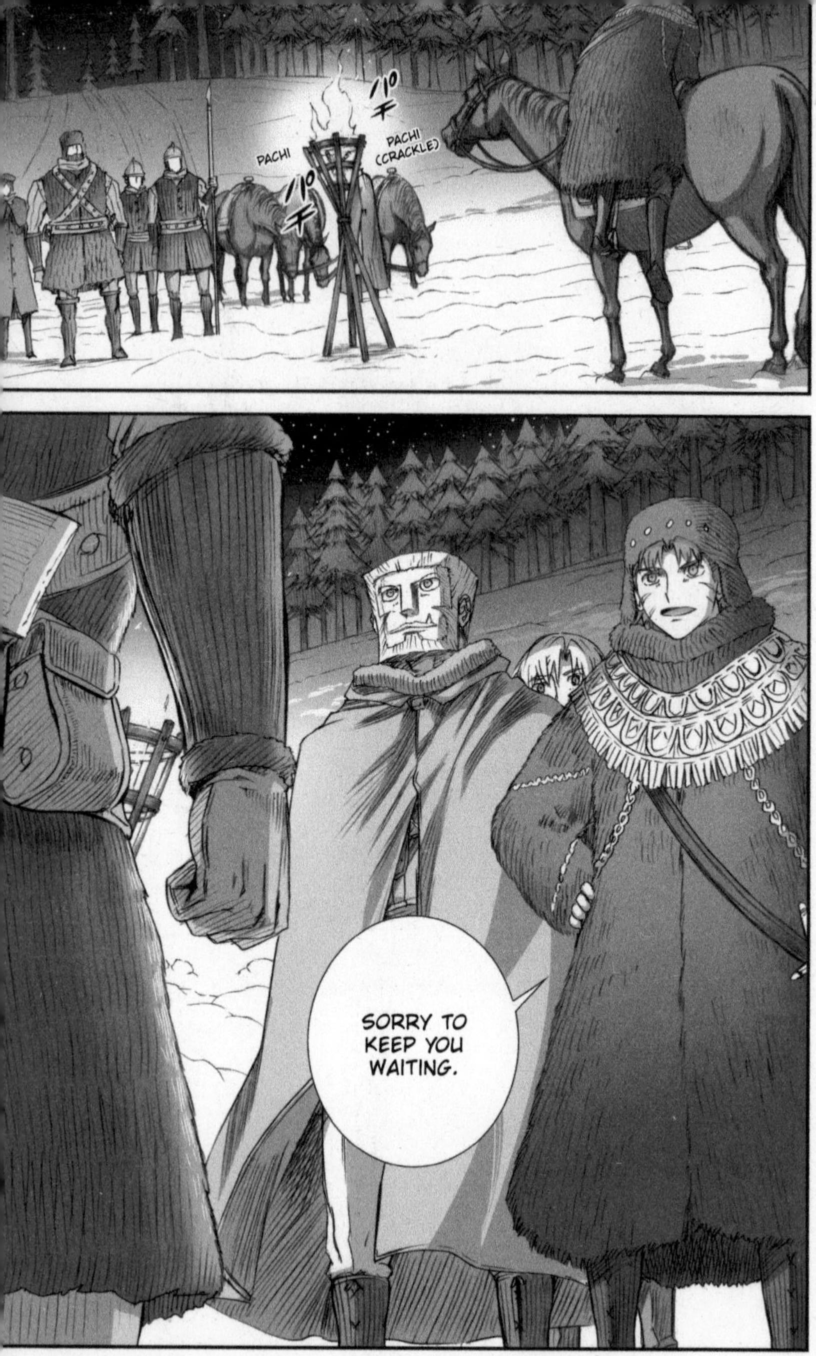

PACHI (CRACKLE)
PACHI
SORRY TO KEEP YOU WAITING.

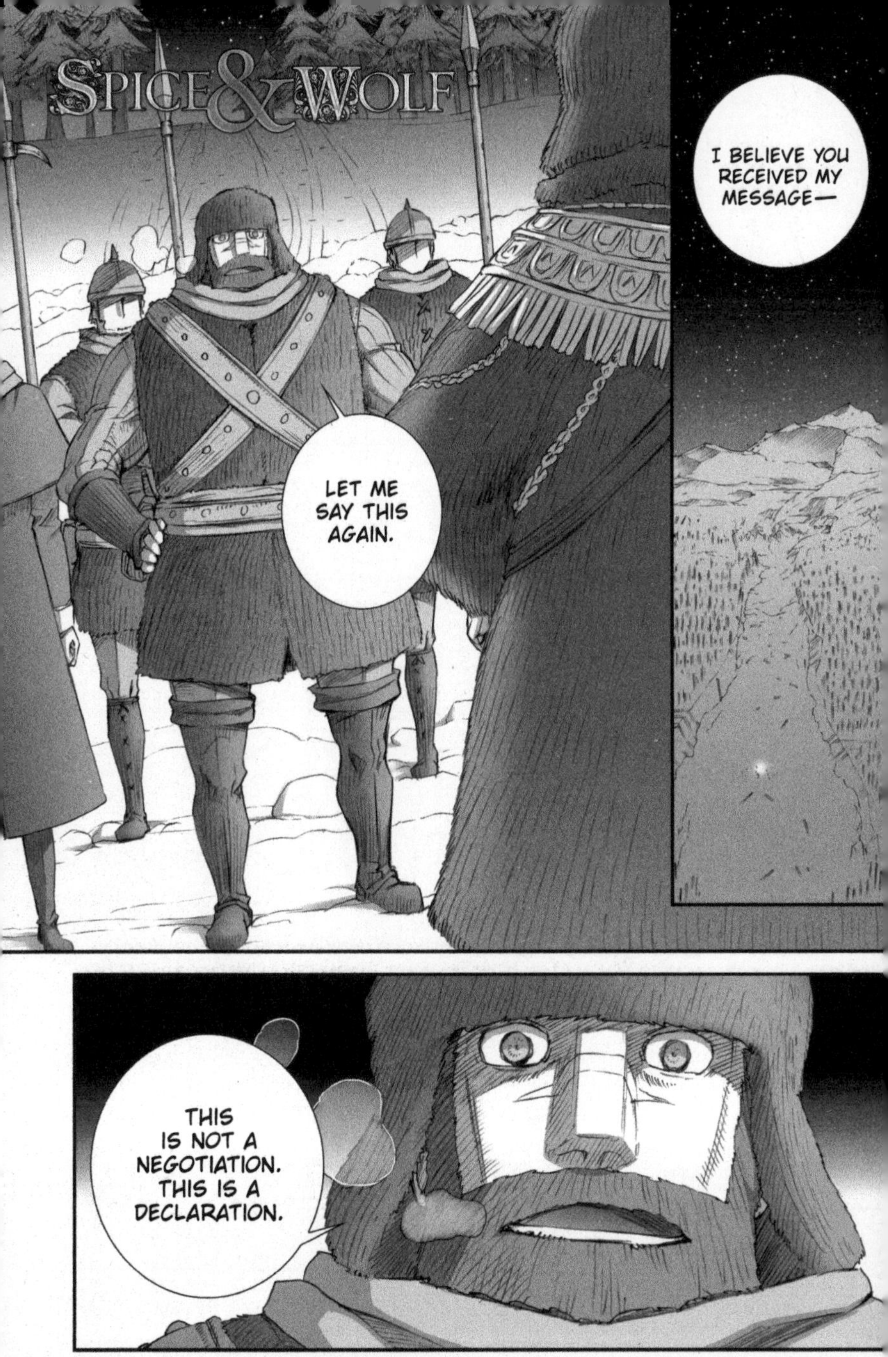
I BELIEVE YOU RECEIVED MY MESSAGE—
SPICE & WOLF
LET ME SAY THIS AGAIN.
THIS IS NOT A NEGOTIATION. THIS IS A DECLARATION.

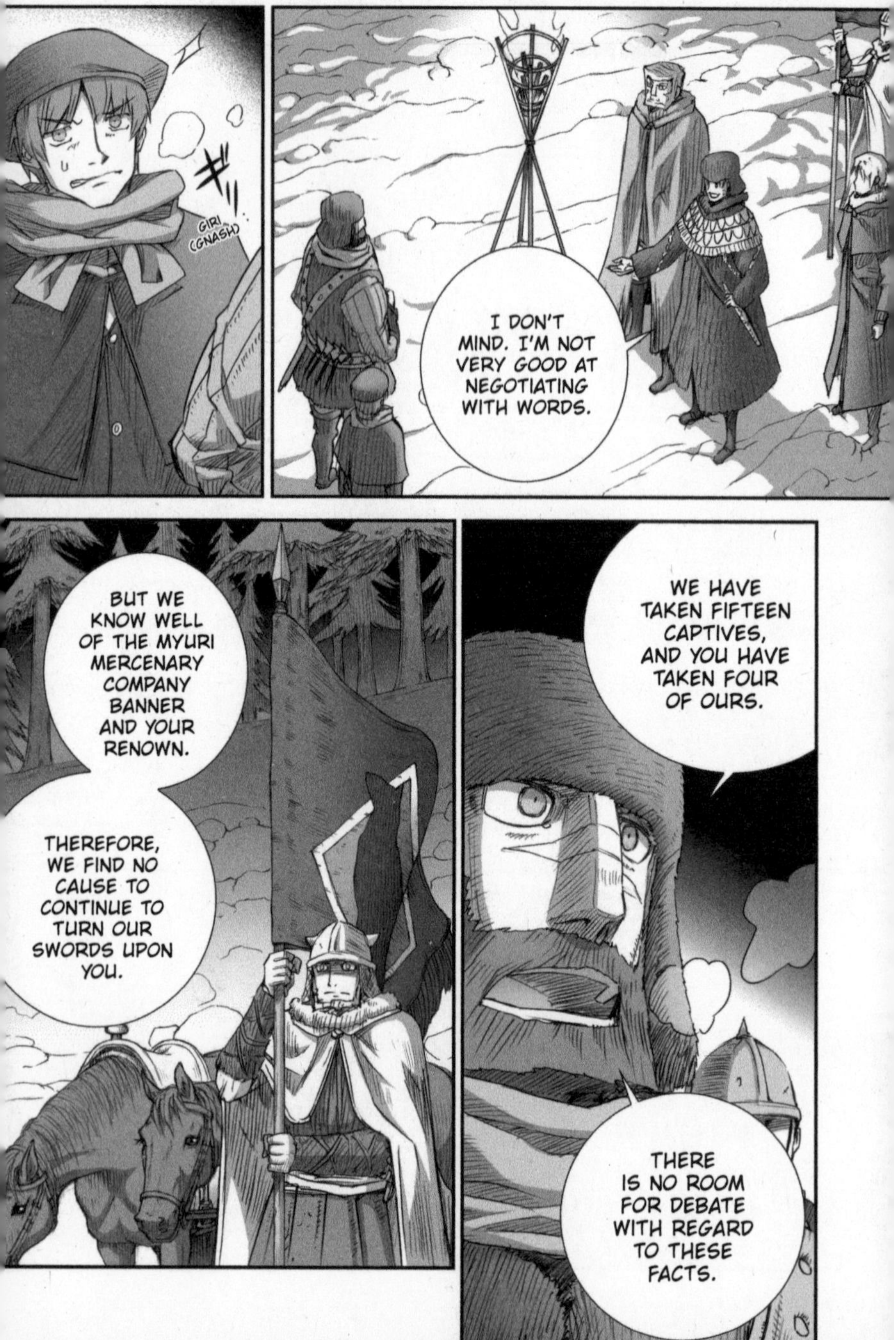
I DON'T MIND. I'M NOT VERY GOOD AT NEGOTIATING WITH WORDS.
GIRI (GNASH)
WE HAVE TAKEN FIFTEEN CAPTIVES, AND YOU HAVE TAKEN FOUR OF OURS.
THERE IS NO ROOM FOR DEBATE WITH REGARD TO THESE FACTS.
BUT WE KNOW WELL OF THE MYURI MERCENARY COMPANY BANNER AND YOUR RENOWN.
THEREFORE, WE FIND NO CAUSE TO CONTINUE TO TURN OUR SWORDS UPON YOU.

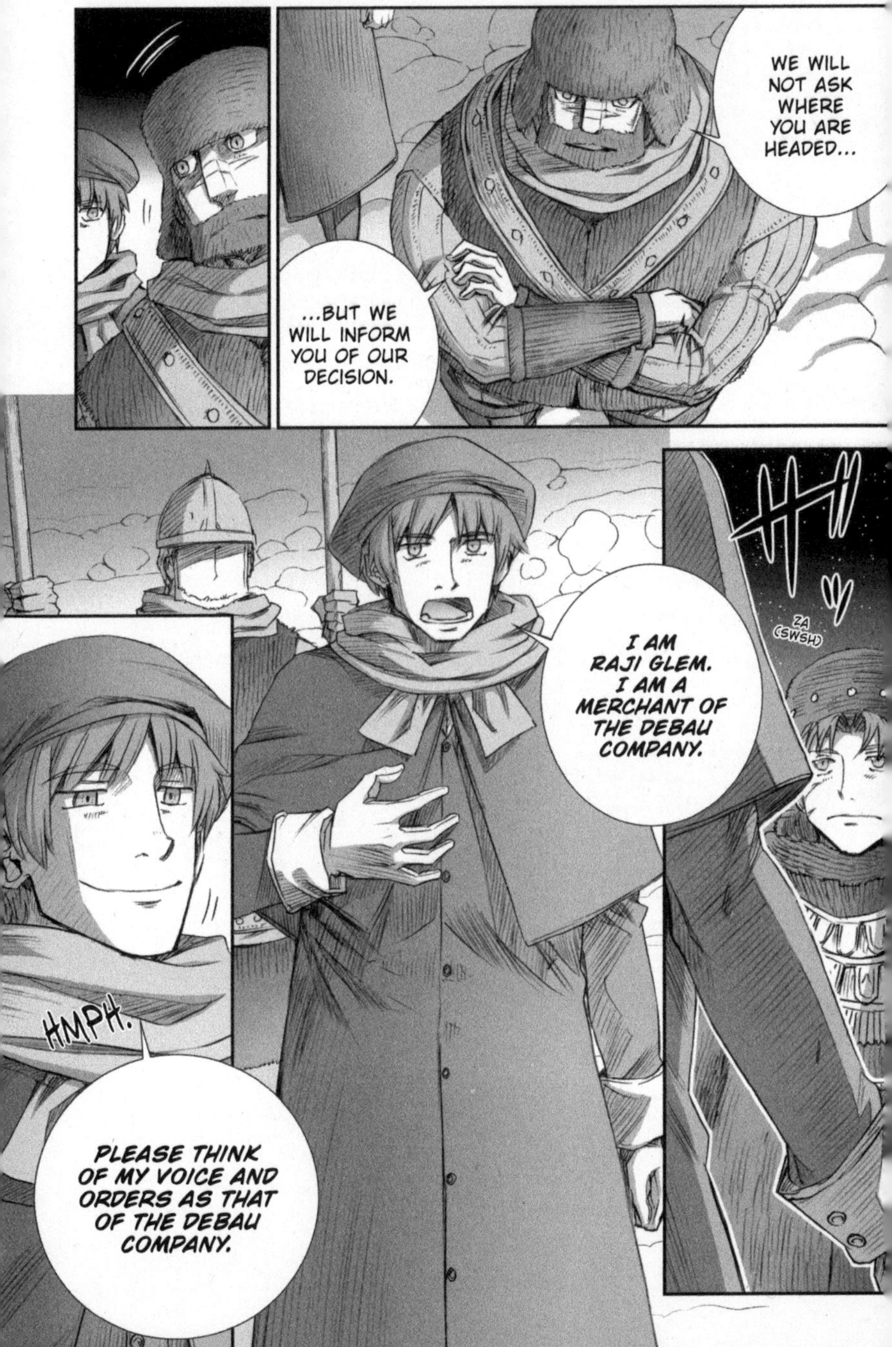
WE WILL NOT ASK WHERE YOU ARE HEADED...
...BUT WE WILL INFORM YOU OF OUR DECISION.
ZA (SWSH)
I AM RAJI GLEM. I AM A MERCHANT OF THE DEBAU COMPANY.
HMPH.
PLEASE THINK OF MY VOICE AND ORDERS AS THAT OF THE DEBAU COMPANY.

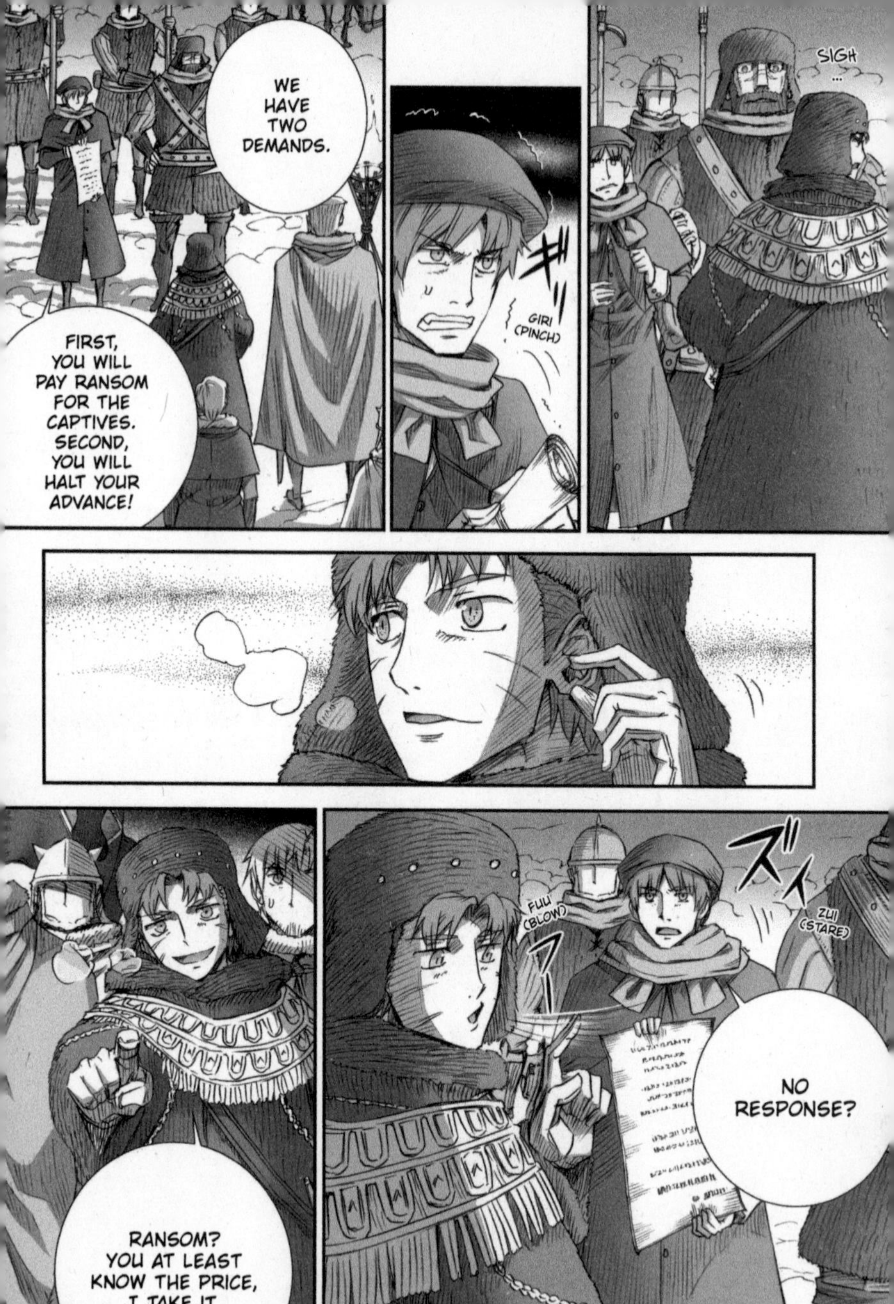
SIGH ...
ギリ
GIRI (PINCH)
WE HAVE TWO DEMANDS.
FIRST, YOU WILL PAY RANSOM FOR THE CAPTIVES. SECOND, YOU WILL HALT YOUR ADVANCE!
ズイ
ZUI (STARE)
FUU (BLOW)
NO RESPONSE?
RANSOM? YOU AT LEAST KNOW THE PRICE, I TAKE IT.

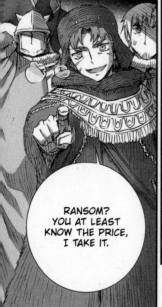

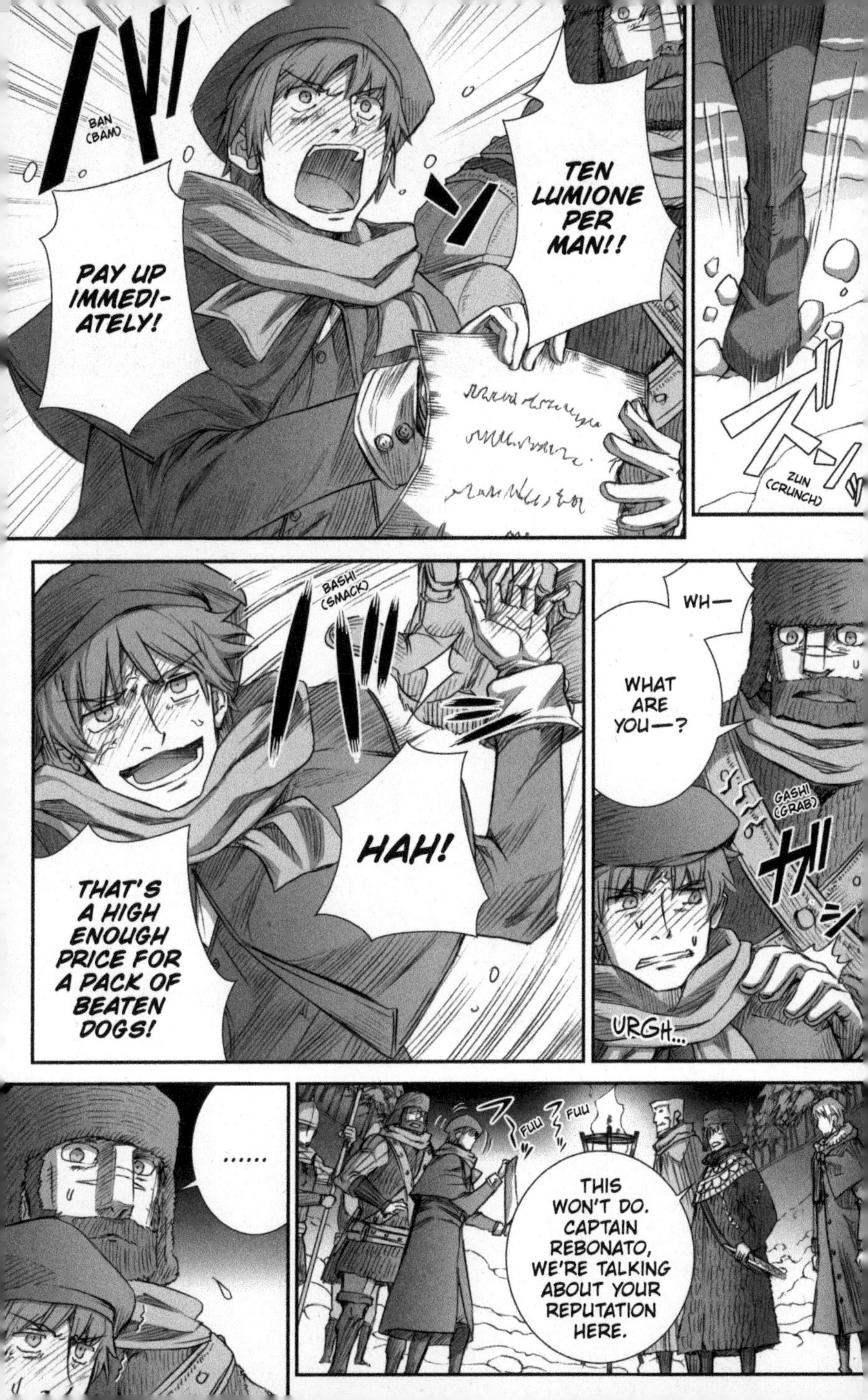
ZUN
(CRUNCH)
TEN LUMIONE PER MAN!!
BAN
(BAM)
PAY UP IMMEDI-ATELY!
WH—
WHAT ARE YOU—?
GASHI
(GRAB)
URGH...
BASHI
(SMACK)
HAH!
THAT'S A HIGH ENOUGH PRICE FOR A PACK OF BEATEN DOGS!
FUU
FUU
THIS WON'T DO. CAPTAIN REBONATO, WE'RE TALKING ABOUT YOUR REPUTATION HERE.
......

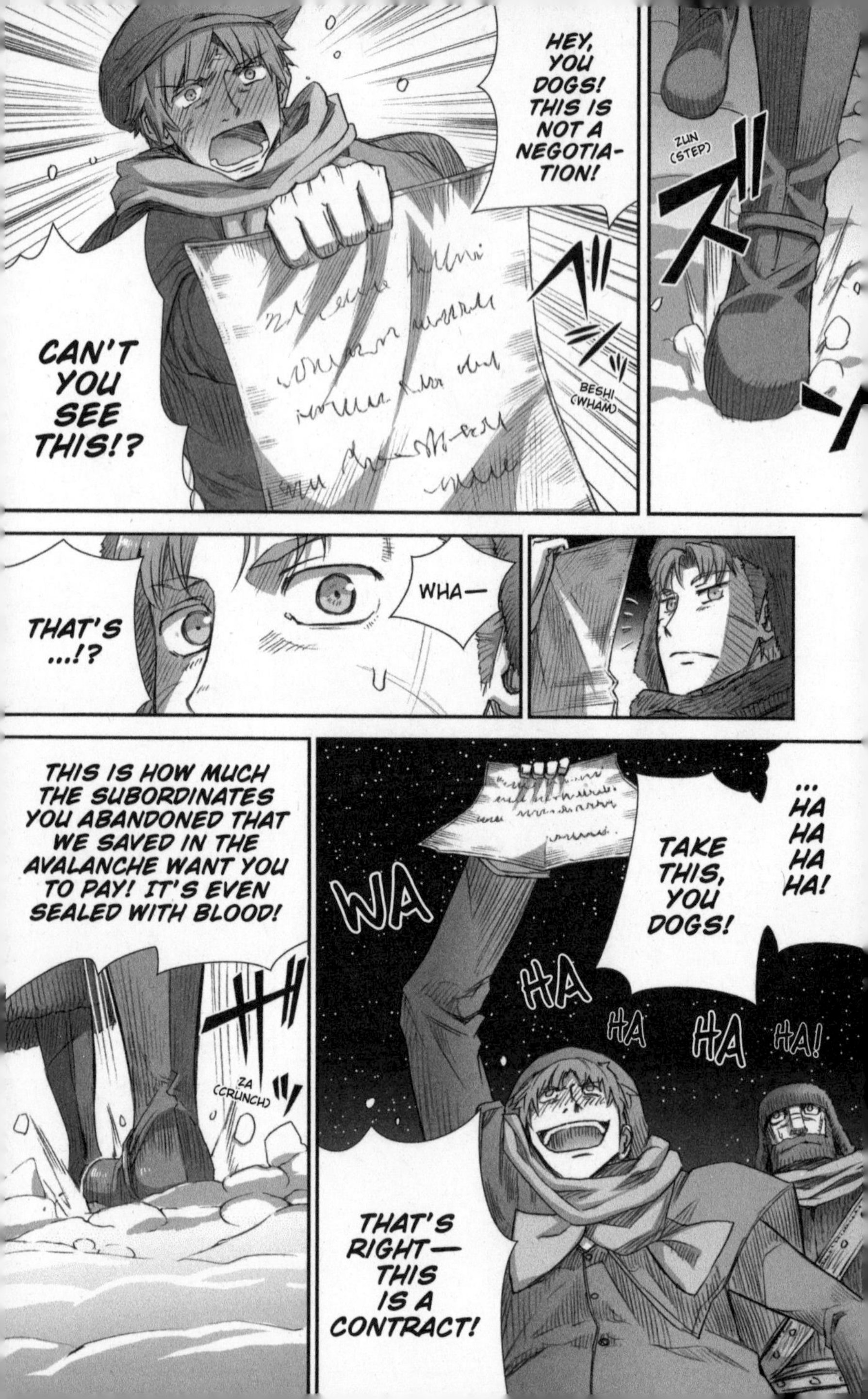
ZUN (STEP)
HEY, YOU DOGS! THIS IS NOT A NEGOTIATION!
BESHI (WHAM)
CAN'T YOU SEE THIS!?
WHA—
THAT'S ...!?
...HA HA HA HA!
TAKE THIS, YOU DOGS!
WA HA HA HA HA!
THAT'S RIGHT—THIS IS A CONTRACT!
THIS IS HOW MUCH THE SUBORDINATES YOU ABANDONED THAT WE SAVED IN THE AVALANCHE WANT YOU TO PAY! IT'S EVEN SEALED WITH BLOOD!
ZA (CRUNCH)

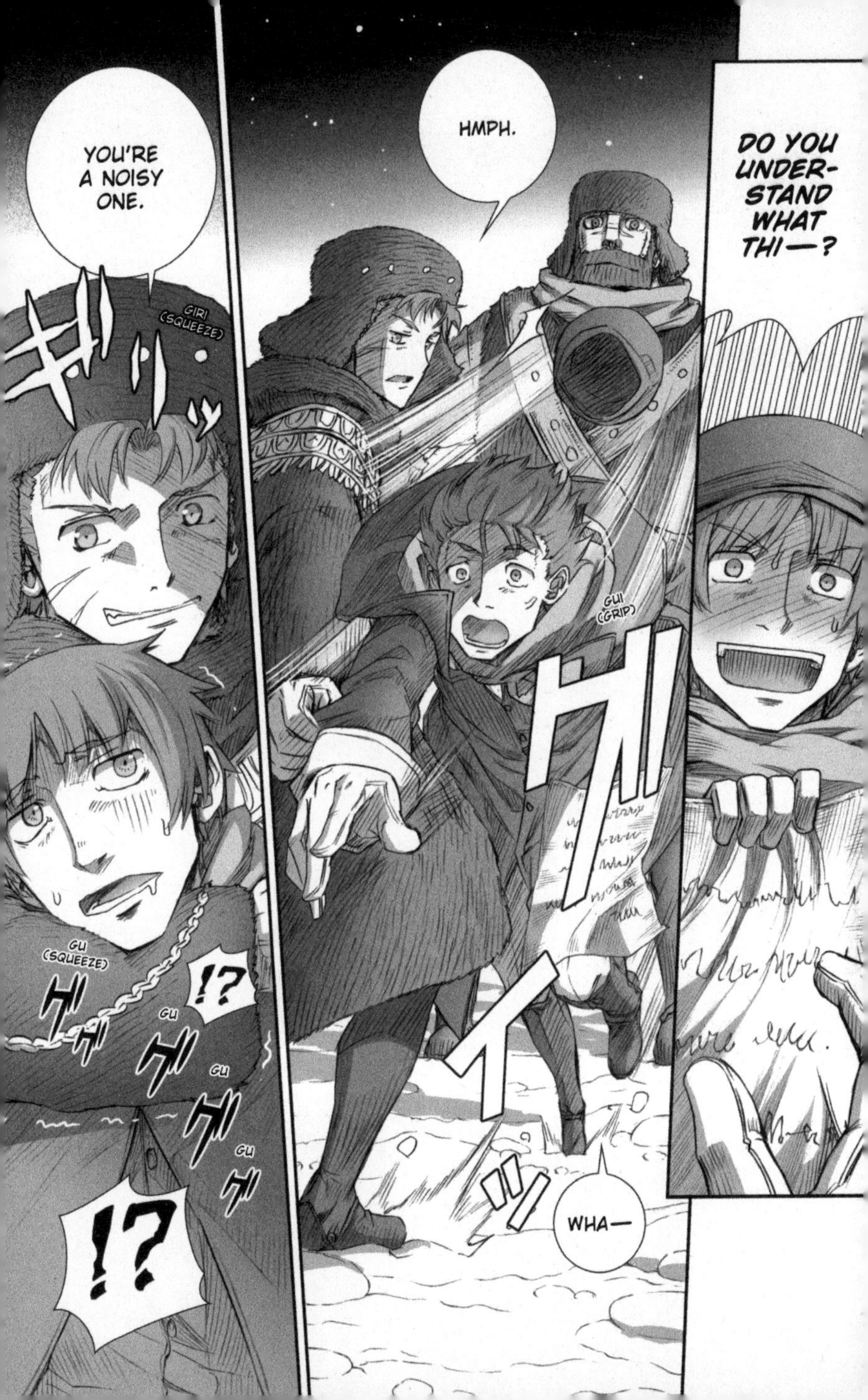

DO YOU UNDER-STAND WHAT THI—?
HMPH.
GUI (GRIP)
WHA—
YOU'RE A NOISY ONE.
GIRI (SQUEEZE)
GU (SQUEEZE)
!?
GU
GU
GU
!?

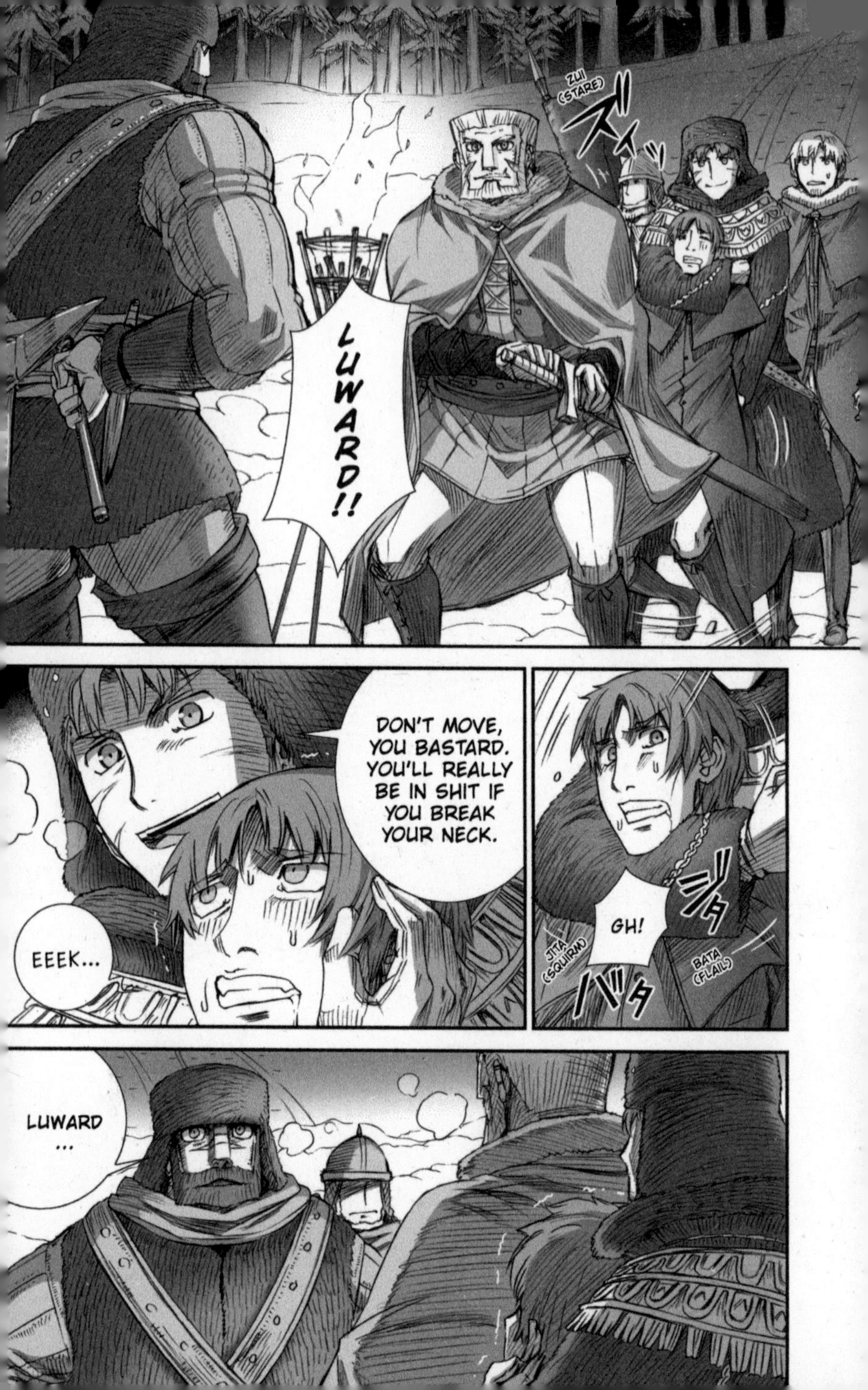
ZUI (STARE)
LUWARD!!
GH!
BATA (FLAIL)
JITA (SQUIRM)
DON'T MOVE, YOU BASTARD. YOU'LL REALLY BE IN SHIT IF YOU BREAK YOUR NECK.
EEEK...
LUWARD ...

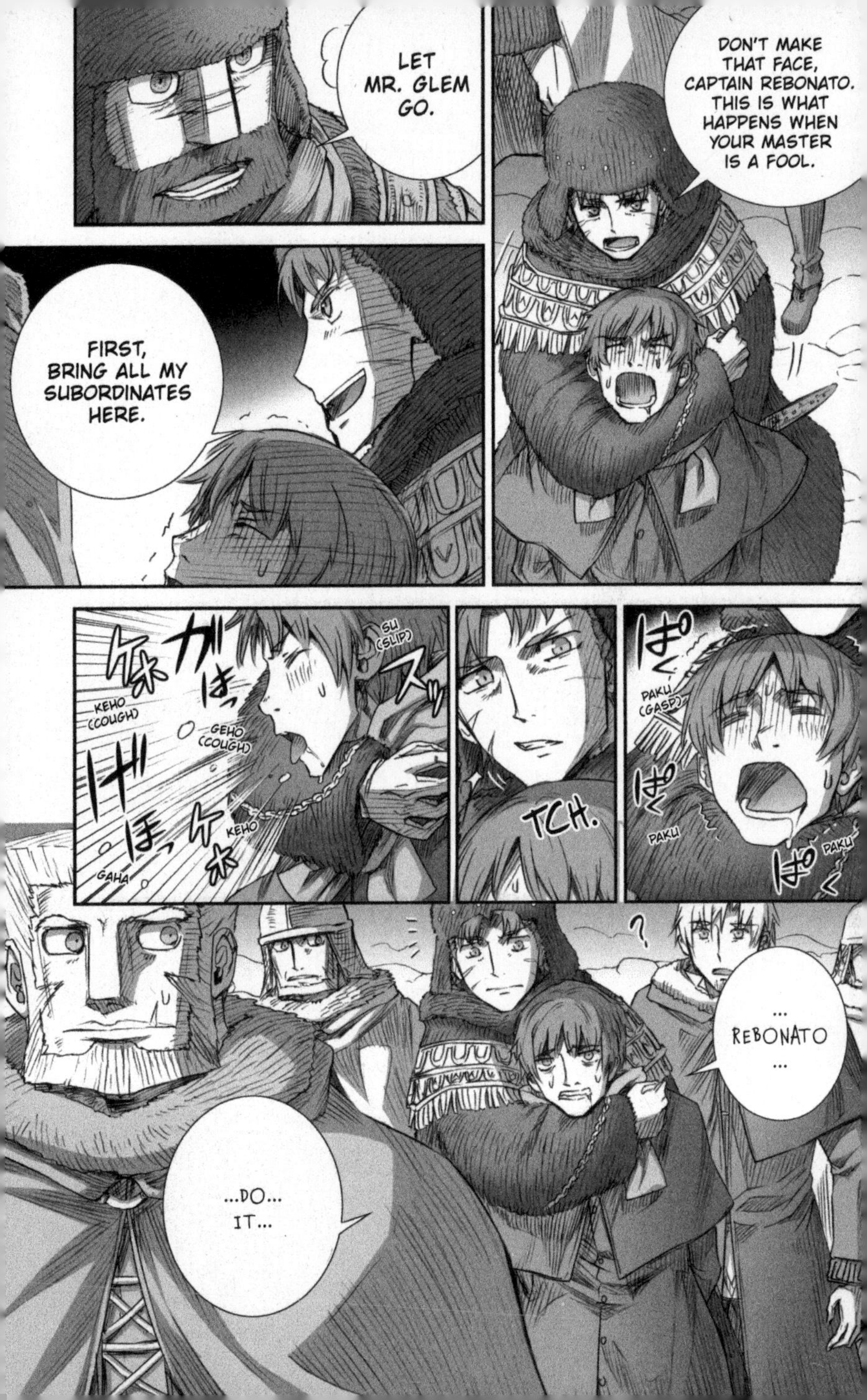
DON'T MAKE THAT FACE, CAPTAIN REBONATO. THIS IS WHAT HAPPENS WHEN YOUR MASTER IS A FOOL.
LET MR. GLEM GO.
FIRST, BRING ALL MY SUBORDINATES HERE.
ぱく
PAKU (GASP)
ぱく
PAKU
ぱく
PAKU
TCH.
SU (SLIP)
スッ
がはっ
GAHA
ケホ
KEHO (COUGH)
げほっ
GEHO (COUGH)
ケホ
KEHO
... REBONATO ...
...DO... IT...

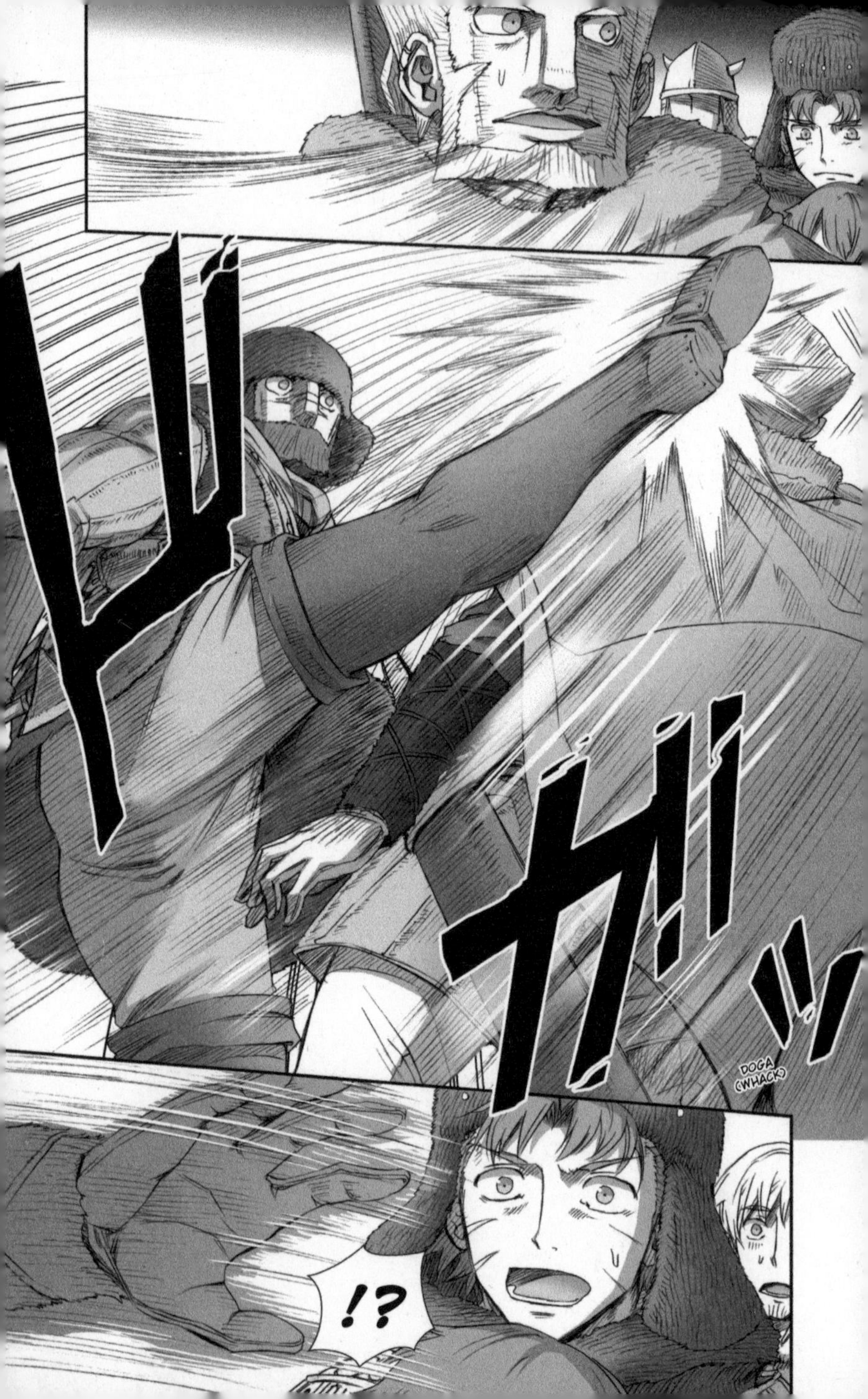
ドガ!!ッ
DOGA (WHACK)
!?

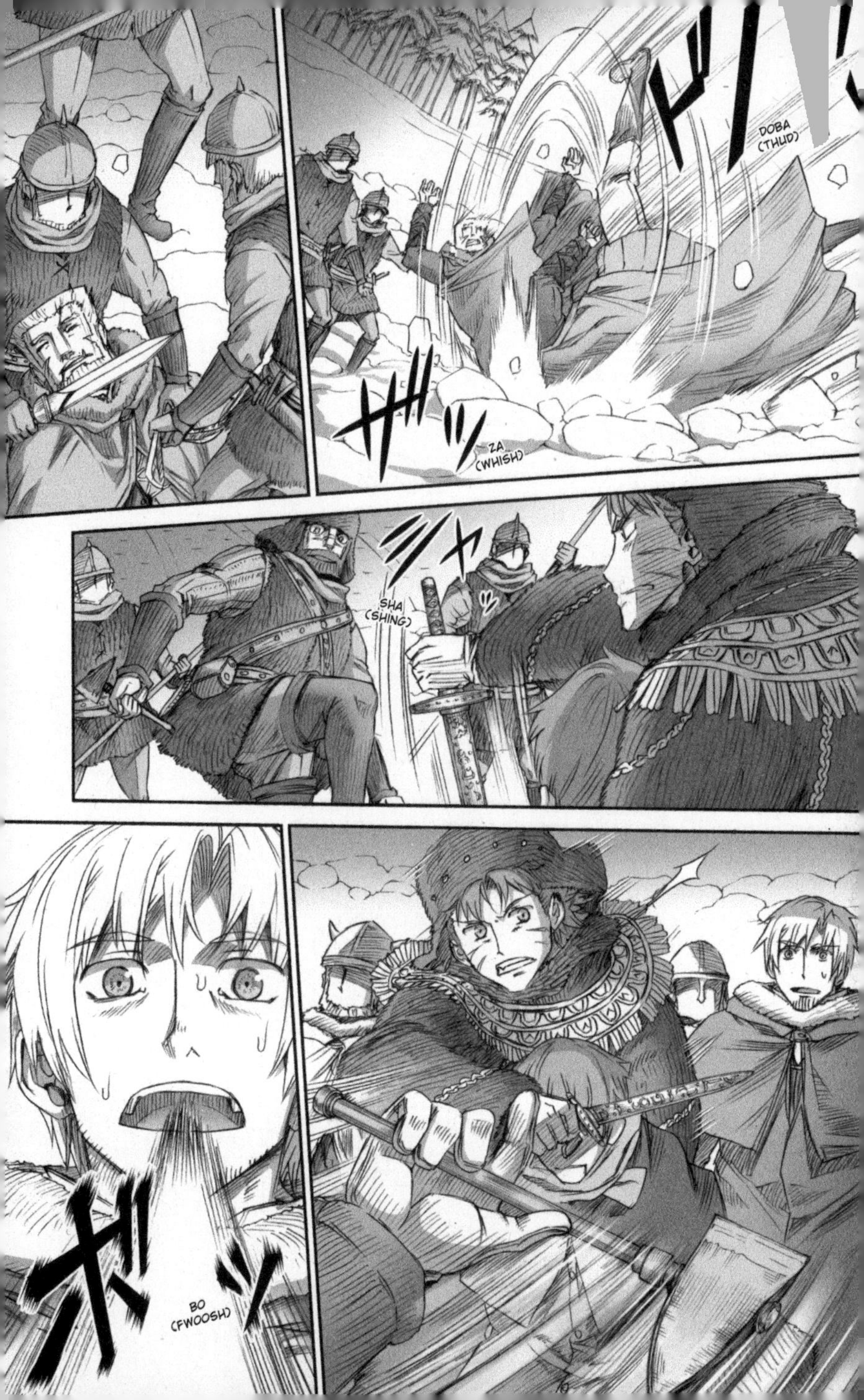
DOBA (THUD)
ZA (WHISH)
SHA (SHING)
BO (FWOOSH)

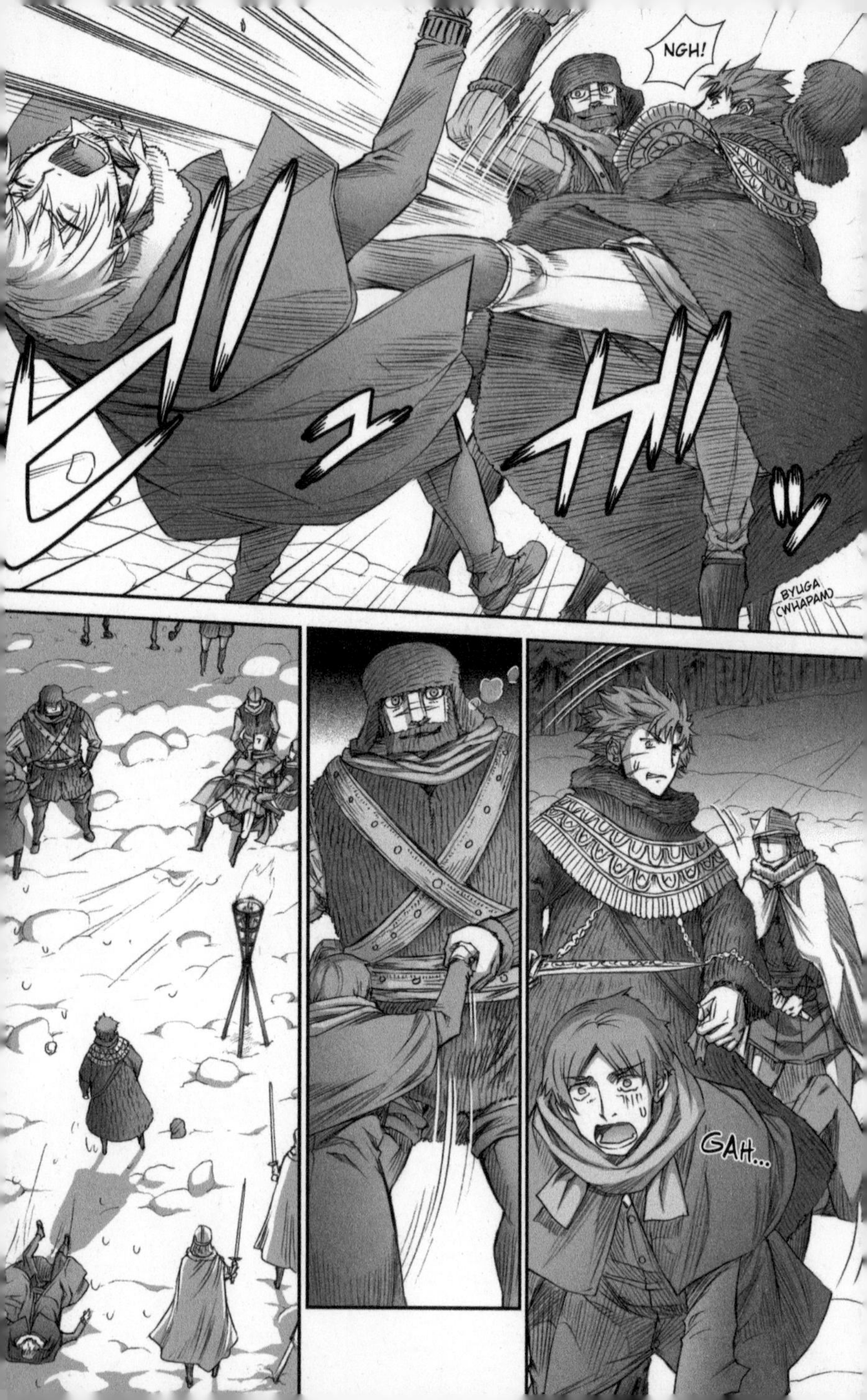
NGH!
BYUGA
(WHAPAM)
GAH...

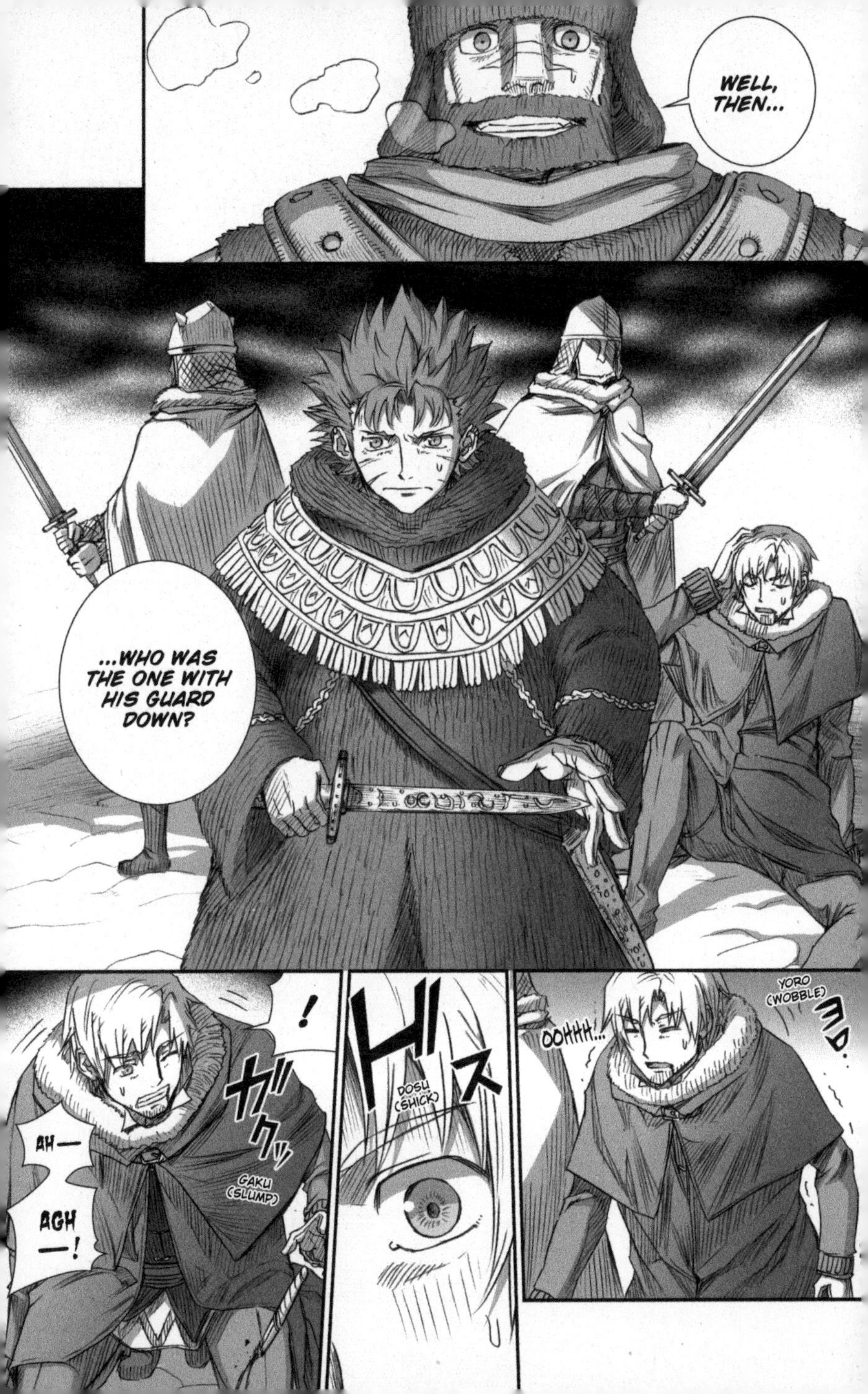
WELL, THEN...
...WHO WAS THE ONE WITH HIS GUARD DOWN?
ヨロ
YORO (WOBBLE)
OOHHH...
ドス
DOSU (SHICK)
!
ガクッ
GAKU (SLUMP)
AH—
AGH—!

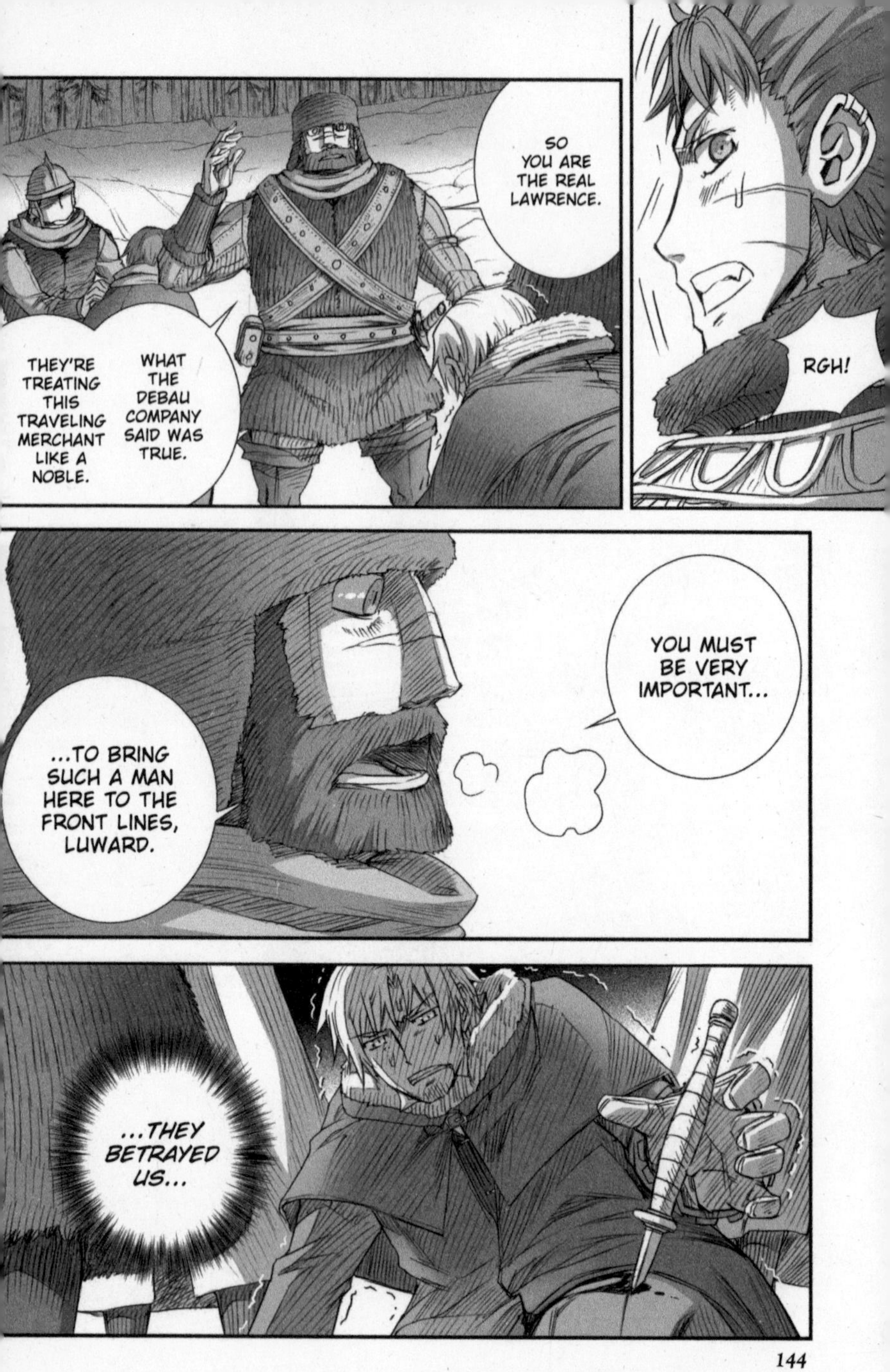
RGH!
SO YOU ARE THE REAL LAWRENCE.
WHAT THE DEBAU COMPANY SAID WAS TRUE.
THEY'RE TREATING THIS TRAVELING MERCHANT LIKE A NOBLE.
YOU MUST BE VERY IMPORTANT...
...TO BRING SUCH A MAN HERE TO THE FRONT LINES, LUWARD.
...THEY BETRAYED US...

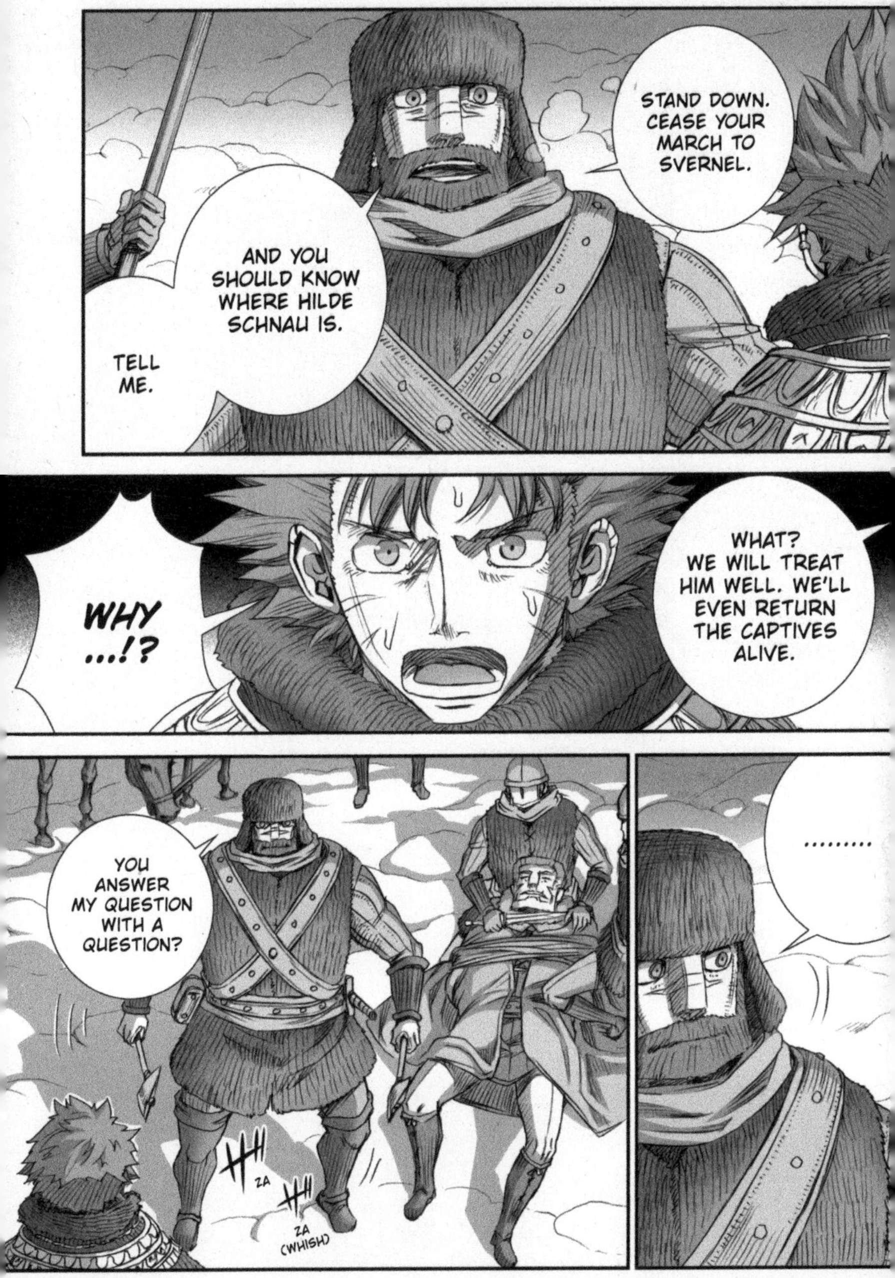
STAND DOWN. CEASE YOUR MARCH TO SVERNEL.
AND YOU SHOULD KNOW WHERE HILDE SCHNAU IS.
TELL ME.
WHAT? WE WILL TREAT HIM WELL. WE'LL EVEN RETURN THE CAPTIVES ALIVE.
WHY ...!?
....
YOU ANSWER MY QUESTION WITH A QUESTION?
ZA
ZA (WHISH)

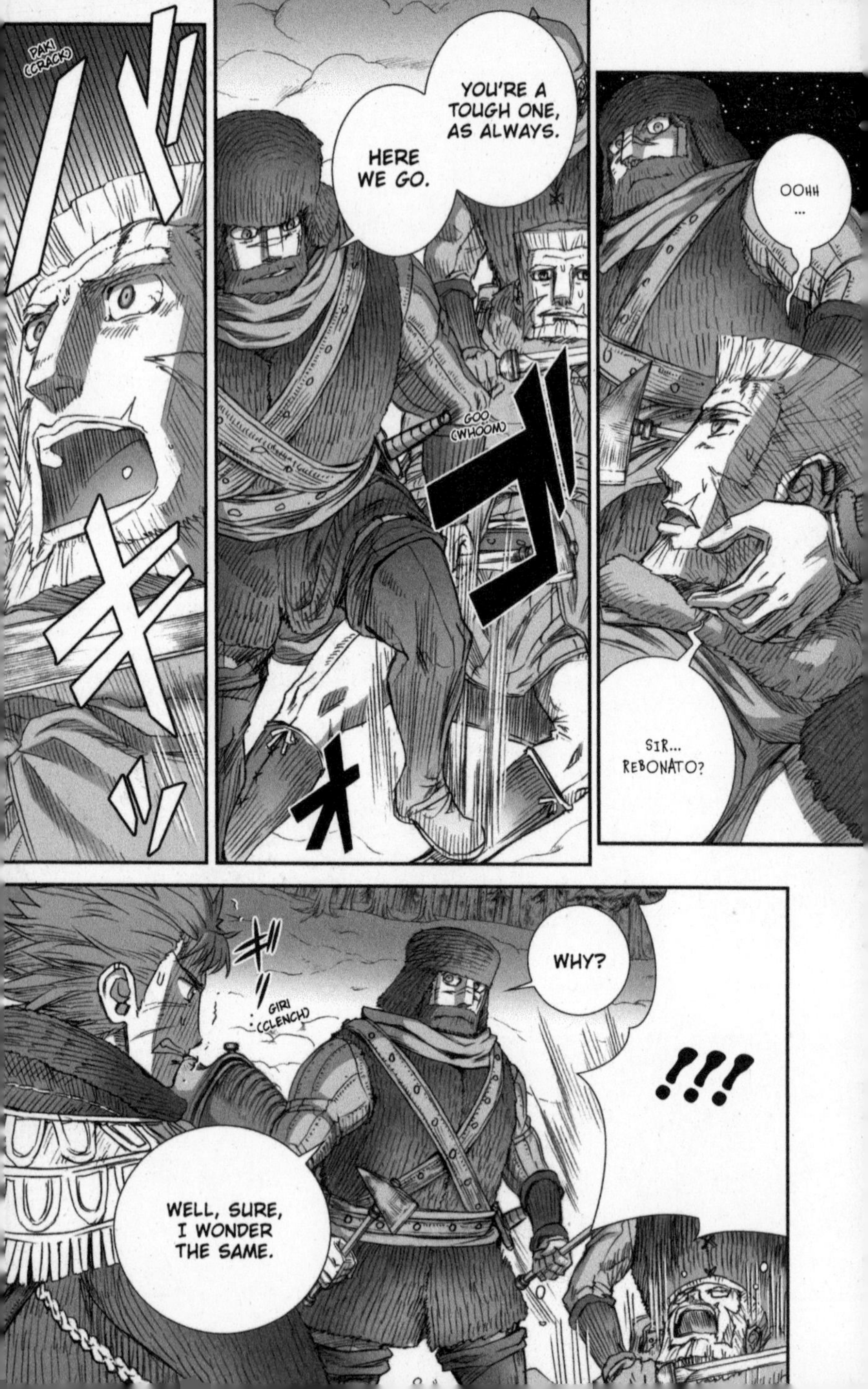
OOHH ...
SIR... REBONATO?
YOU'RE A TOUGH ONE, AS ALWAYS.
HERE WE GO.
GOO (WHOOM)
PAKI (CRACK)
WHY?
!!!
GIRI (CLENCH)
WELL, SURE, I WONDER THE SAME.

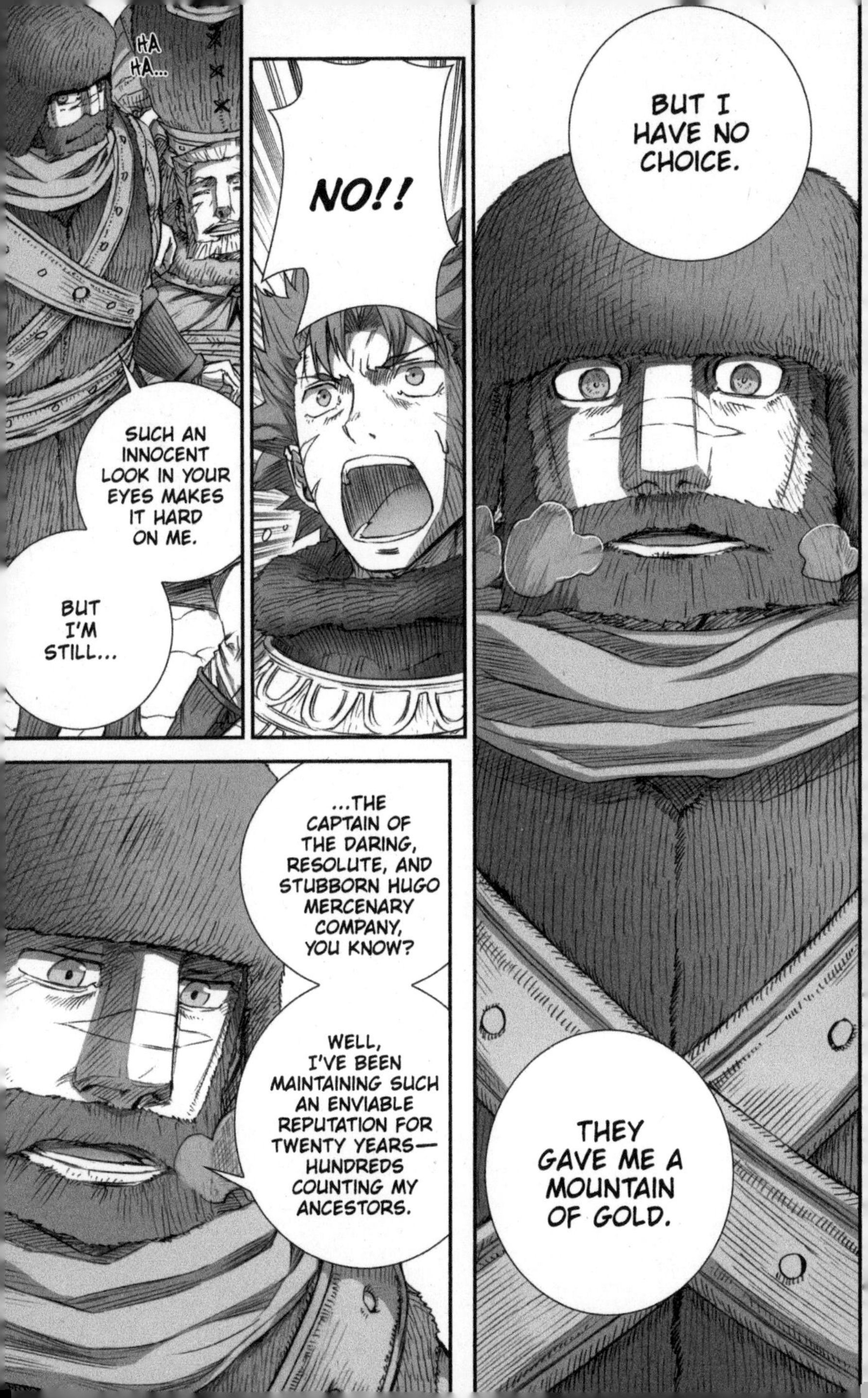
BUT I HAVE NO CHOICE.
THEY GAVE ME A MOUNTAIN OF GOLD.
NO!!
HA HA...
SUCH AN INNOCENT LOOK IN YOUR EYES MAKES IT HARD ON ME.
BUT I'M STILL...
...THE CAPTAIN OF THE DARING, RESOLUTE, AND STUBBORN HUGO MERCENARY COMPANY, YOU KNOW?
WELL, I'VE BEEN MAINTAINING SUCH AN ENVIABLE REPUTATION FOR TWENTY YEARS—HUNDREDS COUNTING MY ANCESTORS.

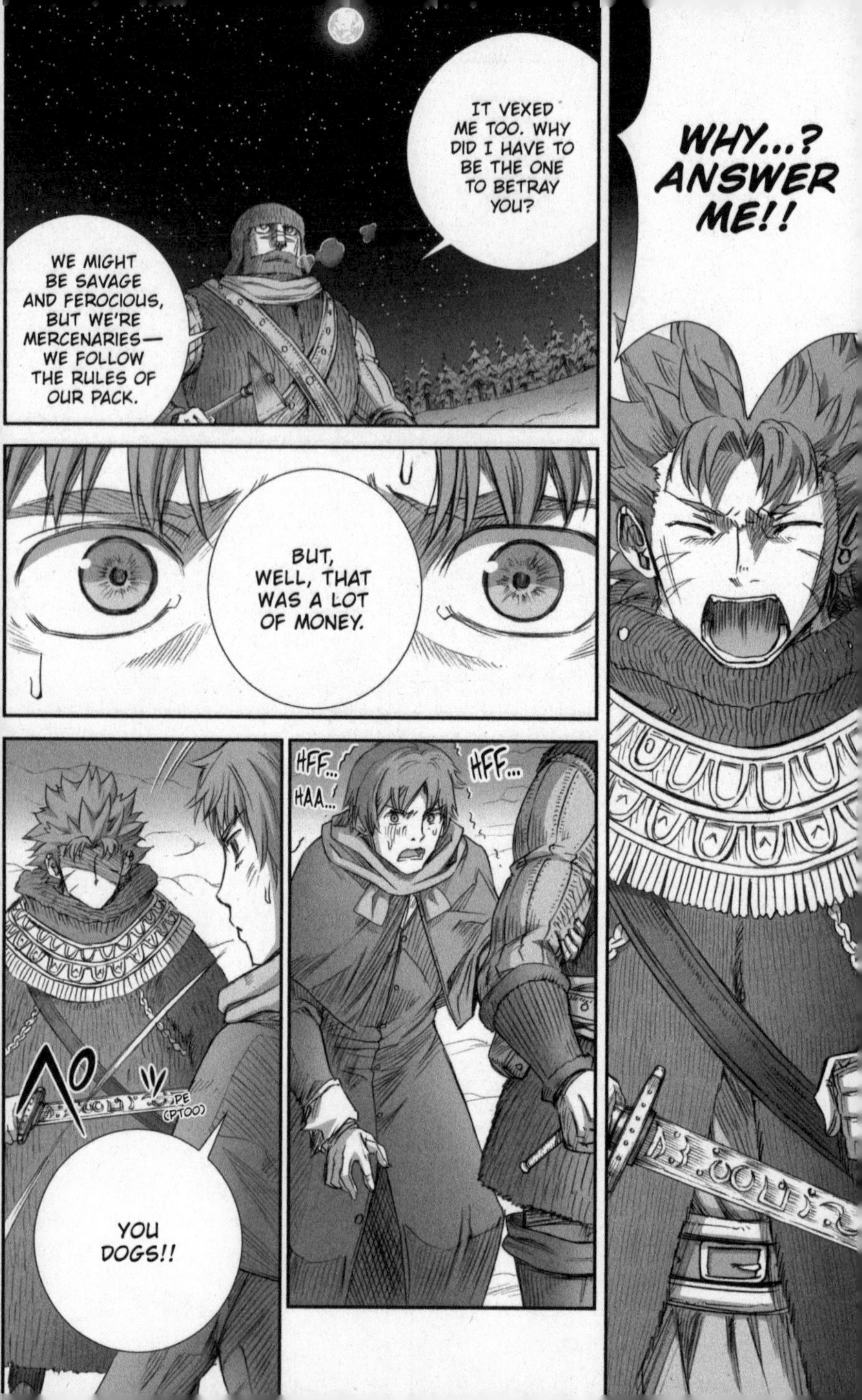
WHY...? ANSWER ME!!
IT VEXED ME TOO. WHY DID I HAVE TO BE THE ONE TO BETRAY YOU?
WE MIGHT BE SAVAGE AND FEROCIOUS, BUT WE'RE MERCENARIES— WE FOLLOW THE RULES OF OUR PACK.
BUT, WELL, THAT WAS A LOT OF MONEY.
HFF...
HFF... HAA...
PE (PTOO)
YOU DOGS!!

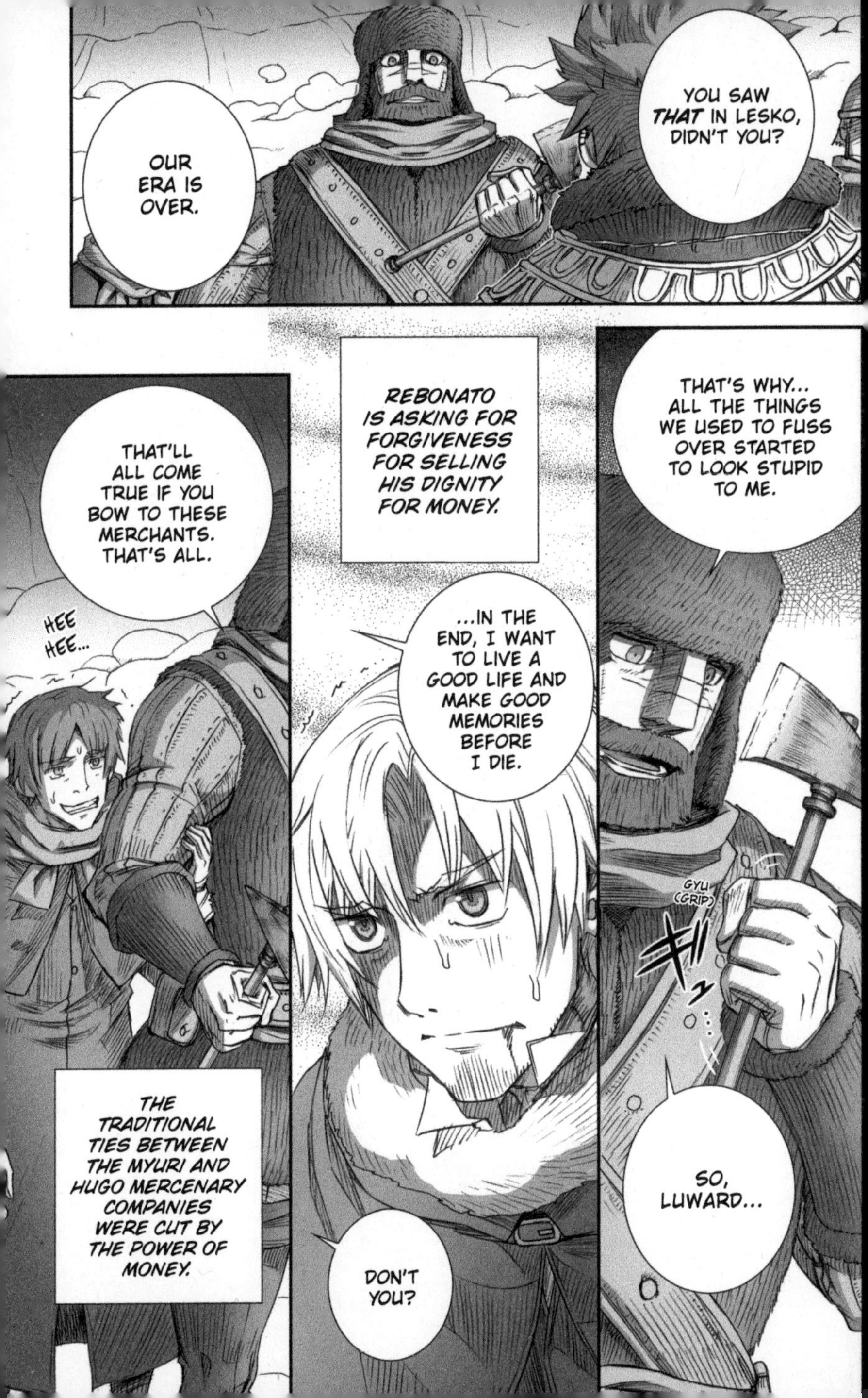
YOU SAW *THAT* IN LESKO, DIDN'T YOU?
OUR ERA IS OVER.
THAT'S WHY... ALL THE THINGS WE USED TO FUSS OVER STARTED TO LOOK STUPID TO ME.
GYU (GRIP)
SO, LUWARD...
REBONATO IS ASKING FOR FORGIVENESS FOR SELLING HIS DIGNITY FOR MONEY.
...IN THE END, I WANT TO LIVE A GOOD LIFE AND MAKE GOOD MEMORIES BEFORE I DIE.
DON'T YOU?
THAT'LL ALL COME TRUE IF YOU BOW TO THESE MERCHANTS. THAT'S ALL.
HEE HEE...
THE TRADITIONAL TIES BETWEEN THE MYURI AND HUGO MERCENARY COMPANIES WERE CUT BY THE POWER OF MONEY.

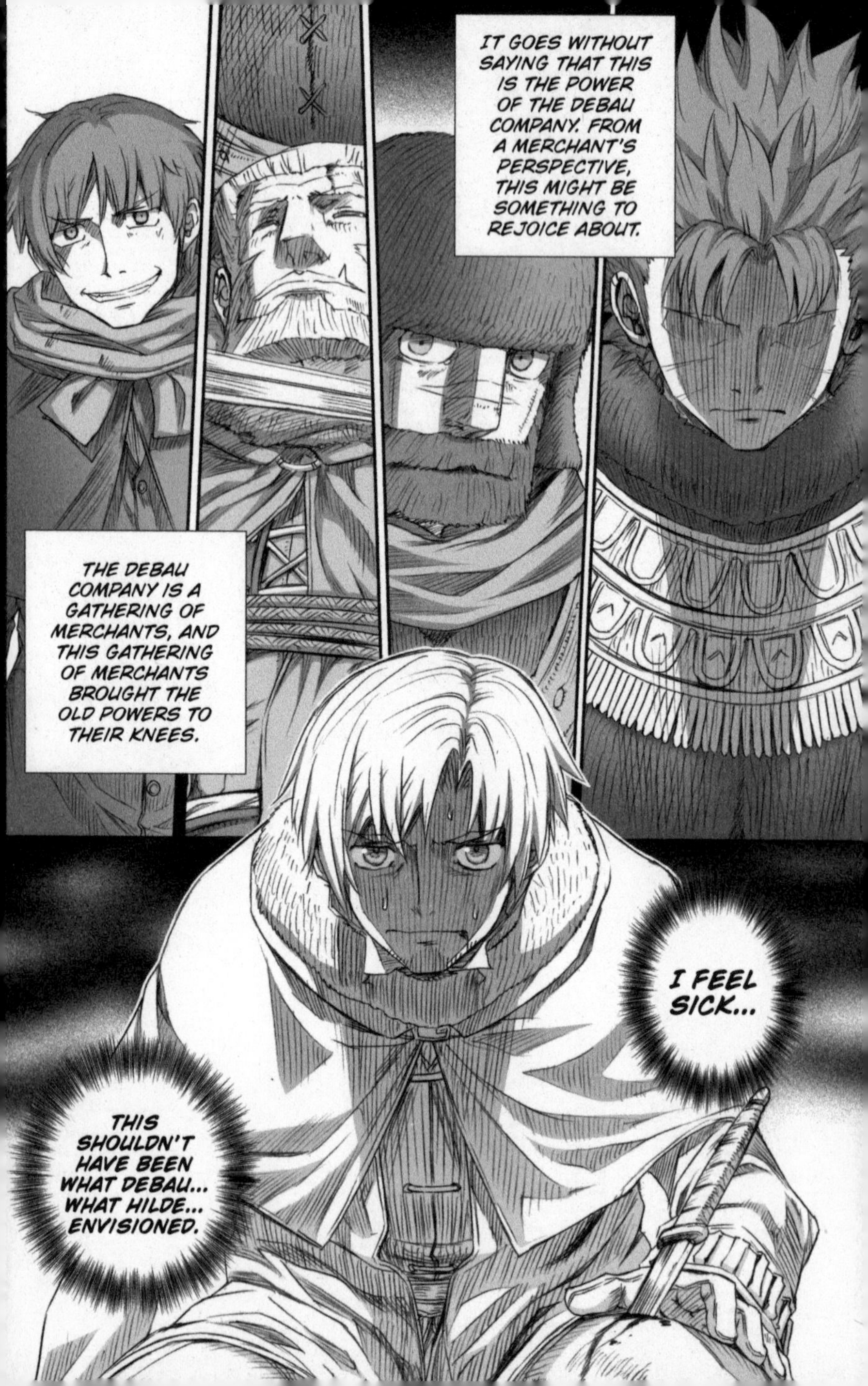
IT GOES WITHOUT SAYING THAT THIS IS THE POWER OF THE DEBAU COMPANY. FROM A MERCHANT'S PERSPECTIVE, THIS MIGHT BE SOMETHING TO REJOICE ABOUT.
THE DEBAU COMPANY IS A GATHERING OF MERCHANTS, AND THIS GATHERING OF MERCHANTS BROUGHT THE OLD POWERS TO THEIR KNEES.
I FEEL SICK...
THIS SHOULDN'T HAVE BEEN WHAT DEBAU... WHAT HILDE... ENVISIONED.

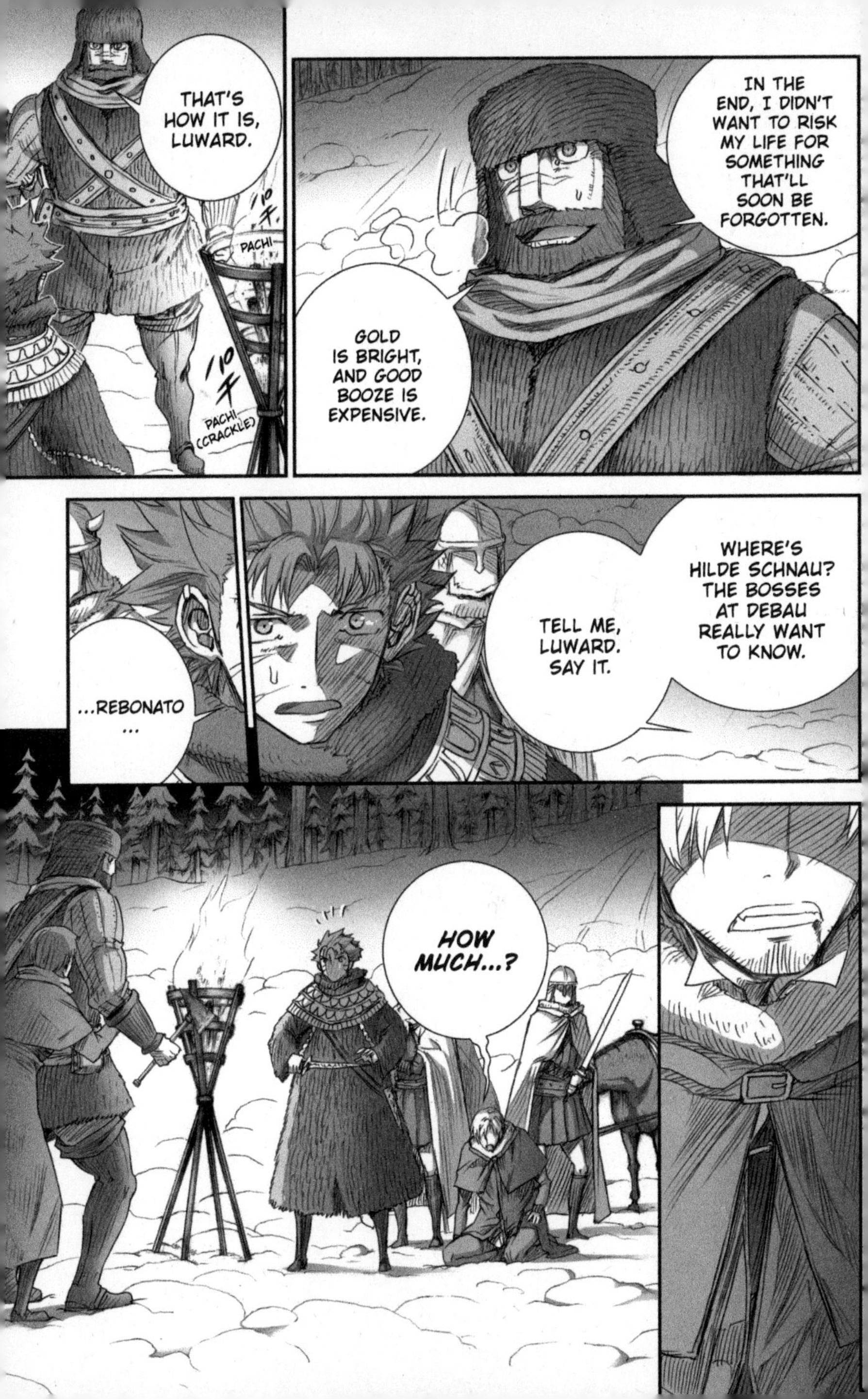
IN THE END, I DIDN'T WANT TO RISK MY LIFE FOR SOMETHING THAT'LL SOON BE FORGOTTEN.
GOLD IS BRIGHT, AND GOOD BOOZE IS EXPENSIVE.
THAT'S HOW IT IS, LUWARD.
PACHI
PACHI (CRACKLE)
WHERE'S HILDE SCHNAU? THE BOSSES AT DEBAU REALLY WANT TO KNOW.
TELL ME, LUWARD. SAY IT.
...REBONATO ...
HOW MUCH...?

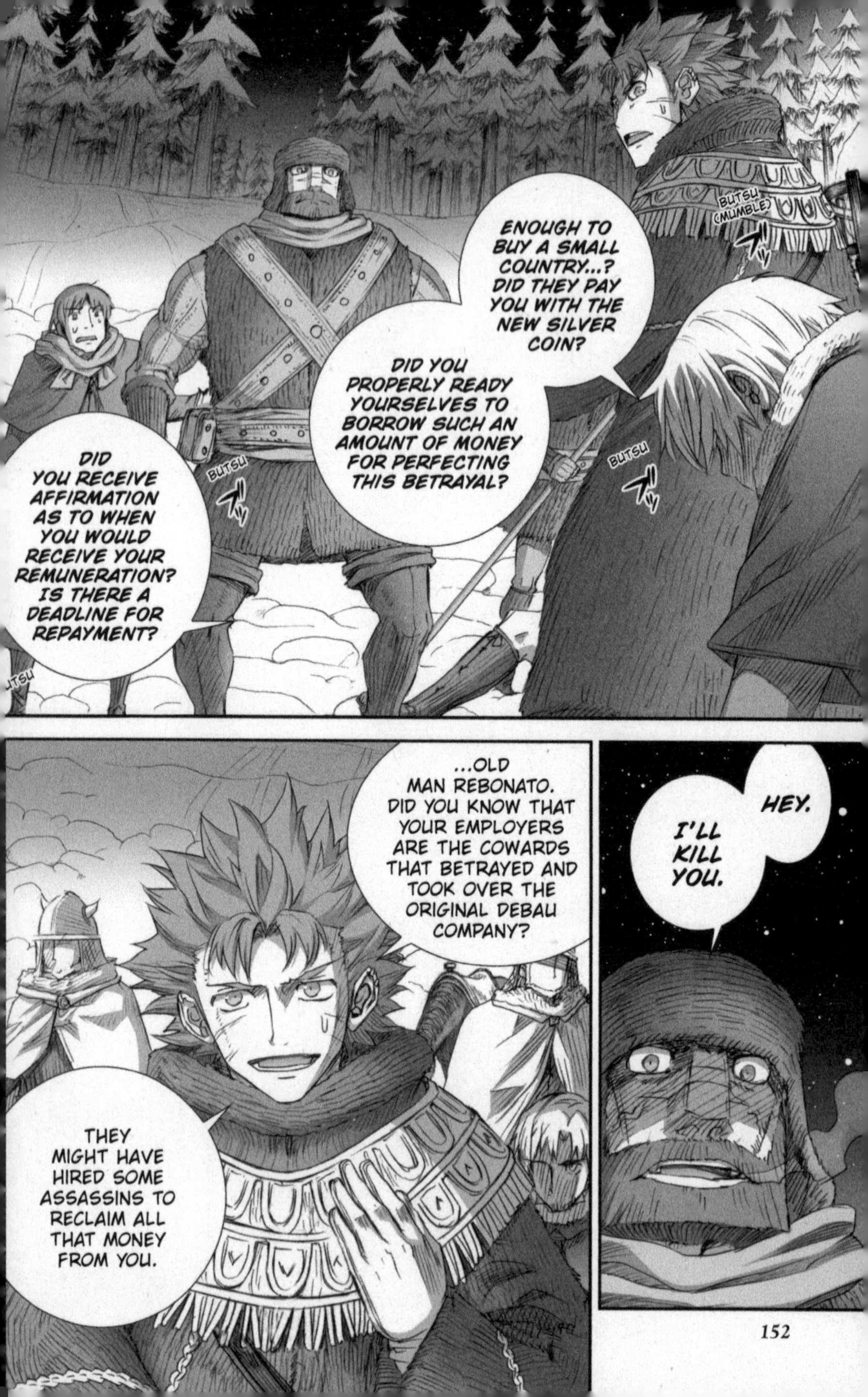

BUTSU (MUMBLE)
ENOUGH TO BUY A SMALL COUNTRY...? DID THEY PAY YOU WITH THE NEW SILVER COIN?
BUTSU
DID YOU PROPERLY READY YOURSELVES TO BORROW SUCH AN AMOUNT OF MONEY FOR PERFECTING THIS BETRAYAL?
BUTSU
DID YOU RECEIVE AFFIRMATION AS TO WHEN YOU WOULD RECEIVE YOUR REMUNERATION? IS THERE A DEADLINE FOR REPAYMENT?
HEY.
I'LL KILL YOU.
...OLD MAN REBONATO. DID YOU KNOW THAT YOUR EMPLOYERS ARE THE COWARDS THAT BETRAYED AND TOOK OVER THE ORIGINAL DEBAU COMPANY?
THEY MIGHT HAVE HIRED SOME ASSASSINS TO RECLAIM ALL THAT MONEY FROM YOU.

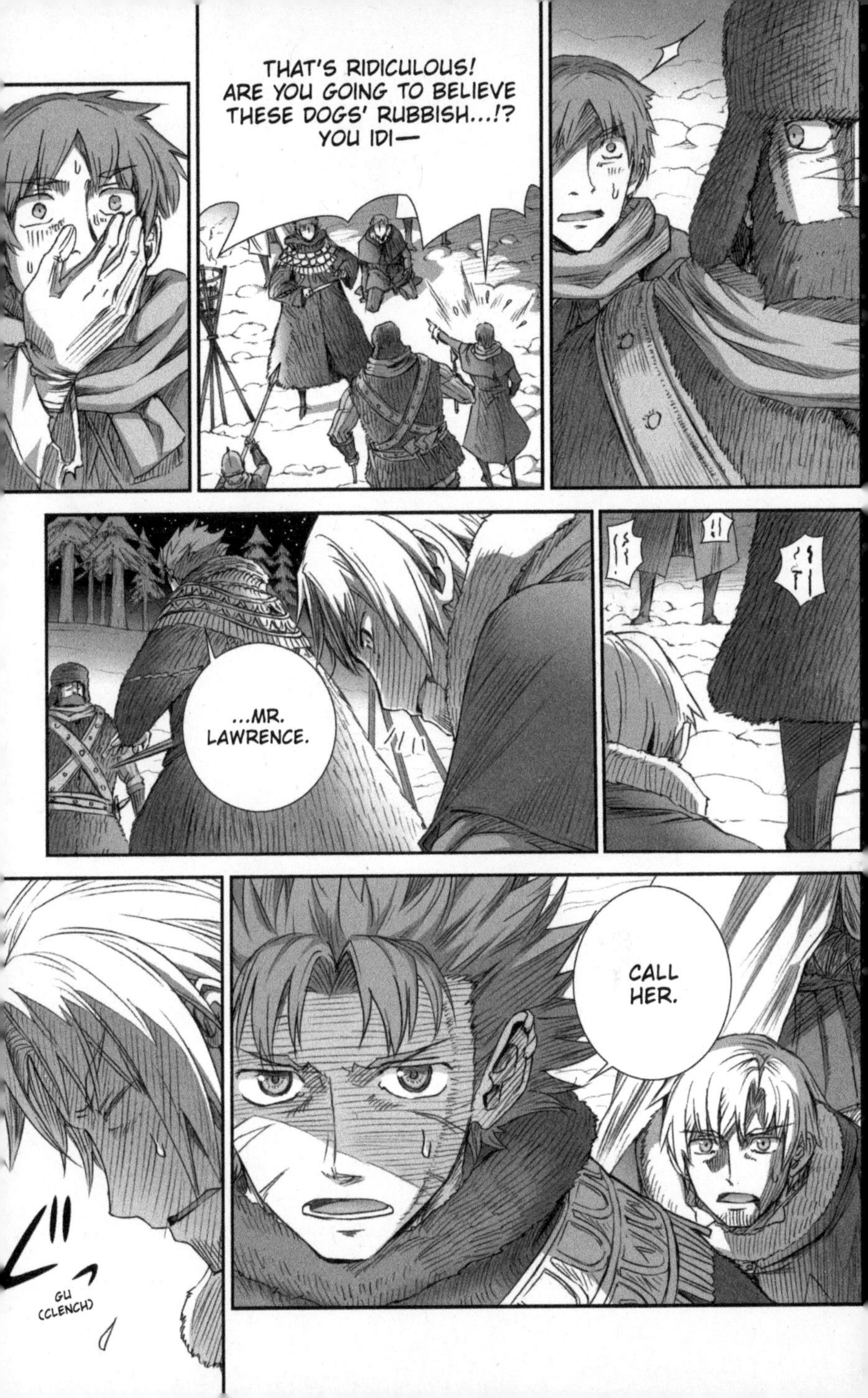
THAT'S RIDICULOUS! ARE YOU GOING TO BELIEVE THESE DOGS' RUBBISH...!? YOU IDI—
...MR. LAWRENCE.
CALL HER.
GU (CLENCH)

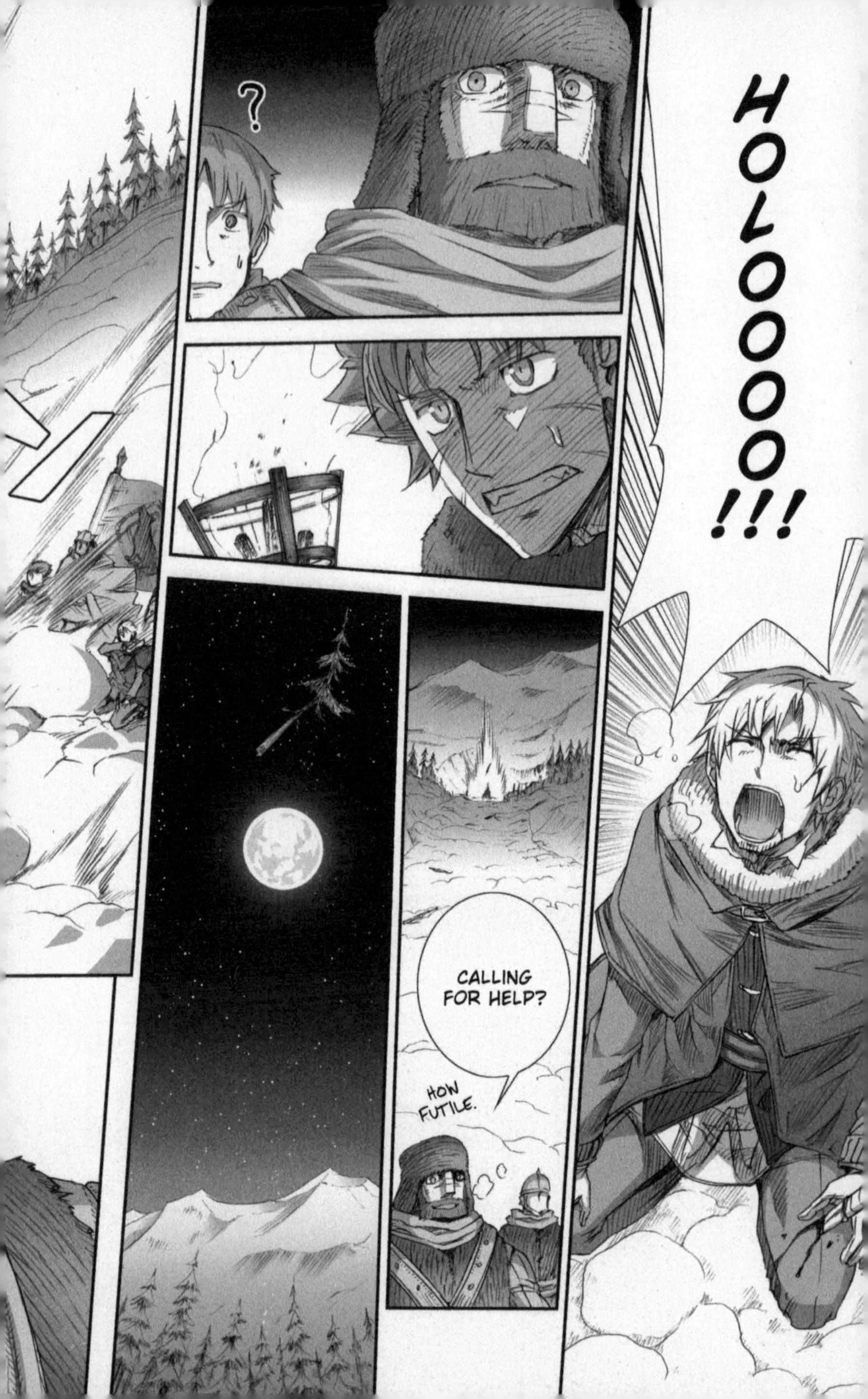
HOLOOOOO!!!
?
CALLING FOR HELP?
HOW FUTILE.

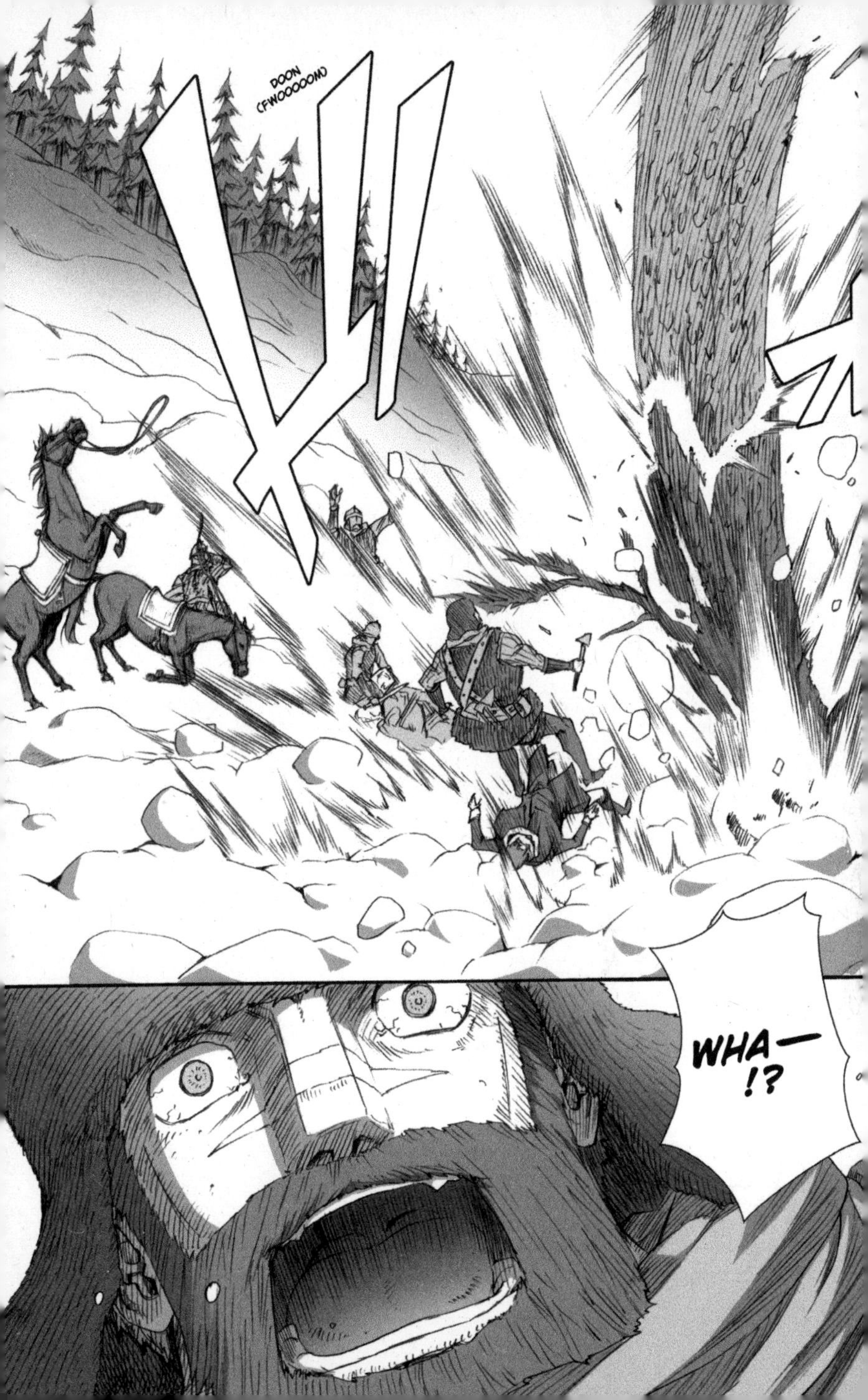
DOON
(FWOOOOOM)
WHA—!?

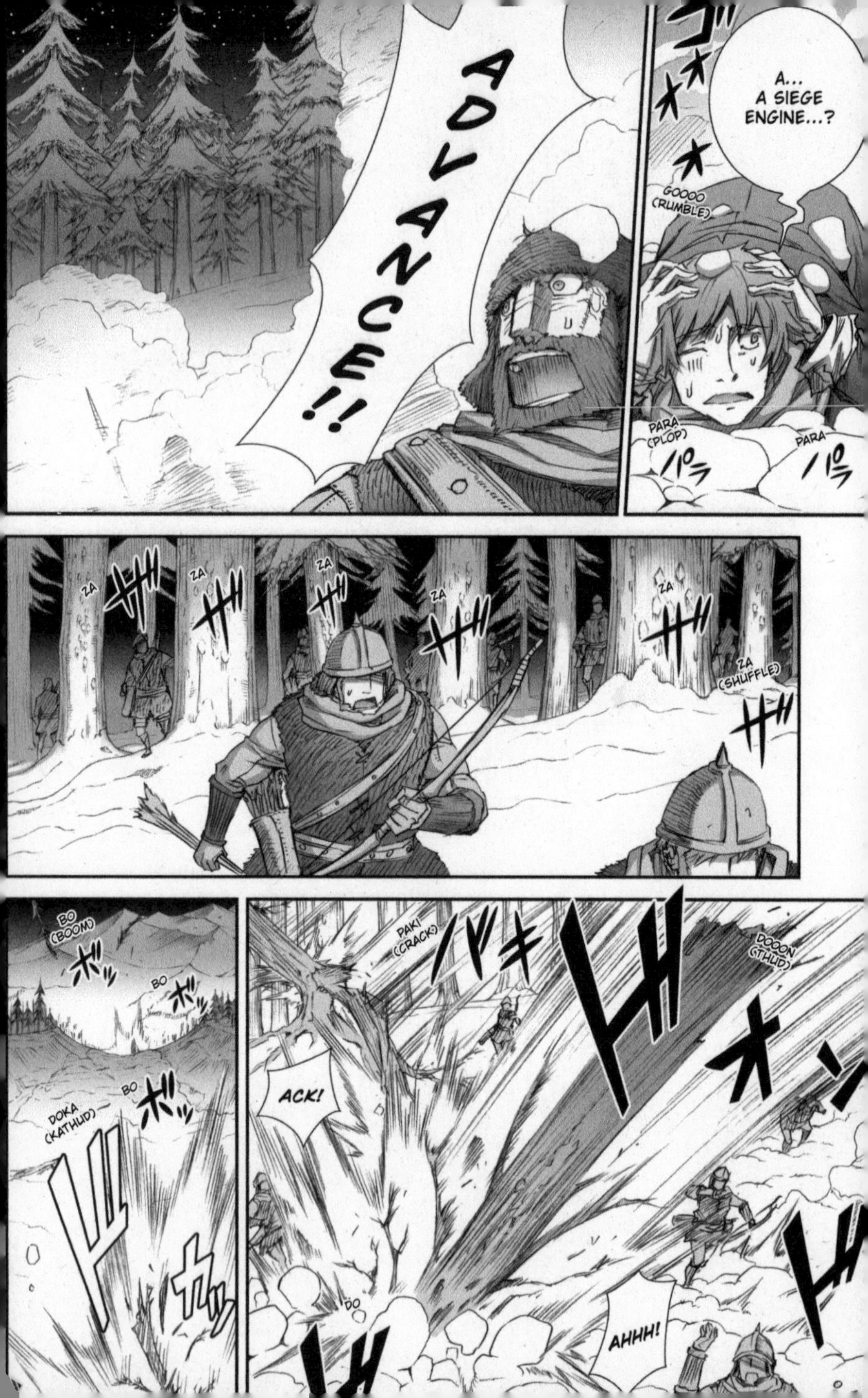

A... A SIEGE ENGINE...?
GOOOO (RUMBLE)
PARA (PLOP)
PARA
ADVANCE!!
ZA
ZA
ZA
ZA
ZA
ZA (SHUFFLE)
DOOON (THUD)
PAKI (CRACK)
ACK!
AHHH!
DO
BO (BOOM)
BO
BO
DOKA (KATHUD)

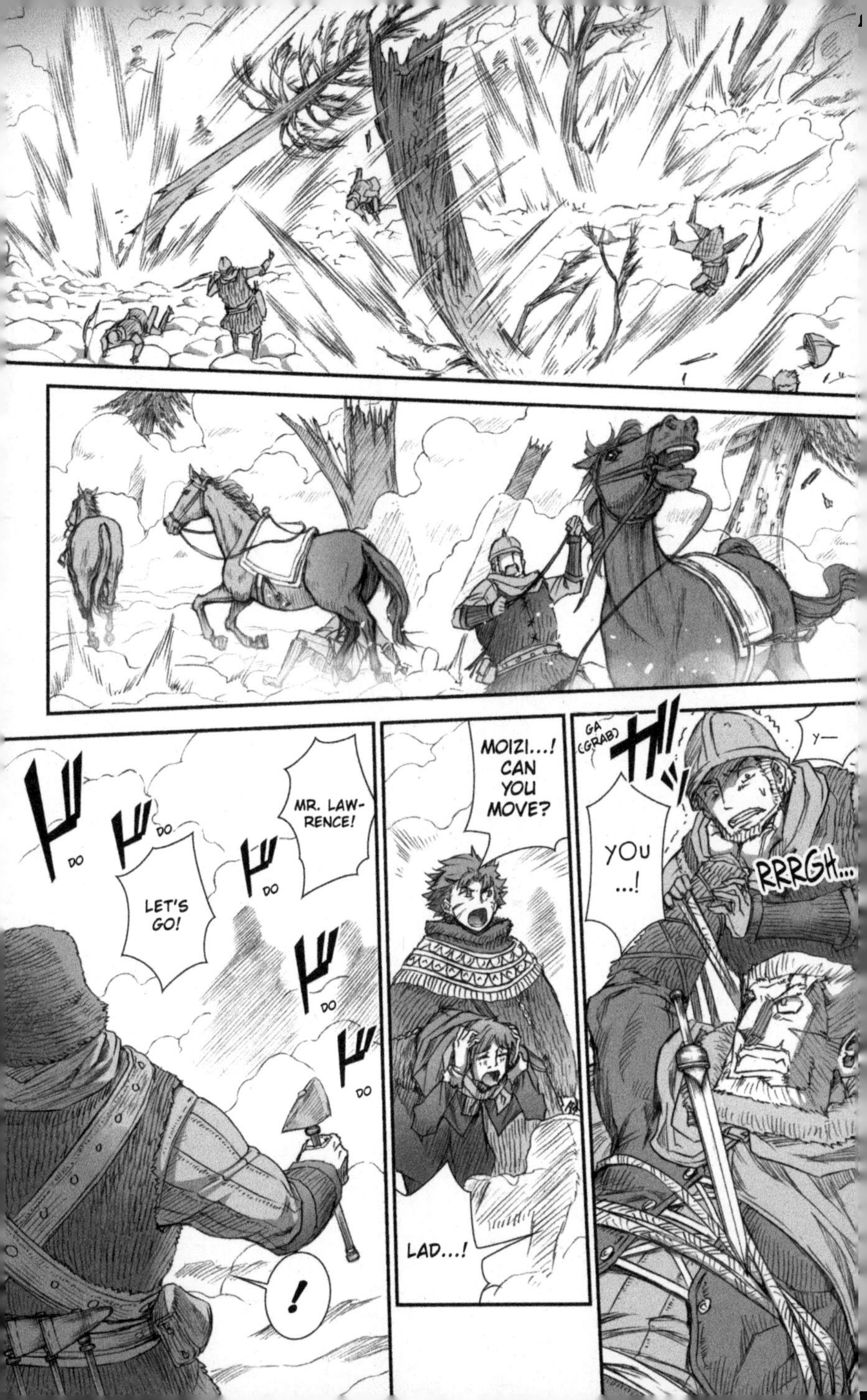
GA (GRAB)
Y—
YOU ...!
RRRGH...
MOIZI...! CAN YOU MOVE?
LAD...!
MR. LAW-RENCE!
LET'S GO!
DO
DO
DO
DO
DO
!

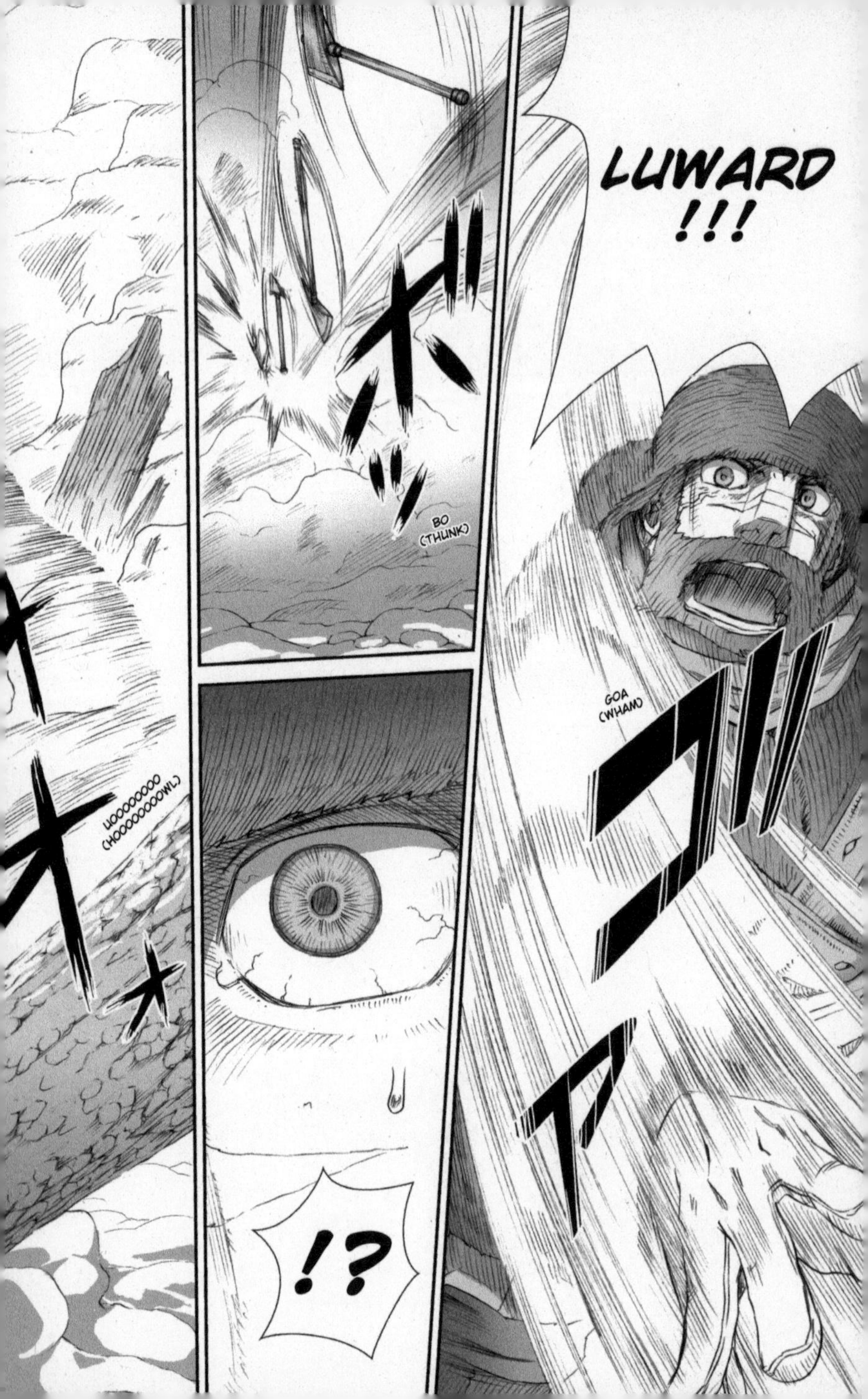
LUWARD!!!
GOA (WHAM)
BO (THUNK)
!?
UOOOOOOOO (HOOOOOOOOOWL)

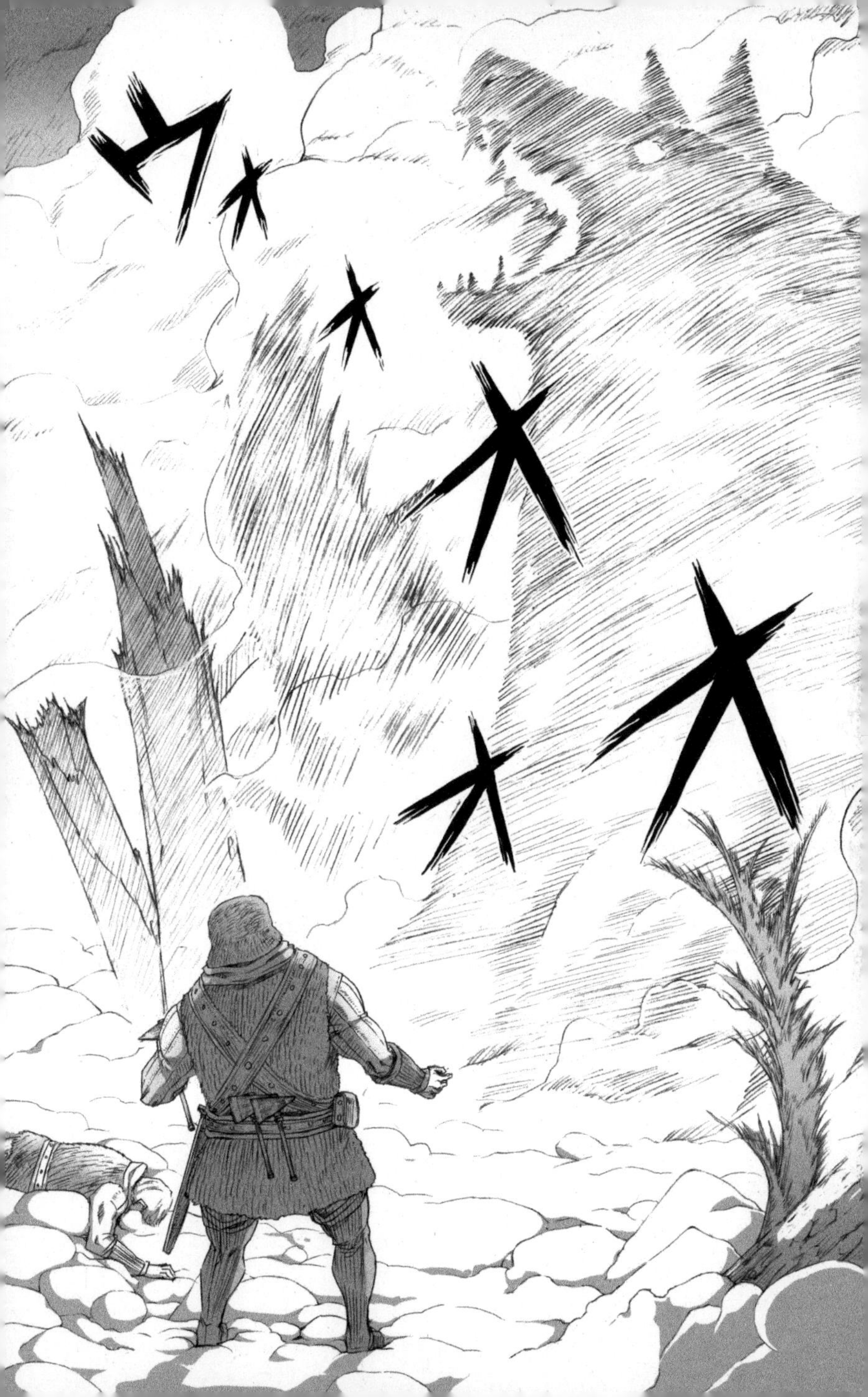
ウォォオオオ

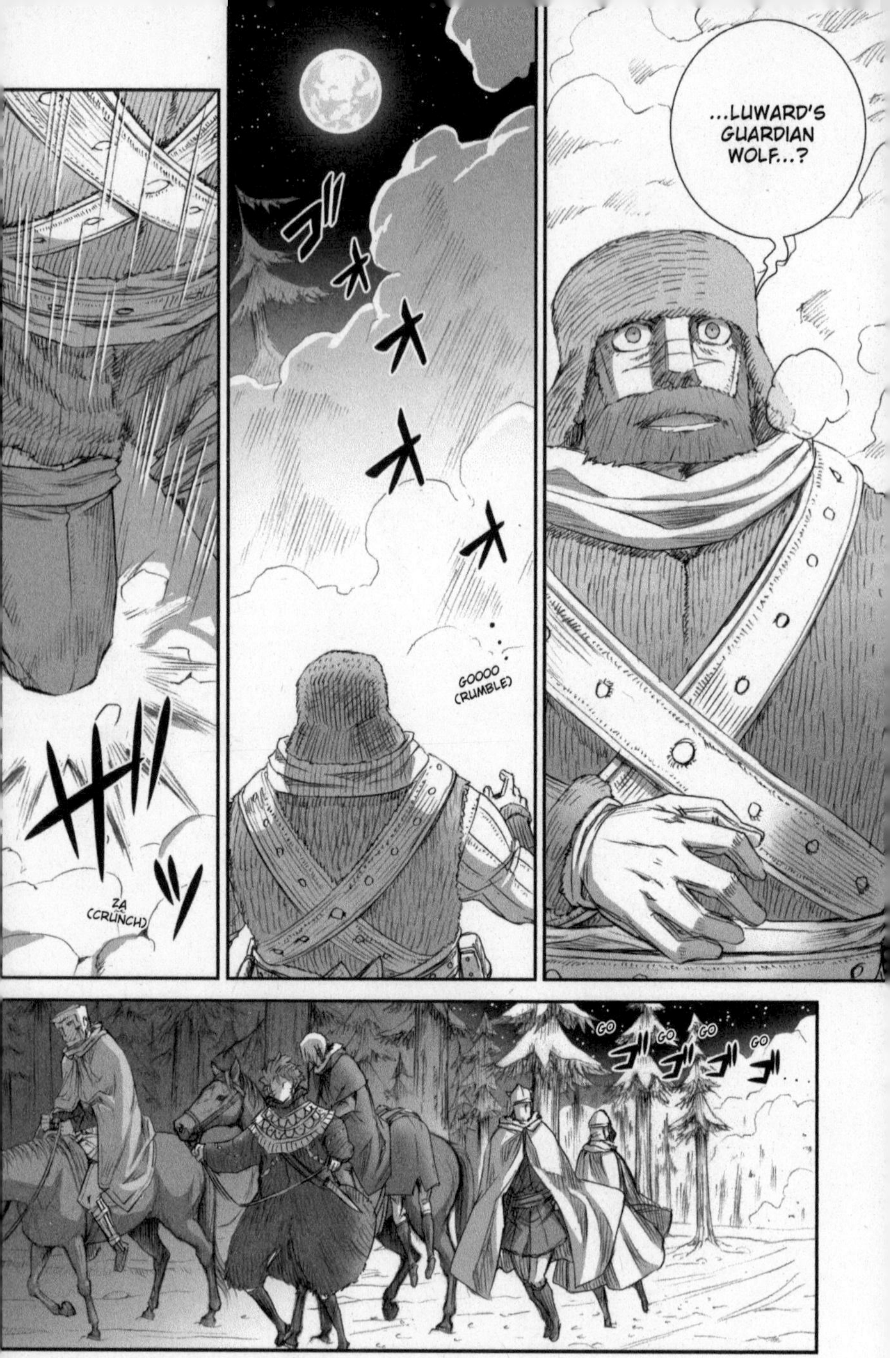
...LUWARD'S GUARDIAN WOLF...?
GOOOO (RUMBLE)
ZA (CRUNCH)
GO GO GO GO

To be continued in Volume 16...

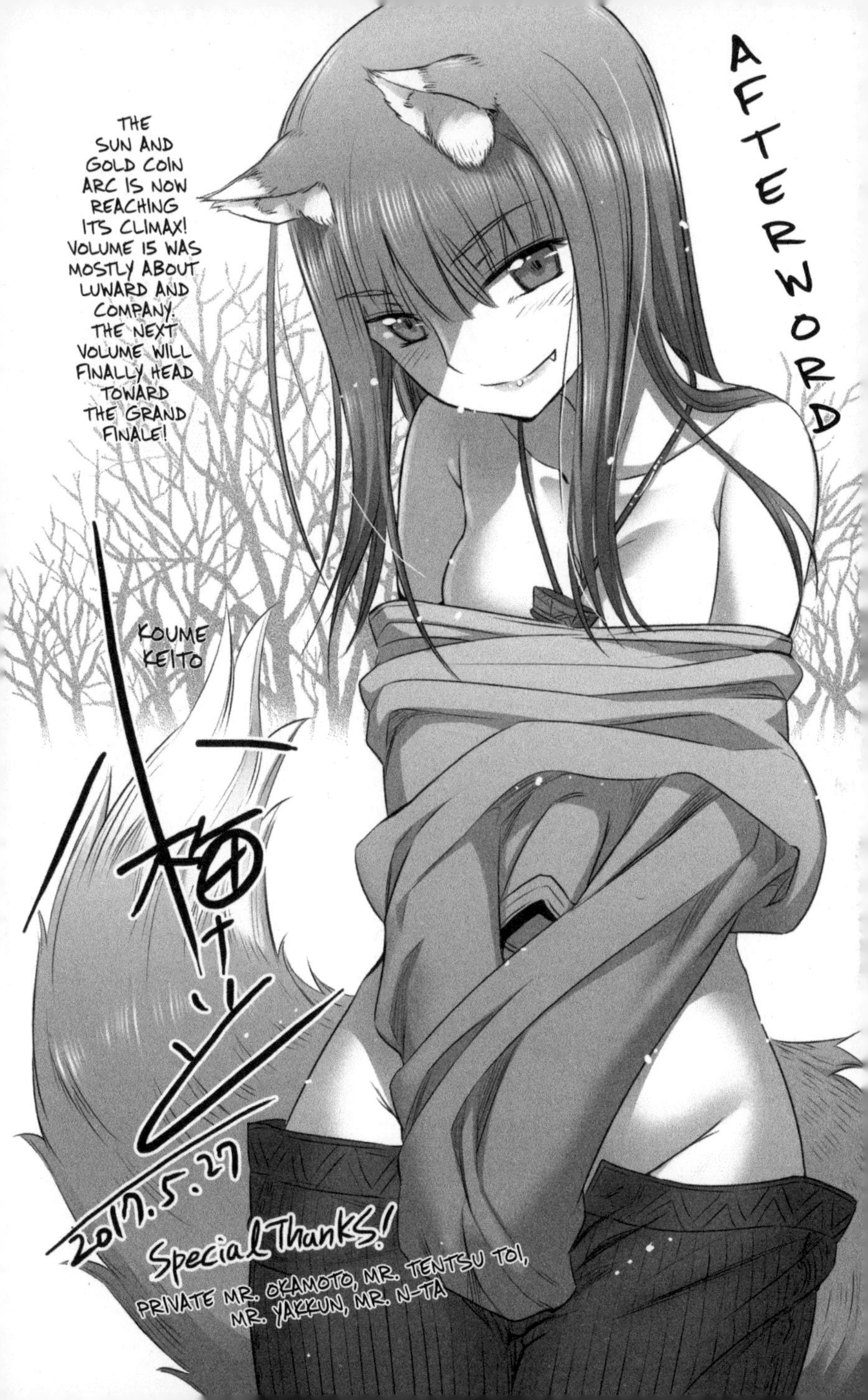
AFTERWORD
THE SUN AND GOLD COIN ARC IS NOW REACHING ITS CLIMAX! VOLUME 15 WAS MOSTLY ABOUT LUWARD AND COMPANY. THE NEXT VOLUME WILL FINALLY HEAD TOWARD THE GRAND FINALE!
KOUME KEITO
2017.5.27
Special Thanks!
PRIVATE MR. OKAMOTO, MR. TENTSU TOI, MR. YAKKUN, MR. N-TA